TEACHERS' RESOURCE BOOK

TEACHER'S RESOURCE BOOK

An Approach to Physical Science

PSNS Project Staff

JOHN WILEY & SONS, INC.   New York • London • Sydney • Toronto

PREFACE

The decision to develop this course was the result of many conferences among physicists and chemists who agreed that the traditional systematic, tightly packed, logical science course is not appropriate for nonscience majors — that is, it is inappropriate for most students. Conventional courses, with their emphasis on the learning of a great many facts, seldom communicate to students any of the spirit of scientific investigation, any of its excitement, any of the scientist's sense of involvement in his work. On the contrary, science courses often tend to increase the aversion to science common among students, and to strengthen their conviction that they cannot understand science and that they should have as little to do with it as possible.

In order to reduce the large number of topics found in traditional physical science courses, and in order to establish a sense of continuity and cohesiveness, which they often lack, we choose to build this course around one "main stem": solid matter. A great deal of thought and many extensive discussions have preceded decisions as to which topics to include and which to exclude; these have been made on the basis of the usefulness of the topic to an understanding of solid matter — not on its traditional place in a physical science course. As a result, vectors, resistance, acids and bases, and valence are among the topics not included, whereas there is considerable discussion of diffraction, kinetic energy, and bonding forces. We hope that, in the interest of maintaining the integrity of the course and of completing it while still allowing ample time for observation and discussion, you, too, will resist the temptation to include material not pertinent to the main stem.

The sequence in which the topics are considered has also been given much thought. In order to spur the students' interests and to motivate them, we have tried to make them aware of the need for each new topic before its introduction. We have tried to establish a "need to know." This is in distinct contrast to many science courses, where topics are brought up, arguments are developed, evidence is marshaled, all in order to demonstrate the logical solution to a problem or question of which the students were previously unaware — the solution is worked out before the puzzle is made known. This is not the way in which science itself develops, nor is it the kind of approach likely to appeal to most students.

During the discussions that led to the decision to develop this course, and during its actual development, we were aware of certain threads running through all scientific work: the usefulness of mathematics in science; the necessity to ask questions of ourselves and of nature; the need to perform experiments in finding answers to questions; and the importance of scientific "modelmaking" and hypothesizing. Throughout the course each of these threads is emphasized by example and by discussion. We feel that the best way for students to gain an understanding of science is for them to actively participate in it, using its tools and its techniques. You will find in Appendix I a discussion of the means by which we attempted to emphasize each of these threads. We urge you to read it before teaching the course.

We firmly believe that experimentation is at the very heart of scientific endeavor, and that the only way for students to get a real feeling for what science is, the only way for them to become personally involved in the study of science, is to provide them with many opportunities to experiment throughout the course. In fact, we made these experiments an integral part of the course and of the text. Altogether we included over sixty of them. Most must be performed as they occur, in order for the students to understand the succeeding discussion. Some of the experiments are intended for presentation in class

v

6096

as <u>demonstrations</u>; about a dozen are designed to be performed by the students on their <u>chair-arms</u> during class or lecture; another dozen or so are designed so that the simple equipment can be given to the students to <u>take home</u> and use there. The largest number, of course, are designed to be performed in a <u>laboratory</u>, which may be very simply equipped. We hope that in all cases the students will be encouraged to experiment freely and to exercise their ingenuity.

There is no question that we could cover more material if we were to have devoted less time to experiments; in some physical science courses, experimentation is left out altogether and students are simply told the results. Such an approach is incompatible with the aims of this course, and inconsistent with the methods of scientific inquiry.

An important feature in the teaching of this course is the pace at which the material is covered. We do not want anyone teaching it to feel pressured to cover any particular set of topics in any particular amount of time. On the other hand, we do feel that the course can and should be essentially completed in a normal school year. A common way of doing this sort of thing is to compare the number of chapters in a textbook with the number of weeks in a school year and then to pace the lectures accordingly. But we made no effort to make all of the chapters in the text equally difficult or time consuming. The density of ideas and material varies from one chapter to another, and sometimes from section to section within a chapter. This was not entirely accidental, for we feel that an occasional change of pace is likely to be stimulating to students. However, the rate of progress cannot be entirely arbitrary, and our experience shows that you should adjust your pace so as to finish Chapter 10 by midyear in order to complete the course by the end of the year.

As a further comment here on the course itself, we point out that, in all probability, more than half of the students who take it will be prospective elementary school teachers. No course could equip them to answer all of the questions that children can ask; no scientist could answer them all, either. As long as they feel that they must provide definite answers to all of the children's questions, they will feel insecure in the classroom during the science period. However, if we can convince them that they will be teaching science best if they adopt the scientist's attitude of "let's try to think of a way of finding out," they may approach it with more enthusiasm. The best preparation we can give them for handling the science period in school is the conviction that leading naturally curious children in their exploration of the world about them can be an enjoyable experience. We are convinced that our approach is equally appropriate for students who do not go into teaching. If we can develop the same open-mindedness in them, if we can reawaken some of their earlier interest and curiousity, we will be helping them to become more effective and understanding as parents and as citizens.

Finally, we will make some comments about the Teacher's Resource Book itself. With an audience as varied in background, interest, and experience as the instructors for whom the book is intended, it is virtually impossible to write anything that will be uniformly valuable to all. It is very difficult to decide what to put in and what to leave out, which topics from the text to discuss in more detail and which to disregard, where to explain a point and where to consider it self-evident. We can only hope that we have done reasonably well — and that you will let us know about those areas in which we have not.

You will find that this book is divided into chapters and sections corresponding to the divisions in the text. Each section includes the questions from the text together with our suggestions for possible answers; a discussion of each experiment of the section including the purpose of the experiment, the required experimental equipment, laboratory notes, and a discussion of the results. At the end of each chapter you will find a list of references with notes on their relevance. The authors, titles, and publishers are given in more complete form in Appendix IV. An annotated list of films as well as information on their availability comprises Appendix III. Appendix II consists of a selection of questions and problems, with answers, that may be useful for making up examinations or special assignments. Appendix I is a fairly detailed discussion of many points having to do with the teaching and administration of the course.

Rensselaer Polytechnic Institute
Troy, New York
January 1969

PSNS Staff

CONTENTS

PSNS STAFF

S. ARONSON
Nassau Community College
Garden City, New York

J. J. BANEWICZ
Southern Methodist University
Dallas, Texas

L. G. BASSETT
Rensselaer Polytechnic Institute
Troy, New York

S. C. BUNCE
Rensselaer Polytechnic Institute
Troy, New York

W. E. CAMPBELL
Rensselaer Polytechnic Institute
Troy, New York

E. L. CARLYON
State University of New York
at Geneseo

M. T. CLARK
Agnes Scott College
Decatur, Georgia

Sister M. de la SALLE, O.S.F.
Alverno College
Milwaukee, Wisconsin

T. H. DIEHL
Miami University
Oxford, Ohio

W. E. EPPENSTEIN
Rensselaer Polytechnic Institute
Troy, New York

D. F. HOLCOMB
Cornell University
Ithaca, New York

H. B. HOLLINGER
Rensselaer Polytechnic Institute
Troy, New York

S. J. INGLIS
Chabot College
Hayward, California

J. L. KATZ
Rensselaer Polytechnic Institute
Troy, New York

H. M. LANDIS
Wheaton College
Norton, Massachusetts

S. H. LEE
Texas Technological University
Lubbock, Texas

A. LEITNER
Rensselaer Polytechnic Institute
Troy, New York

W. J. MCCONNELL
Webster College
Webster Groves, Missouri

H. F. MEINERS
Rensselaer Polytechnic Institute
Troy, New York

E. J. MONTAGUE
Ball State University
Muncie, Indiana

L. V. RACSTER
Rensselaer Polytechnic Institute
Troy, New York

A. J. READ
State University of New York
at Oneonta

R. RESNICK
Rensselaer Polytechnic Institute
Troy, New York

F. J. REYNOLDS
West Chester State College
West Chester, Pennsylvania

R. K. RICKERT
West Chester State College
West Chester, Pennsylvania

R. S. SAKURAI
Webster College
Webster Groves, Missouri

J. SCHNEIDER
St. Francis College
Brooklyn, New York

R. L. SELLS
State University of New York
at Geneseo

L. SMITH
Russell Sage College
Troy, New York

A. A. STRASSENBURG
State University of New York
at Stony Brook and
American Institute of Physics

P. WESTMEYER
Florida State University
Tallahassee, Florida

S. WHITCOMB
Earlham College
Richmond, Indiana

E. A. WOOD
Bell Telephone Laboratories
Murray Hill, New Jersey

E. WRIGHT
Montana State College
Bozeman, Montana

TEACHERS' RESOURCE BOOK

CHAPTER 1

YOU AND PHYSICAL SCIENCE

Chapter 1 is intended to introduce the student to the course. It attempts to set the tone, which is rather friendly and informal. This is but one aspect of our very conscious effort to involve the student in the process of discovery and learning. We hope that our informal tone will help to counteract the disinterest, and even antipathy, so many students have toward science, and will thus encourage them to participate actively. We know and they know that we are not going to make scientists out of them; we know and they will surely know that they are not likely to discover anything not already known to science, that they could gain the same amount of factual information more easily and in less time if we simply gave it to them. But science is not merely a collection of facts. It involves an attitude, an approach to learning as well. It is our belief that students will come to understand and appreciate science more if they participate in some of the same sorts of activities as do professional scientists. It is easy to memorize the value for g, but the whole subject of gravity will be better understood if the student determines g experimentally. Crystals and crystal structure are likely to take on more meaning after one has grown and handled some crystals.

Young children seem to have a lively curiosity and a sense of wonder about the world around them. They constantly ask such questions as "What is lightning?," "What happens to the sugar when you put it in your coffee?," "Where does the Sun go at night?" When they reach college age they seem generally to have lost this interest. There are probably a number of reasons, but we suspect it is very significant that as they grow older they are often discouraged by their teachers and parents from trying things out, from actively seeking answers to their questions. Instead, they are given short factual answers, and more often than not, led to believe that those answers are complete and final. We want to avoid all these impressions. We want the students to know that there are many questions science can answer only tentatively, and vastly more it cannot answer at all. In this text, we avoid the simple statement of fact wherever possible; we try not to be pedantic in answering questions. Instead, we try to lead the reader along a logical course of reasoning from what he knows about a topic toward the answer to the question at hand. Whenever possible, we try to devise ways by which the student can acquire sufficient information by experiment to answer his own questions. We hope that you, the teacher, will share our view and belief; that you will try to lead students to discover the answers for themselves through questions and experimentation; that you will try to develop in them an understanding of what science is, and how it is related to other human endeavor; and that you will try to reawaken in them the healthy sense of wonder and curiosity they had as children.

Section 1-1 ABOUT THIS COURSE

This section serves as a brief introduction not only to the chapter but to the whole course. Some of our aims and methods are discussed. Attention is directed in various ways to the need for accuracy of observation, for clarity of expression, and for precision in the meaning and use of words.

Exposition of complex ideas is difficult in any field of study, and much effort often goes into clarifying the precise meaning an author attaches to a particular word. In some instances precise and very specific meanings have been assigned to common words. This can be a problem for the student. Even though we have tried to define all such words carefully in the text, it will take most students some time to recognize this and to make equally careful use of them. It should be pointed out to them at every opportunity that precision and clarity are lost by careless usage.

The difference between subjective and objective interpretations may need some clarification for the nonscience student. Perhaps a comparison of the scientist and the artist will help. If two artists paint the same scene, their paintings may well be very different, yet it is entirely possible that each could be considered a great work of art. The artist's interpretation of what he sees and his eventual rendering of the scene depends almost entirely on how he feels, how he expresses those feelings, and his materials and technique of painting. And not everyone will respond in the same way to the same painting. The artist's work is subjective.

If two scientists view the same natural phenomenon, their initial interpretations and explanations may differ, for those initial interpretations depend not only on the observer's knowledge and past experience, but to some extent on how he feels. The initial interpretations are subjective. However, the differences will eventually be reconciled as additional experiments are performed and observations obtained. Eventually the explanations must fit in logically with the body of scientific thought. The initially divergent interpretations are modified and brought into satisfactory agreement. When this has been accomplished the interpretations will no longer be subjective in character; they will have become objective.

It is mentioned in the text that mathematics is a tool for science. In a sense this is true, and that will be the only use of it made in this course. It will be used as a shorthand, as a method by which to show clearly the relationships between quantities, and as an aid to clarifying our thinking. But students might be interested to know that mathematics is, in reality, much more than that. It is a language. Not only are many of the ideas of modern physics difficult to express unambiguously in words, but much of it cannot be understood in anything but mathematical terms by scientists themselves. Another aspect of the idea of mathematics as a language is that it has a very special "grammar." This is the set of rules by which mathematical manipulations are made. The rules have no real counterpart in ordinary language, yet they serve the important function of suggesting to theoretical scientists new ways of relating known quantities and properties to one another. Not all such mathematical relationships turn out to have physical meaning; they are, nevertheless, an important source of suggestions for further experiment and investigation.

The discussion of our aims in developing this course is very brief, and our aims and our reasons for fixing our attention on solids may need further clarification. Solid matter is not the only possible route toward our goal, nor is its meaning or significance clear to most nonscientists. To most people wood, glass, steel, diamonds, plastic, gold, ice (anything which doesn't bend or dent easily) are solid, and the uniqueness of our choice escapes them. And we don't exclude liquids and gases from consideration either, although it is true that we discuss them only to help the student understand solids better.

We knew from the outset that it would be necessary to study topics from both physics and chemistry, because both are needed to understand the physical world. In order to gain this understanding and communicate it to others (a particularly important consideration for those students who become teachers), one must have some knowledge of each. We believe that students can best gain this knowledge through experience, and that solid matter is an ideal subject for our purpose. It is an area of interest and significance for both chemists and physicists, an area where the techniques of both are used interchangeably. It is, in fact, an area where the two sciences become indistinguishable; the traditional arbitrary boundaries between them vanish. We hope that students will gradually become aware of the fundamental unity of physical science.

Section 1-2 THE SCIENTIST AS A DETECTIVE

No Comment

Section 1-3 OBSERVATION AND SHERLOCK HOLMES

Scientists are sometimes accused of trying to impose an order or pattern on the world. What they really do is observe nature and from their observations they try to discover patterns in nature's ways. The process of observing and deducing from observation is not restricted to scientists, however. Businessmen, for example, must be keen observers of trends and able interpreters of their meaning in order to be successful. Many other professional people must make use of similar techniques. We have chosen to illustrate the discovery process by referring to the techniques of the detective; we use two quotations from one of the best-known detectives in all literature: Sherlock Holmes. We could, of course, have chosen any one of a number of more recently created fictional detectives, but the Holmes stories are classics, and they illustrate particularly well the points we wish to make.

The question is raised in the text as to what Sherlock Holmes might conclude if he were to observe the same set of clues in a modern office building as were presented to him by the woman in "The Adventure of the Speckled Band." The purpose is to indicate that the answers to questions depend on the environment in which they are asked. Each of the ages of man has responded to the same or similar questions with quite different answers.

It might help students to become better acquainted with observational techniques if they were asked to work out an unambiguous set of clues appropriate to a modern situation. Examples of phenomena that could serve to sharpen their powers of observation are: a burning candle, a carbonated drink in a glass, an open pan of water heated to boiling on a stove, the starting of a fluorescent light. Another interesting example would be to have them identify the locale of a scene in a slide or photograph through an analysis of its characteristics.

Experiment 1-1   The Salol Experiment

This experiment is intended as an introduction to the subject matter of the course. It involves the melting and recrystallization of salol (phenylsalicylate, $HOC_6H_4COOC_6H_5$ — melting point $43°C$). Most students find the experiment very interesting, so it can profitably be used as a curtain raiser for the first meeting of the class. Hopefully it will raise questions in the students' minds — that is one of the purposes of this course. And hopefully not all of the questions will be answered during the first class meeting. A good part of this course is devoted to building a model that describes crystals; this model includes a description of melting and recrystallization.

At this early stage in the course it is much more important to ask questions than to answer them. The answers can follow later, and we hope that the students can be led to answer their own questions; this is another purpose of the course. After all, the scientist must answer his own questions. We also hope that in answering his own questions, the student raises still more questions. This is the way science progresses.

We have classified this experiment as a "chair-arm" experiment. It is one of a number of experiments that can be performed in the classroom as well as in the laboratory. Other experiments are classified as "take-home" experiments. There are a number of advantages to having the students perform experiments at home, not the least of which is the freedom they have to explore without the usual pressure of the laboratory. The use of chair-arm and take-home experiments helps to make the scheduling of experiments more flexible; in addition it extends the experimental work beyond the confines of the lab.

Equipment Needed
(per class of 24 students)   *Cat. Number*

1 glass medicine dropper (Note a)	68845 ✓
1 250-ml beaker (Note a, b)	68815 ✓
24 glass microscope slides (Note a, c)	68850 ✓
1 spatula (or scoopula)	68864
24 magnifiers	68847 ✓
24 boxes, safety matches	68539
30 g, salol crystals (Note a, b)	68546 ✓
24 plastic bags with tie wraps	68853

Laboratory Notes

(a)   It is imperative that the beaker, medicine dropper, and salol crystals used in the preparation of the slides be quite dry. Even small traces of water may prevent the salol from solidifying.

(b)   Thirty grams of salol should be placed in the dry beaker for each group of slides to be prepared. Using a bunsen burner, hot plate, or alcohol burner, heat carefully until all the salol is melted, then remove from heat.

(c)   The slides should be laid on the table, production-line style. Using the medicine dropper, a puddle of liquid salol about the size of a dime is placed on one end of each slide, and a single drop of salol on the opposite end. The slides are then left to cool. On most slides, solidification will probably not occur until each puddle has been seeded. A spatula with some crystallized salol coating on it will probably serve as a seed. The salol will crystallize and stick firmly to the slide.

(d)   The distribution of materials for this chair-arm experiment will be facilitated by putting a magnifier, a box of matches, and a prepared slide in a plastic bag and closing it with the tie wrap. Upon entering the classroom each student can be supplied with a bag of materials. This may tend to encourage the students to retain the slide for use at home; many students appear reluctant to put it in a pocket or purse.

The actual manipulations for the experiment are very simple. Each student is furnished a microscope slide, matches, and a magnifier. The slide will have a dime-sized patch of crystallized salol on one end and a much smaller patch on the other. Students should loosen a bit of salol from the smaller patch with fingernail or pencil point and leave it lying near the point where it was attached. Holding the slide by the end with the smaller patch, the other end should be gently heated with a match flame until the large patch of salol has just melted. (The match should be held far enough below the slide while heating it so that it neither heats the slide too rapidly nor causes an excessive soot deposit on it.) When the salol has melted, the slide should be allowed to cool until it is no longer hot to touch.

Crystals will not form during the cooling even after the salol has cooled below its freezing or solidification temperature. The student, therefore, is left with a supercooled melt on one end of the slide and a small patch of crystals on the other end, with one bit of crystal freed. By moving that bit of crystal into the melt, it becomes a seed crystal, and the melt crystallizes within a few seconds.

The students should observe the crystals carefully while they grow; the magnifier will help. They should be encouraged to remelt and recrystallize the salol as often as they wish, but it is necessary to keep a small piece of crystal to seed the salol each time.

Since this experiment is performed again in Chapter 5, it will be a saving to keep those slides the students don't take home.

The crystals formed will be of many sizes and apparent shape, but closer examination will reveal that a single crystal is shaped like a diamond of the playing card variety (Fig. RB 1-1). The angles are $\alpha = 71°30'$, $\beta = 108°30'$, though this detailed information is not important to the students. All of the other shapes that may be found in a crystallized patch are made up of combinations of this basic pattern.

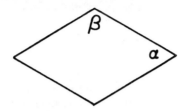

Figure RB 1-1

Some questions to direct student attention along lines we will investigate during the course are: "How does it happen that they all have the same shape?" "Why do they grow with large, flat faces that reflect the light?" It is quite remarkable that out of each formless puddle of liquid salol the same shape of shiny-faced solid is built up each and every time the crystals form.

Throughout the course, the students will watch the growth of other crystals, and they may want to compare both their growth and physical characteristics. To facilitate this comparison, and to establish suitable laboratory technique, the students should be urged to keep a lab book or journal in which they record their observations. The records in the lab book should be simple and straightforward, but they should be complete enough to be understood when referred to weeks after they have been noted. They may, for example, record the size, shape, color, and method of growth of salol crystals to facilitate later comparisons.

The students should be encouraged to discuss their observations and to formulate hypotheses to describe them. They may want to use words such as atom, or ion, or molecule, but we feel such technical terms at this stage should be introduced by the student, not the teacher. The students should be encouraged to record in their notebooks what they consider the best hypothesis, for that record might be of interest later in the course. However, we feel that no final conclusions can be reached at this stage, and certainly none should be handed them authoritatively.

The phenomenon of supercooling is known to occur in some other substances. One of the most important of these is water. Although it freezes at $0°C$ in a vessel, small very clean droplets of water can be cooled to as low as $-40°C$ without freezing. Such supercooled droplets of water sometimes occur in the atmosphere when no bits of dust or salt (from ocean spray) are present to initiate ice formation. Cloud seeding is an attempt to cause these droplets to solidify. Just as we seeded the molten salol with solid salol, it is most effective to seed molten ice (water) with solid ice. However, ice is difficult to transport to high altitudes, so that silver iodide, which has an almost identical crystal shape, is used as a substitute. When the crystals grow large enough they fall, and on reaching warmer air, the ice melts and may initiate rain.

Experiment 1-2 Solution of Powders

The purpose of this experiment is to permit the student to observe large crystals growing over a time interval of some 3 to 6 weeks. The equipment has been selected so that the powders that are dissolved in water when the class is on Chapter 1 should form suitable crystals by the time Chapter 5 is reached. It is in Chapter 5 that these crystals are discussed.

The longer time interval and the resulting larger crystals are a sharp contrast to the salol experiment. But of greater importance is the fact that the salol crystals formed from a melt; the crystals in this experiment formed from a water solution. The distinction between melting and dissolving and between crystallization from melts and solutions is discussed in Chapter 15.

Two sets of crystals will be grown in this take-home experiment. If half of the class grows one set and the other half the other set, the differences may spark some interest and discussion. One of the powders to be dissolved in water is a mixture of copper sulfate, $CuSO_4 \cdot 5H_2O$, and potassium alum, $KAl(SO_4)_2 \cdot 12H_2O$. Copper sulfate is blue and is a triclinic crystal; potassium alum is white (colorless) and is an octahedral cubic crystal. Because of the different crystal structures, the two crystals form separately as the water evaporates.

The other powder is composed of a mixture of chromium alum, $K Cr(SO_4) \cdot 12 H_2O$, and potassium alum. The chromium alum is violet-ruby red and is an octahedral cubic crystal like the colorless potassium alum. Consequently these two crystals grow as a single kind, a solid solution or intermediate crystal $K (Cr, Al) (SO_4)_2 \cdot 12 H_2O$.

> *CAUTION:* Most of the substances used for experiments are poisonous, and all should be handled as if they were. Never try to identify unknown substances by tasting them. Always wash hands thoroughly after working with unknown substances. Never leave unknown substances where others could get to them accidentally.

Neither the names nor the formulas of these compounds are of any importance to the student, so there is no reason to make this information available to them, unless they are curious and ask. The outcome of the experiment should not be told to the students under any circumstances. To do so would defeat the purpose of the experiment, and seriously undermine the philosophy of the course: we want the student to understand through his own observation and experimentation, not simply to remember what he has been told.

It would be desirable for you to grow one or two samples of each kind of crystal as well as to keep a sample of each of the two powder mixtures for later reference and observation. Also, because the students are told in the text not to shake or otherwise disturb the jars during the experiment, it would be worthwhile for you to make up one jar and shake it occasionally in order to show experimentally why they should not. (Many very small crystals will form rather than a few large ones.) Alternatively, an interested student, perhaps one who has questioned the instructions, might be given an extra bottle so that he could report to the class later on the effects of shaking.

Using the equipment suggested below, these crystals take about 3 to 5 weeks to grow. However, it is very interesting to grow some of the alum crystals more slowly by using a narrow-necked bottle to retard the evaporation of water. If the solution is not disturbed and if evaporation is slow, one big alum crystal will grow.

Equipment Needed (per class of 24 students)	Cat. Number
12 bottles, powder A (Note a)	68855
12 bottles, powder B (Note a)	68855
1 extra portion, powders A and B	68855

Laboratory Notes

(a)   You may order the bottles already packed with the proper amount of powder in each. There might be a label attached to each bottle identifying it as "A" or "B." These are used for manufacturing and storing purposes, and should be removed before the bottles are given to the students. Inevitably, some students will lose or spill their solutions. The extra portions of each powder can be used to give these students a second chance.

Should you want to prepare these powders yourself, powder A is composed of 2.5 to 3 grams of potassium alum and 4.5 to 5 grams of copper sulfate per bottle. Powder B is composed of 1.5 to 2 grams of potassium alum and 1.5 to 2 grams of chromium alum. Both components in each mixture should be in powder form before they are distributed to the students; otherwise the crystal shapes are evident from the start. The experiment has been designed to use bottles the same size and shape as those used with the alcohol burners. The opening of the bottle regulates the rate of water evaporation and consequently of crystal growth.

(b) So that these crystals can be of value to the investigations in Chapter 5, they will have to be removed from the bottles and examined closely. Sometimes, however, they stick to the glass at the bottom. Those that stick can be removed by adding just enough water to cover the bottom of the bottle and warming it. The warm water will dissolve a bit of the crystal in contact with the bottom of the jar, but that part is distorted by its contact with the bottom and is of little use in displaying the crystal's characteristic shape.

Experiment 1-3   Formation and Dissolving of Crystals

Part A   The main purpose of this part of the experiment is simply to illustrate the process of diffusion and the fact that a solid goes into solution in the form of imperceptibly small particles. As with any experiment, of course, it also has the purpose of encouraging the student to make a few critical observations. For example, there are definite differences in the way a crystal of potassium permanganate dissolves in cold and in hot water.

Equipment Needed
(per 2 students)   *Cat. Number*

2 250-ml beakers	68815
several crystals of potassium permanganate (Note a)	68EXP
1 spatula (Note b)	68864
1 weighing cup	68823
1 stirring rod	68867

Laboratory Notes

(a) The potassium permanganate can be purchased in 1-oz bottles, one of which is sufficent for over 25 students. The easiest way to dispense the chemical is to give each pair of students a paper weighing cup with 10 or so small crystals contained therein.
(b) The students should be encouraged to use the spatula whenever chemicals are to be transferred to a container. If this point is not emphasized early, they may use their fingers to handle solid substances.
(c) Potassium permanganate solutions deteriorate on standing and have a tendency to stain glassware if left even a day or so. If this should happen, the stain can be removed by covering it with hydrogen peroxide or concentrated hydrochloric acid, and allowing it to stand for a few minutes.

The process of dissolving, if considered in any detail, is a very complicated one. In its simplest terms, it occurs because the molecules of the solvent "get between" the molecules of the solute and reduce the effectiveness of the forces that normally hold them together. In order for this to continue to occur, the dissolved material must be removed from the interface between the solid and the solvent. The motions of the molecules serve to remove this material. The removal will occur more rapidly, and consequently the dissolving will proceed more rapidly, if the solvent is agitated by stirring or heating.

This experiment provides an excellent opportunity for student discussion. After they have performed it, ask the students to propose a model to explain their observations. Because of their varied backgrounds, some students may come reasonably close to the simplified picture just given. But it is a better learning process if they reach that conclusion on their own. Your part should be that of a moderator, keeping the discussion on the track, helping them to see the logic in some of their ideas, the illogic in others. The two or three best models can then be put on the shelf and examined from time to time as the course progresses and further information becomes available for their evaluation.

This sequence of observing, hypothesizing (model making), and testing, followed by further observing, hypothesis extension or modification, and testing, is fundamental to science. The students should have the sequence of steps pointed out to them after they have gone through them, and they should come to realize that they are participating in the same sort of activities as do scientists. Bringing it up again occasionally as the course progresses should serve to reinforce the idea in their minds.

Part B   Part A of this experiment demonstrates the dissolving of crystals to form a water solution. Part B, a take-home experiment, demonstrates the formation of crystals from solution. Experiments 1-1 and 1-2 also demonstrate the formation of crystals; in 1-1 crystals formed from a melt, in 1-2 they formed as the solvent (water) evaporated. In this experiment the crystals form because of the replacement of ions.

Equipment Needed
(per 2 students)   *Cat. Number*

2a 1 formation of crystals kit (Note a)	✓	68834
2 magnifiers		68847 ✓

Laboratory Note

(a)   Each kit consists of a vial containing 1 gram of $CuSO_4 \cdot 5H_2O$ with a 4-penny nail attached to the outside, and a second vial containing 1 gram of $AgNO_3$ with a 2-inch piece of bare copper wire attached.

The powdered crystals should be dissolved in water first and then the piece of metal placed in the solution. The vial should then be left undisturbed so that the students can observe the formation of silver crystals or the plating of copper. The metal ions initially in solution deposit as atoms on the wire or nail; the atoms of the solid metal become ions, replacing the ions that were in solution. Details of this replacement process are complex; the copper plates out with a very uncrystalline appearance, the silver forms a silver tree. The students should look for any changes in the solution. The silver nitrate solution turns bluish as the copper atoms go into solution; the copper sulfate solution becomes less bluish. The equations expressing these reactions are

$$CuSO_4 + Fe \rightarrow FeSO_4 + Cu$$

$$2\,AgNO_3 + Cu \rightarrow Cu(NO_3)_2 + 2\,Ag$$

Students sometimes ask about the effect of putting the iron into the silver nitrate solution. The reaction there is

$$2\,AgNO_3 + Fe \rightarrow Fe(NO_3)_2 + 2\,Ag$$

These equations are for your information. It is much too early in the course for them to have meaning for most of the students, since the appropriate theory isn't discussed until Chapter 14. The students, however, should record their observations carefully in their notebooks in order to be able to refer to them during that later discussion. We have included the experiment here to arouse interest and to give further experience in careful observation.

Section 1-4 ASKING ANSWERABLE QUESTIONS

Astronomers and geologists cannot perform experiments in the sense that they can control or fix different variables successively in order to determine the importance of each in turn, as the laboratory scientist can. However, they can ask questions and formulate hypotheses predicting the answers about phenomena of the physical universe. Though few such questions are answerable with any certainty, some are. They ask answerable questions, obtain answers through careful observations, and then use those answers to extend and modify the hypotheses. The point is that while astronomy and geology are not experimental in the same sense that physics and chemistry are, neither do they involve the mere accumulation of chance data. The data sought are the data known to be necessary for answering specific questions.

The boiling point of water is included in the discussion of this section in order to illustrate the number of variables to be considered in even so familiar a process as boiling. It would be interesting to ask the students which variables they would have included had they been asked to make a list in advance of reading this section. Alternatively, they might be asked to list the variables which would be of potential importance in determining the effect that driving has on tire pressure (there are at least ten), or those which might affect cooking time for some particular kind of vegetable (there are five or six).

Section 1-5 CLASSIFICATION

As already noted, careful observation is not a technique used by scientists alone; it is of value to persons in many fields. It is very difficult, though not impossible, to teach students to become really observant. We do not expect that this section, nor even this chapter, will do it, but the discussion and examples are very useful.

First, this section illustrates the fact that the criteria for classifying or categorizing are quite arbitrary. It has rather simple examples, but the same thing holds true for observations and data of a more complicated nature. Classification is very largely dependent on the observer and what he is seeking; there is seldom only one reasonable choice. The successful scientist is perhaps the one who can best see the natural categories into which a set of observations fall, and who can then select the one with the broadest generality or widest applicability.

The second thing illustrated by this section is the variety of minor differences that may exist between one set and the next. This is, of course, related to the fact that there are often a number of suitable classification schemes for a given body of data. It is also indicative of the clarity of definition and the precision of description needed in scientific work.

Classification schemes are not, *a priori*, correct or incorrect. One generally judges them in any practical situation on the basis of their usefulness in clarifying the data and the relations between them, and in suggesting new relationships or new lines of investigation. However, the examples given serve only to illustrate classification schemes, and there is no way to judge their relative values. Students often feel somewhat frustrated by this, because they have grown accustomed during their prior educational experience to being told the correct answers to all questions and problems. We want to emphasize here that questions often do not have *an* answer. They frequently have several, and the *right* one depends on what one is looking for. However, there can be incorrect answers if, after establishing the criterion, the student does not apply it correctly.

QUESTIONS

1-1   In the photograph which opens Chapter 2 there are many different objects. Classify these objects by grouping them into groups or sets. A set may consist of only one item, although it may have 5, 10, 1000, or more. After carefully observing the objects in the photograph, establish criteria that differentiate some of them as one set, distinct from the others. Indicate what the criterion is and then list the items that fall within that set. Establish several other criteria and classify these same objects into still other sets. How many sets can you establish?

Answer   One possible means by which the measuring apparatus in the photograph can be formed into a set is to use a straight-line scale as a criterion. The objects forming this set are steel measuring tape, thermometer, manometer, vernier calipers, scale to be used with a reversing telescope.

1-2   Following this question are five figures. Classify these figures in sets by establishing criteria that distinguish some from the others. Classify them into several different sets.

Figure RB 1-2

Answer   One possible set for these figures is composed of those which have a circle as part of their structure. This set would, of course, be composed of the first three. But there are other sets composed of those figures which have triangles, those figures which have squares, etc.

1-3   Choose the pattern from the three patterns within the gray area below that best fits into the empty square. Explain why it is best.

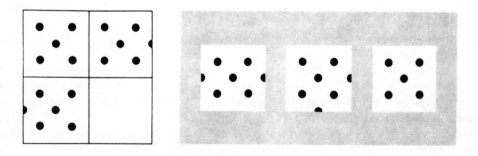

Figure RB 1-3

Answer   The answer to this question depends on the student's sense of symmetry or whether he really likes complete symmetry in such patterns. One possible answer to this question is to consider the four squares on the left as part of a repeat pattern in a wallpaper print. The pattern in the gray area that best fits this wallpaper print might be the right-hand one.

1-4   Choose the pattern from the two within the gray area that fits in the empty square.

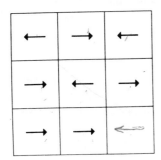 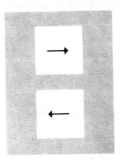

Figure RB 1-4

Answer   The answer to this question depends not on the choice of the right or left hand arrow in the gray area, but on the reasons for this choice.

1-5   Organize or classify into sets the words in List I, then those in List II:

List I	List II	
steam	record	water
gasoline	experiment	kilometer
salt	blue	rainbow
oxygen	Fahrenheit	hearing
water	model	light
mercury	violet	yard
carbon dioxide	crystals	waves
wood	vehicle	question
waves	puzzle	measure
doughnuts	solids	sky
alcohol		
ice		

Answer   There are as many answers to this question as there are criteria.

Experiment 1-4 Classification of Objects

The students are to be supplied with small amounts of nine different fairly common chemicals. They are to group these materials, on the basis of observable properties, into sets according to criteria they themselves establish. One of the objectives of this experiment is to point out that there is no one correct criterion. It would even be desirable to encourage them to develop several sets each according to a different criterion, and then to comment on the relative usefulness of each set as a means of distinguishing between materials.

Preparation time for this lab is approximately 30 minutes for a lab class of 24 students. The chemicals are often dissolved, decomposed, etc., by the students as they devise and test their various classification schemes. If the lab sessions are consecutive, have several sets prepared ahead of time. (See Note b below.)

Equipment Needed (per 2 students)	*Cat. Number*

½ teaspoon of each of the following chemicals, each in its own weighing cup (Note a)

starch	68565
ferrous ammonium sulfate, hydrate	68565
sodium dichromate, hydrate	68565
cobalt nitrate, hydrate (Note b)	68565
sugar	68565
sodium chloride	68565
cupric sulfate, pentahydrate	68565
cupric carbonate	68565
lithium carbonate	68565
9 weighing cups	68823
1 spatula	68864
2 magnifiers	68847

The following items are not specifically called for, but one should have them available in case a student wants to make various tests (Note c)

cups or beakers	68815, 68896
test tubes	68873, 68906
mortar and pestle (not available as PSNS equipment)	
alcohol burners and matches	68810
stirring rods	68867

Laboratory Notes

(a)   Each of these nine substances can be purchased in a one- or two-pound bulk package. The purity need be only technical grade. The weighing cups are best set out in an array. Each pair of students will require nine.

(b)   The cobalt nitrate is extremely hygroscopic. This substance should not be put in its cup until after the lab has started; otherwise, it will absorb moisture from the air and make a mess of things.

(c)   The following criteria may be considered typical: (a) color, (b) crystallinity, (c) odor, (d) melting point, (e) solubility.

It is worth noting in connection with the first of these, that whiteness is in part dependent on the particle size, and that even colored substances tend to appear white if finely powdered. A student who has used whiteness as a category might be encouraged to investigate this effect by grinding his materials with a mortar and pestle. To observe crystallinity a magnifier is a useful way to extend the range of observation beyond that of the unaided eye; a microscope would extend it even further. One finds that many materials appearing to be powdered or amorphous are actually crystalline when examined with these instruments. In fact, crystallinity often cannot be observed without going to the extreme of x-ray analysis, which is in a sense very high magnification. To test for solubility, a stirring rod is useful. Solubility is a property that cannot be observed with any real accuracy with the unaided senses. There is not much to be done at this stage to aid the student in extending his ability to determine solubility more accurately than simply "very soluble" and "apparently insoluble," and he should be made aware that such a classification is very gross.

QUESTIONS

1-6   Using a dictionary or textbook, define each of the following terms: classify, criterion, hypothesis, intuition, phenomenon, property, qualitative, rational, solid.
Answer   Requires only dictionary definitions.

1-7   Suppose you were given a piece of solid, metallic material (two identifying properties are already known). Could you determine easily whether it is iron or aluminum? List as many ways as possible in which these two metals differ.
Answer   Several obvious ways in which aluminum and iron differ are: density, color, hardness, and magnetizeability.

1-8   Classify the following substances as solid, liquid, or gas, and specify the criteria you used to make your decisions: air, chocolate pudding, glass, granite, ice, jello, mercury, milk, oxygen, sand, steam, tar, wood.
Answer   The correctness of the answers is dependent on how well they satisfy the criteria the students themselves set up.

1-9   Devise a means of classifying buildings.
Answer   Same as in Question 1-8 above.

1-10   In Experiment 1-2, you used very hot water to dissolve the powder in the jar. Why? Can you think of an analogous everyday situation that justifies your answer?
Answer   Although many things are more soluble in hot water than in cold, the reasons are too varied and complex to expect the students to know. If the students cannot think of an analogous everyday situation to justify their answer, you might ask them to recall dissolving sugar in hot tea and iced tea.

1-11   Suppose you were asked to explain the physical principles involved in the following phenomena. Try to do this as well as you can, using only terms you can define readily. Later, after further study on your part, you will be asked this same question. It will be interesting to compare your answers then with your answers now.

(a)   It is usually found that after a car has been driven for a considerable distance at high speeds, the pressure in the tires changes.

(b)   Water condenses on the outside of a glass. Before explaining this, it may help to consider the conditions under which this occurs as well as conditions under which it does not occur.
Answer   (a) The friction between the tire and the road surface and the flexing of the sidewalls heat the tire up. This in turn heats the air within. Because the air cannot expand inside the tire, the pressure increases. (b) Moisture condenses on any surface cold enough to chill the air near it sufficiently so that the air cannot retain all of its moisture. That is, the air temperature is reduced sufficiently so that the air becomes saturated.

This question is being asked in Chapter 1 and again in Chapter 7 so that the student will realize that although he may now have a reasonably good idea of the answer to each of these questions, the model developed in this course will permit him to handle these questions with much more confidence.

ADDITIONAL QUESTIONS

1-12   Find the minimum number of criteria needed to differentiate the figures in Question 1-2 into five different sets, one figure in each set.
Answer   Only one criterion is needed. One such criterion is the number of times straight line segments join.

1-13   Six additional groups of patterns to be classified into sets are given in Figure RB 1-5. They can be used in the same way as the ones in the text; they can also be categorized in such a way that each set is divided into five subsets of one member each.
Answer   Suitable categories can be described for each of the examples as follows: (a) the number of regions runs from two to six; (b) the number of regions runs from three to seven; (c) the minimum number of straight lines required for the figures runs from four to eight; (d) the number of straight lines in the figure is: 2, 4, 6, 8, 10; (e) the number of intersections with the outer boundary runs from one to five; (f) the number of identical triangles per figure is 2^n, $n = 0, 1, 2, 3, 4$.

1-14   Construct a set of patterns similar to those of Questions 1-2 to 1-5 in the text. Show it to at least two other students and ask for their responses. Do they correspond to the ideas you had in mind as you constructed the set?

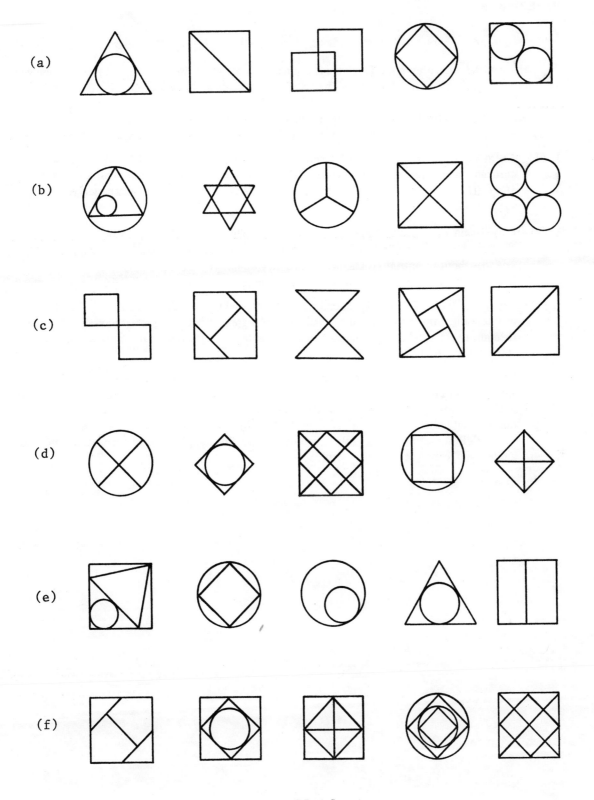

Figure RB 1-5

REFERENCES

Note

Many of the references in the Teacher's Resource Book are those listed in the text itself. These will be indicated by a (T) preceding the author's name. The comments in the text concerning these references apply here also. Additional comments will also be added here for the assistance of the teacher.

The references in the Teacher's Resource Book will be identified in each chapter by the author's name only. The complete identification by author, title, publisher, edition, etc., will be made in Appendix IV.

1. (T)   Chem Study, Chapter 1, Section 1-1, pages 1 to 8. A good illustration of scientific thinking through a simple yet perceptive analogy. There are some similarities to our Sherlock Holmes story. The analogy should be close enough to the beginning student's own experiences to be meaningful.

2. (T)   Christiansen and Garrett, Chapter 1, pages 1 to 13. This chapter gives a preview of some of the organizational aspects of science. Although it is still too early for the students to understand how one goes about organizing (particularly since they do not yet know just what is to be organized), it may be of value for the students to see something of the *nature* of the end product.

3. (T)   Feynman, Chapter 2, Section 2-1, pages 2-1 to 2-21, and Chapter 22, pages 22-1 to 22-10. It might be interesting for the students to be aware of how a great physicist expresses himself in his own field just to get a *feel* for it. The mathematics chapter again focuses on the sense of what constitutes this important discipline.

4.   *Scientific American*, September, 1964. This entire issue is devoted to mathematics, including applications to various disciplines. The treatment is considerably more advanced than is necessary for PSNS, particularly in its use of abstract concepts, but the sense of mathematics comes through quite nicely. This is true of all of the *Scientific American* articles listed here in the Teacher's Resource Book. Thus there will not be any direct application to our teaching, but the indirect application can be very useful.

CHAPTER 2

WHEN, WHERE, AND HOW MUCH?

It is our hope that the laboratory and demonstration experiments accompanying Chapter 1 were each intrinsically interesting to the students as individual physical phenomena. Our purpose, however, is not simply to entertain, but to arouse the students' curiosity with regard to the world about them, to raise questions in their minds. We choose to do this by considering very simple experiments and experimental situations, because we want the students to begin to realize that science is not exclusively concerned with esoteric questions requiring extensive and expensive laboratory facilities for their answers. Much of scientific interest can be learned by observing simple, everyday macroscopic phenomena.

Even though observation is a necessary first step, it leads nowhere without the curiosity to understand – the desire to explain. Science is the systematic attempt to understand and to explain phenomena in general terms that apply to a variety of situations. Observation is the first step in this process. Formulation of a tentative explanation (hypothesis) is next, and this is followed by experimental testing.

Section 2-1 A CONTROLLED ENVIRONMENT, THE LABORATORY

Students need to learn that experiments must be repeatable to be meaningful. That is, an experiment performed in a laboratory at any given time and place must yield the same results when performed at any other time or place and when performed by any other competent experimenter. In order for this to be so, the conditions under which the experiment is performed must be controlled in such a way that they can be accurately specified and duplicated. It is by no means always obvious which conditions must be controlled and which ones are unimportant. Often such distinctions can be made only experimentally. To do so, each potentially important variable must be varied in turn, while all others are held fixed, and the consequent effects on the results noted.

Another common procedure in experimental work is to idealize, to abstract the idea or the object from its surroundings, and to study it free from outside influences. Collisions between air pucks, or free fall in a vacuum are examples. Here, important aspects of the experimental environment are controlled by eliminating them.

Another thing students must come to realize in order to understand the nature of experimental science is the need for quantitative relations. However, the term quantitative relations may not be clear to students reading the text for the first time. A simple example may help to clear it up. For instance, it is a qualitative statement when the instructor says to a student, "I am older than you are." It becomes quantitative when he says, "I am 1.8 times as old as you are." It may be useful to know in a given situation that this object is heavier, or hotter, or larger than that object, but it certainly isn't the sort of information that enables one to establish universal laws.

In order to make use of quantitative relationships, it is necessary to define certain physical quantities and to specify the magnitudes of the units in which they are to be measured. This is done in Sections 2-2 and 2-3 where length, mass, and time are considered. These three quantities are among the most basic to physical measurement. In fact, if we add but one more, to make four of them, then all other and more complicated quantities that science has found it necessary to define can be specified in terms of these four. This fourth quantity is electric charge. (It is not discussed in the text until Chapter 10.)

Two additional concepts, temperature and heat, are introduced in Sections 2-4 and 2-5. It is not the purpose of Chapter 2 to define these two quantities rigorously. They are not defined until Chapters 9 and 10, after the concept of energy and the molecular model have been introduced. But we do talk about them in a nonrigorous sense in Chapter 2. We do consider with care some of the ways to measure these various quantities, and we formulate precise operational definitions for some of their common units.

SECTION 2-2 HOW MUCH?

The discussion of length and of the history of the units in which it is measured has been felt by some students to be too elementary. We have included it, however, to help provide them with a gradual introduction into the substance of the course, and to begin to make them aware of the need for precise definition and usage of words in a scientific context. The point about the need to establish standards for units of measurement is, of course, connected with the requirement that experiments must be repeatable by other investigators.

Density is defined in Section 2-2. This is a new concept to many students, and it is further complicated by our use of the word mass where they are accustomed to using weight. Both words are defined earlier in the section, but they are often confounded in everyday use by laymen and scientists alike. It might be well, therefore, to point out that the mass of an object can be loosely considered as an indication of the amount of matter of which it is made up. Experimentally it is found that at any particular place, bodies of equal mass experience equal gravitational attraction; that is, they have equal weight.

For nonscience students the concept of density requires some clarification because this is the first quantitative relationship to be introduced. The students realize as a result of their experience that the larger a chunk of material is the heavier it is. If we use volume as a measure of largeness and mass as a measure of heaviness, then their experience is described by saying that the larger the volume the larger the mass. To make it still more precise: if the volume is doubled the mass will be doubled, if the volume is tripled the mass will be tripled, etc. This type of relationship is stated more briefly by saying that the mass is directly proportional to the volume, or that the ratio of the mass to the volume is a constant. Such a statement is valid because if the volume is increased by some factor K, the mass is increased by the same factor and the ratio remains the same.

$$\frac{(\text{mass})_a}{(\text{Volume})_a} = \frac{(\text{mass})_b}{(\text{Volume})_b} = \frac{K(\text{mass})_a}{K(\text{volume})_a}$$

One can then say that for a given material the ratio of the mass to the volume is a characteristic constant which is the same for all samples of the material, under the same conditions, but which varies from one material to another. The name given to this ratio is *density*.

QUESTIONS

2-1   A particular iron horseshoe has a volume of 50 cm^3 and a mass of 390 g. An aluminum scoop has a volume of 55 cm^3 and a mass of 150 g. A large nail has a volume of 0.4 cm^3 and a mass of 3.1 g. Some nails are made of iron and others of aluminum. Of which metal is this nail made?

Answer   The purpose of this question is to emphasize the fact that density is a characteristic property of matter that may be used as a means of identifying substances. The method of solving it is simply to calculate the densities of the three objects involved and then to compare the results.

$$\text{density of horseshoe} = \frac{\text{mass of horseshoe}}{\text{volume of horseshoe}}$$

$$= 390 \text{ g}/50 \text{ cm}^3$$

$$= 7.95 \text{ g/cm}^3 = 8.0 \text{ g/cm}^3$$

$$\text{density of scoop} = \frac{\text{mass of scoop}}{\text{volume of scoop}}$$

$$= 150 \text{ g}/55 \text{ cm}^3$$

$$= 2.73 \text{ g/cm}^3 = 2.7 \text{ g/cm}^3$$

$$\text{density of nail} = (\text{mass of nail}) / (\text{volume of nail})$$

$$= 3.1 \text{ g}/0.4 \text{ cm}^3$$

$$= 7.8 \text{ g/cm}^3 = 8 \text{ g/cm}^3$$

From this calculation one must conclude that the nail is made of iron. Because the volume of the nail is given to one significant figure, the density of the nail is accurate to one significant figure, and the difference in the calculated densities is not significant.

2-2   On the basis of your experience, try to arrange the following in order of increasing density: an iron nail, a piece of glass, a feather, mercury, a copper wire, a styrofoam cup, water, an acorn, the human body.
Answer   This question cannot be answered accurately by most students on the basis of previous experience. Its purpose is more to set them thinking about the meaning of density than to induce them to learn its value for an assortment of things.

The given objects listed in order of increasing density are (1) feather; (2) styrofoam cup; (3) acorn (0.4 - 0.7 g/cm^3); (4) the human body (0.95 - 1.05 g/cm^3); (5) water (1.0 g/cm^3); (6) glass (2.4 - 5.9 g/cm^3); (7) iron nail (7.8 g/cm^3); (8) copper wire (9.0 g/cm^3); (9) mercury (13.5 g/cm^3). Estimated densities, where available, are given in parentheses.

Questions may arise about some of these items since, for instance, the density of a bag of feathers depends on how much they are compressed, and the density of a styrofoam cup depends on how much air was incorporated into the styrene when it was prepared. Discussion of these questions should point out the requirement for careful specification of the conditions if one wishes to obtain an accurate answer. The related problem of how to estimate the volume of irregularly shaped objects is considered in the answers to Questions 2-19 and 2-20.

2-3   The density of dry air at normal atmospheric pressure and at 20°C is given as 1.20×10^{-3} g/cm^3. What is the mass of air in one cubic meter?

Answer   The density is given by density = mass/volume; multiplying both sides of this equation by volume we obtain

$$\text{volume} \times \text{density} = \frac{\text{mass}}{\text{volume}} \times \text{volume} = \text{mass}$$

Such an algebraic manipulation is not obvious to nonscience students, so the process and the reason for it should be discussed.

Given
$$\text{density} = 1.20 \times 10^{-3} \text{ g/cm}^3$$

$$\text{volume} = 1 \text{ cubic meter}$$

Substituting these values into the equation obtained above,

$$\text{mass} = \text{density} \times \text{volume}$$

we find that mass $= 1.20 \times 10^{-3} \dfrac{g}{cm^3} \times 1 \text{ meter}^3 = 1.20 \times 10^{-3} \dfrac{g \text{ meter}^3}{cm^3}$

Since this does not come out in grams it is necessary that we convert meter^3 to cm^3, or vice versa, so that the volume units cancel:

$$1 \text{ meter} = 100 \text{ cm} = 10^2 \text{ cm}$$

and

$$1 \text{ meter}^3 = (100 \text{ cm})^3 = (10^2 \text{ cm})^3 = 10^2 \times 10^2 \times 10^2 \text{ cm}^3 = 10^6 \text{ cm}^3$$

Substituting

$$\text{mass} = 1.20 \times 10^{-3} \dfrac{g \text{ meter}^3}{cm^3} = 1.20 \times 10^{-3} \dfrac{g \times 10^6}{cm^3} cm^3$$

$$= 1.20 \times 10^{-3} \times 10^6 \text{ g} = 1.20 \times 10^3 \text{ g}$$

or, since 10^3 g = 1000 g = 1 kg, mass = 1.20 kg.

Because this is one of the first problems involving the conversion of units and the use of exponential notation, it is advisable to take class time to work out the algebra, the conversion of units, and the use of powers of ten. It also emphasizes the use of units to check on the dimensions carried along. It would probably be well to call the students' attention to Appendix A in the text.

Experiment 2-1 Making Measurements

This experiment involves two different determinations of density. That required for Part A is a straightforward evaluation of volume in terms of three linear measurements. This simple procedure is not applicable, however, to the irregular rock fragment of Part B.   Rough volume estimates might be made by making approximations, but the only way to arrive at a quantitative result is by means of a liquid displacement measurement. It may be difficult to lead students to this idea without actually telling them, but the effort should be made.

The balance is used to determine the mass of the samples and this part of the experiment is best done in the laboratory. However, the recommended amounts of the other materials listed are sufficient for the volume determination to be done as a take-home.

Equipment Needed (per student)	Cat. Number
1 balance kit (Note a)	68831
2 aluminum cups (Note a)	68882
1 wooden block (Note b)	68816
4 stone fragments (Note b)	68868
1 styrofoam cup, 6 oz.	68824
1 graduated cup, plastic, 50 ml	68836
1 plastic bag and tie (Note c)	68853
1 plastic ruler, 12 inches	

Laboratory Notes

(a)   The balance is shipped unassembled, but a construction guide is included in each kit. Approximately 15 minutes are required to assemble each one. No tools are required. The balance should be used only in the laboratory and is to be shared by two students. Unfortunately they may tend to think of it not as a delicate instrument but as a toy. Although it is rugged and inexpensive it is well designed and surprisingly sensitive. Manipulated properly, it can be used with masses as small as 10 mg; with a full load of 50 g on each pan, the sensitivity is better than 20 mg.
A discussion of the care and use of a chemical balance would be appropriate here.
Strings of specially selected beads are used in place of standard masses. The masses of the beads are identical to within one part in a hundred (1%). The students should determine or be given the mass in grams of the entire string of beads. Then, after determining the total number of beads, each student is to calculate the mass per bead. The string is then cut to give smaller lengths of 1, 2, 3, 5, 10, 20, 30, 50, 100, etc., beads per chain. These should be stored in the drawer at the base of the balance.

It is recommended that one aluminum cup be used on each pan. These cups are very useful for holding the weighing beads and the chemicals. The stability of the cup can be improved by notching its lip with a pair of scissors. The notch should be just wide enough to fit around the metal rod connecting the pan to the balance arm. If two cuts are made in the lip of each cup and the notch is folded down against the side, the mass of the cup will remain the same and no additional problems will arise when taring the two cups.

(b)   Most students have little trouble using the plastic ruler to obtain the block volume. Note, however, that the blocks do not have the same volume. This is intentional and is designed to encourage students to rely upon their own results.

It is better to use four small pieces of stone instead of the one larger piece mentioned in the text. Water displacement is the best method to use to determine the rock's volume. This technique requires sizable fragments if even moderate accuracy is to be obtained. These bigger stones, however, are normally too heavy for the balance. Thus the four rocks are weighed individually but are used together when the volume is determined.

(c)   If the volume determination of the two substances is to be done as a take-home experiment, all the materials (except the balance and pans) listed under *Equipment Needed* should be bagged to facilitate distribution to the students.

Section 2-3 WHEN?

The answer to the question "What is time?" has yet to be found. It continues to bother scientists and philosophers up to the present day. It is perhaps not intrinsically more difficult to define than length: time is the variable by which we order a succession of events into a sequence, and length is the variable by which we order a succession of points into a series. Only the latter is likely to be a satisfactory definition, however; it is much easier to picture intuitively a location in space than it is to picture mentally a location in time.

Regardless of the philosophical attractiveness and the practical difficulty of defining time, the only aspect of the problem significant for most scientific work is that we succeed in specifying the units and the methods by which we measure it. When we define time in a physical situation, we invariably do so in terms of the measurement of a periodic process: the number of years, or pendulum swings, or clock ticks, between two events. This type of definition is called an *operational definition.*

There are, however, two quite distinct types of definitions. One we might call a fundamental definition, which specifies the essential nature or quality of the thing being considered. This sort of definition is independent of any measurements and makes no mention of measuring units. An example is the definition of length as the spatial extent between two points. Basic as it is, however, such a definition is of little practical use in a laboratory. There we must have an operational definition, which, for instance, says that the unit of length, the meter, consists of a fixed multiple of a certain wavelength of light.

QUESTION

2-4   Think about the possible use of the following phenomena as units of time: (a) the motion of the Moon around the Earth; (b) the rotation of the Earth about its axis; (c) the beating of your heart; (d) the dripping of water; (e) the time between sunrise and sunset; (f) a freely swinging pendulum. *Answer*   Each of these phenomena can be and has been used to measure time. The more nearly constant the period the more satisfactory any particular phenomenon would be for use in establishing a unit of time.

Section 2-4 HOW HOT?

There are several experiments in this section, although only one new concept is introduced. This is temperature, which is brought in empirically, using thermometers, in Experiment 2-2.

Experiment 2-2 Observations of Dissolving Solids

This is an experiment which should serve very well to whet the student's interest even though the results are not explained until Section 15-7.

Equipment Needed (per 2 students)	Cat. Number
2 thermometers, metal backed, -10/ × 110°C	68875
4 test tubes, 25 × 150 mm (Note a)	68873
1 graduated cup, plastic, 50 ml	68836
1 spatula	68864
35 g, sodium carbonate, anhydrous (Note b)	68549
20 g, ammonium chloride (Note b)	68516
2 weighing cups, paper	68823
1 beaker, 250 ml (Note c)	68815
2 pairs, safety goggles	68838

Laboratory Notes

It is recommended that a sufficient quantity of metal-backed thermometers be purchased so that each student has one. The thermometer is inexpensive, durable, and accurate; furthermore, it will be used in many take-home and laboratory experiments.

(a)   This experiment could be performed with only two test tubes for every two students, but the tubes must always be dry on the inside before a chemical is introduced.   Because the test tubes are not damaged in this experiment, extra ones are suggested.

(b)   The quantities suggested are sufficient to allow each student to do both parts. It is not necessary to weigh the chemicals; all that is required is that each pair of students have a sufficient amount of each chemical to fill a test tube to a depth of about an inch.

      The paper weighing cups can be filled ahead of time with the amount of chemical to be used by each pair of students in the lab, and one can be placed at each lab station.

(c)   In this experiment, the beaker is used as a test tube rack.

QUESTIONS

2-5   What is the significant difference in your observations with the anhydrous sodium carbonate and the ammonium chloride? In what ways were you able to determine this?
Answer   When the anhydrous sodium carbonate dissolved, the test tube became hotter than it had been. This was detected by feeling the hotness as compared to the reference test tube and by observing the thermometer. The student should conclude by either observation that the process of dissolving sodium carbonate evolves heat. When the ammonium chloride dissolved, the test tube became colder than it had been. The student should conclude that dissolving ammonium chloride in water absorbs heat from the surroundings.
The first of these processes is *exothermic* and the second is *endothermic.* The description of these processes in terms of energy changes will be given in Chapter 15 but should not be discussed here.

Experiments 2-3 and 2-4 make further comparison between thermometers and the students' sense of touch for determining temperatures. This is followed by a discussion of temperature scales and temperature measuring devices.

Experiment 2-3   A Thermal Illusion

All equipment needed here is supplied by the student.

QUESTION

2-6   In view of the experiment with the three bowls of water, are you justified in relying on the observations made with your hands when you wish to determine temperature?
Answer   The sensations of hot and cold as determined by touch are relative and reasonably useful only for noting changes in temperature. In the experiment one hand feels warmer and the other colder as they respond to changes in temperature, but they lead to different estimates of whether the lukewarm water is hot or cold.

Experiment 2-4 The Temperature Sensitivity Of The Hand

The students' ability to discern differences in temperature is often very strongly affected by whether or not they can see the water being added. The experiment can be made more meaningful and more interesting by blindfolding them as they try to sense the changing water temperature.

Equipment Needed (per student)	Cat. Number
1 thermometer, metal-backed, -10/+110°C	68875

QUESTION

2-7   Make a diagram of a thermometer showing the following points by marks and labels (in degrees) for the Fahrenheit scale on the left side and the Celsius scale on the right side: (a) the boiling point of water;

(b) the freezing point of water; (c) some particular temperature that would be comfortable as a room temperature; (d) the freezing point of mercury (-40°C).

Answer   The conversion can be obtained by laying off two linear scales such that 212° F is equivalent to 100°C and 32°F is equivalent to 0°C. This method is preferable for nonscience students. The 180 divisions between freezing and boiling on the Fahrenheit scale are equivalent to the 100 divisions on the Celsius scale.

Section 2-5 HOW MUCH HEAT?

The distinction between temperature and heat is introduced in this section in two thought experiments which are preliminary to Experiment 2-5. In discussing both of them it should be emphasized that heat flows from the body at the higher temperature (the rock) to the body at the lower temperature (the water). Although this is common experience, few students are likely to have articulated the observation. When the temperatures of the bodies become equal, heat flow stops, and we have thermal equilibrium.

From the second thought experiment we further conclude that the more heat we add to a body, the higher we raise its temperature. The converse to this should also be obvious to the students.

Experiment 2-5 Heat Transfer From Different Substances

Although heat is neither defined nor measured here, an intuitive understanding is developed. Some ideas suggested or illustrated are: heat is detected only when it is flowing from one body to another; its flow depends on the temperature difference between the bodies; it flows from higher to lower temperatures, and not in the opposite direction; the amount of heat energy present in an object depends at least upon its mass, its temperature, and the substance of which it is made.

Equipment Needed (per 2 students)	Cat. Number
6 lead balls	68812
20 glass marbles (Note a)	68848
1 equal-arm balance	68831
1 beaker, 250 ml (Note b)	68815
2 alcohol burners and fuel	68810
1 box, matches	68539
1 burner stand	68810
2 styrofoam cups (Note c)	68824
2 thermometers, metal-backed, -10/+110°C	68875
1 graduated cup, plastic, 50 ml	68836
2 plastic bags, heat resistant (Note d)	68544
2 pairs, safety goggles	68838

Laboratory Notes

(a)   Glass marbles are available in units of 135 black and 15 white (marbles; glass, #68848). They will be needed later, in Experiment 13-1, in bags of ten (9 black, 1 white), so they can be bagged this way for distribution to the students for this experiment. Two students, each with a bag of marbles, should work together.
   It is necessary to use nearly the same mass of each kind of ball in order for the results of the experiment to be meaningful. Ten to fifteen glass marbles is a suitable number; the students should use the balance to determine the number of lead balls needed to match approximately the mass of the marbles.

(b)   The water is to be boiled in the beaker. Start with the hottest water readily available, place the beaker on the burner stand, and use the alcohol burners to maintain boiling throughout the experiment. It requires considerable time to bring a beaker of cool water to a boil if alcohol burners are the only source of heat.

(c)   Styrofoam cups are effective as calorimeters. Use the plastic graduated cup to pour 50 ml of water into each styrofoam cup. The initial temperature of the water should be determined just before the hot spheres are added.

(d)   It is important that the lead and glass balls be kept dry while they are being heated in the boiling water. If this is not done, droplets of hot water will remain on them, and will be introduced into the calorimeter along with them, significantly influencing the results. To prevent this place the glass marbles and the metal balls in separate plastic bags before submerging them in the boiling water. The special, heat resistant bags do not melt and will keep the contents dry.
   The transfer of heat from the water to the contents of the plastic bags is not as rapid or effective as it would be without the bag. In order to insure uniform heating, it is necessary to keep the bags of marbles and lead balls in the boiling water for some time, probably at least 10 minutes.
   After the spheres have reached 100°C they must be poured from the plastic bags into the calorimeter cup as quickly as possible.

QUESTION

2-8   What do you deduce from your experiment concerning the effect of the nature of the material on heat transfer?
   Answer   The heat transferred to its surroundings by a mass of material when it undergoes a temperature change is proportional to the temperature change and to the mass of the object, and it must also depend on the material. Experiment 2-5 shows the difference between glass and lead. The heat transferred by the glass marbles should be considerably more than that by the lead. The quantity being compared in Experiment 2-5 is the specific heat of glass (0.20 cal/g°C) and of lead (0.03 cal/g°C), but it would be confusing here to name the quantity or to give numerical values.

Experiment 2-6 A Study Of Temperature Change During Cooling

As was mentioned earlier, it is obvious to most people that to raise the temperature of something you must add heat and to cool it you must remove heat. What they do not often realize, however, is that the converse statements are not necessarily true. That is, it is not true that when heat is added to a body its temperature must rise, nor that when heat is removed, its temperature must fall. Changes of state (solid-liquid and liquid-gas) require energy changes which involve the transfer of heat without accompanying temperature changes.

Experiments 2-6 and 2-7 are intended to illustrate these phenomena, although there are no actual measurements made on the quantities of heat transferred. In the first of these two experiments the students determine the temperature of a melt as it cools and solidifies. During the portion of the time when the material is solidifying, the temperature remains roughly constant. Let the students discover this, and then draw a graph of the temperature as a function of time. The resulting cooling curve will show a corresponding plateau.

Graphs are used in this experiment for the first time, and a fairly careful class discussion of the drawing and interpretation of graphs, as covered in Appendix B, would probably be very useful. A point which is mentioned there but which might well be further emphasized is that one of the most important effects of graphically representing experimental data is to "average" the errors involved and thus to give a more accurate overall result than can be obtained otherwise. This is what is implied in the phrases "the best straight line" and "the smoothest curve nearest the most points." Students should be made to realize that merely connecting the experimentally determined points completely nullifies this important aspect of graphing.

Equipment Needed (per 2 students)	Cat. Number
1 pegboard kit (Note a)	68852
1 alcohol burner	68810
1 box, matches	68539
1 thermometer, glass, -10 / +360 (Note b)	68874
1 test tube, 25 x 150 mm (Note c)	68873
2 pegboard clamps, large	68532
15 g, *para*-dichlorobenzene (Note d) or napthalene (Note d)	68542 68540
2 pairs, safety goggles	68838
1 weighing cup, paper	68823
1 graduated cup, plastic, 50 ml	68836
4 sheets, graph paper	—
1 plastic ruler, 12 in.	—
(per class)	
1 clock with sweep second hand	68821
2 plastic squeeze bottles, 500 ml (Note e)	68817

Laboratory Notes

(a)   The pegboards must be assembled. Allow about 25 minutes per kit. Each kit consists of a 19-inch long wooden base, and a 12 x 19-inch sheet of ¼-inch pegboard with holes spaced ½ inch apart, a plastic bag of small parts, and assembly instructions. The long, thin bolts and aluminum sleeves come in two different lengths. The shorter bolt and sleeve are used with the larger clamp and vice versa. This places the center of both types of clamps equidistant from the pegboard.

(b)   The thermometer is used in this experiment as a stirring rod; experience shows that the resulting breakage is minimal. While data are being taken, the liquid should be stirred constantly to insure even heat transfer. Do not use the metal-backed thermometer in this experiment. Even with the glass thermometer, the coloring may float out of the markings. Should this happen, recolor using a little graphite in alcohol.

(c)   The test tube should fit snugly in the large clamp. If it does not, the clamp can be closed slightly by squeezing tightly with pliers at its two corners.

(d)   The *para*-dichlorobenze and naphthalene should be measured out ahead of time and the proper amount placed in a paper weighing cup at each lab station. (It is best to alternate chemicals at adjoining stations to discourage the "What temperature are you getting?" talk between students.) The 50-ml graduated plastic cup is useful for measuring out the chemicals; 20–25 ml of *para*-dichlorobenzene are required, and 25–30 ml of naphthalene. The difference comes about because the naphthalene is flaky and less dense as shipped.

If several different lab sections are to do this experiment, it is advisable to have the first section leave the test tubes with the slugs of solidified chemicals in them. The following sections then need only to heat and melt the substance to begin the exercise. In any event, the students should not attempt to clean the test tubes. This should be emphasized, because pouring the molten material down the drain will result in a plugged drain, since both of these chemicals are insoluble in water.

(e)   Plastic 500-ml bottles are recommended for refilling the alcohol burners. If a plastic bottle leaks, screw the cap on tigher. Also cut a little off the end of the spout to enlarge the opening and increase the ease of flow.

QUESTIONS

2-9   You used about 15 grams of solid substance. How would the curve be different if you had used 30 grams?

Answer   The quantity of heat given off as the substance cooled may be divided into three parts: the heat evolved as the liquid cooled to the melting point, the heat evolved as the liquid turned to solid, and the heat evolved as the solid cooled to its final temperature. In each of these three steps the heat evolved is proportional to the mass of the substance. Thus the heat evolved would be twice as much with 30 grams as with 15 grams. The rate of loss of heat to the surroundings depends on the relative temperature of the surroundings, and to some extent on the surface area of the specimen. If the latter factor were the same in both cases, the rate of loss of heat would be the same in both cases, but the resulting rate of decrease in temperature would be about half as much for 30 grams as for 15 grams. Thus the time required to cool through a given temperature change should be roughly twice as great for the 30-gram as for the 15-gram sample. The understanding to be derived from this experiment and from this question is that the loss of heat goes on whether the hot object is cooling or solidifying at constant temperature, as long as its temperature is higher than that of its surroundings.

2-10   What would the curve look like if the test tube containing the melt had been placed in cold water? Would you expect the solidification temperature to change or the plateau to be shorter? Would the temperature of the water change? Give reasons for your answers, then check them by the following experiment. (Experiment 2-7: *A Closer Look at the Plateau.*)

Answer   This question probably calls for more experience and information than most nonscience students have, since it asks for a comparison of the heat transfer between the specimen and the surrounding medium when that medium is air and when that medium is water. The basic process is the same but the amount of heat transferred per unit time per degree of temperature difference may be somewhat greater for water than for air because of the higher rate of heat transfer through the water. The difference between the two cases will probably be small except initially, and certainly there will be no major change in the shape of the curve. The solidification temperature would not be changed since this is a property of the material. The length of the plateau is determined by the heat evolved by the material as it solidifies (this is the same in both cases) divided by the rate of transfer of heat to the surroundings at the melting point (this may be somewhat greater for water than for air). Thus the length of the plateau would probably be somewhat shorter when the tube is surrounded by water than when it is surrounded by air.

Experiment 2-7 A Closer Look At The Plateau

In Experiment 2-6 the melt was in a thermal environment consisting of the air itself, and it was difficult to observe the heat flow between the cooling melt and its surroundings. Our purpose in Experiment 2-7 is to emphasize the fact that during the solidification process, heat does leave the material, even though the temperature remains constant. We do this by placing the melt in a water bath, and then simultaneously following the temperatures of the bath and the melt. The important result is that the water temperature rises while the melt is solidifying at a constant temperature (plateau). Figure RB 2-1 shows qualitatively what one finds. Heat is therefore entering the water, and it clearly must come from the hotter body in contact with the water.

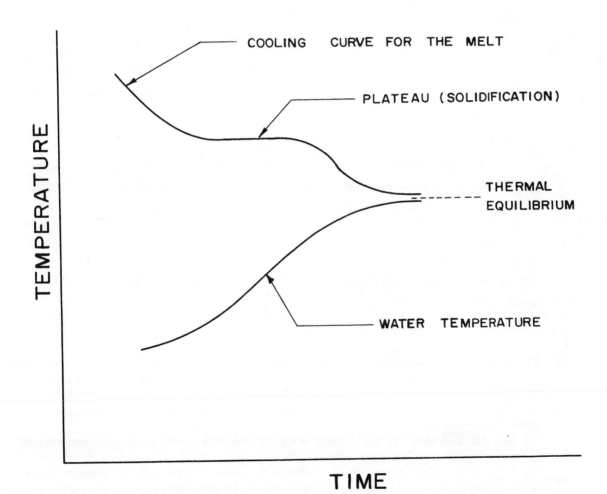

Figure RB 2-1

The amount of heat given off during the solidification process in Experiment 2-7 is rather small and usually results in a water temperature change of only two or three degrees. Students must therefore be very careful in making their measurements to be certain of noticing the effect. When the data on the water temperature versus time is being graphed, the variation can be made more obvious by using a different scale for the water temperature than is used for the melt temperature. If twice as many divisions are used to represent one degree, there is an effective magnification of two in the changes; three time as many divisions per degree gives a magnification of three, and so on. This is a useful technique in situations such as this one; the only caution is that the scale differences   should be clearly indicated on the graph so that the reader will be able to recognize at a glance what has been done.

Equipment Needed	
(per 2 students)	*Cat. Number*
1 pegboard	68852
1 alcohol burner	68810
1 box, matches	68539
2 test tubes, 25 × 150 mm (Note a)	68873
1 thermometer, glass, -10/ + 360°C (Note a)	68874
2 pegboard clamps, large	68532
2 pairs, safety goggles	68838
4 sheets, graph paper	—
1 plastic ruler, 12 in.	—
1 styrofoam cup, 6 oz	68824
1 thermometer, metal backed (Note a)	68875
1 graduated cup, plastic, 50 ml	68836
(per class)	
1 clock with sweep second hand	68821
2 plastic squeeze bottles, 500 ml	68817

Laboratory Notes

(a)   The test tube used in Experiment 2-6 should be reused here. It should still contain a slug of solidified chemical. However, if two test tubes are used, each containing 15 grams of the same chemical, and a thermometer in only one of them, the results will turn out better. The reason is that two test tubes will decrease the amount of water in the styrofoam cup at the same time as they increase the amount of heat to be given off.

The glass thermometer should again be used in the test tube. The metal-backed thermometer should be used to determine the water temperature.

It is not necessary to have exactly 50 ml of water in the calorimeter cup. What is important, however, is to have just enough water in the cup so that the water level and chemical level coincide when the test tube is submerged in the cup.

QUESTIONS

2-11   Is heat continuously evolved by the substance in the test tube during the time of the experiment?
Answer   The temperature of the water rises continuously during the experiment. During the time when the specimen solidifies the temperature of the water continues to rise, which indicates that the water is continuing to absorb heat even though the temperature of the specimen remains constant. Thus the specimen evolves heat while it is solidifying at constant temperature.

2-12   How does the temperature-time curve of the water relate to the cooling curve of the substance in the test tube?
Answer   This question must be discussed carefully so as not to go beyond the abilities of the non-science student. Two relationships are of interest here. The curve for the water continues to rise even though the temperature of the specimen remains constant. This observation is the basis of the answer to Question 2-11. The second fact which should be observed is that the two curves both approach a common final temperature. This equilibrium temperature is the temperature at which neither gives heat to the other.

2-13   Many people say that temperature is a measure of heat. Do the temperature-time curves of this experiment support this suggestion?
Answer   If temperature were a measure of heat, the water would be receiving heat continuously even though part of the time the specimen would not be giving it off. Thus the quantity of heat transferred during a change of state is not related linearly to the temperature. The suggestion is therefore not at all true during changes of state.

2-14   If you put ice in a glass of tap water it will melt. Where does the heat come from to melt that ice? How could you verify your answer?
Answer   When ice melts it must absorb heat to change from solid at $0°C$ to liquid at $0°C$. It is in contact with water at a higher temperature and can absorb heat from the water. It will continue to melt until all of the water cools to $0°C$; then no further melting will take place except by absorbing heat from the surroundings.
This answer can be verified by either testing the water with your hand or measuring the temperature of the water with a thermometer. The thermometer reading will drop to $0°C$ if the ice does not all melt, or to some intermediate temperature if it does. In either case the decrease in temperature of the water is a measure of the loss of heat by the water.

2-15   If a rectangular object has the dimensions 4.0 cm x 2.0 cm x 6.0 cm and has a mass of 144 g, what is its density?
Answer By definition, density = mass/volume.
The mass is given as 144 g, but we must calculate the volume.

$$\text{Volume} \quad = \quad \text{width} \times \text{height} \times \text{length}$$
$$= \quad 4.0 \text{ cm} \times 2.0 \text{ cm} \times 6.0 \text{ cm} = 4.0 \times 2.0 \times 6.0 \text{ cm}^3$$
$$= \quad 8.0 \times 6.0 \text{ cm}^3 = 48 \text{ cm}^3$$

In no stage of the multiplication should there be more than three significant figures, and the final answer should be rounded off to two since only two are given in each dimension. The volume should thus be written as 48 cm^3, not as 48.0 cm^3 or 48.000 cm^3. Even though the mass is given to three significant figures, the density, $144 \text{ g}/48 \text{ cm}^3$, should also be rounded off to two, because no quotient or product can be more precisely known than its least precise factor. The proper form for the answer, then, is density = 3.0 g/cm^3.

2-16   If the density of an object is 0.05 g/cm^3 and its mass is 144 g, what is its volume?

Answer   Volume = $\dfrac{\text{mass}}{\text{density}}$ = $\dfrac{144g}{0.05g/cm^3}$ = 288 cm^3

2-17 Do you think it would make any difference in the results if the density of a cube of copper metal were determined out of doors on a hot day in August (95°F) or on a cool day in November (45°F)? Why?

Answer   By definition, density = mass/volume. The mass of the block will not change with temperature but the length of each side of the cube increases if the temperature increases. Thus the volume will increase if the temperature increases. If the denominator in the expression for the density increases with increasing temperature, the density must decrease with increasing temperature. Since the increase in length is small (less than 0.06%), the decrease in density will also be small (less than 0.20%).

2-18 Scientists are faced with the problem of measuring very small, as well as very large, distances. How would you measure the thickness of a page of a book? What difficulties might be encountered? What experimental procedures take care of these difficulties?

Answer   The thickness of 100 or 200 pages can be measured with a meter stick; the thickness of 1 page can be found by dividing the result by the number of pages. The greater the number of pages the more accurate the value for one page. For example, if 600 pages of a book have a combined thickness of 2.3 cm (two significant figures), then an average page has a thickness of 2.3 cm/600 = 0.0038 cm (two significant figures). Similar procedures are used in measuring atomic distances.

2-19 Calculate the approximate weight per cubic foot of your body. To do this you will need to make some approximations. Try to estimate your body volume by substituting for it a rectangular box having a length equal to your height. Make a reasonable guess as to your average width and thickness. Use these three dimensions to calculate your volume in cubic feet and divide that volume into your weight. The result should be close to the corresponding value for water, 62.4 lb/ft^3. What independent evidence can you give in support of your result?

Answer   height = 5.8 ft   weight = 170 lb

average thickness = 0.50 ft   average width = 1.0 ft

volume = 5.8 ft x 0.50 ft x 1.0 ft = 2.9 ft^3

density = $\dfrac{170 \text{ lb}}{2.9 \text{ ft}^3}$ = 58 lb/ft^3

We know that this is only an approximation; most people can just about float in water, and their body density must therefore be about equal to the density of water.

2-20 The approximation suggested in Question 2-19 is a very crude one. It can be improved by substituting appropriately sized geometrical solids for various parts of the body, in succession, as follows: (a) Consider your trunk from hips to neck to be a cylinder. Determine its approximate length and radius and compute its volume. (The volume of a cylinder is $\pi r^2 l$.) (b) Consider each leg to be a cylinder. Approximate the dimensions and find the volume. (c) Each arm is a cylinder. Approximate the dimensions and find the volume of both arms. (d) What is the approximate shape of the neck? Approximate the dimensions and find the volume of your neck. (e) Your head is approximately spherical. Determine its average diameter. Find the volume of your head (the volume of a sphere is $(4/3)\, \pi r^3$). (f) Now find the total volume of your body and again divide it into your weight. Compare this result with the density of water, 62.4 lb/ft^3.

Answer   (a) Trunk: length = 2.0 ft; radius = 0.40 ft; volume = $\pi x r^2$ x 1 = 1.0 ft^3
                    (b) Legs: length = 3.0 ft; radius = 0.25 ft; volume = 2 x 0.60 ft^3 = 1.2 ft^3

(c) Arms: length = 2.5 ft; average radius = 1/8 ft; volume = 2×0.12 ft^3 = 0.24 ft^3

(d) Head: radius = 4 inches = 1/3 ft; volume = $4/3 \, \pi \times 1/27$ ft = 0.15 ft^3

(e) Neck: height = 0.25 ft; radius = 0.2 ft; volume = 0.03 ft^3

(f) Total: volume = 2.62 ft^3 ; density = $\dfrac{170 \text{ lb}}{2.62 \text{ ft}^3}$ = 65 lb/ft^3

2-21 Someone once proposed using the honeycomb made by honey bees as a standard of length. What factors must be considered to determine if this is a good standard?

Answer   In an individual honeycomb where all bees are of the same species, are all holes of the same size? In a given hive are all holes of the same size? How great is the variation from hive to hive, and from one species of bee to another? Does the size vary with atmospheric conditions? Does the size vary with altitude? These questions must be answered in order to establish whether any honeycomb can be used or only one special one. The honeycomb would be a useful standard if all holes were the same size and if honeycombs were readily available.

2-22 Compare the interval between successive noons with the interval between successive sunrises as a basis for determining a unit of time.

Answer   The interval between successive noons — between successive transits of the Sun across a line passing through a point immediately over head and the North Pole — is the same as all points on the earth and varies but slightly during the year. It would thus be a reasonably good unit of time. The time from sunrise to sunrise, however, varies from day to day and from place to place on the Earth's surface.

2-23 Imagine that you have a small heavy object tied to one end of a string. The other end is held stationary. The object swings with a period (time for one complete back-and-forth motion) of one second. What would you predict would have to be changed to change the period to two seconds? Try it. Work with your pendulum until you have discovered how to change the period from one second to two seconds. Compare as quantitatively as possible the 2-second pendulum with the 1-second pendulum.

Answer   This question forms the basis for an experiment that students can do with a string, several weights, and a watch. The most obvious variables to consider are the mass of the object, the length of the string, and the amplitude of the swing. It is suggested that the student measure the time for 50 swings and then successively double each variable, keeping the other variables fixed at their original value. A few measurements with different lengths may show him that he must increase the length by a factor of four in order to increase the period by a factor of 2. The square of the period is proportional to the length. Changes in amplitude and mass have little effect on the period.

2-24 Why does heating the bottom of a test tube, while the top is still cool, sometimes cause violent ejection of the contents of the tube?

Answer   In Experiment 2-6 the students were cautioned when heating the naphthalene or *para*-dichlorobenze to play the flame over the side and bottom of the test tube to insure even heating of the entire sample. If one portion were heated more rapidly than others it might vaporize, forming a pocket of vapor which would expand considerably, pushing the surrounding material away. If this occurred rapidly enough it might blow the rest of the material out of the tube. If the material is liquefied one must also apply heat gently and uniformly to prevent violent boiling, which has the same effect.

2-25 Draw a heating curve for the substance used in Experiment 2-6. Will there be a plateau? If so, is heat entering the substance during that time? If so, where did this heat come from?

Answer   See Figure RB 2-2. The heating curve is the reverse of the cooling curve. The two curves would be mirror images if the rate of heat transfer were the same in both cases. There is a plateau in the heating curve. While the temperature remains constant at the melting point, heat is being added to the substance to change its state from solid to liquid without changing the temperature. The heat required must be supplied by the burner.

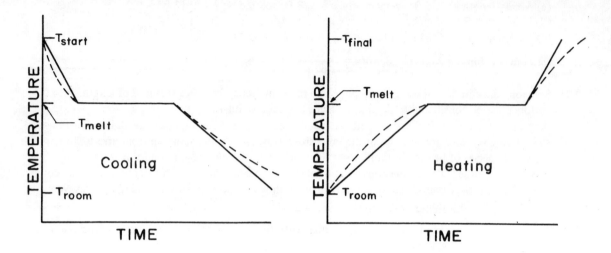

Figure RB 2-2

2-26 In the experiment on cooling curves, Experiment 2-6, is the slope (steepness) of your graph before the plateau greater than the slope after the plateau? Is the slope related in some way to the rate of heat transfer from the substance to the surrounding air? Compare the difference in temperature between the substance and the surrounding air at the beginning and at the end of the experiment. Is there some relationship between the rate of heat transfer and temperature difference?

Answer   The slope of the graph, $\frac{\Delta T}{\Delta t}$ (Fig. RB 2-3) is considerably greater at the start than it is at the end. To show this, lay off two triangles with the horizontal legs Δt being the same for both; ΔT, the vertical leg, is obviously greater for the triangle near the start than for the one near the end. The slope approaches zero as the temperature of the substance approaches room temperature and is greater the greater the difference in temperature between the substance and the surrounding air.

The rate of transfer of heat determines the rate of change of temperature of the substance. The mass of the substance and its character also influence the rate of change of temperature.

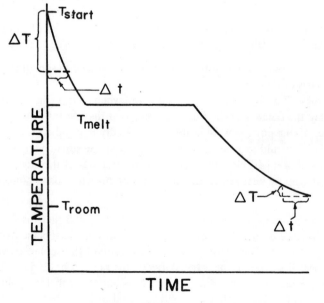

Figure RB 2-3

2-27 Try to think of a situation in which you could control an experiment in some way. Examples might be (a) a variation of a cooking recipe, as in changing the amount of baking powder; (b) checking gasoline mileage by changing only the octane rating of the gasoline, or by changing the average driving speed, etc. Show how the problem is isolated and how the variable you choose can be controlled.

Answer The students should be able to give a variety of such problems related to their diet, their finances, their effectiveness in studying etc.

2-28 Just as density is one of the characterizing properties of a particular substance, so is solubility. For example, carbon dioxide, one of the constituents in soda water, has a solubility in water of 3.48 g/liter at a temperature of $0^{\circ}C$ and at atmosphere pressure. That is, at this temperature and pressure, no more than 3.48 grams of carbon dioxide can be dissolved in 1 liter of water. As with boiling temperatures, solubilities depend on the physical condition of the substance, so these conditions must be stipulated whenever solubilities are given. In this instance, the temperatures and pressure of the water are given.

As a test of your ability to observe and to plan an experiment, outline a simple procedure to find out whether the solubility of carbon dioxide in water increases or decreases when the temperature is raised.

Answer The problem is to find out how much carbon dioxide is dissolved in one liter of water at a low temperature and at a high temperature. The variables to be related are the mass of carbon dioxide dissolved in one liter of water and the temperature of the water. Other variables which may affect the results and which must be kept constant are the pressure on the surface of the water and the rate of evaporation from the surface.

ADDITIONAL QUESTIONS

2-29 The statement is made in Section 2-1 that scientists started to experiment to test their explanations in the seventeenth century, but has not man always experimented?

Answer Answers to this question might include a statement such as, "If one concludes it is hot by touching the alleged hot object, then has an experiment been performed?" If so then man has always experimented in this manner. The reference to the seventeenth century probably refers to what we now mean by an experiment, in which we consciously control the known variables to test an explanation or hypothesis.

This question is included to make students think more clearly and precisely about the meaning and significance of experimentation, and possibly to make them feel that it is not just a thing that scientists do, but something anyone does to "prove" something to himself. A discussion of "good" and "bad" experiments could fit in here.

2-30 What is meant by: natural units? fundamental units.

Answer A natural unit is a unit based on some naturally occurring phenomenon such as the time it takes the Earth to revolve about the Sun or the length of time required for a heartbeat.

A fundamental unit is a unit such as length, mass, or time upon which other units are based. The students are aware of the units of speed: feet per second or miles per hour. Although these units are based on the fundamental ones of length and time, they are neither fundamental nor natural themselves. One might say that fundamental units would more properly be called fundamental concepts, and that their magnitudes are often, though not always, measured in terms of natural units.

2-31 Is there a method for determining the amount of mass an object possesses other than comparing? In determining the amount of anything an object possesses, can this be done by other methods than comparison?

Answer Whenever we measure some quantity, we compare it to some standard whose magnitude we already know. Ask the students to come up with an example where this is not so if they disagree.

2-32 Some people say that our definition of time should not depend on measurements. Do you believe this is necessary? Give reasons.

Answer We want to point out here that a measurement of the size of something is not the same as the idea or concept that the thing itself represents. The units by which something is measured do not define its meaning; conversely, a definition should not depend on measurements.

REFERENCES

1. (T)   Baez, Chapter 7, pages 81 to 93. This is just a collection of various ideas and notions about time. It is very hard to describe the difficult but basic concept of time, so we look for various sources of thought on the concept, and perhaps we profit as we go along.

2. (T)   Feynman, Chapter 5, pages 5-1 to 5-10. Here are more ideas and notions of length and time, and examples of how to measure them. Some ideas of the orders of magnitude for various lengths and times are also given.

3.   Resnick and Halliday, Chapter 1, pages 1 to 12. This reference gives specifications about the standards used for length and time.

4.   Astin, A.V., "Standards of Measurement", *Scientific American,* June 1968, pages 50 ff.

CHAPTER 3

A LOOK AT LIGHT

We will later want to make use of the results of x-ray diffraction studies in our investigations of the structure of solids. To understand this method of analysis, it is necessary to understand the wave properties of light and the interference properties of waves. We take up the first of these topics here, and will begin the second in the next chapter.

Section 3-1 LIGHT AND SOLID MATTER

Since none of the students are likely to know anything about x-ray diffraction methods of analysis, and not many more will know anything about ordinary interference and diffraction, it is difficult to establish a "need to know" in advance. We make an attempt in this secton by means of an experiment involving the interaction between light and photosensitive crystals. The conclusions which can be drawn from the experiment this early in the course are few, but we will refer to it later on. Hopefully it will serve here to indicate that a study of light may have a real bearing on the study of matter.

Experiment 3-1 A Chemical Reaction Produced by Light

The purpose of this experiment is twofold. First, it is graphic proof of the fact that light interacts with matter in such a way as to cause changes in that matter. Later on you can refer back to this as an indication of the fact that light has energy, although the concept of energy has not been brought up as yet. The second purpose of this experiment is that the students will gain additional experience in laboratory techniques and observation. What they observe, of course, is that a piece of paper dipped in one solution and then into another is subsequently affected by light. Light has caused something to happen to the substance on the piece of paper. Why two solutions? Would either alone be affected the same way? This question should certainly arise, but should be answered only by performing the experiment of wetting a piece of paper with one solution and another piece with the other solution and exposing them both to light.

This experiment is suitable either as a take-home assignment or for in-lab performance. In any event, the students should be cautioned to exercise care in handling the materials, particularly the silver nitrate. Besides being poisonous, if it is spilled it will severely stain hands, clothing, etc. Staining can be minimized, however, by immediately washing away any spilled chemical.

Equipment Needed (per student)	*Cat. Number*
contained in the chemical reaction produced by Light Kit (Note a):	68845
1 glass vial with cap, containing silver nitrate (Note b)	

38   A Look at Light

Equipment Needed
(per student)   *Cat. Number*

1 glass vial with cap, containing sodium chloride (Note b)

2 strips, chromatography paper, 8 x 2.5 cm

2 plastic lids (Note c)

1 medicine dropper

2 paper towels

1 plastic bag with wire tie   68853

Laboratory Notes

(a)   As supplied, this package contains sufficient materials to prepare individual kits for 10 students.
(b)   Solutions of both substances are obtained by carefully filling the container vial with water, recapping, and shaking to dissolve all of the dry material.
(c)   Plastic lids are used in place of more expensive watch glasses. One solution is to be poured into each lid. The lids should be marked ahead of time with a ball-point pen to facilitate the identification of the solution and to prevent the possibility of contamination if these materials are used a second time.

When the strip of paper moistened with silver nitrate solution is placed in the sodium chloride solution, the students will observe little change unless the room is very brightly lighted. The darkening of the paper after more extended exposure is caused by the interaction of light with silver chloride. Light causes silver chloride to decompose, ultimately yielding silver metal.

Students who have previously had chemistry may want a chemical explanation of what is happening, and there is no need to withhold this from them if they ask for it. You must be cautious, however, about how you present such information. Most of the students are likely to be frightened if you present chemical equations to them this early in the course. You will have to do it in an offhand manner, with the assurance that you are giving them the information simply because it was requested, not because you expect the class to be responsible for learning it.

The silver chloride which is deposited on the paper when it is submerged in the sodium chloride solution is a fine white precipitate. It is difficult to see, however, and most students will fail to notice it. The equation for the precipitation reaction is

$$Ag^+NO_3^- + Na^+Cl^- \rightarrow \downarrow Ag^+Cl^- + Na^+NO_3^-$$

Under the influence of light the precipitated silver chloride is reduced in a complicated series of reactions to various subchlorides and ultimately to finely divided metallic silver, which is dark in color. The overall reaction for this reduction process may be summarized in the equation

$$2\,Ag^+Cl^- \rightarrow 2\,Ag + Cl_2$$

Other silver halides (silver bromide and silver iodide) behave in a similar manner.

The fact that the substances silver chloride, silver bromide, and silver iodide decompose in proportion to the amount of light to which they are exposed is the basis of black and white photography.

It is asked in the textbook how the photographic record may be made permanent. The students will have observed that so long as the light-sensitive chemical remains on the paper, it will continue to darken. From this observation, perhaps they can be led to conclude that to stop the action all remaining traces of the chemical must either be removed or somehow altered so as to become insensitive to light. Much of the chemical can be washed off the paper, and the "fixer" commonly used in photography is a solution of sodium thiosulfate, $Na_2S_2O_3 \cdot (5H_2O)$. It dissolves the unaltered silver halides (AgC1, AgBr, AgI) remaining in the paper or film. This involves a chemical reaction between the silver ion and the thiosulfate ion. The result is a light-insensitive complex.

Section 3-2 COLOR

The purpose of this section is to pose questions and propose hypotheses about the nature of color, and then to perform some simple experiments to test the hypotheses.

Experiment 3-2 Colored Objects

This is a take-home experiment. Its primary purpose is to test the model presented in the textbook for the interaction between colored objects and white light. The data it yields should be discussed in terms of whether or not they fit the hypothesis that such objects absorb part of the white light and reflect the remainder. The same data can also be checked against other hypotheses suggested in the textbook.

Equipment Needed (per student)	*Cat. Number*
contained in the Colored Objects Kit, (Note a):	68822
1 red crayon	
1 blue crayon	
1 red filter	
1 blue filter	
2 white index cards, 3″ x 5″	
1 plastic bag with wire tie	68853

Laboratory Notes

(a)   As supplied, this package contains sufficient materials to prepare individual kits for 10 students.

The foregoing materials should be packed in the plastic bag to facilitate distribution to the students. They should be returned in good condition because the filters will be useful in several other experiments; it is also recommended that this experiment be repeated as a chair-arm experiment during class discussion of Questions 3-1, 3-2, and 3-3.

The "cornflower" crayon was selected because it reflects about the color range of light transmitted by the blue filter, and the "orange-red" crayon was chosen because it reflects the color range transmitted by the red, although these two color ranges overlap somewhat. These crayons and filters were very carefully matched and any substitutions are likely to work far less well.

QUESTIONS

3-1 Describe the appearance of each mark as viewed through the red filter.
Answer   Viewed through the red filter the red mark is undetectable; both the blue and the black marks appear black. Through the blue filter the blue mark is invisible, and the red and the black marks are black.

3-2 Is the first hypothesis in agreement with your experimental results? the second? Discuss the evidence.
Answer   On the basis of the first hypothesis — that colored objects add colored light to white light — the red mark would add red light to the white light illuminating it. It would therefore be expected to appear brighter than its surroundings when viewed through the red filter, since the filter would add red color equally to everything viewed through it. Similarly, the blue mark would be expected to appear bluer than its surroundings when viewed through the blue filter. The blue mark viewed through the red filter and the red mark seen through the blue filter should, on the same basis, have a reddish-blue appearance.

The observations are in accord with the second hypothesis, that colored objects remove all colors except their own characteristic color from white light.

3-3 Can you explain why there is so little contrast between the red mark and the white paper when both are viewed through the red filter?
Answer   The red mark reflects only red light, which is passed by the red filter. The white paper reflects all colors equally, but the filter absorbs all of them except for red, so that again only red light gets through. If there is no significant difference in reflecting ability between the paper and the red mark, then there will be no noticeable contrast between them.

An interesting demonstration with which to extend the discussion of color is to place a piece of deeply colored plastic on the bed of an overhead projector and then disks of other deeply colored filters on top. It is difficult to obtain complete color cancellation in practice, however, because the color density of most filters is too low.

The discussion may go in the direction of physiological optics. This can be followed up by suggesting that the students examine traffic lights through the red and blue filters. They will find that, generally, the green light has large blue content whereas the red and the caution light have none. These shades have been formulated so as to be distinguishable by people having the more common kinds of color blindness.

Experiment 3-2 can be extended to include an examination of colored marks illuminated by colored light. To do this effectively, all other illumination must be eliminated. Probably the easiest way for the students to do this themselves is by cutting a 1-inch diameter hole near one end of a cardboard mailing tube or any other cardboard tube, such as those obtainable from rolls of paper towels, and then covering this hole with one of the colored filters. The tube should be placed upright over the colored marks or patches to be examined, with the hole turned in the direction of the light source (see Fig. RB 3-1). Looking down the tube, with the eye close enough to its upper end to block off the light which would otherwise enter there, the student can observe the same effects as are obtained in Experiment 3-2.

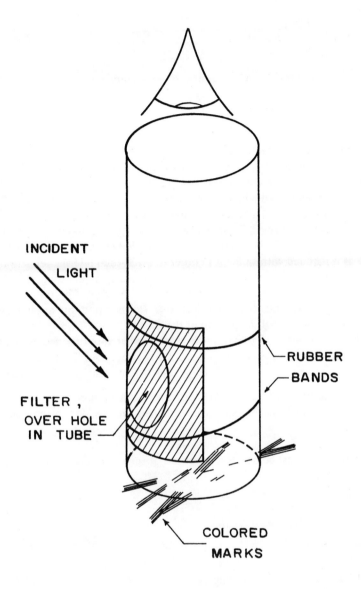

INCIDENT
LIGHT

RUBBER

BANDS

FILTER ,
OVER HOLE
IN TUBE

COLORED
MARKS

Figure RB 3-1

Experiment 3-3 Breaking Up White Light

Part A   This is intended as a take-home experiment, but it can also be done as a demonstration. Its purpose is to show the students how simply one can demonstrate the breaking up of white light into the colors of the spectrum without special equipment. You will probably think of a variety of ways in which to extend the investigation; several suggestions are included.

Equipment Needed
(per student)   *Cat. Number*

1 clear glass or plastic tumbler (to be supplied by each student)   —

1 set of colored filters (used in Experiment 3-2)   68822

When using an ordinary glass of water to break up the light of the Sun into its component spectrum of colors, the Sun must be low in the sky, at an altitude of somewhat less than 30°. Otherwise total internal reflection will occur, and no simple spectrum will appear.

The experiment can be performed when the Sun is higher by tilting the glass away from the Sun, or by using a wine or champagne glass having straight, slanted sides, such as the one pictured in Figure RB 3-2. The experiment can be demonstrated even in cloudy weather if a narrow intense beam of light, such as that from a slide projector, is used as a substitute for sunlight. The light source must be directed at the surface at the same low angle as is required with sunlight in order to avoid total internal reflection.

Can the students get only the red or only the blue part of the spectrum using the filters from Experiment 3-2? Does it matter on which side of the glass the filters are placed? Can they establish the path of the light through the water by marking off various portions? Do they find that anything unusual happens when they cover the right or the left half of the top of the glass?

Fancy glasses give very different shapes of rainbows, but what about the sequence of colors? What differences in pattern are produced by different glasses? What effect does the height of the water or the diameter of the glass have on the rainbow? What happens as the Sun's altitude increases?

Part B (A demonstration)   This demonstration requires, in addition to the two prisms, a fairly intense, narrow light source. This is very satisfactorily obtained with a slide projector and an opaque slide having a narrow vertical slit in it.

Note: The two prisms must be constructed ahead of time. The epoxy cement requires at least 24 hours to set.

Equipment Needed
(per class)   *Cat. Number*

1 Liquid Fillable Prism Kit, consisting of: 68856

    12 lantern slide glasses

    2 packages, epoxy cement

    6 rubber bands

    6 toothpicks

    slide projector   —

Laboratory Notes

Four pieces of glass are required for each prism. Extra glass has been provided because of the possibility of breakage.

The body of the prism is made first. Take three plates of glass and stack them like a pack of cards with the edges aligned. (Small sheets of paper should be inserted between the plate faces to prevent sticking.)

Figure RB 3-2

Place several rubber bands around the stack of glass plates such that the bands make contact with the longer edge of the plates. The three pieces of glass can now be moved apart and opened to form a 60° triangular prism which is held together by the rubber bands. Make the body of both prisms before proceeding.

The epoxy cement must be prepared according to the directions on the package. Once the two cement components are mixed, the epoxy will start to set. Thus, two packages of cement are furnished, one for the body seams and one for the floor seams.

The toothpicks are used to place the cement in the inside seams. Apply the cement carefully and use no more than necessary. During the time required for the cement to harden, the glass plates should be held securely by the rubber bands.

Once the body has been completed, it is floored with the fourth glass plate. Here, however, the cement will probably have to be applied to the body-floor seams from the outside. Furthermore, to demonstrate successfully that light may be recombined by a second prism after it has been separated by a first one, the two prisms must be placed very close together (see Fig. RB 3-3). This requires that you construct your fillable prisms in such a way that one of the vertical sides of each is parallel to and right along an edge of its base. In other words, one side of the base of each prism should have little or no projecting lip. The prisms are ready for use as soon as the epoxy has hardened. It is advisable, however, to fill them with water and check for leaks before using them in any demonstration.

In this demonstration the effect of one prism is shown first by casting the spectrum on a piece of white paper or a screen some distance away. Then to check the hypothesis suggested in the textbook — that if one prism adds color, two should add more — a second prism can be placed next to the first. The two

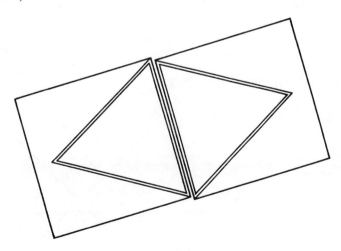

Figure RB 3-3

prisms must be quite close to each other so that the divergence of the beam between them will not cause trouble. The recombined light beams will then give you white light again on the paper. A way to demonstrate that the second prism simply recombines what the first one separates is to remove some of the colored light from the first before it gets to the second. You can do this if you block off some of the colored light by using a sheet of paper or a card between the prisms. The recombined beam will then no longer be white.

Students may wish to know more about the bending of light at prism-air interfaces, as well as more about the way in which the prism breaks up the light. Unfortunately, there is no simple explanation. It can only be explained meaningfully in terms of the interaction of oscillating electromagnetic fields with the charged particles which make up the material of the prism. The analogous case of refraction of water waves at interfaces is discussed in some detail in PSSC *College Physics,* Chapter 7.

The production of the rainbow by water drops can be simulated with an intense narrow beam of white light and a spherical (preferably) or cylindrical glass container of water. A 2 × 2 slide projector is again a very suitable source; it should be used with a slide consisting of a 2 x 2-inch piece of cardboard having a ¼-to ½-inch circular hole in the center to restrict the size of the beam. A 200-ml or larger Florence flask or a small spherical fishbowl is an excellent analog to a spherical raindrop. If no spherical container is available, a cylindrical one such as a beaker can be substituted, but this is equivalent to a two-dimensional model (looking down from above) of a raindrop, rather than a three-dimensional one.

A diagram of the arrangement of the apparatus used to demonstrate refraction by a sphere, as well as the paths of the light rays through it, is shown in Figure RB 3-4. If a white sheet of paper is held in either

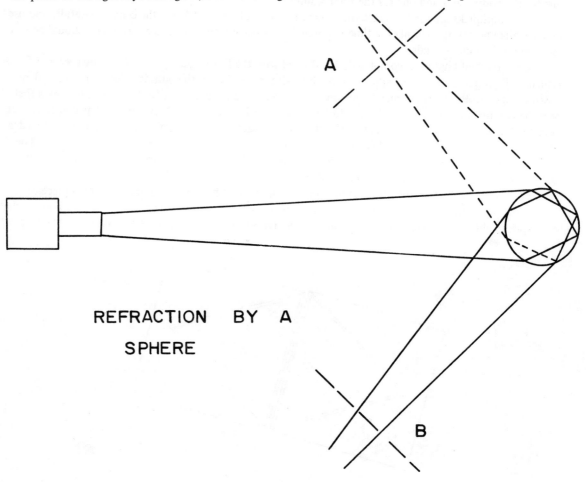

REFRACTION BY A

SPHERE

Figure RB 3-4

region A or B, two spectra can be seen. The outer one, the source of the primary rainbow, will be the brighter one because it suffers one less loss by reflection than the other. The actual formation of a rainbow from the cumulative effects of many raindrops is shown in Figure RB 3-5.

Section 3-3 MECHANICAL WAVES

You might begin this section by asking your students what kinds of waves they know of, what they think the characteristics of wave motion are, what they think there is about a moving wave. It is likely that water waves would be among the first mentioned; others might be sound waves, radio waves, shock waves, waves on strings or springs, possibly infrared or ultraviolet radiation, or even x rays. The subsequent discussion should include consideration of the significant differences between the types of waves mentioned as well as their common characteristics. It is not, of course, technical understanding which is sought here. It is simply desirable to encourage the students to think about waves and to gather their previous observations and experiences.

To extend our knowledge of waves, we will need to make some controlled observations on them; that is, we will need to perform some experiments. Water waves are the easiest type to work with at an elementary level, and we will shortly investigate some of their important properties, in both this chapter and the

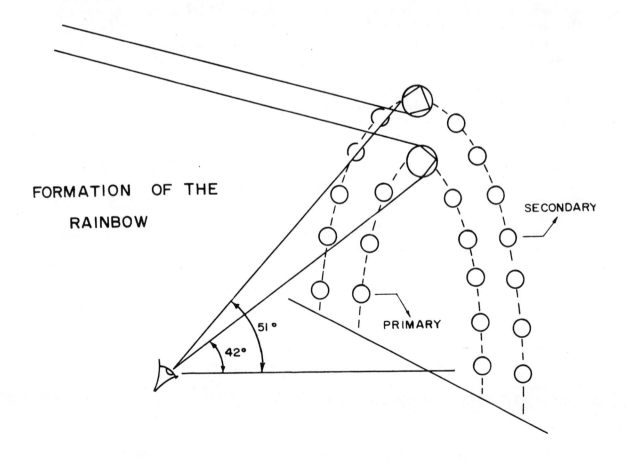

Figure RB 3-5

next. It is for this reason that much of the discussion in the text deals with water waves and that many analogies are drawn from them.

The discussion about a boat bobbing up and down on the ocean but not moving horizontally with the waves may need reinforcement for many students. Most people are aware of the fact that floating objects are gradually washed up on beaches, and it is only natural for them to attribute this to the motions of the waves. There are actually several effects which contribute to this drifting, including, in shallow water, the motions of the waves themselves. In deep water and in the absence of wind and current, however, floating objects have essentially no horizontal movement. You can demonstrate this fairly convincingly by floating a bit of cork in a ripple tank, or by suggesting to your students that they attempt to cause a cork to move on a puddle by dropping stones into it and thus making ripples on its surface.

Experiment 3-4 Water Waves

The students will supply their own equipment for this experiment. It is a take-home experiment which directs students' attention to waves on the surface of water. The directions suggest the use of a pie pan, wash basin, bathtub, or other large container. The questions are all qualitative, and with the apparatus the students will use, their discussions will necessarily be restricted to qualitative comments.

Because of the variety of types of containers students will use, it will help to tie things together if you use a ripple tank or a flat-bottomed glass dish to project some wave patterns with an overhead projector. (The ripple tank will be used in Chapter 4 where we study water waves in greater detail.) An eye dropper serves as a convenient way of dropping drops of water into the dish to generate waves. A piece of rubber tubing can be joined end to end to form a circular reflector. Circular waves reflecting from an elliptical reflector (formed with rubber tubing) also produce interesting patterns. The students should look at them in terms of the concepts which have been discussed in the text: wavelength, frequency, velocity, and amplitude. The PSSC *Physics*, D. C. Heath, Chapters 15 and 16, and the teacher's guide for the corresponding sections may provide ideas which are useful to you here and in Chapter 4.

The textbook points out that the larger the container, the better. The students might be asked, after they have experimented with a variety of containers, why this is so. What happens as they progress to larger and larger containers? They should be able to see that reflections from the walls usually interfere less with the initially generated waves in the bigger containers, unless the container happens to have some special shape which can focus the reflected wave. This might help them to understand better the construction of the ripple tank and the purpose of nonreflecting barriers at its edges. The same general approach is sometimes used in the construction of hi-fi speaker housings; an absorbing baffle is placed behind the speaker so that there will not be a reflected wave to interfere with the forward wave.

Experiment 3-5 Waves in a Spring

This experiment is designed to give the students an opportunity to generate and observe pulses and continuous waves in a one-dimensional medium. In addition, the students attain a deeper understanding of the concepts of wavelength, amplitude, frequency, and wave velocity.

Equipment Needed (per 2 students)	*Cat. Number*	
1 wave demonstrator, 1 inch in diameter, 6 feet long	68826	✓
clock or watch with sweep-second hand	68821	

The spring is to be stretched between the two students. If one end should become loose the person at the other end could be hurt by the spring as it snaps back. Also, it is to be shaken for lengthy periods of time during the performance of the experiment. The spring has been designed to minimize these problems if it is held properly. Each end has a wire loop. The student should insert his little finger through the loop and place the body of the spring across the palm of his hand. Closing his hand, he will obtain a firm grip, with his little finger acting as a safety catch to prevent an accidental release of the spring.

Suggested Sequence of Manipulation

(a) *Pulses.* After properly gripping each end, the students should move apart until the spring is stretched to approximately twice its original length. The person at one end should then sharply strike the spring with the edge of his free hand. The pulse generated will traverse the length of the spring several times before finally dying out. The students should be encouraged to describe the effect on the shape of the pulse when it is reflected at each end. At this point, simple statements such as, "The pulse comes down on the left but goes back on the right," are adequate.

The speed of the pulse should then be determined. This is accomplished by measuring the separation distance between the two partners and then determining the time required for the pulse to make one or more round trips.

Finally, the phenomenon of *superposition* should be introduced (without being specifically named) by showing that pulses will pass through one another. The people at each end of the spring should strike it sharply at the same instant. The two pulses thus formed will travel in opposite directions and pass through each other at about the middle. The complex pulse then generated, plus the emergence of the two original pulses, is readily observed by anyone who is at either end and looking approximately along the spring. Much more is made of this topic in Chapter 4, so this prior introduction is useful.

(b) *Standing waves.* To produce a standing wave, one end of the spring should be held still while the other person moves his end of the spring up and down with a steady, rapid rhythm. With just a little practice most students are able to obtain a standing wave.

The analysis of wave characteristics is facilitated if the first standing wave studied is one wavelength from student to student. Knowledge of the separation distance between the students gives a quantitative result for the wavelength. A numerical value for the frequency is obtained by timing ten or more oscillations of the spring. The product of these two measurements yields the wave velocity. If the students' separation distance is the same during the production of standing waves and pulses, the velocities obtained for the two processes will be very nearly identical. This fact is seldom anticipated by the students and comes as an interesting revelation.

The students can be led to associate amplitude with energy by having them observe the effect on the wave form of shaking the spring more vigorously at the same frequency.

Finally, the students are encouraged to shake the spring with different frequencies to obtain standing waves with different wavelengths. A quantitative evaluation of each new frequency and associated wavelength will yield velocity values that are identical to within experimental error.

The quantitative relation between the length of the spring and velocity is not part of this course, but it may be of interest to show that there is a way of varying velocity.

QUESTIONS

3-4 If the wave pulse travels down the spring as a crest, does it reflect and travel back as a crest or as a trough?

Answer   It returns as a trough.

3-5   Does the speed of the wave pulse increase or decrease as the spring is pulled tighter?
Answer   The speed increases with increasing tension.

3-6   If you were actually to set these waves traveling down a very long spring, and if you were to hold the tension in the spring constant, the wave speed would be constant. What would happen to the wavelength of those waves if you were to increase the frequency of the waves?
Answer   The product of the wavelength and the frequency is equal to the speed: $\lambda f = v$. Since v is a constant for constant tension, the wavelength must become smaller if the frequency becomes greater.

3-7   If you were to hold the frequency constant but increase the wave speed, would the wavelength increase or decrease?
Answer   Using the same relation as above, $\lambda f = v$, we see that for constant frequency an increase in the wave speed requires a corresponding increase in wavelength.

Demonstration of Wave Machine

Equipment Needed (per class)	*Cat. Number*
1 traveling sine wave machine	68881
1 overhead projector	–
1 clock with sweep-second hand	68821

The sine wave machine consists of a wooden platform (12–14 inches long) with arms rigidly attached to each end forming a short wide U. In one arm is a hook which is free to rotate. The opposite arm is fitted with an identical hook to which a handle has been added. The machine is supplied with two segments of slinky spring. Each segment can be stretched between and attached to the hooks.

To use the apparatus, a spring segment is inserted and the machine is placed on the platform of the overhead projector. Properly positioned, the edges of the wooden frame rest upon the edges of the projector and the spring is suspended over the illuminated glass platform. The focus is adjusted until a sharp shadow of the spring is observed on the projection screen. The shadow closely resembles the diagrams used to represent waves.

Turning the handle causes the spring to rotate and the projected wave image appears to move across the screen. If an opaque pointer is placed on the platform while the handle is being rotated, the waves appear to move steadily past the pointer. The students can count the number going past during a definite period of time and thus obtain the frequency. The frequency multiplied by the wavelength, which was measured earlier, yields the wave velocity.

Another extremely effective demonstration can be obtained by sticking a small bit of paper to one of the slinky loops. The spring shadow is again on the screen, and the students are asked where the paper will go when the handle is again rotated. The illusion of motion across the screen is so strong that most people state that the bit of paper will move over to the edge and there fall off. The handle is then rotated to show the paper moving up and down with simple harmonic motion although the wave moves across the screen.

The second spring segment has a different number of loops; when it is used, a different wavelength is obtained.

The following analogy is suggested as a means of helping students understand the transition from spring waves to water waves.

Imagine that we are in a large empty room and that we have 30 or 40 identical springs of the same type as used in Experiment 3-5. One end of each spring is attached to a small central ring, and the other end is given to a student who walks radially away from the ring. The situation now resembles a bicycle wheel where the small central ring represents the hub, the stretched springs the spokes, and the students are in a circle suggesting the rim.

A sharp vertical blow is given to the ring, causing it to vibrate up and down. What is observed by each student if he looks only at his own spring? What is observed by a person in the balcony if he looks at all the springs simultaneously?

This type of approach has proven very successful in helping students to concentrate on the common characteristics of wave phenomena without undue concern about changes in the propagating media.

Section 3-4 THE WAVE MODEL OF LIGHT

In connection with the idea that color is dependent on wavelength, it might be pointed out that the perception of color is a physiological phenomenon. An interesting article by Edwin Land on the subject of color vision is referred to in the References at the end of this chapter. An excellent discussion of the physiology of vision is contained in *Feynman's Lectures on Physics*, Addison-Wesley, 1963, Vol. I, Chapters 35 and 36.

Mention of the speed of light may very well bring up the question of how it is determined. A brief description and discussion of the classical method used by Michelson should soon make it clear to the students that it is a difficult problem requiring precise and highly refined equipment. It is then interesting to point out that an approximate determination of the speed of light was made by Roemer as early as 1675.

QUESTIONS

3-8   How many wavelengths of monochromatic orange light of wavelength $\lambda = 6.0 \times 10^{-7}$ meter are there in one meter? in one centimeter? How many wavelengths of monochromatic green light of wavelength $\lambda = 5.0 \times 10^{-7}$ meter are there in one centimeter?
Answer   For orange light of 6.0×10^{-7} meter wavelength:

$$\frac{1.0}{6.0 \times 10^{-7}} = 1.67 \times 10^6 \quad = 1.7 \times 10^6 \text{ waves/meter}$$

$$= 1.7 \times 10^4 \text{ waves/centimeter}$$

For green light of 5.0×10^{-7} meter wavelength:

$$\frac{1.0}{5.0 \times 10^{-7}} = 2.0 \times 10^6 \text{ waves/meter}$$

$$= 2.0 \times 10^4 \text{ waves/centimeter}$$

3-9   Suppose you are wearing dark green sunglasses as you drive along a street in town. You come to a traffic light. On what basis would you make a decision to drive through this intersection?
Answer   What would you see when the yellow light is on? What would you see when the red light is on? In both cases, nothing. What could you see when the green light is on? A green light. Therefore stop when you do not see a light, go when you do see one. In actual practice, most green sunglasses are light green, so that other colors are also somewhat visible.

3-10 Another hypothesis concerning colored objects might be that a colored object changes all white light into its particular color. How could you show that this hypothesis is untenable?

Answer   It was demonstrated that white light is made up of all colors. If colored objects turned all white light into their own characteristic color, they would also turn each of its components into their own color. But if we illuminate a colored object with light of any other pure color, it appears black.

3-11 Draw a diagram of the light rays in Experiment 3-3. Use a side view. Show how the water in the glass acts like a prism; that is, diagram the light-ray path through the prism and also through the water, and show how these diagrams are similar. Can you explain the fact that the spectrum from the glass of water is curved?

Answer   The curvature of the spectrum comes about because, although the bending of the light is the same around the edge of the water, the edge of the water prism is curved. See figure RB 3-6.

3-12 We have stated that all wavelengths of light have the same speed in a vacuum. The colors have different wavelengths, however, as shown in Table 3-1. What can you say about the frequencies of the various colors? That is, which color has the greatest, and which color has the lowest frequency? Is the frequency of an x ray greater or less than that of visible light?

Answer   From Equation 3-1 we have that $f \lambda = v$. If v is constant we can write

$$f = \frac{v}{\lambda} = \frac{\text{constant}}{\lambda}$$

Therefore, as λ becomes larger, f becomes smaller, and vice versa. Violet has the shortest wavelength of visible light; thus it has the highest frequency. So the frequency of violet light is the highest, and that of red light is the lowest, in the visible spectrum. Since x rays have very small wavelengths compared to those of visible light, they have much higher frequencies.

3-13 In any equation, the units of the left-hand side of the equation must equal the units of the right-hand side. Show that this is true for the wave equation $v = f \lambda$. (Note: This is a necessary but not sufficient condition for the validity of any equation.)

Answer   You may need to explain the meaning of dimension to the students before they do this problem. Give examples, such as length, mass, time, etc. Point out that in science, a dimension is not necessarily restricted to length, width, and height.

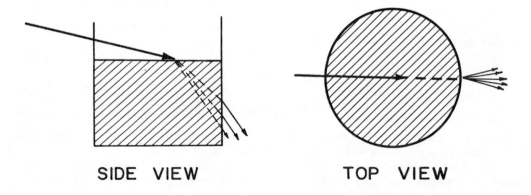

SIDE VIEW   TOP VIEW

Figure RB 3-6

The dimension of v is length/time. The dimension of f is 1/time. The dimension of λ is length. If we use brackets to denote "dimension of," then

$$(v) = \left[\frac{length}{time}\right], (f) = \left[\frac{1}{time}\right], (\lambda) = \left[length\right]$$

and

$$(f\lambda) = \left[\frac{1}{time}\right] \cdot \left[length\right] = \left[\frac{length}{time}\right]$$

Therefore,

$$(v) = (f\lambda)$$

3-14 The wavelength of orange light is about 6000 Å, or 6.0×10^{-5} cm; the speed of light is 3.0×10^{10} cm/sec. What is the frequency of light of this color?

Answer $\quad f = \dfrac{v}{\lambda} = \dfrac{3 \times 10^{10} \text{ cm/sec}}{6 \times 10^{-5} \text{ cm}} = 0.5 \times 10^{15}/\text{sec}$

3-15 Determine the wavelength of the radio waves which are transmitted by radio stations having the following frequencies:

(a)   a standard (AM) broadcasting station at 810 kilocycles per second (kilo means thousand).

(b)   an FM broadcasting station at 90 megacycles per second (mega means million).

Answer   (a) $f = 810$ kilocycles/sec $= 810 \times 10^3$ cycles/sec

$$= 8.1 \times 10^5 \text{ cycles/sec}$$

$$\lambda = \frac{v}{f} = \frac{3 \times 10^{10} \text{ cm/sec}}{8.1 \times 10^5 \text{ cycles/sec}} = 0.37 \times 10^5 \text{ cm}$$

(b) $f = 90$ megacycles/sec $= 90 \times 10^6$

$$= 9.0 \times 10^7 \text{ cycles/sec}$$

$$\lambda = \frac{v}{f} = \frac{3 \times 10^{10} \text{ cm/sec}}{9.0 \times 10^7 \text{ cycles/sec}} = 0.33 \times 10^3 \text{ cm}$$

If this problem brings up questions about the difference between AM and FM transmission, it would probably be best to restrict your answer to the simple definitions: AM means Amplitude Modulation, FM means Frequency Modulation. Anything more is likely to prove very confusing to students with no background in science.

3-16 Analogous to a pendulum, the period of a wave is defined to be the time for one complete cycle of oscillation. Thus for the sailboat example in Figure 3-3, the period is the time required for the boat to bob from a crest to a trough and back to a crest. For that example and using the data given in the text, answer the following questions.

(a)   What is the period of oscillation of the sailboat? (Hint: How are period and frequency related? Reason it out.)

(b)   How far did the boat travel during one period?

(c)   What is the average speed of the sailboat going up and down?

(d)   Compare this with the speed of the wave going horizontally.

Answer   (a) period $= 1/f$. Reasoning might include use of dimensions, such as saying period is measured by time (seconds), frequency by one over time, (sec^{-1}), thus they are reciprocals. Alternatively, if two crests pass per second, one crest should pass in one half second. Therefore, period $= \frac{1}{2}$ sec $= 0.5$ sec.

(b) Up from center to top = 5 ft
      top to center   = 5 ft
      center to bottom   = 5 ft
      bottom to center   = 5 ft
      total   = 20 ft

(c) He traveled 20 feet in ½ second, so average speed is

$$\frac{20 \text{ ft}}{0.5 \text{ sec}} = 40 \text{ ft/sec}$$

(d) v = 20 ft/sec (as shown in text).

3-17 (a) It is possible to perform Experiment 3-5 quantitatively by actually measuring the wave speed, the frequency, and the wavelength of the standing wave. Suppose that you had set up a standing wave with a frequency of 4 cps and found that two loops had formed in your spring stretched to 3 meters long. What would the speed of the waves be in that spring?

(b) If the tension of the spring in part (a) were held the same, with what frequency would you need to oscillate it to set up a standing wave with three loops?

Answer   (a)   We are given the information that λ = 3 meters and f = 4 cps. Therefore the speed is given by

$$v = \lambda f = 3 \times 4 = 12 \text{ meter/sec}$$

(b) The speed is the same, the new wavelength is λ = (2/3) 3 meters = 2 meters. The frequency is thus

$$f = \frac{v}{\lambda} = 6 \text{ cps}$$

3-18 The speed of sound in air is about 1100 ft/sec. If the frequency of middle C on the piano is 256 vibrations per second, what is the wavelength of the sound wave?

Answer $\lambda = \dfrac{v}{f} = \dfrac{1100}{256} = 4.3$ ft

ADDITIONAL QUESTIONS AND PROBLEMS

3-19 An old theory of vision states that we see things by sending light out from the eyeball, then detecting the reflected light. Discuss this theory.

Answer   This theory cannot account for variations of brightness. In the extreme case we might wonder why we can't see in the dark.

3-20 One can form a colored beam of light by passing white light through a filter of the desired color.
(a)   Can the same result be obtained by reflecting a white beam of light from the same filter?
(b)   What colors will a colored glass filter reflect?
(c)   How could you check this experimentally? Are you sure that your method will lead to unambiguous results?
(d)   Is there any difference in the process of reflection by a colored piece and a clear piece of glass? What colors will a clear piece reflect?

Answer   (a) No, almost no light will be reflected — all colors except the filter color will be absorbed, and the filter color will pass through without significant reflections. A red filter looks red in transmission of red, not in reflection.
(b)   None; see part (a).
(c)   Put the filter up against a strongly absorbing black background. This is ambiguous because there is always some reflection when light hits any object.

(d)   Difference due to colors being absorbed by the substances used to color the filter, but not in the glass itself. Clear glass reflects all colors.

3-21   White light shines on two pieces of glass, one of which is clear, the other colored blue. Which becomes hotter: the clear glass, the blue glass, neither?
Answer   The blue glass. Since the blue *absorbs* light (absorbs energy), it must get hotter than the clear glass which absorbs almost none.

REFERENCES

1. (T)   Baez, Chapter 13, Sections 13.1 through 13.5, pages 159 to 168. This is a generally nonmathematical introduction to vibrations and waves. One of the fundamental wave equations is derived verbally. There may be some difficulties here, though, since the author uses some concepts such as force, velocity, etc., which the student has not yet encountered in the course. There has to be some intuitive feeling for these concepts.

2. (T)   Feynman, Chapters 35 and 36, pages 35-1 to 36-12. These chapters are not directly related to our treatment of light and color, but Feynman's presentation should be interesting as an example of how the various sciences are interrelated.

3. (T)   PSSC, Chapter 3, Sections 3-1, 3-2, pages 43 to 45. This is a simple introduction to color very much like our treatment.

4.   Resnick and Halliday, Chapter 19, Sections 19-1 through 19-3, pages 463 to 470. This is a more mathematical introduction to waves. It includes a mathematical description of a traveling wave.

5.   Bascom, W., "Ocean Waves", *Scientific American*, August 1959, pages 75 ff.

6.   Land, E. H., "Experiments in Color Vision", *Scientific American*, May 1959, pages 84 ff.

CHAPTER 4

INTERFERENCE OF LIGHT

The measurement of intermolecular distances is a vital part of the study of the solid state of matter. In practice, these measurements are made by means of x-ray diffraction techniques. By acquiring an understanding of wave motion in general, and of the interference and diffraction phenomena associated with light waves in particular, the student should be in position to understand and to appreciate x-ray diffraction measurements.

Chapter 4, then, serves as the link between Chapter 2, a general discussion of measurements, and Chapters 6 and 15, the discussions of how x-ray diffraction is used to determine the distances between the lattice planes in a crystal. Chapter 3 establishes an understanding of wave phenomena in general, and therefore it leads directly into Chapter 4.

Section 4-1 INTERFERENCE

Young's double-slit experiment serves two important purposes in this chapter. Not only does it clearly demonstrate that light possesses properties which cannot be accounted for except on the basis of wave characteristics, it also furnishes the background necessary for the study of Bragg's law in Chapter 6 and for an introduction to the x-ray study of crystals in Chapter 15.

Experiment 4-1   Young's Double-Slit Experiment

The purpose of this experiment is to acquaint the students with the overall principles of Young's double-slit experiment. It also serves as a pedagogical device for introducing and discussing the wave model of light.

This experiment is best performed in a darkened room.

Equipment Needed *(per 3 students)*	Cat. *Number*
1 Optical Slits Kit, consisting of:	68863
1 ceramic socket with power cord	
1 straight filament lamp	
10 double-edge razor blades	
6 coated glass microscope slides (Note a)	
1 package, red and blue cellophane (Note b)	

Equipment Needed (per 3 students)	Cat. Number
3 magnifiers	68847

Besides these items, the following materials should be readily available:

1 bottle, graphite in alcohol (Note a)	68531
24—30 glass microscope slides, uncoated (Note a)	68850
1 roll, cellophane tape	—
3 rubber bands	—

Laboratory Notes

(a)   There should be a sufficient number of coated-glass microscope slides in the box to allow each student to make his own double slit. If there are not enough, however, additional opaque slides can be made by painting one side of a clean microscope slide with a suspension of graphite in alcohol. Two thin coats are superior to a single thick one.

Once a student has produced a satisfactory slide and has had it checked by the instructor, it should be protected. This is best done by placing a second, uncoated slide over the prepared one, with the opaque face sandwiched in the middle. The two slides can then be held together by wrapping strips of cellophane tape around each end.

Care must be taken in making the double slits, and most students will have to make several attempts before they succeed in producing good ones. They may need to be shown the interference pattern formed by a good pair before they can recognize that theirs is not satisfactory. You should check closely to be sure that each group of students does succeed in producing a satisfactory set.

(b)   The cellophane supplied in this kit can be used, but the colored filters used in Experiment 3-2 are better.

The differences between the interference patterns formed using the red and then the blue filters are not obvious to the casual observer. To carry this experiment out successfully demands careful observation; otherwise it will not be possible to notice that the red interference pattern spreads out more than the blue.

QUESTION

4-1   What type of pattern would you expect to see if the light were considered to be a large number of small particles coming through the two slits? Does this agree with your observations?
Answer   If light were composed of particles that behave as marbles do, the student would probably expect to find two bands of light with perhaps a slight overlapping, but certainly with no destructive interference. This does not agree with observation.

Section 4-2 SUPERPOSITION OF WAVES

The study of transverse waves on a spring is an important step in the study of wave motion. The students should consider the photographs carefully.

The determinations of wave speed from Figure 4-3 are relatively easy. Pick a point on the pulse and measure to determine how far it travels during the time interval between frames.

QUESTIONS

4-2   Assume that the picture in Figure 4-3 is one-tenth actual size. Determine the speed of the wave pulse for various time intervals. Record your results. Is the speed constant?
Answer   The speed of the pulse is constant. This can be verified by laying a straight edge along corresponding points on each wave.

4-3   Measure the amplitude of the wave at time 0 and at time 8—24 sec. Does the amplitude change with time? If so, how?
Answer   There is no appreciable decrease, but during the measuring process students will find that the spring to the left of the pulse does not line up with the spring to the right. They will have to be careful, therefore, to use the same reference line in making each of the measurements of amplitude. Ultimately, of course, such a pulse would die out, but it would apparently take longer than 11/24 sec.

4-4   Assuming that Figure 4-4 is again one-tenth actual size, determine the speed of each pulse and compare the two.
Answer   The speeds of the two pulses are the same. A straight edge can again be used to advantage in locating corresponding points on each of the pulses in successive frames.

4-5   Examine the same point on the spring in all other frames of Figure 4-5. Does the superposition principle hold in each frame?
Answer   The superposition principle does hold for the same point in each of the frames. See the discussion of Question 4-6.

4-6   Make measurements of any other point where the waves cross to check whether the superposition principle applies in general.
Answer   The superposition principle does hold for different parts of the spring in the same frame. Questions 4-5 and 4-6 are asked to generalize its application. It applies for the same part of the spring as the pulse passes by, and it applies for the different parts of the spring at any one instant of time.

Section 4-3 INTERFERENCE REVISITED

The ripple tank is first introduced in this section, although experiments using it could well be done in Chapter 3. For example, it could be used to measure wavelength and to determine wave speed. A detailed description of it is included here, however, because of its great importance to this chapter, and because it is first used extensively here.

Water waves in a ripple tank interact optically with the illuminating light source to produce the light and dark bands seen in the photographs beginning with Figure 4-7. This is illustrated in Figure RB 4-1, where it can be seen that the crests act in the same way as positive or converging lenses, and that the troughs behave as negative or diverging ones. This means that, as one looks down from above, the crests will appear brighter than the troughs, simply because they concentrate the light rather than disperse it.

Most of the students will have little real knowledge of the workings of lenses, but diagrams of the two types shown in Figure RB 4-2, with the appropriate ray patterns, may not be completely unfamiliar. Sample lenses might also be made available to them.

The students, incidentally, might well be asked to determine whether or not obstacles and slits have any effect on the wavelength of the incident waves, in addition to their effect on their direction. They can make the necessary measurements on Figure 4-7.

The great value of the ripple tank is that it uses water waves to demonstrate with striking clarity wave phenomena of many kinds, and in general these phenomena correspond to the wave properties of light. Emphasis should be placed on diffraction in shadow formation, diffraction in waves passing through a slit,

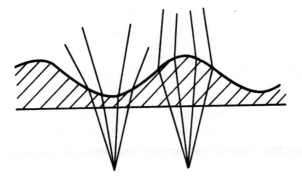

Figure RB 4-1

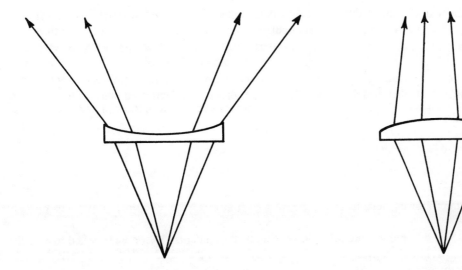

Figure RB 4-2

and of prime importance, the formation of an interference pattern in the water-wave analog of Young's double-slit experiment. Not only are constructive and destructive interference clearly seen, but the general shape of the interference pattern is quite evident.

To show all of the phenomena discussed in this section a rectangular ripple tank is recommended. In setting up the equipment it is best to bear in mind that:

1. The glass should be clean on both sides.
2. The depth of the water should be kept at about one-half centimeter for all demonstrations unless otherwise noted.
3. The tank must be level. A carpenter's level is best for this, but the tank itself can be used. The glass bottom is level when the water has a uniform depth.
4. The water should be changed after each day's use. Distilled or deionized water is better than tap water (which may be hard) because no deposit will form on evaporation.

A number of demonstrations and experiments with the ripple tank are discussed briefly below. In each case an appropriate film loop is suggested for class showing, but note that these loops should not be shown until after each of the demonstrations has been carried out.

Generating Straight Pulses

If a dowel rod is used to produce a straight pulse, soak it in water for several hours before using. This reduces the roughness of the rod and improves the quality of the pulse.

Place the dowel rod parallel to and near one end of the tank. A straight pulse can then be generated by giving a quick, short, rolling motion. The orientation of the dowel can be changed so that the direction of pulse travel is not normal to the reflector. (A plane, vertical barrier must be set up as a reflector; the sloping sides of a ripple tank will not work.) By doing this the angles of incidence and reflection can be compared. (See film loop *Reflection of Plane Waves from Straight Barriers in a Ripple Tank.)**

Generating Circular Pulses

Circular pulses can be produced by using your finger, a pencil, or a drop of water from an eye dropper as a point source. Students should observe that circular pulses retain their circular form even after reflection from the straight sides of the ripple tank. It is interesting to have the students locate, as best they can, the center from which the reflected circular pulses appear to radiate. This can be studied in some detail by varying the distance of the source from the refecting surface. Careful analysis of the experimentally produced patterns will indicate that the imaginary center of the source of the reflected pulses is the same distance behind the reflector as the real source is in front of it. (See film loop *Reflection of Circular Waves in a Ripple Tank.)*

Waves and Obstacles

In this and the following demonstration the wave generator is to be used since continuous waves are required.

Having viewed the formation and reflection of pulses, the students might now be asked to speculate about what happens as straight waves pass an obstacle. How does the "shadow" of an obstacle depend on the wavelength of the waves?

* An annotated list of useful films and film loops, with information as to running time, rental cost, and rental source comprises Appendix III.

Place a small barrier (about ½-cm wide) in the tank, send plane waves toward it, and observe the shadow. Change the frequency of the generator — thereby changing the wavelength — and note how the shadow changes.

The size of the obstacle in the ripple tank can also be varied. The range of variation here should be from the very small — much less than one wavelength, to the very large — several wavelengths or more. From this the students should be able to conclude that even with ideal optics an object must be at least as large as the wavelength of light used if it is to be detected. They might then be asked to estimate the maximum wavelength of radar used by police to detect automobiles.

Next, the effect of an obstacle on a wave can be "reversed" by letting the waves pass through a small opening, equivalent to a slit. After observing waves of different wavelength pass through a slit, the students can be asked to predict the effect of keeping the wavelength constant and varying the slit width. How does the shape of the wave depend on the relationship between wavelength and slit width?

These observations on diffraction effects in shadow formation and in waves passing through a narrow opening are of prime importance to this chapter and to Chapters 6 and 15. (See film loop, *Diffraction and Scattering of Waves Around Obstacles.*)

Superposition

The usual ripple tank will not demonstrate the phenomena shown in E.S.I. Film Loop #80-239, *Superposition of Pulses,* so it is best to show the film rather than to attempt a demonstration. In this film loop single pulses are generated by two independent sources, and the loci of their intersections are drawn on the film. Multiple pulses from two sources are then shown. These build up to periodic waves, and an interference pattern develops.

Two Point Sources

As an introduction to the interference effects due to two point sources, it is instructive to show, if possible, the wave pattern of first one and then the other of the two point sources alone. The student should recognize that the two patterns are the same except that one is displaced from the other. Then, after the patterns are seen individually, let both point sources produce waves simultaneously so that interference effects will be seen. The frequency dependence of the interference pattern for two point sources is similar to that shown in Figure 4-10.

The important thing for the students to understand, of course, is that although the circular waves are still traveling out from the point sources, the two sets together produce a constant pattern. They may be helped in this if you point out explicitly which regions of the pattern constitute constructive interference and which constitute destructive. The regions of alternate light and dark strips correspond to constructive interference. They are due to the light-focusing effects of the crests and troughs resulting from the constructive addition of the two circular wave patterns. The intervening clear regions between these rays correspond to destructive interference; neither crests nor troughs are formed here and thus the light is not focused sharply into light and dark areas. These points should be made to facilitate the comparison of Figures 4-9 and 4-10.

QUESTIONS

4-7   Describe the motion of a bit of cork placed on the water surface in the ripple tank shown in Figure 4-10 at either of the positions marked 1. Describe the motion of the cork if it were placed midway between the 0 and the 1.

Answer   This question is included to encourage students to look closely at Figure 4-10. A bit of cork placed at either of the positions marked 0 or 1 would bob up and down as the crests and troughs proceed outward from the region of the double source. A bit of cork placed halfway between would not bob up and down, for that is the region of destructive interference.

4-8   Now pick a point in Figure 4-9 where two crests coincide on one of the rays immediately adjacent to the central ray and along which constructive interference takes place. Mark it lightly by circling it with your pencil. Count the number of wavelengths from this point back to slit S_1 and also the number back to slit S_2. What do you find? Now using a ruler, measure (in either inches or centimeters) the distance back to slit S_1 and to slit S_2. The difference in the distances is called the *path difference*.

Repeat these same counts and measurements for other points along this same ray and along the other ray adjacent to the central ray. What statement can you make about the points along these rays? Can you establish a relationship between the wavelength and the path difference?

Answer   If the point P is chosen at the intersection of the crests farthest to the right along the ray immediately adjacent to and below the central ray, the number of waves to S_1 is 13, the number of waves to S_2 is 12. The number of waves differs by one; this is on the first ray adjacent to the central ray of constructive interference. The distance PS_2 subtracted from PS_1 yields the path difference for rays from the two slits to point P. It will be found to be one wavelength, equal to the distance from crest to crest. All other path differences along the same ray are also one wavelength.

4-9   Now do the same for each of the second rays from the central ray. What statement can you make about the points on these rays along which constructive reinforcement takes place? Make a statement about the third rays.

Answer   The path difference $PS_1 - PS_2$ for points chosen along the second rays of constructive interference on either side of the central ray is 2λ; the path difference for the third ray is 3λ.

4-10   You are now in a position to sum up all your results in a general statement that says what must be true about a point where constructive interference takes place between the waves from S_1 and the the waves from S_2. Write this statement referring to Figure 4-9.

Answer   A statement generalizing the measurements made for Questions 4-8 and 4-9 might be: "The path differences $PS_1 - PS_2$ for any point on a ray of constructive interference is given by the relationship

$$PS_1 - PS_2 = n\lambda$$

where n takes on the values 0, 1, 2, 3, . . . ; for the central ray, $n = 0$ for the first rays on either side of the the central ray, $n = 1$ for the second rays $n = 2$, etc."

4-11   Refer to your record of Experiment 4-1. How did the spacing between the bright bands change when you doubled the distance between the slits in that experiment? Compare this result with the effect of doubling the spacing between the vibrators in Figure 4-10(a). In Figure 4-10(c) the wavelength is twice as large as that in Figure 4-10(b), but the spacing is the same in each. Has doubling the wavelength increased or decreased the size of the angles the radiating rays make with the central ray?

Answer   When the distance between the two slits was doubled in Experiment 4-1 by using a third razor blade as a spacer, the interference pattern was compressed. This corresponds to the difference between Figures 4-10(a) and 4-10(b); the distance between the sources in 4-10(b) is greater than that in 4-10(a), and the rays of constructive interference in 4-10(b) are closer together than in 4-10(a). In Figure 4-10(c) the angles which the radial regions of constructive interference make with the central ray are greater than in 4-10(b); they are, in fact, the same as in 4-10(a) because the wavelength and source spacing have the same ratio in Figures 4-10(a) and 4-10(c).

4-12 Changing the angle between each of the rays of constructive interference and the central ray of the interference pattern in the ripple tank (Figure 4-10) is equivalent to changing the spacing between each band and the central band you saw during the performance of Experiment 4-1, Young's double-slit experiment. Refer to your notes of that experiment. Did increasing the wavelength increase or decrease the spacing of the bands?

Answer   The interference pattern for red light was more spread out than that for blue light. The measured wavelength of red light is greater than that of blue light. This corresponds to the difference between Figure 4-10(b) and 4-10(c). The separation of the sources is the same in each figure, but the wavelength in 4-10(c) is greater than that in 4-10(b), consequently the interference pattern is more spread out there.

If you choose, you can profitably repeat the measurements made in Question 4-8 by making similar ones directly from a ripple tank in the laboratory. This will help to dispel any unease the students may have about the relationship between the diagrams and reality. To make the measurements, simply place a large piece of white paper on the floor underneath the tank and, with illumination from above, mark the locations of the two sources and appropriate points along the center lines of various rays of constructive interference. The results of these measurements can serve, in conjunction with the observation that the ratio λ/d is the same for Figures 4-10(a) and 4-10(c), as the basis for a useful discussion. Since the interference patterns are also the same in the two figures, such a discussion can lead to the generalization that it is this ratio which determines the general shape and character of two-slit patterns.

The derivation of the relation $n\lambda = d\sin\phi$ is not at all easy for students in this course. To help them better understand its meaning, it is often useful to make a point of the fact that the sine of an angle is only a name; it is the name of the ratio of the lengths of two particular sides of a right triangle. It has no mystical meanings which are hidden from them because of their lack of background in mathematics. The only reason that we use the term, sine, instead of writing out the ratio each time is because it applies to all right triangles and our results are not restricted to some particular triangle having two particularly labeled sides. Problem 4-17 has been included to help reduce students' fears which arise from our using such terminology.

Experiment 4-2   Measuring the Wavelength of Light

In determining the wavelength of light in this experiment, students will come to the realization that measurements of very small quantities, of the order of 10^{-5} cm, can be made with essentially homemade equipment. Nothing is required beyond a meterstick, a pile of razor blades, and the double slit made for Experiment 4-1. However, the nature of some of the measurements involved does not warrant any expectation of high accuracy. The results may occasionally be in error by as much as a factor of 2 of 3, although they should certainly be within an order of magnitude. It is, then, an order-of-magnitude experiment. The requirements for its successful performance are simply a good pair of slits and care in making measurements.

Equipment Needed *(per 3 students)*	*Cat. Number*
Optical Slits Kit, consisting of:	68863
1 ceramic socket with power cord	
1 straight filament lamp	
20 double-edged razor blades (Note a)	
red and blue cellophane fitters (Note b)	
1 meter stick	68849

Equipment Needed *(per 3 students)*	*Cat. Number*
1 double-slit slide, prepared for Experiment 4-1	–
Slide projector, 35 mm	–
Graphite in alcohol	68532
Clean glass slides and cellophane tape, for additional slides	68850

Laboratoy Notes

(a)   The experience of previous teachers indicates that it is best to have the students determine d, the distance between the slits, as a class project. Place 20 razor blades and a ruler or meter stick at some central spot in the room. Then during the lab period, have students go there one at a time and measure the thickness of the pile of blades. After they all have had an opportunity to measure, they should record this information and determine the average value of the blade thickness d. This value should then be used by all students.

Alternatively, a slide projector can be used to obtain a direct measurement of d. Insert a transparent ruler in the projector and focus the image on a far wall. Use a meter stick to determine the separation on the screen of any two divisions on the image of the ruler. The ratio of this measurement to the size of the divisions gives the magnification. Thus, if two marks on the ruler, known to be one centimeter apart, appear 75 centimeters apart on the screen, the magnification is 75.

Next remove the ruler and replace it with a prepared double slit. The only thing seen on the screen will be two thin lines of light, the separation of which can be measured. This number, divided by the previously obtained magnification, yields the actual slit separation d.

(b)   The best contrast is obtained when the lamp is covered with the red filter. Also, several pieces of the filter should be fastened with rubber bands to the bulb to prevent any white light from getting to the eye of the observer. Looking at unfiltered light while trying to make a measurement makes the measurement more difficult.

After the wavelength of red light has been determined, place a blue filter above the red filter with their edges in contact, so that the observer sees red and blue light simultaneously. Then, by counting the number of blue bands that occupy the same distance as 10 red bands, a ratio can be obtained from which one can compute the approximate wavelength of blue light. Most students find it very difficult to make a direct determination of the wavelength of blue light because the interference pattern obtained with the blue filter is faint and has very little contrast.

It is important, of course, that the students first understand why they are making each measurement. The distances OP and SP (refer to Figure 4-14) are needed to determine $\sin \phi$ in the equation $n\lambda = d \sin \phi$. But in order to specify OP correctly, it is necessary to count the corresponding number of bands n. The remaining unknown quantity is d, the distance between the slits. It might be well to measure it first.

The method used here in measuring the slit separation d depends on the assumption that it corresponds exactly to the thickness of one razor blade (see Figure 4-13). If the thickness of a pile of twenty razor blades is determined, even with a meter stick, the thickness of one of them is one-twentieth of the total thickness. Students may question the use of a meter stick for measuring such a small quantity. However, this is intended as an order-of-magnitude experiment, not a precise determination of the wavelength of light. Later on in the course, measurements of atomic distances are discussed. If students realize what can be accomplished using something as common as a meter stick, they will then be better able to appreciate the fact that measurements of atomic distances can be relied on when more sophisticated tools are used. Even so it might be of interest to some of them to be allowed to repeat the measurement of the thickness of one razor blade using a micrometer, although it should not be done until after they have completed the determination in the prescribed manner. It is also true that the improvement in overall accuracy may not be as great as would be expected, because the spacing of the two slits depends partly on how the blades are held when they are drawn across the glass slide.

A method is described in the text book for identifying the central band of the interference pattern; a small window, a couple of millimeters on a side, is scratched near the top of and overlapping the double slits. In this way the observer can see both the lamp filament and the interference pattern at the same time. The band which lines up with the filament is the central one in the pattern. It is from it that the number of bands n are counted to the right or to the left.

The distance OP, from the central band out to band number n, and the distance SP, from the slits to the meter stick, must be measured while the observer remains in one position. The latter of these two measurements can be carried out by using a string which does not stretch. The observer must hold one end of it at the double slits while his partner holds the other end tautly on the meter stick at the location of the nth band. Another method for determining the same quantity is to premeasure a distance to a mark on the lab bench, or to one on the back of a chair, or to any point where the observer can consistently position the slits in order to look through them. The distances SP and SO are so nearly the same that it is reasonable to consider them identical for the purposes of this experiment. The remaining distance needed, OP, is measured very simply if the observer looks through the window and slits simultaneously and indicates to his partner where the central and the nth bands fall on the meter stick. The ratio of these two distances, $\frac{OP}{SP}$, is $\sin \phi$.

Although these are far from precise measurements, the error they introduce into the results will be very small if they are made with even moderate care. The most important sources of error are the determination of the distance OP and the determination of the slit separation d. But even though we cannot count on accurate results, we hope the students will acquire a sense of accomplishment and understanding when they realize that they have measured something as small as 10^{-5} cm using a meter stick. You might want to take the first available set of student measurements and use them to run through the calculations for the entire class. If this is done early enough in the laboratory session, it may well help others to understand what they are doing, as well as to give them an idea of the sort of magnitudes and results they should expect. Even so, each group of students should perform several trials of the experiment, with each student taking a turn as the observer.

The students should realize that the very small separation of the slits can also be measured by using a source of light of known wavelength. This is analogous to measuring the separation of lattice planes in crystals by using x-ray diffraction techniques. Commercial sodium vapor lamps, for example, are nearly monochromatic sources, radiating at an average wavelength of 5893 Å.

Experiment 4-3 Measuring the Separation of the Wires in a Wire Mesh (A Demonstration)

Equipment Needed	*Cat. Number*
wire screens: 250, 500, 1000 mesh	68827
slide projector, 35 mm	—
1 meter stick	68849
1 opaque slide with pinhole in the center	—

The slide projector is used with an opaque slide having a 1/16- to 1/8- inch hole in it. The small spot should be focused on a screen or wall; one of the fine wire screens held immediately in front of the lens will then cause a colored interference pattern to appear where the white spot had been.

First, use the 250-, 500-, and 1000-mesh (lines per inch) screens to show that the spacing between the spots of the diffraction pattern on the screen is larger for the finer mesh screen and smaller for the coarse mesh.

Next, obtain the two-dimensional diffraction pattern using the 1000-mesh screen. The center spot (0 order) will be white, but all other spots will be spectral. Using the first-order spot on either side of the central white one, measure the distance from the red part of one to the red of the other.

We solve the equation $n \lambda = d \sin \phi$ to obtain

$$d = n\lambda/\sin \phi$$

In this example $n = 1$

λ = whatever value the class obtained for red light in Experiment 4-2, probably about 6500 Å

$$\sin \phi = \frac{\frac{1}{2} \text{(distance between right and left red spots)}}{\text{distance from projector to screen}}$$

SUMMARY

We have dealt in this chapter with the phenomenon of interference. We first observed the interference pattern created by light passing through a double slit. Then, making use of the models and analogies of water waves in a ripple tank and pulses on springs, we demonstrated the principle of the superposition of amplitudes. We also considered in some detail the nature of constructive and destructive interference. By inference we have showed light to have a wave character.

Somewhat more particularly, we showed qualitatively the dependence of the shape or size of an interference pattern on the wavelength and the slit spacing. We also indicated the essential equivalence between obstacles and slits. These results will be of special importance when we discuss x-ray crystallographic measurements in Chapter 15.

We have had a gentle initiation into the use of mathematics, including a little trigonometry. We have also performed the first experiment requiring real care and some dexterity. These should both serve as a foundation for more of such work as the course progresses.

QUESTIONS

4-13 Two waves travel along a rope in opposite directions, as shown in Figure 4-16.
(a) Draw the shape of the rope when the leading half of the left wave coincides with the leading half of the right wave.
(b) Draw the shape of the rope when the two waves coincide completely.
(c) Draw the shape of the rope when the trailing half of the left wave coincides with the trailing half of the right wave.
(d) What point(s) on the rope always remains at rest (never moves up and down).
Answer   (a), (b), (c), see Figure RB 4-3. (d) That point which is symmetrically located with respect to the two waves. It is the point midway between their leading edges.

4-14 Consider Figure 4-6. Make a tracing of the 3/24 sec and the 7/24 sec frames. In what direction (up or down) is each part of the spring going? Put arrows on your tracings of these frames to show the directions.
Answer   See Figure RB 4-4.

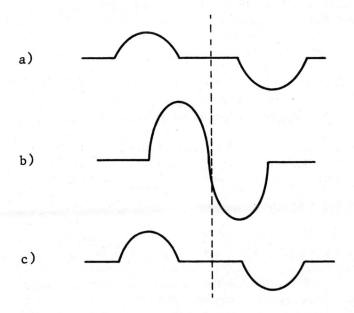

Figure RB 4-3

Figure RB 4-4

4-15 Consider Figure 4-9. Take a piece of tracing paper and trace out *every other* circular arc to the right of screen B. These circular lines are twice as far apart as those in the original. (Note: use a pencil or pen which gives a dark line.)

(a)   If these lines represent wave crests, what is the wavelength of these waves compared to the original? How does their frequency compare with that of the original? (The velocity of all electromagnetic waves, regardless of wavelength, is equal to 3×10^{10} cm/sec in vacuum.)

(b)   When you sight along the right edge of this new pattern, how does the alternation of light and dark rays compare to the original?

(c)   Can you predict qualitatively what the pattern would look like if you used every third circular line? Twice as many circular lines as shown in Figure 4-9?

Answer (a)   The wavelength of the waves on the tracing is twice that of Figure 4-9; the frequency is one-half.

(b)   The interference pattern in the tracing is spread out more than in Figure 4-9. The tracing bears the same relationship to Figure 4-9 that Figure 4-10(c) bears to 4-10(b).

(c)   Using every third line, the wavelength would be three times that in Figure 4-9 and the interference pattern would be spread out still more. If twice as many circular lines were used, the wave pattern would become more compressed.

4-16 As in Question 4-15, trace out *every other* line in Figure 4-9. On another piece of paper trace out the remaining lines in Figure 4-9. Now you have two figures with the same wavelength, but the waves of one figure have traveled ½ of a wavelength farther than the other. Now look along the rays of both figures. Are the light and dark bands of reinforcement and cancellation at the same angles in the two drawings? What can you conclude from this?

Answer   The directions of the rays are unchanged. Making the drawings as directed is essentially equivalent to taking two photographs of the same interference pattern at different times: the locations of the individual waves change, but the pattern of interference is constant.

4-17 Using a protractor, construct a right triangle with an angle of 30°. Measure the appropriate sides to determine the sine of 30°. Do the same for an angle of 37°, 45°, 60°. What is the sine of 90°? 0°?

Answer

$$\sin 0° = 0 \qquad\qquad \sin 45° = 0.707$$

$$\sin 30° = 0.500 \qquad\qquad \sin 60° = 0.866$$

$$\sin 37° = 0.602 \qquad\qquad \sin 90° = 1.000$$

4-18 Using the definition of the sine of an angle in a right triangle as the side opposite the angle divided by the hypotenuse, determine $\sin \phi$ for the rays of constructive interference in Figure 4-10(b). Compare this with the value obtained by measuring d and λ and using a form of Equation (4-1), $\sin \phi = n\lambda/d$

Answer   The students should make dots along the right edge of Figure 4-10(b) where the middle of each ray of constructive interference intersects the edge of the photograph. These points are indicated approximately by the numbers 3, 2, 1, 0, 1, 2, 3. A straight line connecting each point and the point midway between the two sources indicates a direction of constructive interference. The distance along the right-hand edge of the diagram, from 0 to the intersection with such a line, divided by the length of the line, is $\sin \phi$.

To measure the value of the wavelength λ, it is best to measure the length of, say, ten consecutive waves, and take one-tenth of that distance as the length of one wave.

The values of $\sin \phi$ will not be equal to the values of $n\lambda/d$ for the reason that the assumptions made in the derivation of the equation $n\lambda = d \sin \phi$ are not applicable to Figure 4-10, which includes a region only a few wavelengths from the slits. (See discussion in Section 4-3.)

4-19 Measure the angles ϕ of the corresponding rays of reinforcement in Figures 4-10(a) and 4-10(c). Are the angles in one figure equal to the corresponding angles in the other figure? Why?

Answer   The angle between the central and the first ray of reinforcement is the same for Figures 4-10(a) and 4-10(c), because the ratio of λ/d is the same for both.

4-20 Draw a diagram similar to Figure 4-13 and indicate the separation distance between two slits made with the third blade used as a spacer. How does this separation distance compare with the separation when no spacer is used?

Answer   The separation distance with the spacer of one razor blade is twice that with no spacer. See Figure RB 4-5.

4-21 Suppose the sharp edge of the razor blade is not half way between its two sides, but one-fourth of the way from one side to the other. What can you say about the separation of slits made with a pair of such razor blades held together? How could you find out that the razor blades you used were not made this way?

Answer   If the edge of the razor blade is midway between the sides, the slit will always equal the thickness of the blade. If, however, the edge is one-fourth of the way from one side to the other, the separation of the slits may be one thickness of the blade, but it also may be one-half the thickness or it may be one and one-half times the thickness, depending on the orientation of the two blades when the slits are made.

4-22 In the experiment where you measured the wavelength of light, why were you told not to use the slits which you had made with a spacer?

Answer   The slits made with the spacer are twice as far apart as those made without the spacer. Consequently, the interference pattern will be more compressed. This would make counting the bands more difficult and the measurement of *OP* less accurate.

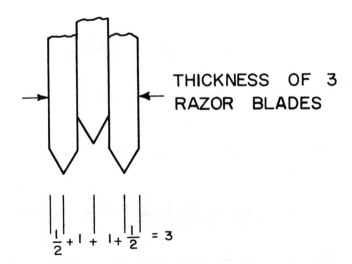

Figure RB 4-5

4-23 When you performed the double-slit experiment to measure the wavelength of light, what was the distance (approximately) between your eye and the slits? How many wavelengths of red light were there in this distance? Compare these numbers with the number of wavelengths shown in the photograph, Figure 4-10(b).

Answer   In the experiment to measure the wavelength of light, the distance between the eye and the double slit might have been one or two centimeters. If it had been 2 cm, and we assume the wavelength of red light to be 7000 Å, then there would have been roughly 2.9×10^4 or 30,000 wavelengths of red light in that region. In Figure 4-10(b) there are between 15 and 20 wavelengths depending on which part of the diagram is considered. The reasons why the equation $n \lambda = d \sin \phi$ does not apply for this figure should be made clear through a consideration of this question and the discussion in Section 4-3.

4-24 A source of red light (λ = 6500 Å) produces interference through two narrow slits separated by a distance $d = 0.01$ cm.

(a)   Suppose that the pattern produced was projected onto a screen. How far away would the screen have to be so that the bands near the central band would be 1 cm apart?

(b)   If you viewed the source by placing one eye directly behind the slits, as you did in Experiment 4-2, how far should the slits be from the source so that the bands near the central band appear to be 1 cm apart?

(c)   Why do you think we used the method described in part (b) of this question instead of that in part (a)?

Answer   (a) Since the bands are to be 1 cm apart, the distance OP to the first ray ($n = 1$) adjacent to the central one must equal 1 cm (See Fig. 4-14). The distance from the double slits to the screen is essentially the same as the distance SP, and it is this distance which we have to find. From the relationship

$$\sin \phi = (OP) / (SP)$$

we obtain

$$SP = OP/\sin \phi$$

From

$$n \lambda = d \sin \phi$$

we have

$$\sin \phi = n \lambda / d$$

Therefore

$$SP = \frac{(OP)}{n \lambda / d} = \frac{d(OP)}{n\lambda}$$

The values given are

$$\lambda = 6500 \text{ Å} = 6.5 \times 10^{-5} \text{ cm}$$

$$d = 0.01 \text{ cm} = 10^{-2} \text{ cm}$$

$$(OP) = 1 \text{ cm}$$

Therefore

$$SP = \frac{(10^{-2} \text{cm}) (1 \text{ cm})}{(6.5 \times 10^{-5} \text{ cm})} = 150 \text{ cm} = 1.5 \text{ meter}$$

(b)   Using the relationship derived in part (a) and solving the problem for $\lambda = 6.5 \times 10^{-5}$ cm, and assuming that the slit separation is 0.01 cm = 10^{-2} cm, we find again that

$$SP = \frac{(10^{-2} \text{ cm}) (1 \text{ cm})}{(6.5 \times 10^{-5} \text{ cm})} = 1.5 \text{ meter}$$

(c)   To project the interference pattern upon a screen 1.5 meters away and still be able to see it, a very intense source of light would be required. By viewing the source of light through the double slits, the eye can easily see the interference pattern which is projected directly on the retina of the eye. These bands would appear to be 1 cm apart against a meter stick placed at the source of light, as was done in the experiment.

4-25 A knowledge of technical terms is not one of the primary goals of this course, but studying new terms whose meaning has been essential in the development of Chapters 3 and 4 would be a useful way of reviewing the material of those chapters. Make a list of these terms.

Answer   A list of new technical terms in Chapter 3 might be:

spectrum	amplitude
crest	frequency
trough	wave pulse
vacuum	wave speed
wavelength	standing wave
monochromatic light	

A list of new technical terms in Chapter 4 might be:

interference pattern	constructive interference
superposition	transverse wave
point source	destructive interference
diffraction	path difference
opaque material	sine of an angle

4-26 What concepts from Chapter 3 were necessary to the understanding of Chapter 4?
Answer
1. White light is an appropriate mixture of all the colors of the spectrum.
2. A transverse wave involves vibrations at right angles to the direction in which it travels.
3. Waves traveling in the same medium can pass through a given point at the same time and continue on undisturbed. In the region where they intersect, their amplitudes add. This addition of amplitudes may lead to constructive interference or it may lead to destructive interference.

REFERENCES

1. (T)   Baez, Chapter 23, Sections 23.1, 23.2, pages 281 to 285. Young's experiment. These sections assume that interference between two sources is understood. The value of these sections is the diagrammatic justification for the necessity of coherence (constant phase difference) between the two sources.

2. (T)   PSSC, Chapter 6, Section 6-1 through 6-3, pages 87 to 93. The same treatment as ours—perhaps a bit more detailed. Also, see the good illustrative color plates between pages 132 and 133.

3.   Resnick and Halliday, Chapter 19, Sections 19-4 and 19-7, pages 470 to 472 and 478 to 481. Also, Chapter 43, Sections 43-1 through 43-4, pages 1068 to 1082. These sections give a more

detailed and mathematical description of superposition, interference, coherence, and Young's experiment.

4. (T)   Shamos, Chapter 7, pages 93 to 107. Some history.

5.   Stevenson and Moore, Chapters 17 and 18, pages 398 to 447. An intermediate treatment of waves and wave phenomena. These chapters contain more than is necessary for our treatment, but it would probably be better to preserve continuity by reading the whole two chapters.

CRYSTALS IN AND OUT OF THE LABORATORY

In Chapter 4 we set up models for the nature of light consistent with our observations. In this chapter we begin to do the same for crystals. These two lines of thought converge in Chapter 6 with the application of x-ray diffraction to the study of crystals.

After the relatively theoretical discussion in Chapter 4, Chapter 5 returns to simple direct observations. In this sense, it tosses the ball again to the students. The goals of the chapter from the student point of view are briefly stated at the beginning: for the students to take a closer look at crystals they have grown, as well as at other crystals, and to think about how they grow and what we can learn from our observation of them.

Section 5-1 CRYSTAL GROWTH

The students' experience with growing salol crystals was at the very beginning of the course when everything was new and strange. They have by now had an opportunity to learn something about performing experiments, and a repetition of the salol experiment can very well lead them to make more extensive observations than they made the first time.

Section 5-2 HARVESTING YOUR HOME-GROWN CRYSTALS

The salol crystallization (Experiment 1-1 and repeated in Section 5-1) takes place in the melt while the crystals resulting from Experiment 1-2 and discussed in this section grow in a solution. Several of the questions in the body of the text in this section relate to the differences between these two methods of growing crystals.

In seeking answers to questions about the differences between these experiments, you have an opportunity to underline the differences between observation and interpretation. What students observe, for example, is the difference in the rate of crystallization. They could also observe that one starting liquid was formed by adding water to the crystals, the other was formed by adding heat. How many pure observations can be listed? Where does interpretation begin?

A worthwhile discussion can be built upon the observation that in some jars two kinds of crystals grew, whereas in others a single kind grew, intermediate in color between the two original constituents. Students should be encouraged to suggest hypotheses, but it would be wise not to endorse any interpretation nor to yield to their request for the right answer.

The request for a mental model of what is happening when the solid is dissolving may cause the student to recall the diffusion of potassium permanganate in water. Hopefully, the students will begin to set up alternative models such as: (a) some sort of little particles of both substances mingling together (they have no *evidence* yet for atoms and molecules, and should be challenged for their definition of these terms and evidence for the presence of either if they glibly say these are the mingling particles); (b) both substances are continuous with no spaces whatever. Their difficulty here will be one of scale. They can't see any spaces. They may not feel that two continuous substances could not mingle. Consider smoke in air, milk in water. If some of the students do not see these as mixtures of particles, and an argument develops among them, this is fine. They are likely to argue about it among themselves later and in so doing they will develop their capacity to think about matter on an unfamiliar scale.

Experiment 5-1 Sugar and Salt

This is an experiment designed to give the student additional experience in growing crystals, this time using familiar materials. The evaporation and crystallization require several days; the time factor and the availability of materials make this an ideal take-home experiment.

Equipment Needed (supplied by the student)	Cat. Number
3-4 glasses or paper cups	68896
4-5 teaspoons, table salt	—
½ glass, sugar	—
2 stirrers (spoons)	—

Salt is almost as soluble in cold water as in hot, but sugar is much more soluble in hot water than in cold. A clear sugar solution can be obtained with very little water if the mixture is gently heated. Variously colored sugar crystals for decorative purposes are obtainable in supermarkets. Seeding the clear sugar syrup with these opens up a wide variety of possibilities for interesting observations. Sometimes they dissolve partially and the color diffuses through the viscous solution slowly. Can the students grow colored sugar crystals? Colored salt crystals? Will ink be accepted or rejected by the growing crystals? How about food coloring? The possibilities are almost endless.

Experiment 5-2 Packing of Spheres

The purpose of this experiment is to give students the experience of seeing an array of close-packed spheres, and thus to help them to visualize the regular structure resulting when uniform particles are arranged in a repeating pattern. The close-packed arrangement assumed by uniform spheres is typical of some metals and is encountered in Chapter 17, but care must be taken that the students realize that under other circumstances other arrangements are possible.

Equipment Needed (per student)	Cat. Number
1 Packing of Spheres Kit (Note a)	68866
1 magnifier	68847

Laboratory Notes

(a) The plastic boxes are supplied with an appropriate number of glass spheres contained therein. A small piece of cellophane tape seals the box to prevent it from being opened accidentally. The dimensions of the box and spheres are such that the student may obtain an array that is at least three spheres deep.

The arrangement assumed by the spheres is closest-packing. Each sphere in a layer touches six neighboring spheres in that same layer. If another layer is placed on the first, the spheres of the upper layer lie in alternate depressions of the lower. Each sphere thus touches three others in the layer below. If this second layer has a third on top of it, each sphere in the intermediate layer would touch three spheres in the layer above it, three in the layer below, and six spheres in its own layer, making twelve nearest neighbors in all. The counting of nearest neighbors helps to distinguish between different crystal forms.

Section 5-3 HARVESTING CRYSTALS GROWN IN NATURE

Those of your students who become elementary-school teachers will certainly have stones brought in to them by children in their classes, who will want to know what kind they are. But for young children especially, attaching a name to a specimen is not as fruitful as examining it closely and thinking about the processes that led to its formation. It is usually hard to see the individual grains of the minerals that make up the rock without breaking such a specimen so as to expose a fresh, unweathered surface. If the stone is small and composed of easily weathered minerals, the weathering may have progressed through the whole specimen, but usually a fresh break will disclose unweathered mineral grains. The blunt end of a geological hammer is best, but an ordinary hammer will do. Shield the eyes from flying chips.

Boulders and stones made of sedimentary rocks are usually rather flat, like a well-used cake of soap. This is because these rocks tend to split along the sedimentary layers. The grains of sediment may be very small, discernible only with a strong magnifier, or large like sand grains, or so large that individual rounded pebbles are evident.

Boulders of igneous rock are usually more rounded and difficult to break. When molten rock cools quickly, so many crystal nuclei are formed at once that the crystal grains are very small. Such a rock is usually dark, but some fine-grained igneous rocks are light in color. Coarser igneous rocks may have a pepper-and-salt look and the different kinds of mineral grains (usually only two or three different types) are discernible in them. Names are not important, but the most common rock-forming minerals are quartz, feldspar, and mica.

Nearly all white pebbles are composed entirely of the mineral quartz (SiO_2), which looks glassy when broken. It does not exhibit cleavage. A quartz pebble may be made from one single continuous crystal throughout or from several intergrown crystals, but generally it is not possible to detect the boundaries between the crystals. Feldspar is dull, opaque, and light colored. It may be chalky white or flesh colored or pink. It has two different cleavage planes. Mica has one excellent direction of cleavage and splits easily into very thin sheets. There are many varieties of mica, but the two commonest varieties are *muscovite* (silver gray, colorless in thin sheets) and *biotite* (black, dark in thin sheets).

Metamorphic rocks are commonly slabby like sedimentary rocks, but composed of crystals that have grown as the result of metamorphism. Therefore, whether changed from an originally sedimentary rock or an originally igneous rock they will not show rounded grains; they commonly contain a good deal of mica.

If you live where outcrops of the bed rock (everywhere present beneath the soil mantle) are exposed, you may enlist the aid of the geology department in planning a field trip for your class.

In the quotation from Holden and Singer, *Crystals and Crystal Growing,* the physicist is quoted as saying that a cut glass bowl is not solid because it is not crystalline. Not all physicists would agree that glass is not a solid. Some call it an amorphous solid, a formless solid, because its atoms are in a disorderly array. Those who agree with Holden would say that glass is just a stiff liquid, so stiff that it does not flow at ordinary temperatures and pressures. It has no proper melting point; it just gets gradually less stiff with increasing temperature.

Section 5-4 BREAKING CRYSTALS

This section deals with the strictly observational aspect of cleavage planes and the fact that some crystals have them while others do not. Any attempt to explain cleavage is strictly speculation at this stage, since such an explanation must be based on crystal structure and the bonding forces discussed in Chapters 15, 16, and 17. Such speculation should not be discouraged, however, since it points in the direction in which the course is heading; it involves the construction of some sort of model, and it indicates what must be studied before a sound explanation of cleavage can be attempted.

At this point an operational definition of *cleavage plane* is appropriate: a cleavage plane is any one of a series of closely spaced parallel planes along which it is possible to split a crystal. These cleavage planes must bear some relationship to the basic structural unit of the crystal.

Experiment 5-3 Cleaving Crystals

This experiment is designed to let students examine crystals and discover for themselves the cleavage planes characteristic of each. It may be used effectively as a chair-arm or as a take-home experiment.

Equipment Needed (per student)	*Cat. Number*
1 sodium chloride crystal, 1-inch cube (Note a)	68820
1 calcite crystal, 1-inch cube (Note a)	68820
1 razor blade, single-edged (Note a)	68820
1 plastic bag with tie	68853
1 hammer or metal block (Note b)	68840
1 magnifier	68847
crystals of quartz, mica, or feldspar (Note c)	—

Laboratory Notes

(a)   The materials for this experiment are available in bulk form in the Cleaving Crystals Package, Stock No. 68820. Each package contains 10 halite cubes, 10 calcite crystals, and 10 single-edged razor blades.

(b)   The recommended quantity of materials for this experiment is sufficient to permit the student to do it at home or in the dormitory. The hammer, however, is suggested for use in the laboratory only. It is to be used again for experiments in Chapters 8 and 16.

(c)   Quartz, feldspar, or mica crystals are not available as PSNS materials.

Both calcite and sodium chloride cleave so well that they often break cleanly if dropped or struck a light blow with a hammer. Nevertheless, students will need to exercise considerable care to cleave them successfully and consistently. If the razor blade is not placed accurately parallel to a cleavage plane, the crystal may crush rather than cleave. Worse yet, if struck very hard, the razor blade may fracture and send small fragments of steel flying dangerously. This is particularly true if quartz or other noncleaving crystals are tested. The likelihood of fracturing the blade can be reduced almost to zero, however, if it is struck only lightly; the screwdriver handle recommended in the text is ideal. It should be made clear to the students that if a light tap on the razor blade is not sufficient to cleave a crystal, then the blade is probably not parallel to a cleavage plane or the crystal does not have a cleavage plane.

The specimens of calcite and sodium chloride in the Cleaving Crystals Kit are cleavage fragments from larger specimens; they can be cleaved again and again, until only tiny fragments remain. You might have fun discussing whether such fragments are also crystals. The orderly arrangement is still there. Each piece is certainly as orderly a solid as the original. Most crystallographers would speak of any such a fragment as a crystal.

If quartz, mica, or feldspar are available, you can use them to demonstrate that not all crystals have three sets of cleavage planes. Quartz for instance has none. This fact will be useful in Chapter 15 when cesium chloride will be used as an example of a cubic crystal with no cleavage. Mica will prove helpful for the discussion of graphite (Chapter 17) which also has only one cleavage plane.

QUESTIONS

5-1   How many differently oriented cleavage planes did the crystal have? (Parallel planes have the same orientation. These constitute one set of parallel cleavage planes, but are usually referred to as one direction of cleavage or simply one cleavage plane.) If you were given more than one kind of crystal to break, you should answer this question for each crystal.
Answer   The cleavage planes of the crystals used may be summarized as follows:

Crystal	Number of Planes
quartz	none
mica	one
feldspar	two
calcite, sodium chloride	three

5-2   Can you predict how a particular piece will break, that is, what the orientation of the surface of the break will be?
Answer   The purpose of this question is to focus the attention of the students on what they have learned from cleaving crystals; to make them aware that they now know where the potential planes of breaking lie in the still unbroken crystal.

5-3   Do the remaining pieces still have cleavage planes along which they would break if you tried to break the piece? If so, how many?
Answer   Many students will say there is an infinite number of cleavage planes in the crystal. This is not so. The crystal cleaves between planes of atoms and there is a finite (though very large) number of such planes. The number in a given direction can be calculated by dividing that dimension of the crystal by the spacing between the atoms; determining that spacing is the subject of Chapter 15.

5-4   If you crush some of the cyrstal so that it is too small for you to detect its shape, can you predict what it would look like if you examined it with a magnifying glass? Try it.
Answer   The purpose of this question is to encourage the students to make predictions on the basis of repeated observations. This is a simple prediction which they can quickly and easily check. Their success should give them confidence. It would be well to call to their attention that they have here gone through a process of: (1) repeated observations of experimental results (cleaving), (2) predictions of a result beyond the scale of direct observation with the unaided eye, and (3) checking the prediction by using an instrument (the lens).

5-5   How small a bit of the crystal do you think would still be bounded by cleavage faces oriented in the same way as these you have been observing?
Answer   Here they are asked to extend their predictions beyond their powers of observation with instruments. There is no right answer to this question. No one knows just how small a particle of crystal could be and still be bounded by cleavage faces.

The cleavage planes of crystals are not necessarily parallel to the sides of the repeat unit of which the crystal is composed, but all cleavage planes are related to these repeat units. The discussion in Section 5-4 points this out. The fact that such surfaces appear smooth and regularly reflecting to the eye is then used to place an upper limit of roughly 6500 Å on the size of the repeat unit.

QUESTIONS

5-6   In Experiment 1-2 all jars originally contained a mixture of a colored powder and a colorless powder. In some of the jars crystals intermediate in color between the two powders grew. In other jars two different kinds of crystals grew: one blue and one colorless. Suggest a model or models to describe these results.
Answer   This is an open-ended question. It is not expected that they will all arrive at the same model. Class discussion of the merits of various models might prove fruitful. At this stage probably the farthest they can go on the basis of their experience would be to suggest that in those jars where the crystals were of two distinct types, they were made of structural units that were different from each other, whereas in those jars in which one kind of crystal grew from two original constituents, either they got together to form one building block or there were two building blocks that somehow fit well together.

5-7   You have observed that in certain cases, two types of crystals were formed separately in the jars. However, when the original solids were dissolved in water, the solutions were homogeneous. Describe a model which would be consistent with this behavior.
Answer   There must have been an intimate mingling of different kinds of constituents in the solutions which later separated in some way to form two different solid structures.

5-8   In the topaz crystal in Figure 5-4 it was shown that the slopes of the crystal faces were related as 1 to 2. Draw a diagram of the same crystal with faces whose slopes are related as 1 to 3.
Answer   See Figure RB 5-1.

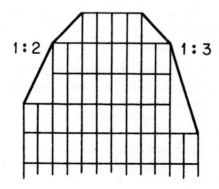

Figure RB 5-1

5-9 Suppose you lower the temperature of a solution of common salt (sodium chloride) until it starts to freeze. Design an experiment to determine whether the first ice crystals formed contain any salt.
Answer   One possibility is to put a fairly concentrated salt solution into a freezer (in a flexible plastic container) until it begins to freeze. A qualitative answer can then be gotten simply by tasting the first crystals to form. They should be noticeably less salty than the starting solution.

5-10 Assume that each of the following figures is the outline of the top view of a solid figure resting on the paper. Furthermore, assume that each of the figures is composed of building blocks smaller than the figures. What shape must those building blocks be, and what arrangement must they take in each figure, if all of the building blocks are identical, and if:
(a)   all the building blocks are oriented in the same way, that is, the top always stays on top,
(b)   any orientation is permissible.
Answer   See Figure RB 5-2.

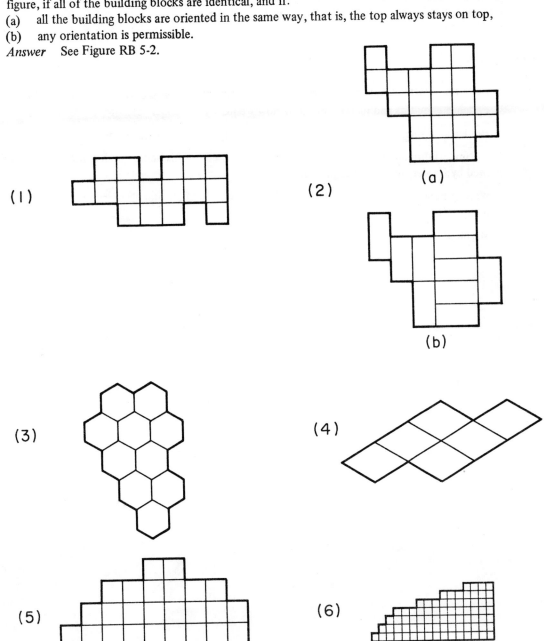

Figure RB 5-2

5-11 Recall Experiment 5-1 in which you grew some salt and sugar crystals from solution. Do you suppose the solutions were more concentrated near the bottom or near the top? Propose an experiment that might permit you to answer this question were you able to perform it. How would this experiment help you answer the question?

Answer Probably the simplest procedure would be to take a sample drop from near the top of the solution and another from near the bottom, using an eye dropper. Placing the two drops on a microscope slide and evaporating them to dryness would make it possible to compare the amount of residue in each. (The students would have to be careful not to stir the solution when withdrawing the samples.) The result should indicate that there is no difference in concentration; molecular motion in the solution will keep it essentially homogeneous throughout.

REFERENCES

1. (T)   Baez, Chapter 10, Sections 10.1, 10.2, pages 120 to 127. These sections show how we look at evidence — by bits and pieces, and show how we justify the conclusions we reach.

2. (T)   Holden and Singer. A fine, simple description of crystals and crystal growing.

      Note: Edmund Scientific Company sells a kit based on this book which contains the chemicals used by Holden and Singer in growing their crystals.

3.   Wood, Chapters 1 and 2, pages 1 to 29. The focus of these chapters is on symmetry, and symmetry in crystals.

4.   Mason, B. J., "The Growth of Snow Crystals," *Scientific American,* January, 1961, pages 120 ff.

CHAPTER 6

WHAT HAPPENED IN 1912

Section 6-1 THE STORY

This chapter deals with the discovery that an x-ray beam falling on a crystal may result in a pattern of diffracted x rays which gives information about the structure of the crystal. It is primarily a historical account of the way in which this discovery came about. The events related are typical of the manner in which many scientific discoveries are made. Several lines of investigation are developed to an appropriate stage, and someone aware of both explores the possibility of combining them.

The state of knowledge of students who have followed through Chapters 1 to 5 of this course is similar to that of chemists, crystallographers, and physicists in 1912: a repeating unit had been hypothesized as the basis of crystal structure, but its dimensions were not known except that they had to be much smaller than the wavelength of visible light. With regard to visible light, the phenomena of diffraction and interference had been observed and explained. With regard to x rays, some properties were known, but their electromagnetic nature had not been established nor was there more than a very rough estimate of their wavelength. This chapter is an account of how von Laue was able to suggest an investigation which, ultimately, gave answers to both uncertainties.

It is hoped that the students in this course will be able to get some feeling for the nature of scientific discovery as they read this chapter. This feeling and sense of discovery would not be possible if we were to pursue further our discussions in Chapter 4 and Chapter 5. In the latter chapter a discussion of crystal structure in terms of atomic arrangements would have been out of place since such knowledge has been obtained largely by the use of diffraction techniques. The atomic basis for crystal structure should not be presented in this chapter since the nature of atoms and their properties are not presented until Chapter 13. The properties of atoms, the nature of an x-ray diffraction analysis, and the resulting knowledge of the structure of crystals are discussed in Chapter 15 and should not be attempted at this stage.

Section 6-2 THE NATURE OF DIFFRACTION

In keeping with the philosophy of the course, the subject of multiple-slit interference was not treated in Chapter 4, where it would seem logically to fit, but is presented only at the moment that the student needs to know about it. It may seem that it would have been easier or better to lay the groundwork before starting the story, but laying groundwork for something before there is any apparent need for it often makes a course dull and meaningless for the student.

A discussion of the reason why the diffraction grating spacing must be larger than the wavelength of the light to be diffracted, but not much larger, is usually difficult for nonscience students to follow. This point is central, however, to the appreciation of the use of x rays for diffraction patterns from crystals and is worth taking time to develop. The first part of the argument demonstrates nicely the power of the simple Equation 4-1 in making it clear that the wavelength must not be longer than the spacing d.

In connection with the second part of the argument, that λ must not be so much smaller than d that the diffracted beams are crowded inconveniently close together, you might remind them of the experiment in which they measured the wavelength of light. The red light pattern was more widely spread out and thus more easily measurable than the pattern of the shorter wavelength blue.

The following experiment is discussed in the textbook, and its performance is important to the logical development of the argument even though it is not numbered.

The Diffraction Grating

Diffraction grating is discussed in Section 6-2, and the double-slit interference equation $n\lambda = d \sin \phi$ is applied to the case of the large number of slits in a grating. Spectroscopes (also used in Experiment 13-3) should be passed out to the students. The textbook suggests first that they examine the grating and then that they use the spectroscope to observe the diffraction patterns produced by light from various sources. The grating can be examined without removing it from the spectroscope (Note b).

Equipment Needed	*Cat. Number*
grating spectroscope (1 per student) (Note a)	68865
light sources (1 of each per class, placed in front of classroom)	
fluorescent light	68891
uncoated fluorescent tube for mercury spectrum	68892
neon discharge tube	68851
sodium arc	—
incandescent line-filament bulb	68863
red and blue filters	68822

Laboratory Notes

(a)   The diffraction grating spectroscopes are supplied in sets of six, each set consisting of:
    6 cardboard tubes 10 inches long and 1 inch in diameter
    12 tube caps to fit over ends of tube
    1 envelope containing:
        1 card with six-inch discs, each with a slit cut along a diameter
        2 cards, each with three double circles with ½-inch holes cut out of their centers
        2 sheets of plastic grating replica, each sheet divided into six 5/8-inch squares
To assemble the spectroscopes, remove the slit disc from the card, punch (or push) out the slit, and insert the disc into the open end of a tube cap. Place one such tube cap over the end of each tube and press on until the slit disc is held tightly between the tube and the flange of the tube cap.

Separate six of the plastic replica gratings. Remove the double circles from the card and clean out the central ½-inch holes. Fold one circle on top of the other at their junction. Place one grating between the two circles and insert in the open end of a second tube cap. Slide this grating-equipped cap over the other end of the cardboard tube and press until the grating holder seats firmly between the tube and the flange of the tube cap.

To observe a spectrum, hold the spectroscope with the grating near the eye and line it up with the light source so that you see the light through the slit. By maintaining this position of the source, the spectroscope, and the eye, the spectrum should appear to be along the inside of the tube about half way between the slit and the eye. A line through the center of the slit and perpendicular to it should also pass through the center of each of the spectral lines to obtain maximum spread of the spectrum. If this condition is not met the spectroscope should be adjusted by rotating the tube cap carrying the grating holder.

(b)   The extra grating supplied with each spectroscope may be passed out to the students so that they can examine it and use it as directed in the beginning of Section 6-2, or they may be instructed to examine the grating already mounted in the spectroscope. In either case they should not rub the grating with their fingers or any hard object.

It is useful to compare the patterns observed in this experiment with those observed in the experiments of Chapter 4. In Chapter 4, because of the small ratio of λ/d, even large values of n (up to 10–20) gave small values of ϕ. In the present case λ/d is much larger, so that even with $n = 1$, ϕ is a large angle. The second difference is in the width of the lines. In obtaining the equation $n\lambda = d \sin \phi$, only two slits were considered. The same equation also locates the positions of complete constructive interference for a grating. However, a detailed consideration of the many-slit case (the grating) leads to the fact that very close to the positions of maximum intensity, and everywhere in between, there will be almost complete destructive interference of the waves coming from all slits. This then leads to extremely narrow lines in a grating pattern, in contrast to the gradual change in intensity with angle which is observed in the pattern for the double slit.

No attempt should be made to explain the origin of the spectral lines for mercury, neon, and sodium. Such an explanation requires the use of some atomic model. This model is developed in Chapter 13 where spectra provide important information upon which to base the construction of a model. At this time the discussion should be restricted to the phenomenon of diffraction.

The diffraction pattern produced by a two-dimensional wire mesh in Experiment 4-3 might be mentioned at this time and used as an introduction to the three-dimensional grating represented by a crystal.

QUESTION

6-1   Figure 5-5 is a good model of the regular, step-like nature of the face of a crystal. If the faces of the crystal you grow have a regular array of steps and niches, why do they not act as diffraction gratings for visible light?

Answer   The purpose of this question is to develop students' understanding of the scale of roughness of a crystal face. Now that they have found that the spacing of a diffraction grating must be greater than the wavelength of the radiation being diffracted, they can say that the step-to-step distance on the surface of a crystal face must be smaller than the wavelength of light, since crystals do not diffract light. If they were much larger than the wavelength of light they would appear as visible roughness. This was an important conclusion that crystallographers had drawn just prior to 1912.

Section 6-3 THE IDEA

Having considered the physical principles involved in the formation of a diffraction pattern by a grating, we return to the story of Section 6-1. If some time has elapsed since that section was discussed, it would be well to refresh the students' minds by recalling the main ideas.

Section 6-4 THE EXPERIMENT

The experiments of Friedrich and Knipping are briefly described. These may be visualized by returning to the consideration of the double slit and grating experiments. The first experiment attempted unsuccessfully to observe x-ray diffraction with $\phi = 90°$. The second experiment produced x-ray diffraction with small values of ϕ, and this indicated small values of λ/d. Each spot in any given direction from the central ($\phi = 0$) spot was due to a different value of n.

The pattern of spots observed in experiments similar to those of Friedrich and Knipping are now referred to as Laue patterns. Since neither Laue nor powder patterns will be used as the basis of crystal analysis later in this course, there is no need to go into the details of either the apparatus or the analysis. Students raising questions about these methods may be referred to elementary texts on crystal structure.

The remainder of this chapter is used to develop the Bragg equation. This is the basis of the method of determination of crystal structure which will be used in Chapter 15. In that chapter the experimental details as well as an analysis of the data for NaCl and CsCl are discussed.

Section 6-5 DIFFRACTION FROM A REGULAR ARRAY OF OBJECTS

This is the second of the two derivations encountered in the first seven chapters of the text. It should be worked through in class carefully and with considerable discussion, since it forms the basis for the crystal analysis in Chapter 15.

Referring to Figure 6-3, the text states that the direction of travel of the diffracted wave makes the same angle with the row of posts as does the direction of travel of the incident waves. Students will probably assume incorrectly that this is true because the waves are reflected by the row of posts. Actually reflection is not involved at all. The wave diffracted by each row must result from the superposition of the waves scattered by each post in that row. The following analysis, which is not recommended for the students, shows that for maximum intensity the angles made by the incident ray and the diffracted ray must be equal.

Consider the rays r_1 and r_3 (Figure RB 6-1) incident on the adjacent objects A and E, and making the angle θ with the row. Consider also the rays r_1' and r_3', scattered in the direction making the angle Ψ with the row. Draw AF perpendicular to r_1 and r_3, and EG perpendicular to r_1' and r_3'. Then the difference in the distance traveled by the two rays is AG-FE which, in terms of AE and the angles θ and Ψ, is

$$AG - FE = AE \, (\cos \Psi - \cos \theta)$$

For r_1' and r_3' to interfere constructively, the difference in the distance they travel must be an integral number n' of wavelengths. Thus, for a maximum intensity of the diffracted wave, we must have

$$n' \lambda = AE \, (\cos \Psi - \cos \theta).$$

This equation must be satisfied, as must a corresponding one for the difference in distance traveled by ray r_1, and the distance traveled by ray r_2, which is scattered by object C.

$$n \lambda = AC \, (\sin \theta + \sin \Psi) = BC + CD$$

The intensity will be a maximum if $n' = 0$ so that $\Psi = \theta$. Under this condition the second of the two equations becomes the Bragg equation. No other values of n' can be found such that both equations can be satisfied simultaneously.

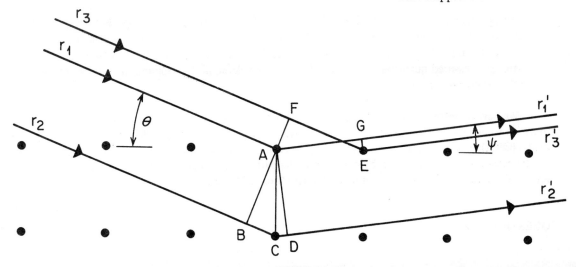

Figure RB 6-1

Following the derivation of the Bragg equation (6-1), the question is asked how the definition of θ (Equation 6-1) differs from the definition of the angle ϕ for the double-slit equation $n\lambda = d \sin \phi$ (Equation 4-1). If the students cannot answer this you can be sure that either they have not followed the development of the Bragg equation or they have not checked the way in which ϕ was defined, or both. The angle ϕ is defined in Figure 4-11 as the angle between the direction of travel of the undeviated ray through the slits and the ray diffracted to the point P. The angle θ, on the other hand, is the angle between the incident ray and the row of obstacles.

QUESTION

6-2   Suppose that a beam of monochromatic x rays of wavelength $\lambda = 3.4 \times 10^{-10}$ meter are used to determine the spacing d between the rows of regularly spaced units in a crystal. Those x rays are observed to diffract when they are incident on the crystal at an angle of $37°$ with one of the cleavage planes of the crystal; $\sin 37° = 0.60$. The x rays are not diffracted for any angle less than $37°$, so n must equal 1. Calculate the spacing d between the parallel rows of units that make up this hypothetical crystal.

Answer   The problem requires the use of the Bragg equation

$$n\lambda = 2d \sin \theta \qquad \text{(Equation 6-1)}$$

and states that $n = 1$, $\lambda = 3.4 \times 10^{-10}$ meter, $\sin \theta = \sin 37° = 0.60$. Solving (6-1) for d by dividing the equation by $2 \sin \theta$, we have

$$d = \frac{n\lambda}{2 \sin \theta}$$

Substituting the given values for n, λ, and $\sin \theta$, we obtain

$$d = \frac{1 \times 3.4 \times 10^{-10} \text{ meter}}{2 \times 0.60} = 2.8 \times 10^{-10} \text{ meter}$$

Actual division of 3.4 by 1.20 yields 2.83333 . . ., but since the problem gives both λ and $\sin \theta$ to two significant figures the answer for d indicates the true precision by using two significant figures, 2.8 rather than 3 or 2.83. (The factors of 1 and 2 in the solution are both known to be integers and are not measured quantities. They are thus not considered in determining the number of significant figures used to express d.)

We have indicated how x-ray diffraction establishes the size and structure of crystals. We must now move on to other studies of crystals in order to arrive at an understanding of their constitituents, the forces which hold them together, and their structure. We will investigate these problems first by observing the effects of heat on solids and then by considering the particles of which all matter is composed. We will then return to a consideration of x rays and crystal structure in Chapter 15.

QUESTIONS

6-3   With lights out in your room at night, look at a distant bright light through a window screen, a thin woven curtain, or a tightly stretched linen handkerchief. Describe the pattern that you see and draw a sketch of it. Interpret it in terms of the wave model of light.

Answer   The pattern observed will be similar to that shown in class in Experiment 4-3 and will depend on the distance between the wires or threads. In general the students should see a cross or plus sign with the arms of the cross parallel to the wires or threads. If the screen is sufficiently fine, each arm should consist of a series of closely spaced spectra. The spectra will not be equally spaced in the two directions unless the wires or threads have the same spacing in the two directions. If the light source is sufficiently bright, the spectra should be visible and it should be possible to see other spectra between the arms of the cross. Figure 4-15 shows the pattern obtained for a relatively coarse mesh in which the individual spectra would probably not be visible.

6-4   (a) In an experiment such as that shown in Figure 6-3, suppose the spacing d between rows of posts is 2 cm and the wavelength of the water waves is also 2 cm. For $n = 1$, what angle do the incident ray and the diffracted ray make with the rows of posts?

(b) What is the longest wavelength for which a diffracted ray could occur from rows of posts with $d = 2$ cm $(n = 1)$?

Answer   (a) $n\lambda = 2d \sin \theta$

$$d = 2 \text{ cm}$$
$$\lambda = 2 \text{ cm}$$
$$n = 1$$
$$1 \times 2 = 2 \times 2 \sin \theta$$
$$\sin \theta = 2/4 = 1/2$$
$$\theta = 30°$$

Before assigning this problem to students, give them the sines of a number of angles or remind them that the sines of a number of angles were calculated in Problem 4-19.

(b) This question will be difficult for nonscience students. They will not know how to go about it and the instructor will have to show them how to tackle such a problem by breaking it down into subproblems as follows: (1) Inspect the equation $n\lambda = 2d \sin \theta$. For this problem, it becomes $\lambda = (4 \text{ cm}) \sin \theta$. As λ becomes larger, what happens to $\sin \theta$? (It gets larger.) (2) What is the largest value $\sin \theta$ can have? Many students will not know this. It would be fruitful to construct a set of right triangles in which the sine is increasing. Students should be able to deduce the maximum value, that is, the limiting value the sine approaches. When they are convinced that the maximum value is unity, they can proceed to the next step. (3) $\lambda_{max} = (4 \text{ cm}) \sin \theta_{max} = (4 \text{ cm}) \times 1 = 4$ cm.

REFERENCES

1. Andrews and Kokes, Chapter 8, pages 188 to 218. This chapter describes various types of crystals and includes sections on crystal energy and on the Bragg equation. There is much more here than is necessary for our treatment, and it anticipates much in our later chapters, but it should be of value as a preview of what we are driving at.

2. (T) Baez, Chapter 23, Section 23.3, pages 285 to 288. The diffraction grating, the next step beyond two-slit interference. Also, page 596 shows a typical von Laue photograph (of rutile).

3. (T) Christiansen and Garrett, Chapter 25, Section 25-8, pages 435 to 438. This is a standard treatment of the Bragg equation and von Laue's experiment following a short description of x rays.

4. Resnick and Halliday, Chapter 41, Section 41-2, pages 1018 to 1020; Chapter 42, Section 42-1, pages 1035 to 1038; Chapters 44 and 45, pages 1099 to 1143. Huygen's principle, diffraction, and diffraction gratings, plus x-ray diffraction. These are more advanced and comprehensive treatments than ours. Page 1136 shows a sodium chloride diffraction pattern.

5. (T) Shamos, Chapter 14, pages 198 to 209. More history.

6. Stevenson and Moore, Chapter 18, Section 18.6, pages 441 to 446. Diffraction.

7. Bragg, L., "X-ray Crystallography," *Scientific American,* July 1968, pages 58 ff. A review of various methods used for determining crystal structure using x-ray diffraction.

CHAPTER 7

A CLOSER LOOK AT DIFFERENCES

In the previous chapters attention was focused on waves and light, particularly those aspects having to do with the use of light in the study of crystalline solids. This led into the discussion of x rays and x-ray diffraction in Chapter 6; we will come back to them again in Chapter 15 when the necessary information about mechanics and mechanical models has been accumulated.

In Chapter 7 students study the effects of heat, which was first introduced in Chapter 3. This leads directly to the observation of the liquid and gaseous states. In order to develop a model that will account for the properties of solids, we first develop a model for the gaseous state. The reason for this detour is that the gaseous state is simpler and it is more instructive to examine the simplest case first and then to proceed to more complex situations. We show it to be simpler by showing that the interaction between the constituent particles of a gas must be less important than those between the particles of a solid. This discussion further amplifies the concept of the particulate nature of matter which was hypothesized in Chapter 5. We then find that there are a number of things we need to understand before we can develop our particle model fully: force, mass, acceleration, pressure, and energy. The chapter thus leads directly to the classical mechanics of Chapters 8 and 9, and to the kinetic-molecular model introduced in Chapter 10.

Section 7-1 THE NEED TO QUESTION

This section involves a return to the point of view of Chapter 1, but it now emphasizes the need to perform experiments as well as to make passive observations. Observation of the properties of a rubber band was chosen as an example with which all students would be familiar. However, even though they are familiar with its properties, they are probably not familiar with the precise scientific way of describing them. The term *stretchability* is coined as a label for the relationship between stretch and applied force. *Elasticity* is used, properly, to designate the property of returning to initial shape after the distorting force is removed. The behavior of a rubber band may then be described in terms of these two properties. Care must be exercised that classroom discussion of this section does not go too far. It is intended as an example to indicate the need for careful measurements and for precise definitions of terms (more restrictive than the common usage). A discussion of the scientific usage of stretchability and elasticity requires establishing stress-strain relationships, hysteresis losses, etc., and would be out of place in this course. It would be preferable to restrict the discussion to letting the students develop concepts by answering Questions 7-1, 7-2, and 7-3.

QUESTIONS

7-1 Do you think that a quantitative definition of stretchability is possible? What factors would have to be taken into account? How would you define quantitatively the stretchability of a rubber band? Several equally useful definitions are possible.

Answer   The stretchability of a given sample can be quantitatively defined as

$$\text{stretchability} = \frac{\text{elongation}}{\text{applied force}}$$

Materials for which this ratio is a constant are said to obey Hooke's law. For other materials such as rubber, however, the relation between the elongation and the applied force is nonlinear, and a precise definition must, in some way, take into account the initial amount of stretch present when a further stretching force is added. It is also true that for any material Hooke's law applies only over a limited range. Elongation beyond the *elastic limit* for the sample is nonlinear and leads to permanent distortion.

7-2   Suppose you were given a rubber band, a nylon thread, a cotton thread, and a leather thong. Can you devise a simple experiment that would enable you to arrange these materials in order of decreasing stretchability? Do you think the order would be the same if they were ranked according to elasticity?
Answer   It is most convenient to start with samples all of the same length. In order to avoid difficulties due to kinkiness, etc., this initial length should be determined under a light load. The relative stretchabilities could then be found by adding a small force to each and measuring the resulting elongations. For small loads and elongations one could make the approximation that Hooke's law holds, so that the definition given above would be suitable. If the samples are not all of the same cross section, the ratio of elongation to applied force for each sample should be multiplied by its cross-sectional area in order to have a meaningful comparison.

Stretchability was defined in Question 7-1 as elongation/applied force; elasticity is defined as the property of returning to the original length when the stretching force is removed. There is no obvious reason why these two properties should be related. Steel has a low stretchability and high elasticity. Putty on the other hand has a high stretchability but practically no elasticity, since it exhibits little tendency to return to its original shape. It is therefore unlikely that a list ranking the materials in order of increasing stretchability would be the same as a list ranking them in order of increasing elasticity.

7-3   One might wonder why or how a rubber band can be made to stretch. Suppose research on the structure of a hypothetical rubber band revealed that a model of it could be considered to be composed of discrete balls held together by springs. A section of such a model might be represented as in Figure 7-1. Using this ball and spring model, can you suggest what might happen when you stretch a rubber band?
Answer   (See Figure RB 7-1) This is the model of the macromolecular structure of rubber and plastics which will be brought up again in Chapter 17. In the unstretched condition, the molecules may be thought of as being kinked, or even coiled up. Stretching such substances a moderate amount simply tends to straighten out the molecules. Excessive stretching will cause some of the molecules or some of the cross links to break, so that there will be some permanent distortion. This question is included not to form the basis for a discussion of the way in which models are developed, but rather as an example of the use of molecular models to describe macroscopic behavior.

Figure RB 7-1

Section 7-2 ANOTHER WAY TO EXPLORE DIFFERENCES

Experiment 7-1 The Distillation of Wood

Although this experiment is seldom included in chemistry courses because students get little precise chemical knowledge from it, there are valid reasons for its inclusion here. It generates much interest on the part of most students, it is an experiment whose outcome they cannot predict in advance, and it requires careful observation in its performance. It has an additional advantage from the point of view of this course in that it requires the use of several standard techniques used in chemistry: collecting gases, distillation, the assembly of glass apparatus.

An excellent way to introduce the experiment is through a discussion of Question 7-4.

QUESTION

7-4   Before you read on, try to predict, on the basis of your experience, what will happen to the wood.
Answer   Be sure to discuss this question before carrying out the experiment. It is unlikely that any of the students will have the sort of background experience necessary for making real predictions. However, a discussion on the basis of their experience with ordinary combustion can lead to some tentative suggestions of possible results. Although the students have all had experience with the burning of wood in the presence of air, it should soon become apparent to them, through such a discussion, that they cannot generalize very much or with much confidence to an experimental situation where the air supply is quite limited. In the process they ought to come up with a number of questions and tentative predictions concerning effects, products, etc., which can only be answered by performing the experiment.

It should be made clear to the students during this pre-lab discussion that this is an experiment with no predetermined results to be obtained or verified, that there is no standard answer or result that the students are to obtain. For this reason their performance can only be judged on the basis of the care with which they work, the keenness of their observations, and the clarity of their exposition.

The complete experiment takes about 60 minutes: 30 to 40 minutes to set up equipment and collect the gas and liquid; 15 to 20 minutes for the distillation of the liquid. Details of the experimental setup are shown in Figures RB7-2, 7-3, and 7-4.

Equipment Needed* (per 2 students)	Cat. Number
3 test tubes, 25 x 150 mm (A) (Note a)	68873
1 pegboard	68852
4 pegboard clamps, large (B) (Note b)	68852
2 rubber stoppers, no. 4, 1-hole (C) (Note c)	68869
1 rubber stopper, no. 4, 2-hole (D) (Note c)	68870
3 pieces, hard glass tubing, 6 mm OD (E) (Note d)	—
1 piece, rubber tubing 6 mm ID x 18 inches (F)	68860

*Capital letters in parentheses will be used to indicate the location of the particular piece in the corresponding apparatus diagrams

Equipment Needed (per 2 students)	Cat. Number
1 styrofoam cup (G) (Note e)	68824
2-3 boiling chips (H) (Note f)	68518
1 gas collecting bottle (I) (Note g)	—
1 polyethylene pan, 5 qt.	68895
2 alcohol burners and fuel (K) (Note h)	68810 - 68515
20 wood splints (L) (Note i)	68562
2 pairs, safety goggles	68838
1 box, matches	68539
cloth or paper towels	—
cold water	—
aluminum foil, 3 x 3 inch square (Note j)	—

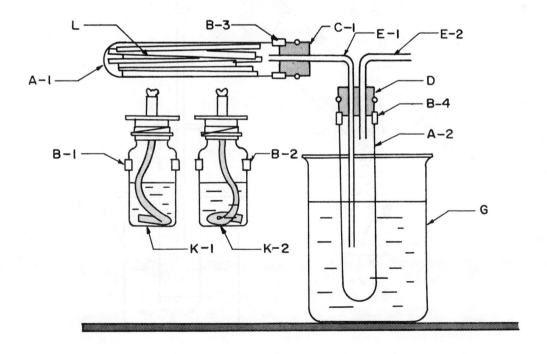

Figure RB 7-2

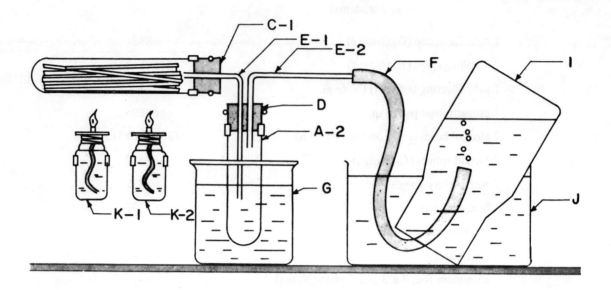

Figure RB 7-3

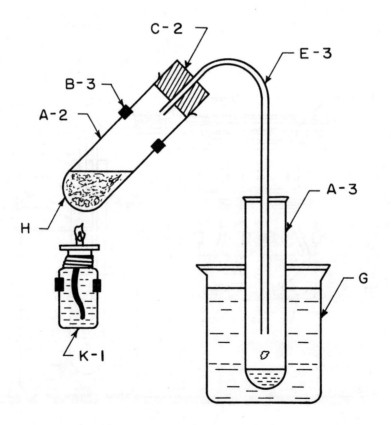

Figure RB 7-4

General Precautions

(1) The gas produced is somewhat noxious and should be prevented from escaping into the room by burning or collecting it.

(2) The glass tubing will often break as the student tries to insert it into the stopper. A little water or glycerine on the tubing and in the stopper hole will reduce the breakage, but it is well to have an ample supply of extra glass bends. Students should be provided with and required to use cloth or paper towels to hold the tubing as it is being inserted into the stopper.

(3) Be sure to remove the stopper and glass tubes from the condensing tube before the heating of the splints is stopped. This will prevent the cold liquid from being pushed up into the hot test tube.

(4) *Safety glasses should be worn during this experiment.*

Laboratory Notes

(a) The test tubes, rubber stoppers, rubber tubing, and glass tubing can be rinsed out in a detergent solution and reused for this experiment, but the distillation products cannot be completely removed. These items can be wrapped and stored for subsequent years but cannot be used for other experiments.

(b) The large pegboard clamps hold the burners, but the jaw size may require reduction to fit the test tubes. Follow previous instructions for this. A fifth clamp may be required to support the lower end of the test tube containing the wood splints.

(c) The three no. 4 stoppers must have holes to accept 6-mm OD glass tubes. They will not be usable for other experiments.

(d) A total length of about 3 ft of 6-mm OD glass tubing is required for each laboratory setup, with an extra length for each four setups to allow for breakage. (The extra length for each four setups should be allowed for each laboratory section.) Thus, if a laboratory section accommodates sixteen students and the equipment is used by three sections, the tubing requirement is

> sixteen students — eight setups: eight 3-ft lengths
> two replacements per section: six 3-ft lengths
> TOTAL fourteen 3-ft lengths

Each length should be cut, using a triangular file or tubing scorer, into three pieces, two 11 in. long and one 14 in. long. The ends should then be fire polished. These pieces should be bent as shown in Figure RB 7-5. The 11-in. pieces should be given a 90° bend 3.5 in. from one end and the 14-in. piece a 135° bend 3.5 in. from one end.

The fire polishing and bending can best be done in a Meker burner, which has a broader and hotter flame than a Bunsen burner, although the latter can be used with a flame spreader. Hold the tubing at each end so that the section to be bent is at the tip of the bright blue flame. Rotate the tubing between the fingers until the tube glows a dull red, then remove it from the flame and bend the tube to the desired angle. When the bend has been made it should be rotated in the cooler part of the flame for 15 seconds or so in order that the tubing does not cool too rapidly. It should then be placed on an asbestos sheet to cool.

To fire polish the tube ends, hold them immediately above the hottest part of the flame for about 30 seconds while rotating the tube between the fingers. This will permit the sharp edges to soften and flow slightly.

With a little practice the cutting, fire polishing, and bending should not require more than five minutes per set of three pieces.

(e) The styrofoam cup is the same as the one used earlier and replaces the beaker shown in the figures. It is a little small for the purpose, so to compensate for the small volume of water it will hold, the initial temperature of the water should be as low as possible.

(f) The boiling chips must be used to prevent violent boiling during the redistillation process. They are quite inexpensive and should be discarded after one use.

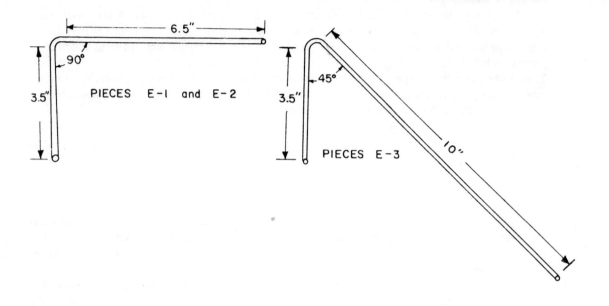

Figure RB 7-5

(g) The gas collecting bottle is indicated as a wide-mouthed bottle. Any transparent bottle may be used as long as its volume is several times that of a test tube. A catsup bottle or colorless pop bottle would be satisfactory.

(h) The alcohol burner is equipped with a brass sleeve stuck through a large washer. This sleeve and washer are designed to keep the flame from reaching the bottle. Care should be exercised that the wick does not extend more than ¼ inch above the sleeve or fuel may run down over the sleeve and bottle and cause excessive heating.

The burner fuel evaporates quite rapidly so the burners should not be filled until the day of the experiment. One filling of a burner will last for 30 to 45 minutes; thus they may require refilling during an experiment.

(i) The splints should be of soft wood. Popsicle sticks, tongue depressors, etc., will serve the purpose. The length should not exceed 100 cm. If they are longer they should either be cut to length before the laboratory period, or the students should be instructed to break off the ends so that the rubber stopper fits snugly into the tube.

(j) The square of aluminum foil is used to cover the bottle of gas collected during the experiment. It will prevent the escape of gas into the room. The covered bottle should be placed outdoors before the cover is removed. New pieces of foil may be needed for successive laboratory sections.

The post-lab discussion can conveniently be based on Questions 7-5 to 7-8. The first three are designed to stimulate careful observation, but 7-8 refers back to Question 7-4 and should serve as a summation of the experiment.

QUESTIONS

7-5   Look at the gas you have collected. (a) How does its volume compare to that of the splints you used? (b) What is its color? (c) Is it soluble in water?
Answer   The gas collected by water displacement is much greater in volume than the wood that produced it. It is colorless, and is thus not the smoke ordinarily produced by the combustion of wood. It has an unpleasant odor (and is probably somewhat poisonous, since it is likely to contain some carbon monoxide). It is not very soluble in water, or it would not have been possible to collect it satisfactorily over water.

    A complete analysis of the gas is, of course, possible, but it would be difficult and quite out of place here. Such an analysis would probably show it to contain carbon monoxide, carbon dioxide, water vapor, methane, and many other components.

7-6   Without shaking the liquid in the upright test tube, examine it carefully. (a) Is it one liquid or more than one? Disconnect the tube containing the condensed liquid and put a few pieces of broken porcelain in it. Connect the apparatus as shown in Figure 7-4 and gently heat it. Once it boils, the porcelain chips will keep it boiling more evenly. Continue to boil it gently until about half the liquid has evaporated. (b) What happens? (c) Is the liquid that condensed in the right-hand test tube the same as that in the left-hand one? (d) How do the two liquids compare? (e) What happens if you mix them together?
Answer   The liquid condensing in the test tube appears at first to be homogeneous, but it separates into two distinct layers if allowed to stand.

    The students will speed up the process by redistilling the original liquid. A light-yellow liquid is distilled off and condensed in the new test tube. A brown liquid remains in the original test tube unless the distillation is allowed to proceed too long.

    If the two separated liquids are mixed and thoroughly shaken, the original brown mixture seems to be obtained again.

7-7   After the test tube containing the wood has cooled, examine the remains. (a) What is the appearance of the solid remains of the wood splints? (b) Take one piece and hold it in a flame. Does it burst into flame? Does it burn at all? Does it leave any ash? Does it resemble any substance you know of?
Answer   The solids remaining in the heating tube burn if heated sufficiently. They burn without a flame — like charcoal bricquets in a charcoal broiler — and a small amount of white ash is all that remains.

7-8   Refer to your predictions in Question 7-4. (a) Did you predict that all these gases and liquids would be obtained from the wood? (b) Can you get the wood back by mixing all the substances you have collected? (c) Were these substances actually present in the wood or were they formed by heating? Have you any evidence for your answer?
Answer   Without previous information, it is impossible for a student to know what substances were originally present in the wood. Most students are surprised to see the results.

    It is impossible to say if the products obtained by the destructive distillation of wood were there all the time or if they were formed because of heating.

    The wood cannot be reconstructed by mixing together the products of the distillation.

    Having discovered that wood is a complex substance and that complicated results are obtained by heating it, the next step is to observe the effect of adding heat to a number of less complicated substances.

Experiment 7-2 Effect of Heat on Various Solids

Part A General Observations. This experiment is intended to give the students more experience in careful, accurate, but nonquantitative observations. At the same time, they will have a chance to observe some of the effects that can occur when heat is applied to matter.

In preparation for the first part of the experiment, each student should set up in his notebook the table suggested in the text. The three columns should be headed *Substance, Appearance, Effect of Heat.* The first column should be filled in before starting, listing the nine substances and leaving several lines for each. The students should be encouraged to list in the second column as many distinguishing properties or characteristics for each substance as they can identify; they should record in the third column all of the changes in the listed properties that occur upon heating.

About 45 minutes of laboratory time (5 minutes per sample) should be sufficient for heating and observation.

Equipment Needed (per 2 students)	*Cat. Number*
9 test tubes, 13 x 100 mm (Note a)	68906
1 400-ml beaker, to serve as test tube rack	68884
1 pinch-type clothes pin, to serve as test tube holder	—
1 pair forceps to hold magnesium during test	68833
1 cork to fit test tube containing iodine	—
1 alcohol burner and fuel (See note h, Experiment 7-1)	68810 - 68515
1 spatula	68864
2 pairs, safety glasses	68838
1 china marking pencil	—
9 weighing cups (Note c)	68823
1 stainless steel wire, 30-cm long (Note b)	68561

Materials Required (per pair of students) (Note c)	
mossy zinc (a few pieces)	68564
mossy tin (a few pieces)	68558
magnesium ribbon (5-mm length)	68537
zinc chloride (¼ test tube)	68563
sodium chloride (¼ test tube)	68566
naphthalene (¼ test tube)	68540
iodine (3-5 small crystals)	68533
sugar (¼ test tube)	68554
para-dichlorobenzene (¼ test tube)	68542

General Precautions

(1) *Safety glasses should be worn during this experiment.* Heating too rapidly may cause violent splattering.

(2) The only dangerous materials are the magnesium and the iodine. Distribute only the specified amounts of each. Place the iodine crystals in a lightly corked test tube. Urge the students to heat the iodine with the cork loosely in place; this will help to confine the vapor.

Laboratory Notes

(a) Of the nine test tubes required, only the two used for sodium chloride and sugar can be cleaned using water. The tube for magnesium is simply a container and is reusable. The tubes containing zinc and tin may be emptied by tapping but will probably have an uncleanable coating of oxide. These tubes may be reused for subsequent lab sections doing this experiment. The other four cannot be cleaned easily. Thus for repeat lab sections, an additional four test tubes are required per lab position.

(b) It may be difficult for students to determine when a metal has melted, and they may wish to use the stainless steel wire as a probe to check its state as it is heated.

(c) Materials may be dispensed in paper weighing cups if the bottom of each cup is numbered to correspond to the number of the material. This is the most economical method in terms of preparation time. Issue each pair of students a set of nine cups.

   The most expeditious method in terms of lab time, however, is to measure out the materials directly into the test tubes. Number each test tube with a china marking pencil to correspond to the material number. Issue each student a beaker containing the nine numbered and filled test tubes.

   The post-lab discussion should bring out the types of changes of state which are possible and, in so far as possible, the conditions under which they occur. The discussion should be based on macroscopic observations and not on such concepts as phase diagrams or a microscopic model except as the students bring them up. Questions 7-9 to 7-11 will serve as a good starting point for the discussion.

QUESTIONS

7-9 Sugar and salt (sodium chloride) look the same. Did they behave similarly upon heating?
Answer Sugar decomposes upon heating. As it melts, it caramelizes. Although salt can be melted, the temperature attainable with an alcohol burner is insufficient to do so.

7-10 A solid is said to sublime if, when heated, it passes directly (without liquefying) from the solid to the gaseous state and, on cooling, condenses directly to the solid state again. Did any of the solids you heated sublime? Can you think of any other solids that sublime?
Answer Iodine sublimes under ordinary conditions. Students should be encouraged to think of other substances that do also. The one that first comes to mind is dry ice (solid carbon dioxide), but moth balls, camphor, and menthol are other fairly common substances that also sublime slowly. So, for that matter, will ordinary ice or snow, which is why snow will gradually disappear in the winter time even if the temperature is constantly below freezing.

7-11 You have seen that the nine solids you tested demonstrated marked differences in behavior when they were heated. You can now answer such questions as: "Do all the solids melt when heated in an alcohol flame?" "What happens when you heat magnesium?" What questions have been raised by your observations? Make a list of questions for possible future study.

Answer   Various questions concerning the detailed mechanism of changes in state should come up, including the relationship between vaporization, sublimation, and melting. A very pertinent question would be, "What happens to the heat supplied by the alcohol flame?"

In the discussion of the observed changes in state the terms melting point and boiling point should arise and be interpreted as characteristic properties of the various substances. Reference may be made to Experiments 2-6 and 2-7 as previous observations of a melting point. The next experiment is designed to illustrate the sharp melting point of pure substances and to permit observation of the variation in melting point with composition of a mixture.

Experiment 7-2 Effect of Heat on Various Solids

Part B The Melting Point of a Mixture. Although this is a repetition of Experiment 2-6 the improved method and the anticipated improvement in the students' experimental abilities permit much greater precision in the determination of the melting point. The most obvious source of error comes from heating the sample too rapidly. It is easy, even with an alcohol lamp, to cause the temperature of the sample to rise much too rapidly for the thermometer to follow it closely. This will lead to an apparent melting range, rather than a melting point, and successive trials will not agree with one another. If it is done carefully, however, comparison of the results of his own successive determinations, and comparison of his own work with that of other equally careful workers should convince the student that the melting point of a pure substance is every bit as much a distinguishing characteristic as is its crystalline form, for instance.

A second purpose of the experiment is to acquaint the students with the fact that the melting point of a mixture depends on its composition and, strangely, is not necessarily intermediate between the melting points of the components.

The text suggests that the students be divided into four groups, each group using a different sample. If there is a sufficient number of students in a laboratory section it would be desirable that the melting points of more than four samples be determined, but in any case it is essential that two pairs of students make determinations on each mixture. About 30 minutes of lab time are necessary to allow for 3 separate heatings for each sample.

Equipment Needed (per 2 students)	Cat. Number
1 pegboard	68852
2 small clamps (A)	68852
1 split cork (B), to carry thermometer	–
1 test tube, 25 x 150 mm (C)	68873
30 cm, Stainless steel wire (D) (Note a)	68561
2 small rubber bands (E)	68860
1 capillary tube, closed at one end (F) (Note b)	68819
naphthalene	68540
para-dichlorobenzene	68542
1 mortar and pestle	–
2 glass plates or squares of aluminum foil	–

Equipment Needed (per 2 students)	Cat. Number
1 china marking pencil	—
alcohol burner and fuel (G) (See Note h, Experiment 7-1)	68810 - 68515
1 thermometer (H), -10°C to 360°C	68874
2 pairs, safety glasses	68838

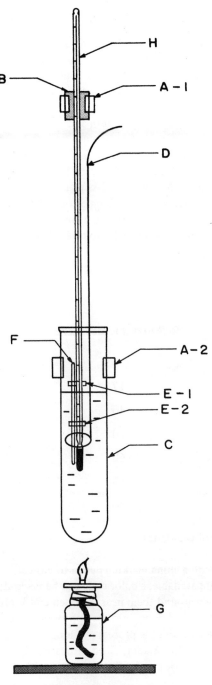

Figure RB 7-6

General Precautions

(1) *Safety glasses should be worn while performing this experiment.*
(2) Students should be cautioned to attach the capillaries to the thermometer with the open ends up.
(3) The slower the heating near the melting point, the more precise the results.

Laboratory Notes

(a) Stirrer (D): A 30-cm length of stainless steel wire (the same wire used in Part A) is bent with a loop 1 or 2 cm in diameter at its lower end with the plane of the loop at right angles to the length of the wire. The other end of the wire may be bent to form a handle.

(b) Preparation of samples: About 2 minutes of pre-laboratory time per sample is required for preparing the capillaries and filling them. Each laboratory station requires a pair of capillaries, and some allowance must be made for breakage.

   The naphthalene is commonly in flake form and the *para*-dichlorobenzene in large crystals. Grind about 100 grams of napthalene into a fine powder in a mortar. (Alternatively the grinding may be done on a glass plate with a spatula, but this is less effective.) Empty the powder onto a glass plate. Clean the mortar and pestle. Then grind about 100 grams of *para*-dichlorobenzene crystals into a fine powder and empty this onto a second glass plate.

   The following table illustrates suitable sample compositions, but how many different ones can be used will depend on the number of students in a lab section. It is preferable to have two pairs of students measure the melting point of each mixture. Weigh out the amounts needed to make up the number of mixtures appropriate to your class. It is most convenient to place the weighed samples on a glass plate; after thoroughly mixing the powders in each sample, scrape the sample into a small pile.

Mixture		Students/Lab Section				
% Naphthalene	% *Para*-dichlorobenzene	12	16	20	24	28
100	0	X	X	X	X	X
83	17		X	X	X	X
60	40				X	X
50	50	X		X		X
40	60				X	X
17	83		X	X	X	X
0	100	X	X	X	X	X
Required number of capillaries		9	12	15	18	21

   Mark the capillaries with a china marking pencil to indicate which type of sample each will contain. (If several colors are available, a color code can be devised; otherwise they may be coded by the number of rings drawn around them near the open end.) Fill three or four capillaries with each sample by pushing the open end down into the appropriate pile of power. The powder can then be packed down with a fine wire and the process repeated. Each lab station should be provided with one filled capillary, and there should be some filled capillaries in reserve for use in case of breakage. The students can attach the capillaries to the thermometers with the rubber bands provided.

The same capillaries may be used in successive laboratory sections but they should be checked before each class for breakage, loss of sample, or loss of markings.

After the students have completed their measurements (each student is instructed to obtain three good values of the melting point) the instructor should tabulate on the blackboard all measured values for each sample. If the above scheme has been followed there will be six readings for each. Variations within the six should serve as a basis for a brief discussion of the precision of the measurement and of the sources of error (usually too rapid heating or cooling, a failure to stir the water bath, or too much of the capillary out of the water bath). Determine the average after discarding values which are obviously in error.

Plot on the blackboard a graph of melting point versus percent composition, locate the experimental points, and sketch the form of the curve.

The discussion should center around the fact that the melting point of a crystalline material is a characteristic property of the material and that usually the addition of a second substance to a pure material results in a lowering of the melting point. Other examples are the use of salt to melt ice and the addition of alcohol or anti-freeze materials to water in an automobile radiator. The explanation of these two experimental observations must be delayed until after a knowledge of crystal structure has been developed in Chapter 15. Students may advance hypotheses to explain this behavior but they cannot be verified at this time.

Questions 7-12 to 7-14 may serve as a basis for discussion to bring out these points.

QUESTIONS

7-12 How precisely do you know the melting point of each sample? For each sample specify a range of temperatures within which you are confident the melting point lies.

Answer   For pure crystalline substances the method used is capable of a precision of $1°C$ or less. The results of students will probably be less precise depending on the care with which they did the experiment. Even if the precision is lower it is fruitful to discuss ways in which they could improve their techniques.

7-13 Compare the melting temperatures of the pure substances and the mixtures. Did the melting temperatures of the mixtures follow your expectations? Can you form a model that describes the differences in the melting temperatures between the pure substances and the mixtures? The melting process is not simple, but our investigations will eventually lead you to a deeper understanding of this experiment.

Answer   Accurately determined melting points fall on the solid curve as shown in Figure RB 7-7. Without having performed the experiment, one might predict that the melting points of the mixtures would change according to the dashed line shown.

The development of a consistent model which has the observed behavior will be an aim of Chapter 15. At this point all that can be said is that somehow the presence of a foreign crystal makes it easier for a given crystal to come apart, lose its structure, and melt, or that the foreign particles weaken the bonding between the particles of a crystal.

7-14 How would you need to modify the apparatus you used to be able to determine melting points greater than $100°C$?

Answer   It would be necessary to use a transparent liquid having a higher boiling point than water. For substances melting at much higher temperatures, entirely different techniques would be required.

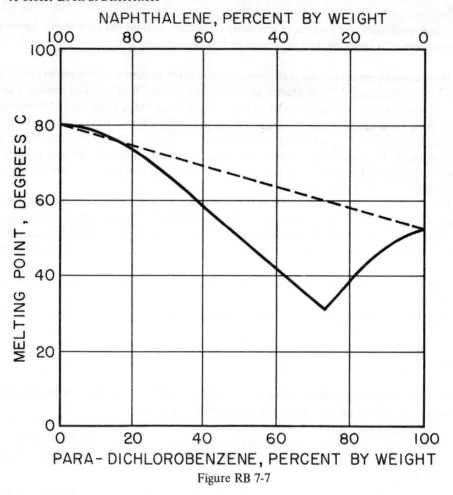

Figure RB 7-7

Section 7-3 COMPARISON OF SOLIDS, LIQUIDS AND GASES

As was mentioned earlier, it is convenient to begin one's study of a subject with the simplest example or situation available, and then to progress to more and more complex cases. We are now in a position to begin studying the structure of matter in detail, and since the gaseous state is the simplest, we start with it.

The reasons for our choice will not be at all obvious to the student. Solids can be seen, handled, and measured easily. The difficulty is that these measurements and observations are not easily related to structure. Gases can't be seen or handled, nor are their properties easily measured. But even though the measurements are more difficult, the physical properties which they define are closely similar for all gases, and are easily related to structure. The purpose of this section is to lead the students to this conclusion. The emphasis must be on the simplicity of the gas structure as evidenced by the lack of interaction between particles, and the lack of dependence of gas properties on the nature of the particles. The former comes about because of the larger distance between particles in the gaseous state. This increase in distance is indicated by Experiment 7-3 and further demonstrated by the consideration of gaseous, liquid, and solid diffusion.

Experiment 7-3 The Vaporization of a Liquid

This experiment illustrates, in a semiquantitative way, the extreme volume difference between the liquid and gaseous states. An estimate of the magnitude of this change can be made fairly readily by a simple computation of the volume of the plastic bag when it is filled with vapor. It certainly won't be highly accurate because of leakage, recondensation on the inner walls of the bag, and errors in approximating its expanded dimensions, but a good "ball-park" estimate can usually be made without much trouble.

Equipment Needed (per 2 students)	Cat. Number
1 pegboard	68852
2 small pegboard clamps	68852
1 test tube, 25 x 150 mm	68873
2 wire ties	68853
3-4 boiling chips	68518
2 plastic bags, heat resistant (Note a)	68544
1 alcohol burner and fuel	68810 - 68515
1 ruler	—

Laboratory Notes

(a) The plastic bag will melt if exposed to excessive heat, so care must be taken that it does not get into the burner flame. The problem can be minimized if one corner of the bag is attached to a clamp mounted at the top of the pegboard. The second wire tie may be used for this purpose. However, a second plastic bag should be available in the event that holes do develop in the first.

(b) The students are asked to make an estimate of the volume of gas produced. They can measure the length, width, and thickness of the filled bag, but the irregular shape precludes more than a rough estimate. One can assume it to be rectangular and use the product of these three measurements or make some other approximation. The experimental value for the ratio of the volume of vapor to the volume of liquid will probably be much smaller than the theoretical value of 1800. The discrepancy is principally due to escaping vapor, but inaccurate volume estimates and errors due to condensation of the vapor on the walls of the bag also contribute.

The students should be able to observe a considerable increase in volume when the water vaporizes and a corresponding decrease when the vapor is condensed. If a larger bag were used, more water would vaporize and the bag would still be filled. There is a fixed relationship between the mass of water that will evaporate, and the pressure, volume, and temperature of the vapor. The plastic bag does serve as a container limiting the volume occupied by the vapor, and if it is stretched it makes a small contribution to the pressure, increasing it somewhat above atmospheric pressure. Once equilibrium is established, any further water that vaporizes in the test tube is reduced by water that condenses on the walls of the bag and runs back down.

The emphasis in the discussion should be on what happens to the individual particles as one causes a substance to go through a change of state.

Section 7-4 ALTERNATIVE MODELS OF A GAS

This section is an exercise in the construction of models. Two are suggested for the structure of a gas, either of which could be used to answer satisfactorily the questions posed in Experiment 7-3. They are (1) the particle size remains constant while the spacing between them increases, or (2) the separation between the surfaces of individual particles remains essentially constant but their size increases. Other intermediate models might be advanced, but these are the extremes.

The difficulty with this approach is that most students are already sufficiently familiar with the terminology and the main points of the atomic and molecular description of matter that they are sure the first alternative is right and the second one is artificial and contrived. Thus, some effort must be made to convince them that Experiment 7-3 is explained equally well by either. Further, they must be brought to the realization that we are very much concerned in this course not only with what we know, but with how we know it; not only with the answer to a question, but with how we go about deciding which of several alternative answers is the most satisfactory.

We immediately proceed, through a discussion of a series of demonstration experiments, to prove to the student what he already believed, namely, that only the first model accounts for the expansion noted in Experiment 7-3 and the diffusion found in the demonstrations. You must be very careful here not to lapse into the usual authoritative presentation, but rather to go very carefully through the logical reasoning which leads to the kinetic-molecular model. This section can be effective only if this care is taken. The discussion is valuable because it provides the first example of model building encountered in the course, and students need to understand both the process and its importance in the development of scientific theory.

Five diffusion experiments are described and discussed in the text, and as many of them as possible should be performed for the class. It is important to the continuity of the course that the bromine experiment be done. The diffusion of ammonia can be done simply with minimal equipment. The other three experiments should also be performed if the necessary time and equipment are available.

Diffusion Demonstration Experiments

Part 1: Diffusion of Ammonia Vapor from an Open Dish. The diffusion rate for this gas can be demonstrated by having each student raise his hand when the odor reaches him. This provides a clearly visible indication that the students can easily remember.

Equipment Needed	Cat. Number
1 flat dish such as the plastic disc used in Experiment 3-1	68845
1 bottle, aqueous ammonia solution (household ammonia is satisfactory)	—
1 classroom clock	68821

Part 2: Diffusion of Ammonia and Hydrogen Chloride in a Glass Tube. Fasten a wad of cotton on each of two rubber stoppers (using a thumb tack works very well), and place one at each end of a large-bore (1 to 2 inches inside diameter) glass tube (see Figure RB 7-8). Pour ammonia solution on one and dilute hydrochloric acid on the other. Then put the stoppers and cotton into the two ends of the tube simultaneously; very quickly a ring of fog will form where the two vapors meet, though it may be necessary to illuminate the central section of the tube in order to make it clearly visible.

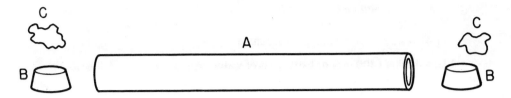

Figure RB 7-8

Equipment Needed	Cat. Number
1 glass tube (A), 3-4 cm diameter x 30-40 cm long (special electrolysis apparatus)	68900
2 rubber stoppers (B)	68900
2 cotton plugs (C)	—
aqueous solution of ammonia	—
aqueous solution of HC1	—

This experiment is a less direct method of observing the diffusion of gases; but it has the advantage of showing that different gases diffuse at different rates. The ring of fog will be formed at a point such that its distance from the source of the gas is proportional to the rate of diffusion.

Part 3: Diffusion of Ink in Water. A simple demonstration of liquid-into-liquid diffusion. From this and the next demonstration the students should conclude that diffusion in liquids is a very slow process. From this, in turn, they ought to be able to conclude that the motion of particles in liquids is quite restricted.

Equipment Needed

1 glass

3-4 drops of ink from fountain pen or bottle

This experiment can be performed at home or in the laboratory; subsequent discussion can bring out the restricted motion of particles in liquids. This will assist in building the model of molecules of a fixed size, with a spacing that depends on the state.

Part 4: Diffusion of Potassium Permanganate in Water. This is a large-scale repetition of Experiment 1-3, the difference being that we are now using the experiment as a means of answering a specific question, and not simply as an exercise in observation. A large beaker or battery jar should be filled with water well in advance of the time it is to be used, and it should then be allowed to sit undisturbed until it is needed, so the effects due to currents will be minimized. A few crystals of permanganate dropped into the water leads to a slow uniform spread of color, primarily horizontally.

Equipment Needed	Cat. Number
3 or 4 crystals of potassium permanganate	68545
1 large beaker (400 ml) or battery jar of water	68884

The students should be made to realize that in this case the diffusion must be preceded by solution so that the actual diffusion process is again that of a liquid into a liquid.

Part 5: Diffusion of Bromine in a Vacuum and in Air. This experiment demonstrates the large difference in diffusion rates when bromine is released in a vacuum and in air. In combination with either of the diffusion in liquid experiments it will demonstrate very rapid diffusion if there is no other material present, slower diffusion if a gas is present, and much slower diffusion if a liquid is present. All three must be shown if the desired point is to be made. Students seeing only the bromine experiment get the idea that diffusion takes place slowly in air but the important idea is that diffusion is faster in a gas than in a liquid.

Equipment Needed	Cat. Number
2 modified Victor Meyer tubes (A), 110 cm long x 2 cm diameter, closed at one end, open at the other, with two 0.8 cm diameter side arms, 6 cm long (see Fig. RB 7-9)	68828
2 glass stirring rods (C), 0.5 cm diameter x 15 cm long Insert through rubber tubing into one side arm so that it extends across inner side of Victor Meyer tube.	68828
2 stop-cocks, 0.8 cm OD and overall length 20 cm Insert into rubber tubing to butt against side arm.	68828
8 pieces of copper wire about 20 cm long (E) Wrap tightly around rubber tubing near the ends as shown in Figure RB 7-9.	68561
2 glass ampules containing liquid bromine (F) Place in top of tube so that they rest on glass stirring rod.	68828
2 solid rubber stoppers (G), to close open end of tube after insertion of liquid bromine ampules	68828

Not Shown in Diagram:

1 ring stand or vertical rod at least 1 meter high, to support Victor Meyer tubes	–
4 clamps, to attach tubes to vertical rod	–
1 vacuum pump with rubber hose about 150-cm long, for attaching to the glass stop cock of one tube	–
alcohol burner fuel, 400 ml	68515
2 beakers, 400 ml	68884
2 latex tubing, 6″ x ¼″ ID	68828

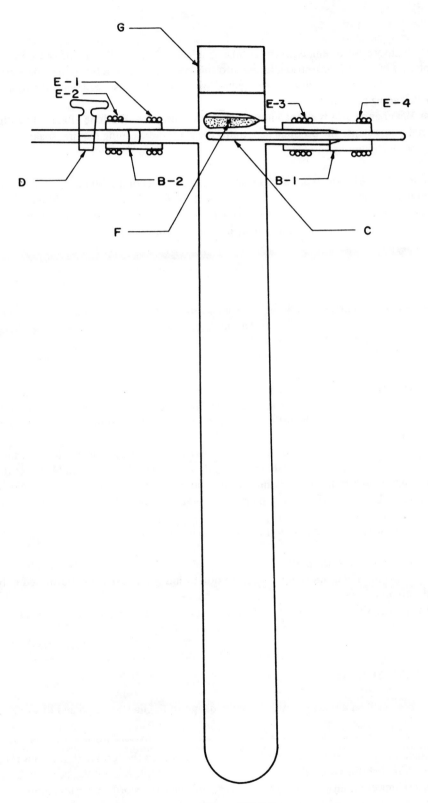

Figure RB 7-9

General Precautions:

It is a wise precaution to immerse the bottom inch of the Victor Meyer tubes in a beaker of alcohol to catch the glass and absorb the bromine gas if the tube should break when the ampule is dropped.

Upon completion of the demonstration, let air into the evacuated tube, remove the stoppers, and pour the alcohol into it. The alcohol will dissolve the bromine, preventing its escape into the room and also assisting in the cleaning process.

If the Victor Meyer apparatus is cleaned immediately after use it can be done effectively with soap and water. If several hours elapse the bromine penetrates the glass and cleaning requires soaking in a hot concentrated solution of sodium hydroxide.

The discussion of the diffusion experiments should bring about a comparison of the relative abilities of the models formulated to explain the results of Experiment 7-3 (see Question 7-14). The students should thus be aware that the model of particles of a fixed size, in rapid motion, with the average distance between them depending on the state, is consistent with their observations.

QUESTION

7-15 Which model of a gas is consistent with the experiment showing the diffusion of bromine when air has been pumped out of the tube? when air has not been removed? Does the same model explain both situations? Are both models reasonable?

Answer   The rapid diffusion of bromine vapor into a vacuum is explained equally well by saying that the particles of bromine expand when it vaporizes, or by saying that they suddenly move farther apart. However, the slow diffusion of fromine through air cannot be easily explained if one assumes that the particles have expanded, because the tube would also be filled with similarly large air particles and there would be little or no space between them through which the bromine vapor could move.

On the other hand, assume the size of the bromine particles is the same in the gaseous as in the liquid state, and simply much more widely separated in the former. Then we would expect them to move through air, though rather slowly, since it too would be expected to consist of small and widely spaced particles. The diffusion occurs much less rapidly when air is present than when it is not, because of the collisions between the particles.

The experiments lead to a model with the following characteristics:

(a)   Liquids and gases consist of small particles.
(b)   The particles are in continuous motion with the motion of individual particles interrupted only by collision with other particles.
(c)   The size of the particles is independent of the state but they are farther apart, on the average, in a gas than in a liquid.

Section 7-5 WHICH MODEL SHALL WE CHOOSE

This section is essentially a discussion of the answer just given to Question 7-15 and of some of its consequences.

Note that the term *molecule* as introduced here is synonymous with *particle* in the model just developed. Many students will thus relate the particles of our gas model to the term molecule as it is used in a chemical sense. Although the connection between these two concepts has not yet been established in this course, there is no important difference between them, and since the word would undoubtedly come up anyway, there is no reason to try to avoid using it.

Brownian motion is introduced in this section as concrete evidence that the molecules are in motion. It is desirable that the students see this movement, but, in so doing, they must be made aware that they are seeing a result of molecular motion and not the molecules themselves. For classroom use this phenomenon is best shown by means of a film. The first part of *Behavior of Gases* does this well. The phenomenon may be seen directly by students if microscopes are available. Students may be invited to the apparatus lecture desk to observe or may be set up in one corner of the laboratory. Directions are given in the text.

The actual motion of the molecules cannot be described quantitatively at this point. This will have to wait until the concepts of velocity and kinetic energy and their dependence on temperature have been developed. At this stage the motion must be described only as random, quite rapid, and impeded by collisions.

Section 7-6 VOLUME CHANGES OF A GAS

This section and Experiment 7-4 are intended to be a first step in determining the macroscopic properties of a gas. Because students generally have a fair intuitive concept of volume and temperature, we begin with them. The third important macroscopic variable, pressure, is introduced after completing the volume-temperature experiment. Pressure, however, cannot be understood without making use of the concept of force. Thus a study of the structure and behavior of gases requires a prior understanding of force. In this way we establish a need to know for the material of the next two chapters.

Experiment 7-4 Effect on a Gas of a Change in Temperature

This is likely to be a difficult experiment for nonscience students. It is quantitative and they are unskilled in manipulating equipment and making accurate measurements; it requires graphical analysis of the data, and they are inexpert at graphing.

It will be helpful to most students to study Appendix B, Graphing, before attempting to perform the experiment. It will also be useful for you to go over with them in detail the material in the text on how the measurements are to be made. Such a discussion should lead them toward an understanding of the desired relationship in a gas. They should also become clearly aware of the need for slow heating and frequent stirring so that all measurements are made under conditions of thermal equilibrium.

About 30 minutes of lab time is required for pre-lab discussion. About 15 minutes is required for students to assemble the apparatus. Another 30 to 45 minutes is required to perform the experiment and 30 to 45 minutes to analyze the results and discuss them.

Equipment Needed (per 2 students)	*Cat. Number*
1 volume-temperature apparatus (Notes a, b, c, d)	68879
1 test tube (B), 25 x 150 mm	68873
1 pegboard	68852
2 clamps (C)	68852
1 split cork (D), to hold thermometer	—
1 thermometer, -10°C to 360°C (E)	68874
1 wire stirrer (F)	68561

Equipment Needed (per 2 students)	*Cat. Number*
2 small rubber bands (G), to attach gas tube to thermometer (Note e)	68860
1 alcohol burner and fuel (Note h, Experiment 7-1)	68810 - 68515
ice	—
2 sheets, graph paper	—
1 plastic ruler	—

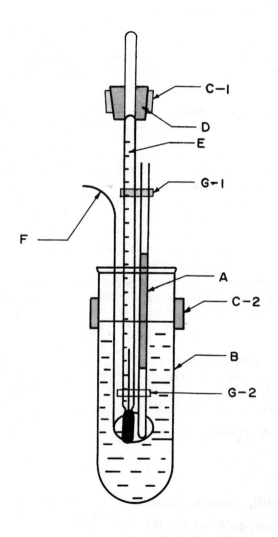

Figure RB 7-10

Laboratory Notes

(a) Preparing the glass tubing: Pieces of soft glass tubing 10-cm long with an outside diameter of 3 mm and an inside diameter of 1 mm are required. The small inner diameter is essential; capillary tubing must be used. One end must be closed if this has not been done. This can be accomplished by heating the tube in a Bunsen burner flame at a point about 5 cm from one end. A 1 to 2 cm section should be heated to prevent strains, but as small a region as possible should be melted. When the glass is melted, pull the tubing apart and close the end of the resulting capillary by melting in the flame. It is desirable to maintain an even bore as near as possible to the end of the enclosed volume; this can be achieved by flattening the end of the tube against a metal or carbon block while it is still soft. The tube should be annealed by slow cooling in the cooler parts of the flame.

(b) Filling the tube: One must place enough oil in the tube to produce a column 1 to 2 cm long (Duo-Seal vacuum-pump oil is recommended). This oil may be injected into the tube with a hypodermic needle. An alternative method is the following: Place oil in the bottom of a beaker to a depth of 1 or 2 cm. Holding the tube vertically with the closed end up, heat the closed end gently with a Bunsen flame until the air inside the tube is heated. Quickly place the tube with the open end down in the beaker of oil. The air will contract on cooling and some oil will be pushed into the tube. The tube should be removed from the oil as soon as the oil column is 2-cm high. Extra oil may be removed by heating the air in the tube.

(c) Adjusting the length of the air column: A fine stainless steel wire which will fit inside the tube may be used to adjust the length of the air column. Hold the tube with the closed end down and use the wire to remove a bubble of air if the length is too great. Hold the tube with the closed end up and use the wire to add a bubble of air if the length is too small. If the column of oil is separated into two or more pieces by a bubble of air, the same method may be used to work the air bubble out of the column.

(d) A 6-cm air column will expand to 8.2 cm if the air is heated from $0°C$ to $100°C$. A smaller length will yield increases in length that are difficult to measure. Lengths greater than 7 cm at $0°C$ will cause difficulties because the whole length of the air column may not be in the water bath.

(e) The tube should be attached to the thermometer with small rubber bands. One rubber band should be over the middle of the air column and the other near the top of the tube. In this way the rubber bands will not interfere with reading the positions of the oil column.

The students are asked to devise a means of measuring the length d of the air column. Ordinary plastic rulers cannot be used because they will not fit into the test tube. The students may come up with any of a number of alternatives:

(1) Obtain a small plastic ruler or cut one so it will fit inside the test tube and can be secured to the gas tube and thermometer. This will provide a direct and accurate means of measuring d.

(2) Some students may wish to mark a wooden stir stick with even divisions using a metric ruler. Then attach the stick to the gas tube and thermometer. This also provides a direct but less accurate means of measuring d.

(3) Assuming that the divisions of the thermometer are equally spaced, a student may use the thermometer scale to measure d in terms of scale divisions. No conversion to centimeters or millimeters is necessary because all that is needed is a number proportional to the length. Because the tube must be mounted in such a way that the major portion of the air column is adjacent to the únmarked portion of the thermometer stem, a subsidiary measurement must be made before the thermometer and gas tube are inserted in the water. With the gas tube fastened tightly to the thermometer, use a ruler to measure the distance L in centimeters from the bottom of the air column to the $0°C$ mark on the thermometer (See Fig. RB 7-11). This distance must then be converted to thermometer scale divisions, which can be done by using the ruler to find, on the thermometer scale, the number of scale divisions L' that are equivalent to L in centimeters. (In Fig. RB 7-11, L' is 70 scale divisions.) When the thermometer and gas cell are immersed in the water, one can obtain the length d of the

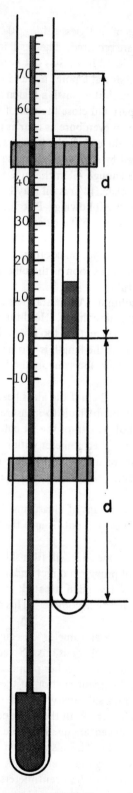

Figure RB 7-11

air column by reading the position of the bottom of the oil drop ($10°$ in Fig. RB 7-11) and adding this reading algebraically to L' (in Fig. RB 7-11, $d = 10° + 70° = 80°$).

CAUTION: The position of the gas tube relative to the thermometer scale should not be changed during the experiment since this would change L'.

In order to obtain the maximum change in temperature, be sure that the students start with ice water. A large beaker containing ice and water can serve as a source for the whole class.

Initially the air column must be sufficiently low in the test tube that when its length increases by 3 cm, the whole air column will still be immersed in water. In order to insure thermal equilibrium for a reading, students should remove the burner and stir the water for 10 to 15 seconds before reading the thermometer.

After the experiment has been completed, show the students how to plot and analyze their data. The methods are outlined in the text, but if you take the data obtained by one pair of students and go through the whole procedure, it will become much clearer to them. Such discussion will also serve to lead directly into Questions 7-16 through 7-19.

A typical set of student data is given in the accompanying table. It illustrates one feature of good technique and two examples of poor technique. First, the air column lengths are given to a tenth of a millimeter as measured with an attached ruler whose smallest division was a millimeter. Admittedly the last digit is an estimate and may be in doubt by 0.02 or 0.04 cm, but it gives a better knowledge of d than if it were omitted. The fact that the air column length does not exceed 4.6 cm is an example of poor technique, since a larger value of d would give higher precision. The temperature range is 21 to $89°C$, whereas a range of 5 to $95°$ would allow better extrapolation.

Temperature in $°C$	d in cm	Temperature in $°C$	d in cm
21.5	3.71	57.0	4.22
22.5	3.73	66.0	4.35
25.0	3.80	73.0	4.42
32.0	3.85	80.0	4.50
35.0	4.01	89.0	4.58
43.0	4.05	89.0	4.61
50.0	4.12		

These data are plotted in Figure **RB** 7-12 using the method outlined in the text. The straight line drawn through the experimental points intersects the temperature axis at $-281°C$. It is obvious that this extrapolation is somewhat uncertain. It is equally obvious that the extrapolation would be subject to less uncertainty if the data points were spread over a larger range of temperature and over a larger range of lengths. In any case, values between $-200°C$ and $-350°C$ may be expected.

QUESTIONS

7-16 What do your results show about the relationship between the volume of a gas and its temperature on the Kelvin scale if the pressure and mass are constant?

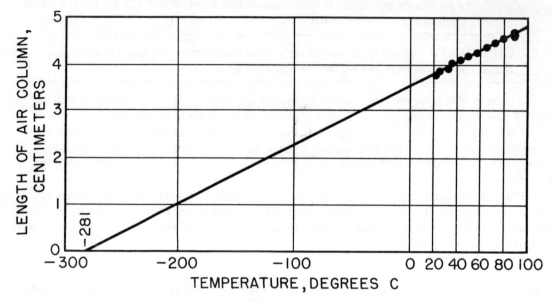

Figure RB 7-12

Answer   The drop of oil was a freely moving piston, so the pressure was constant; if no air leaked out, its mass was constant. The experimental results show that the volume of the gas is directly proportional to the Kelvin temperature.

7-17   Referring to your graph, does the volume of the confined gas double if its temperature doubles?
Answer   The volume of confined gas doubles with doubled temperature only if the Kelvin, or Absolute, scale is used. With any other scale, the volume-temperature relationship is linear, but it includes an additive constant: $V = aT + b$. From this we see that changes in volume are directly proportional to changes in temperature: $\Delta V = a \Delta T$

7-18   From your own graph predict what the volume of the trapped gas should be at $-273°C$. Why do you suppose you were not asked to measure the volume of the gas at temperatures near this value?
Answer   Highly accurate data would yield zero volume at $-273°C$, but there will be wide variations in the results obtained from this experiment. This is due to experimental uncertainties, which are greatly magnified by the extrapolation.

Aside from the obvious technical problems involved in reaching temperatures of the order of $-273°C$, there is also the fact that all gases liquefy when they are cooled sufficiently. That is, it is not possible to have a gas at $-273°C$. Actually the gas would depart from a linear volume-temperature relationship as it approached its liquefaction temperature. For real gases, the relationship holds only at temperatures considerably above that at which they liquefy.

7-19   Why were you advised to wait 10 to 15 seconds after you stopped heating before taking the temperature reading?
Answer   The instructions suggest that heating be stopped 10 to 15 seconds before determining the temperature and volume in order to allow the system to come to thermal equilibrium. The transfer of heat through glass is relatively slow, and time must be allowed for all parts of the apparatus to come to the same temperature.

SUMMARY

In this chapter we have proceeded from very general experiments involving the effects of heat on solids to very specific questions about the structure of gases. We tried to indicate to the students that this transition was really a step in the direction of simplicity, that some of the details we want to know about the structure of solids can be learned more easily by studying gases first. Models were constructed and evaluated, and one was tentatively adopted: small constant-sized particles that become more widely separated from one another as the temperature is increased at constant pressure.

Experiments on volume-temperature relationships for a gas at constant pressure led to the question of pressure-temperature relationships at constant volume. We immediately found, however, that our knowledge of the basic concepts of force and mass is insufficient for carrying out the experiments we would like. We must first learn something more about simple mechanics. This we will do in the next two chapters.

QUESTIONS

7-20 How did you decide whether the gas evolved in Experiment 7-1 was soluble in water?
Answer   It is difficult to measure accurately the solubility of a gas in water. If it is very soluble, the size of the bubbles will decrease as they rise through the liquid. If it is moderately soluble and is left stored over water, one observes a change of water level with time. Neither of these effects was observed with the gas in Experiment 7-1, so we may assume that it is not significantly soluble.

7-21 In Experiment 7-2 was there any substance for which you could say there was more than one effect due to heat? If so, write out a plan for a way to isolate one effect from the other.
Answer   When the metals were heated they developed a coating or crust which did not melt when they did. *Hypothesis:* The crust resulted from an interaction with the air at elevated temperature. *Test:* Heat the metal in the absence of air. If a crust is still formed, it is due simply to heating; if not, it can be attributed to the air.

7-22 Consider the two alternative models of a gas as stated in Section 7-4. List all the evidence in some organized fashion to show the superiority of one model over the other.
Answer   See discussion of Question 7-15.

7-23 Summarize in tabular form all of the properties in terms of which solids, liquids, and gases are (1) similar to and (2) different from each other.
Answer   This is a good question for class discussion but should be restricted to a qualitative level within the experience of the students. A typical tabulation follows.

Property	Solid	Liquid	Gas
Density relative to water	About 0.7 for wood up to 21.5 for platinum	About 0.7 for oil up to 13.6 for mercury	Very small
Compressibility	Small	Small	Very large
Expansion with increase in temperature	Small, varies with substance	Small, varies with substance	Relatively large, same for all
Observable structure	Crystals, amorphous or cellular	None	None
Transmission of light	Most opaque, some translucent, a few transparent	A few opaque, some translucent, most transparent	Transparent

Property	Solid	Liquid	Gas
Ability to flow	May flow under great pressure	Flows more or less easily but depends on substance	Flows very easily with negligible viscosity
Shape or form	Independent of container	Retains same volume, assumes shape of container	Assumes volume and shape of container

7-24 You test a hot iron by wetting your finger and touching it to the bottom of the iron. Suppose you hear a hissing sound when you do this. Give all the information you can about the temperature of the iron.

Answer   If the temperature of the iron is above approximately 100°C, the moisture on your finger will vaporize. The hissing noise is simply the escaping steam. There is probably some correlation between the sound of the hiss and the temperature of the iron, because a hotter iron would be expected to cause faster vaporization.

ADDITIONAL QUESTION

7-25 Consider Experiment 7-3. The 5 ml of water occupied only a small fraction of the test tube. (a) Can you state qualitatively what effect the air in the tube would have on the experimental results? (b) Can you say anything about it quantitatively?   (c) Suggest an experiment to check your predictions.

Answer   (a) The expansion of the air upon heating contributes slightly to the expansion of the baggie. (b) Because its temperature increases by about one third of its initial temperature (i.e., from about 290°K to about 373°K), its volume should also increase by about one third. (c) Heat an empty test tube with the baggie attached.

REFERENCES

1. (T)   Greenstone, et al., Chapter 8, pages 127 to 128, 138-139; Chapter 12, pages 194, 195; Chapter 24, pages 391 to 392. Standard treatments of various items contained in our Chapter 7.

2. (T)   Lehrman and Swartz, Chapter 9, pages 245 to 253. A standard treatment of some heat effects.

3.   Sienko and Plane, Chapter 7, Sections 7.1 through 7.7, pages 151 to 163. Liquids and changes of state.

4.   Chalmers, B., "How Water Freezes," *Scientific American,* February, 1959, pages 114 ff.

5.   *Scientific American,* September, 1967. This entire issue is devoted to materials and their properties. Again the treatment is considerably more advanced than PSNS, but like many articles in this magazine, very readable. This issue can be returned to repeatedly throughout the year.

CHAPTER 8

MATTER IN MOTION

This chapter introduces the student to the mechanics of macroscopic objects; the emphasis is on fundamental understanding of Newton's laws of motion. This must be done without the use of the complicated mathematics of vector dynamics.

Students begin by observing, first hand, the motion of objects subject to varying degrees of outside influence; this should lead them easily to Newton's first law of motion. Then, to describe these external influences, the concept of force is introduced. An arbitrary unit of force corresponding to a certain stretch of a rubber band is used at first, and Newton's second law is developed from the results of experiment.

The chapter ends with an application of Newton's second law of motion to a freely falling object. The distinction between weight and mass is pointed out.

Section 8-1 SOME SIMPLE KINDS OF MOTION

Experiment 8-1 Motion of Objects on a Horizontal Surface

The purpose of this experiment is to help students visualize force-free motion by extrapolating from observable examples to the friction-free idealized situation. Not more than ten or fifteen minutes are required to perform it. It is important that each student have an opportunity to play with the carts so that he can directly observe what happens when retarding external influences (friction) are made negligible.

If there is a linear air track, an air table, or a set of air pucks available it would be worthwhile to use them to complete the extrapolation to friction-free motion. A new, improved air puck using a ballon for the air supply can be purchased through John Wiley & Sons.

Equipment Needed (per 3 students)	Cat. Number
dynamic lab cart (Note a)	68829

Laboratory Note

(a)   The dynamic carts are shipped unassembled and must be prepared by a lab assistant. For this experiment, only the wheels are to be attached.

The U-bolt and hook must be added for Experiment 8-3. Each U-bolt is locked in place with four pal-nuts. Start by threading a nut as far as possible up each leg of the U-bolt. Then shove the bolt through the holes in the body of the cart. Reposition the nuts until each leg of the bolt extends about ¼ inch below the bottom of the cart body. Affix a pal-nut to each end of the protruding bolt and tighten the nuts.

Students quickly conclude that as frictional effects are reduced, an object moves farther and farther, and in the limit of no external influences, the object would travel at constant speed indefinitely. Some will recognize that the freely moving object does not change its direction of motion. Others will have to be helped to this important conclusion.

Questions about the nature of friction may arise, but no more than a very elementary discussion should be attempted. It can perhaps best be viewed as a phenomenon which is discovered experimentally, and one whose details can only be discerned by further experimentation.

The difference between speed and velocity is sometimes troublesome. Some students may know that the word *scalar* refers to quantities that have a *magnitude* (and appropriate units) only, and that the word *vector* refers to quantities that have the properties of both *direction* and *magnitude* (and appropriate units). Many of the quantities used to describe interactions and motions are vector quantities and must be handled according to the rules of vector algebra. Because of the difficulty experienced in learning the mathematics of vectors, we restrict our discussion to motion along a straight line (rectilinear motion). This allows us to illustrate most of the physical principles of kinematics and dynamics, and the vector nature of the directed quantities involved can be handled simply by using positive and negative signs.

Note that we have deliberately chosen *not* to elaborate on the distinction between average speed and average velocity, or that between distance covered and what other texts might call displacement. This presents no difficulties because all the examples of motion that are considered, except for a brief treatment in Section 8-4 and in several questions, do not involve reversals in the direction of motion.

QUESTIONS

8-1   For the puck whose successive positions are indicated in Figure 8-2, calculate the average speed for the time interval between 1.0 second and 2.0 seconds, and for the interval between 1.0 second and 3.0 seconds.
Answer   The average speed v_{av} of the puck for any time interval is given by Equation 8-1, $v_{av} = \dfrac{\Delta s}{\Delta t}$

For the time interval between 1.0 sec and 2.0 sec we have

$$v_{av} = \frac{(40 - 20) \text{ cm}}{(2 - 1) \text{ sec}} = 20 \text{ cm/sec}$$

For the time interval between 1.0 sec and 3.0 sec,

$$v_{av} = \frac{(60 - 20) \text{ cm}}{(3 - 1) \text{ sec}} = 20 \text{ cm/sec}$$

8-2   When the average speed of an object has the same value for all time intervals, we say the speed of the object is constant or uniform. Is the speed of the air puck whose positions are illustrated in Figure 8-2 constant over the time interval shown in the figure?
Answer   You can't tell. From the data given you can only determine that the average speeds over any time intervals separating known positions as seen in the figure are the same. However, the puck could have moved nonuniformly between these positions, and thus average speeds over other time intervals may have been different.

8-3   What can you say about the average speed of the puck over the time interval from 0 to 5.0 seconds?
Answer   Nothing. The purpose of this question is to alert students to unwarranted extrapolation. Because we have no record of where the puck is at the time t = 5.0 seconds we cannot determine the average speed between the times t = 0 and t = 5.0 seconds.

Section 8-2 FORCES

In Section 8-1 and Experiment 8-1 we concluded that when there is no external influence, an object maintains a constant velocity. This section extends this idea to objects whose velocity is zero. The situation is illustrated by a hanging object at rest under the influence of a rope pulling upward and the Earth pulling downward. The magnitudes of these two forces are equal, the directions are opposite; the object remains at rest.

Most students understand the static equilibrium situation described above – no net force on the object, no motion. They do not realize that an object in uniform motion is also in equilibrium – no net force, no *change* in velocity.

Now, we ask, what happens if there is an unbalanced force acting on the object? We expect the object to change its velocity and it does. The remainder of this section is given over to developing a way to measure the effect of an unbalanced force (expressed in units of stretch of a standard rubber band). A method of describing quantitatively the rate of change of velocity is also introduced.

Analogously to the definition of average velocity, average acceleration is defined as the change in velocity divided by the associated time interval (see Equation 8-2). The discussion is, however, limited to velocities that change uniformly with time, and thus to motion with constant acceleration.

Most students find it easier to understand acceleration as the slope of a velocity-time graph rather than in terms of the mathematical definition $a = \Delta v\ /\ \Delta t$. To some, however, steepness and slope will be new words in the context used here. These words have been taken over from common engineering usage. The definition of both steepness and slope is the ratio of the vertical rise to the horizontal run of a road or a hill. The slope on a graph is defined the same way. The units in which the slope is expressed depend on the units of the quantities plotted along the vertical and horizontal axes. Often they are in the same units, and the slope is dimensionless. In science, however, we are frequently interested in the relationships between quantities which are different in kind from one another. If two such quantities are graphed against one another, the slope will have the units of the ratio of these two quantities. In Experiment 2-6, for example, the slope of the temperature-time curve had units of °C/sec; in Experiment 7-4 the slope of the volume-temperature curve had the units of length/°K, since the volume of a column of constant cross-sectional area was measured in length units.

The units for the slope of Figure 8-6(c) are the ratio of the vertical units to the horizontal units, or (velocity) / (time) = (cm/sec)/sec. This is written simply as cm/sec^2. These are, of course, the units of acceleration.

One other quantity can be obtained from the velocity-time graphs of Figure 8-6. The area under any one of the curves in Figure 8-6 gives the distance traveled by the object. This is not useful to us here because we have a direct measure of the position of the object from the tapes, but there are situations in which it is important.

QUESTIONS

8-4   Calculate how far the puck traveled during the first 2 seconds of travel.
Answer   The data of Table 8-1 indicates that the puck traveled 0.6 cm the first second and 1.9 cm the second second, therefore it traveled 2.5 cm during the first 2 seconds.

8-5 Using the information obtained from Figure 8-6(b) find: (a) the average velocity during each of the ½-second intervals and (b) the distance the puck traveled by the end of the first 0.5 second; by the end of the first 1.00 second; by the end of the first 1.50 seconds.

Answer   (a) The following average velocities were read from Figure 8-6(b) for each ½-second interval:

Intervals, in seconds	Average velocity in cm/sec
0 - 0.5	0.3
0.5 - 1.0	0.9
1.0 - 1.5	1.6
1.5 - 2.0	2.2
2.0 - 2.5	2.9
2.5 - 3.0	3.5
3.0 - 3.5	3.9
3.5 - 4.0	3.9
4.0 - 4.5	3.9
4.5 - 5.0	3.9

(b) The distance traveled during any interval is equal to the average velocity over that interval multiplied by the length of that interval.

Interval, in seconds	Distance traveled during interval, in cm	Cumulative distance traveled, in cm
0 - 0.5	0.15	0.15
0.5 - 1.0	0.45	0.60
1.0 - 1.5	0.80	1.40

8-6 Using the information now available to you, can you find out how far the puck traveled during the first 1.20 seconds? In order to make this calculation, you could assume that it traveled with the average velocity for the first second indicated in Table 8-1 (and in Figure 8-6 (a)) and calculate the distance traveled during that first second. Then you could assume that it traveled with the average velocity indicated for the time interval 1.00 - 2.00 seconds for the remaining 0.20 second of travel. The two distances added together would approximate the total distance traveled during the first 1.20 seconds. Calculate the total distance.

Answer   One cannot calculate the exact distance traveled during the first 1.20 seconds from the information given. Using the assumptions suggested, the approximate distance can be calculated as follows:

For interval from 0 - 1.00 sec

$\Delta s = 0.6 \times 1.00 = 0.60$ cm

For interval from 1.00 to 1.20 sec

$\Delta s = 1.9 \times 0.20 = 0.38$ cm

For the interval from 0 - 1.20 sec

$$\Delta s = 0.60 + 0.38 = 0.98 \text{ cm}$$

8-7   Repeat the calculations you made in Question 8-6 for the distance traveled by the puck, but this time use the intervals and average velocities obtained in Figure 8-6(b), and again estimate how far it traveled during the first 1.20 seconds.

Answer   For interval from 0 - 1.00 sec

$$\Delta s = 0.6 \times 1.00 = 0.60 \text{ cm}$$

For interval from 1.00 - 1.20 sec

$$\Delta s = 1.6 \times 0.20 = 0.32 \text{ cm}$$

For interval from 0 - 1.20 sec

$$\Delta s = 0.60 + 0.32 = 0.92 \text{ cm}$$

8-8   Of the two answers to Questions 8-6 and 8-7, which do you think is closer to the "actual" distance traveled by the "real" puck during the 1.20 seconds?
Answer   The answer to Question 8-7 is probably closer to the actual distance because it made use of data corresponding to smaller time intervals, and therefore the average velocities used are probably closer to the velocities one needs to compute correct distances for small time intervals.

8-9   Calculate the acceleration during each of the 5 seconds of travel of the puck in Figure 8-5. Then make a graph of the acceleration versus the time. Does the acceleration change at all during the first 3 seconds? during the last 2 seconds? What can you say about the acceleration at time t = 3.0 seconds? How does the acceleration compare with the force applied? What conclusions can you draw?
Answer   To obtain the acceleration, Figure 8-6(c) is useful. From Equation 8-2

$$a = \frac{\Delta v}{\Delta t} = \frac{v_2 - v_1}{t_2 - t_1}$$

Acceleration for first second $= \dfrac{(1.3 - 0.0)\text{ cm/sec}}{(1.0 - 0.0)\text{ sec}} = 1.3 \text{ cm/sec}^2$.

Acceleration for second second $= \dfrac{(2.6 - 1.3)\text{ cm/sec}}{(2.0 - 1.0)\text{ sec}} = 1.3 \text{ cm/sec}^2$.

Acceleration for third second $= \dfrac{(4.0 - 2.6)\text{ cm/sec}}{(3.0 - 2.0)\text{ sec}} = 1.4 \text{ cm/sec}^2$.

Acceleration for fourth second $= \dfrac{(4.0 - 4.0)\text{ cm/sec}}{(4.0 - 3.0)\text{ sec}} = 0.0 \text{ cm/sec}^2$.

Acceleration for fifth second $= \dfrac{(4.0 - 4.0)\text{ cm/sec}}{(5.0 - 4.0)\text{ sec}} = 0.0 \text{ cm/sec}^2$.

Note that by taking the velocity measurements from Figure 8-6(c) to only two significant figures the acceleration during the third second does not equal that during the first second, or the second second. However, since the graph is a straight line, we may assume that the acceleration is actually constant. During the last two seconds the velocity remains constant at 4.0 cm/sec, as is shown in Figure 8-6(c). Therefore, the acceleration is constant and equal to zero. The graph of acceleration as a function of time is shown in Figure RB 8-1.

One can say very little about the acceleration at the time t = 3.0 seconds since there is a discontinuity in the curve at that instant. However, objects in the real world do not behave in such a

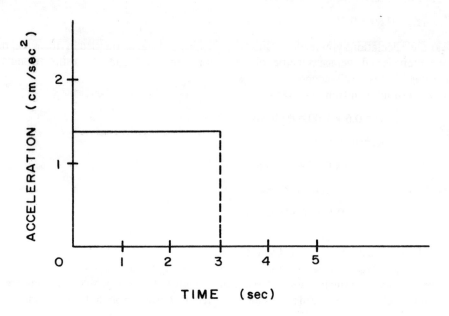

Figure RB 8-1

discontinuous fashion. Accelerations do not jump instantaneously from one value to another, because forces cannot change instantaneously from one value to another.

8-10 Propose, by means of a velocity-time graph, a description of the motion of the puck (without a film of air to float on) under the following conditions. The puck is first accelerated by a constant force, and then after 3.0 seconds the force ceases to operate. The puck, however, continues to move for 2.0 seconds before coming to rest. Assume that the force of friction is constant throughout the motion.

Answer   See Figure RB 8-2; note that numerical value of the velocity of the puck is unknown. The purpose of this question is merely to see if the student can qualitatively relate a velocity-time curve to the forces that accelerate (or decelerate) the object.

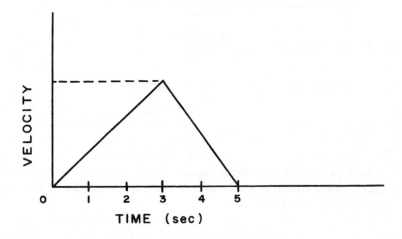

Figure RB 8-2

Experiment 8-2 Acceleration of Falling Objects

In this experiment the students use a method of detecting the position of a moving object at different times. They are to observe the familiar motion of an object dropped from rest and to determine its position, velocity, and acceleration as time goes on.

You might begin this lab by having the students drop an object from a distance of about 1 meter above the floor and see if, by using a second hand and meter stick, they can locate it at various times during its fall. Have them estimate the total time of fall, which is about ½ second. This indicates the need for a timer with intervals much shorter than ½ second if we are to find out what kind of motion is taking place. The timer used in this experiment is a doorbell clapper and its operation is described in the text.

Equipment Needed (per 3 students)	*Cat. Number*
1 Timer Kit (Note a)	68876
6 washers (Note b)	68876
4 batteries	68813
1 battery box (Note c)	68814
3 plastic rulers	—
2 paper clips (Note d)	—
1 C-clamp, 4 inch (Note e)	68829
6 sheets, graph paper	
Optional	
1 ring stand with crossbar (Note f)	
1 pair, scissors	

Laboratory Notes

(a) The timer kit includes the timer, paper tape, carbon discs, and steel washers. Position a carbon disc and a short strip of paper tape on the striking block of the timer and then adjust the bell clapper to obtain the minimum pressure required to give a visible record when the clapper is vibrating. If this is not done, appreciable friction is introduced each time the clapper strikes the tape.

(b) The number of washers recommended was determined experimentally. If one is careful to reduce frictional forces as much as possible, six washers will pull the tape through the timer with an acceleration of 900-plus cm/sec^2.

You may want to assign a different number of washers to various groups within the lab class. Thus one group of students would be given three washers, a second group six, and a third group nine washers. When the results of each group are compared, one should find that the acceleration increases as more washers are used. Further analysis, however, should disclose that a maximum acceleration is reached and then not exceeded, regardless of the weight attached to the paper tape. This clearly indicates the presence of a frictional force, the magnitude of which is appreciable when compared to the weight of only three washers.

(c) The timer operates quite nicely on one battery; it should not be attached to the battery any longer than necessary. The use of more than one battery increases clapper friction noticeably.

(d) Make a small, open loop at one end of the tape and inset the short end of the loop in the holes in the washers; then close the loop and hold it shut by clamping it with a paper clip.

(e) The C-clamp is a part of the dynamic cart kit. It is used here to hold the timer in position at the edge of the lab table.

The timer must be mounted so that the paper tape feeds through vertically and not horizontally.

Do not apply so much pressure with the clamp that the body of the timer is broken.

(f) The paper tape that is to pass through the timer must be held vertically. If the tape leans slightly, it will rub against the timer body as it falls, thus generating appreciable friction. If a ring stand is available, the upper end of the tape can be temporarily attached to the crossbar, allowing the students to check carefully on the vertical alignment of the tape before starting each run. If a ring stand is not available, one of the students in each group will have to hold and position the tape.

When students analyze the tape of a falling object, encourage them to cut it at every other dot and construct a velocity-time bar graph similar to that of Figure 8-6(b). You may have to remind them that the best straight line indicating the instantaneous velocity-time relationship should pass through the midpoint of the end of each bar.

The results obtained may include low values for g (usually caused by a large friction effect) as well as high values (usually caused by improper calibration of the timer).

Do not become involved with the dynamics of the problem at this time. The purpose of this experiment is to familiarize the students with a way to measure the location of an object over short time intervals and from this information to determine the velocity and acceleration of the object at different times. After the concept of force is introduced and a relation between force, mass, and acceleration is found, we will return to the falling object and discuss its motion in terms of dynamics.

QUESTIONS

8-11 For your timer, how many ticks are there in 5 seconds?

Answer Different timers give different numbers of ticks per second. Also, the vibration rate of an individual timer varies with the applied voltage. Actual results for one timer yielded 415 ticks in 5 seconds, or 83 ticks per second.

8-12 How much time (in seconds) is 1 tick?

Answer This is just the reciprocal of the number of ticks per second computed in Question 8-11. For that example,

$$\text{number of seconds per tick} = 1 \text{ sec}/83 \text{ ticks} = 0.012 \text{ sec/tick}$$

8-13 From the record of dots on the tapes, how can we tell whether the velocity of the falling object is increasing or decreasing?

Answer If the distance traveled during successive time intervals (i.e., the space between successive dots) increases, then the velocity is increasing; if the spacing decreases, the velocity is decreasing.

8-14 How can we tell whether or not the velocity of the object changed uniformly with time?

Answer This requires a closer analysis of the information on the tape than that needed to answer Question 8-13. By plotting the average velocity versus time, we obtain a bar graph similar to Figure 8-6(b). If we obtain from it a straight-line relationship between v and t, we can conclude that the velocity changed uniformly with time.

8-15 What was the acceleration of the single object in cm/sec^2? in meter/sec^2?

Answer Inasmuch as the velocity of the falling body increases uniformly with time, the acceleration (the slope of the velocity-time curve) will be constant, the same for any time interval. Choose a conveniently large time interval Δt so that the change in velocity Δv during this time is easily measurable from the graph. Substitute into the equation

$$a = \frac{\Delta v}{\Delta t}$$

Using their own experimental data, students will obtain values ranging from 300 cm/sec^2 to 1100 cm/sec^2. Values greater than 900 cm/sec^2 probably indicate a mistake in the measurements or in the calculations.

8-16 What was the acceleration of the double object in meter/sec^2? How does it compare with the acceleration of the single object?

Answer   Analyzing the tape of the falling double object in the same fashion as was done for the single object should yield somewhat larger values, since the approximately constant frictional forces are smaller in comparison to the weight.

Section 8-3 FORCE, MASS, AND ACCELERATION

This section develops Newton's second law from the results of Experiment 8-3, where various masses are acted upon by various forces and the resultant acceleration is measured. An arbitrary standard unit of force is established by stretching a rubber band a fixed amount. In the first part of the experiment the students determine the acceleration, by means of the ticker-tape record, and find that it is constant and that it is in the same direction as the applied force.

Next we exert different forces on the object to see how the acceleration is related to the force. At this point we cannot measure any force other than our standard unit. We may, however, assume that forces are vectors so that two equivalent rubber bands, each stretched by the standard amount and pulling in the same direction, will exert two units of force. Similarly, if three identical bands, each stretched by the standard amount, act in parallel on an object, they exert a force of three standard units.

A graph of the relationship between the force F exerted by a rubber band and the amount by which it is stretched ΔL will show that a greater stretch produces a greater force, but the relationship will not be a linear one. Since establishing the form of the force-stretch curve requires only a few rubber bands and a meter stick, it is useful to suggest to interested students that they make the measurements at home. Three bands can be connected as shown in Figure RB 8-3, with the circle representing a heavy paper clip or metal ring. If the two bands in parallel are each stretched by a standard amount ΔL_s then the stretch ΔL_2 in the single band is that produced by the force $2F_s$. If the single band is stretched by ΔL_s then the stretch ΔL_1, in each of the other bands is that due to a force of $F_s/2$. Proceeding in this way with additional bands, a number of corresponding values of F and ΔL can be measured and a curve plotted.

Experiment 8-3 Force and Motion

Using the definition of force given above, the students can now apply different forces to the same object, the same force to different objects (different masses), measure the resulting accelerations, and see how force, mass, and acceleration are related.

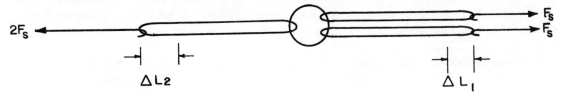

$2F_s$ ΔL_2 F_s F_s ΔL_1

Figure RB 8-3

Equipment Needed
(per 3 students)

	Cat. Number
1 dynamic cart (Note a)	68829
1 recording timer	68876
1 battery box	68814
4 batteries	68813
1 C-clamp, 4 inch (Note b)	68829
3 rubber bands, 30-cm long	68829
1 meter stick	68849
2 or 3 bricks (Note c)	—
2 or 3 plastic or paper bags (Note c)	—
1 dust rag	—
6 sheets, graph paper	—
3 plastic rulers	—
1 or 2 (per class) platform balances and weights capable of measuring up to 2 kilograms	—

Laboratory Notes

(a)   The carts are those used in Experiment 8-1, but for this experiment they should have a U-bolt mounted at each end. The experiment should be performed on a smooth level table at least 2 meters long. If tables this long are not available, it would be best to try to perform it on the floor.

(b)   The timer is to be clamped to the table top. Be sure the jaw of the C-clamp is over the solid portion of the timer base in order to prevent the timer body from becoming cracked.

(c)   The bricks should be wrapped in paper before being used. As they are used, however, they will chip and tear the wrapping paper, permitting brick dust to accumulate on the table top. This dust should be wiped away before each run to prevent damage to the table top.

To determine the acceleration of the cart the students will use the same techniques and the same timer as used in Experiment 8-2. They will, however, need to calibrate the timer again, because (1) they may have a different timer than the one they had in Experiment 8-2; (2) the time interval of a specific timer depends on the applied voltage, which will vary as the batteries age; (3) the timers are now mounted horizontally rather than vertically, and one should check to see if this changes the rate of vibration.

The students should be instructed to label the tapes as soon as they are made. If the tape is no good, throw it away immediately. Students have a tendency to finish this lab with a large number of tapes and no idea of which ones contain good data.

Students are usually reluctant to spend time familiarizing themselves with the apparatus or making practice runs. It is particularly important in this experiment that they do both. Otherwise, their data are certain to be poor. For instance, it is important to synchronize the towing and the release at the start of each run, and to maintain a constant stretch in the rubber band during the run.

As was mentioned in the text, laboratory time can be saved by letting half of the class determine acceleration as a function of force, with constant mass, while the other half investigates acceleration as a function of mass with constant force, This division of labor can profitably be carried even further. Let each group of three students make its measurements at only one fixed pair of values for force and mass, every group having a different pair. If the students are careful in their work, and if the whole class uses the same standard stretch (say 25% of the length) of the rubber bands, their independently obtained data will all lie on one or the other of the two graphs they are asked to draw. This result, the excellent agreement between the whole class' independent measurements, makes quite an impression on them.

Students should express the acceleration in meter/sec^2, the force in units of standard stretch, and the mass in kilograms. The proportional relationships between the variables can then be established effectively by class discussion of their tabulated results. The discussion should bring out the following points: (1) the experiment lacks precision, as indicated by the scatter in experimental results; (2) acceleration is directly proporational to the force if the mass is constant; (3) acceleration is inversely proportional to the mass if the force is constant.

The two proportionalities

$$a \propto F, \qquad m \text{ constant}$$

$$a \propto \frac{1}{m}, \qquad F \text{ constant}$$

imply that $a \propto F / m$ or $F \propto ma$.

Any proportionality can be converted into an equation by introducing a proportionality constant k. So,

$$F = kma$$

In terms of the units used thus far (F in force units of a standard stretch, m in kilograms, and a in meter/sec^2) one could determine k; the value would, in general, not be 1, and it would have units of $\left(\frac{\text{standard force}}{\text{kg-meter/sec}^2}\right)$.

At the end of this section the mks unit of force, the newton, is introduced by letting the constant k be dimensionless and equal to 1. Thus by definition,

$$k = \frac{1 \text{ newton}}{\text{kg-meter/sec}^2} = 1$$

This, of course, also serves to define the newton:

$$1 \text{ newton} = 1 \text{ kg-meter/sec}^2$$

Using these values, the rubber band unit of force employed in Experiment 8-3 is shown to have a value of about 0.5 newton.

QUESTIONS

8-17 Does it appear from your average velocity-time graph that the velocity of the cart changed uniformly with time?
Answer   If the experiment has been performed with care, the increase in distance traversed by the cart during successive tenticks is about the same for all measured intervals. Thus the average velocity is increasing uniformly with time.

8-18 Examine how well the straight line of the instantaneous velocity-time graph fits the points of the average velocity-time graph. Was the acceleration of the cart constant during the application of the constant force?

Answer   A straight line drawn with a slope matching the increasing height of the steps of the average velocity-time graph will come close to the midpoints of the top of each step, missing a few on the high side and a few on the low side. If the sizes of these misses seem reasonable in terms of the accuracy of the experiment, it is reasonable to conclude that the acceleration of the object was constant.

8-19   Those students who applied a constant force and varied the mass should connect the three points of the mass-acceleration graph with a smooth curve. Try to predict the general shape of the curve for increasingly larger and then decreasingly smaller masses. You may find it helpful to determine the product of the mass and acceleration for each of your three values.

Answer   A typical graph of mass versus acceleration is shown in Figure RB 8-4; of *ma* versus *a* in Figure RB 8-5.

Figure RB 8-4 shows that as the mass increases the acceleration decreases; Figure RB 8-5 suggests that (*ma*) is constant, independent of acceleration, as long as the accelerating force is constant.

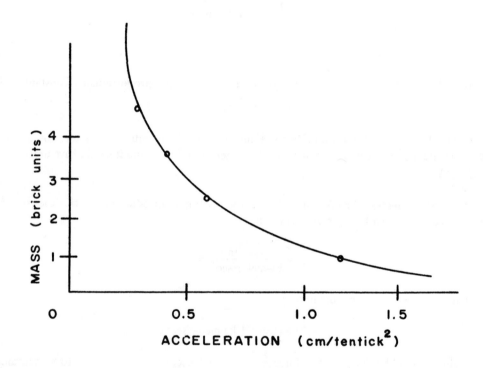

Figure RB 8-4

8-20   Those students who applied different forces to a constant mass should connect the three points on the force-acceleration graph with a smooth curve. Try to predict the general shape of the curve for increasingly larger and then decreasingly smaller forces. When you use a constant mass, how does the acceleration depend on the force?

Answer   For constant mass, the acceleration increases uniformly with the unbalanced force. Since the graph is a straight line, the acceleration is directly proportional to the force, or $a \propto F$. (See Fig. RB 8-6.)

8-21   According to your force-acceleration curve, what acceleration will result when a zero force is applied?

Answer   As we see from Figure RB 8-6, when a zero unbalanced force acts, the acceleration is zero. Therefore, the object will move at a constant velocity, which may be zero.

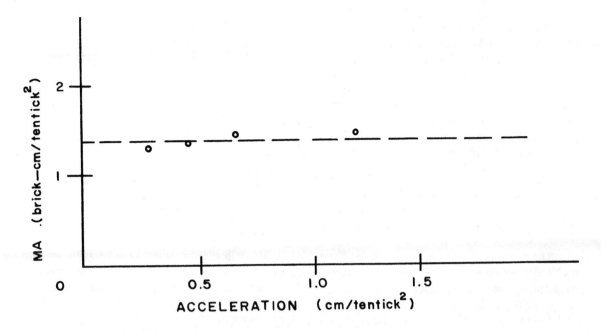

Figure RB 8-5

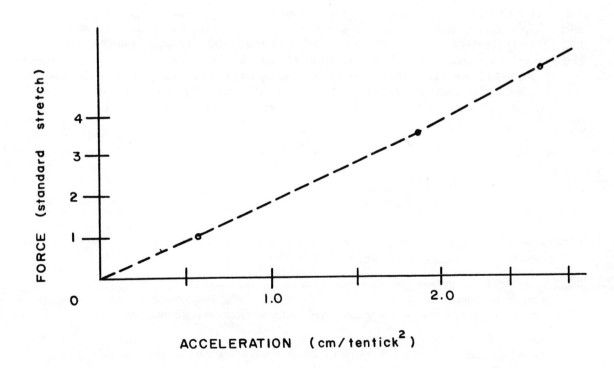

Figure RB 8-6

8-22 Referring to your data in Experiment 8-3, calculate the force exerted by one rubber band when stretched to your standard stretch.
Answer   If, for example, the measured mass of the cart plus 2 bricks was 4.8 kg, and the acceleration when using the rubber band with one standard stretch was 0.28 meter/sec² then, by Newton's second law,

$$F = ma = (4.8 \text{ kg})(0.28 \text{ meter/sec}^2) = 1.3 \text{ kg-meter/sec}^2 = 1.3 \text{ newton}$$

8-23 How great a force is required to accelerate a car of mass m = 2000 kg (this car would weigh 4400 pounds) at a rate of 5 meter/sec² ?
Answer   Using Equation 8-3 we have

$$F = ma = (2000 \text{ kg})(5 \text{ meter/sec}^2) = 10,000 \text{ kg-meter/sec}^2 = 10,000 \text{ newton}$$

Section 8-4 THE MOTION OF A FALLING OBJECT

The experiment by which we arrived at Newton's second law involved exerting a horizontal force on an object thus forcing it to move on a horizontal surface. In this section we apply Newton's second law to freely falling objects, investigated in Experiment 8-2. There we found that the gravitational acceleration at a given location is the same for different objects, independent of their masses. Calling this acceleration g, and letting the weight of the object w represent the force producing it, we have

$$F = ma$$

$$w = mg$$

In Chapter 11 this gravitational force between an object and the Earth will be related to the mass of the object, the mass of the Earth, and their separation from one another. It is inappropriate to discuss this relationship, or the relationship of gravitational mass to inertial mass, at this time, since it contributes nothing to an understanding of the dynamics we require. Gravitation can be accepted simply as a force that produces an observed acceleration of unsupported objects.

At this point in the text, there is a brief discussion of the motion of a ball thrown *up*. This is the only place in this chapter where we treat motion in which the direction of travel reverses. This is done in preparation for a development in Chapter 10 where molecules bounce off a wall.

QUESTIONS

8-24 During its ascent, does the ball have a positive, a negative, or zero acceleration?
Answer   By the convention adopted, that the positive direction is toward the Earth, the acceleration is positive.

8-25 During its descent, does the ball have a positive, a negative, or zero acceleration?
Answer   It is still accelerated downward, so it is still a positive acceleration.

8-26 At the very top of its flight, when its vertical velocity is zero, does the ball have a positive, a negative, or zero acceleration?
Answer   Its speed is still increasing downward, so the acceleration is still positive.

8-27 Sketch a velocity-time graph for the motion of the ball. Remember that its velocity is initially negative and then becomes positive. Negative velocities appear below the time axis, positive velocities above it. The acceleration of the ball is the slope of the velocity-time curve. Is that curve a straight line? Is the acceleration constant? Is the force acting on the ball constant? Is its mass constant?

Answer   See Figure RB 8-7. The curve is a straight line because the velocity changes at a constant rate. That is, gravitational acceleration is a constant. The force must be constant, because the mass and the acceleration are both constant.

8-28 A man of mass 70 kg hangs from a rope tied around his waist. What forces act on him? Calculate in newtons the magnitude and specify the direction of each force.

Answer   The two forces acting on the man are his weight acting downward and the force F of the rope pulling upward. If the man is not accelerating, then these two forces are equal in magnitude. Therefore

$$F = w = mg$$
$$= (70 \text{ kg})(9.8 \text{ meter/sec}^2)$$
$$= 690 \text{ newton}$$

8-29 Compare the average speeds of a good 100-yard-dash runner and a good mile runner. If you do not know the times in which these distances are run, now is the time to consult your athletic-minded friends. Calculate the ratio of the speed of the dash runner to the speed of the miler.

Answer   A good 100-yard runner may run the distance in 9.5 seconds; a good miler may run the mile in 4.0 minutes. To make the comparison meaningful, however, we must convert both distances and times to the same units; here we will use feet and seconds. 100 yards equal 300 ft, one mile equals 5280 ft. Therefore the speed of each is

(a)   the dashman:

$$v = \frac{\Delta s}{\Delta t} = \frac{300 \text{ ft}}{9.5 \text{ sec}} = 31.5 \text{ or } 32 \text{ ft/sec}$$

(b)   the miler:

$$v = \frac{5280 \text{ ft}}{4 \times 60 \text{ sec}} = 22 \text{ ft/sec}$$

The ratio of the speed of the dash runner to the speed of the miler is 32/22 or about 1.5/1.

8-30 If the initial speed of the puck in Figure 8-3c was 10 cm/sec, estimate the final speed v_f and the change in direction of the velocity that results from the push.

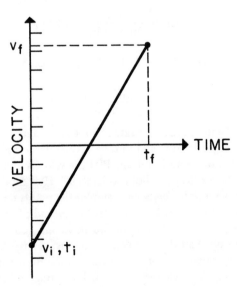

Figure RB 8-7

Answer   Assuming that the arrow representing the initial velocity is 1.3 cm long and that representing the final velocity is 2.0 cm long, we can set up the following ratio

$$\frac{v_i}{1.3 \text{ cm}} = \frac{v_f}{2.0 \text{ cm}}$$

Therefore

$$v_f = \frac{(2.0 \text{ cm})(v_i)}{1.3 \text{ cm}}$$

And since $v_i = 10$ cm/sec

$$v_f = \frac{(2.0 \text{ cm})(10 \text{ cm/sec})}{1.3 \text{ cm}}$$

$$v_f = 15.4 \text{ or } 15 \text{ cm/sec}$$

The direction of travel has changed by approximately 22°.

8-31 A road up a hill is 5 miles long. If you drive up the hill at a steady speed of 30 mph, and then drive the 5 miles down the same hill at a steady speed of 50 mph, what is your average speed for the whole trip? Note: this is a famous problem since it is a bit tricky. Be careful. The answer is *not* 40 mph.
Answer   The car spends more time traveling at the slower speed than at the faster speed. We must first find the time spent going up the hill and then the time spent going down the hill. The average speed is the total distance for the round-trip divided by the total time. First the time to travel up the hill:

$$v = \frac{\Delta s}{\Delta t}$$

$$\Delta t = \frac{\Delta s}{v} = \frac{5 \text{ mile}}{30 \text{ mile/hr}} = 0.17 \text{ hr}$$

The time to go down the hill is found by the same method to be

$$\Delta t = \frac{5 \text{ mile}}{50 \text{ mile/hr}} = 0.10 \text{ hr}$$

The total time for the round trip is thus 0.27 hr. The total distance traveled is 10 mile; therefore

$$v_{av} = \frac{10 \text{ mile}}{0.27 \text{ hr}} = 37 \text{ mph}$$

8-32 A hot-rod enthusiast accelerates his car at a rate of 30 ft/sec², starting from rest. Fortunately, however, he runs out of gas 5 seconds later, and thus he decelerates as he coasts to a stop. His rate of deceleration is one-half that of his acceleration. Plot the velocity-time curve for his motion. What is the distance he travels during his period of acceleration? How far did he travel altogether?
Answer   To plot the velocity-time curve, one can plot the points representing the velocity each second. At the end of the first second it is 30 ft/sec, at the end of the second second it is 60 ft/sec, at the end of the third second it is 90 ft/sec, the fourth second 120 ft/sec, the fifth second 150 ft/sec. The deceleration is one-half the acceleration, that is −15 ft/sec². The negative sign indicates that the deceleration is opposite to the original acceleration. By the same process as above the car will come to a stop in 10 sec. Because the curves are both straight lines, this gives enough points to make a plot.

The distance traveled during the acceleration is obtained by multiplying the time by the average speed. Since the acceleration is constant in both cases, the average speed is one-half the sum of the initial and the final speeds:

$$(5 \text{ sec}) \times (\frac{150}{2} \text{ ft/sec}) = 375 \text{ ft}$$

Similary, for the distance traveled during deceleration,

$$(10 \text{ sec}) \times (\frac{150}{2} \text{ ft/sec}) = 750 \text{ ft}$$

The total distance traveled is thus

$$375 + 750 = 1125 \text{ ft}$$

8-33 Describe Newton's first law in terms that would be understandable to an untutored layman. (Try it on a friend.)

Answer   This question can be answered many different ways, but it is hoped that the student will have acquired enough background by this time to give a reasonable description of this law.

8-34 A tennis ball, initially moving to the right at 30 meter/sec, strikes a wall and rebounds with the same speed of 30 meter/sec.
(a)   What is the velocity after rebounding?
(b)   What is its change in velocity Δv?
(c)   If it made contact with the wall for a time interval of 0.01 sec, what is its average acceleration during this time?
(d)   What is the average force of the wall on the tennis ball during this time? Assume the mass of the ball to be 0.02 kg.

Answer   The purpose of this question is to give the student some practice in handling rebound problems, so that he will better understand how the kinetic theory of gases (discussed in Chapter 10) explains gas pressure.
(a)   The negative of the initial velocity, since the direction is opposite.
(b)   The change in velocity is

$$\Delta v = v_2 - v_1$$

$$= (+30 \text{ meter/sec}) - (-30 \text{ meter/sec}) = +60 \text{ meter /sec}$$

(c)   The average acceleration a is defined as

$$a = \frac{\Delta v}{\Delta t}$$

$$\Delta v = +60 \text{ meter/sec and } \Delta t = 0.01 \text{ sec} = 10^{-2} \text{ sec}$$

$$a = \frac{+60 \text{ meter/sec}}{10^{-2} \text{ sec}} = 6000 \text{ meter/sec}^2$$

(d)   The mass is $m = 0.02 \text{ kg} = 2 \times 10^{-2} \text{ kg}$; the acceleration is $a = 6 \times 10^3 \text{ meter/sec}^2$, so we have

$$F = ma = (2 \times 10^{-2} \text{ kg}) (6 \times 10^3 \text{ meter/sec}^2)$$

$$= 120 \text{ newton}$$

8-35 If your moving car should collide with a bridge abutment, the car is likely to be wrecked. Analyze this in terms of Newton's second law.

Answer   The moving car would be brought to rest, that is, the car would decelerate (this may be considered a negative acceleration). The sudden deceleration of the car is the result of the force exerted by the bridge abutment, which is likely to be more than the car is able to withstand.

8-36 A body is moving 10 ft/sec at the start of an interval. Five seconds later, it is traveling 75 ft/sec in the same direction.
(a)   If the acceleration is constant during this period, what is the average velocity?
(b)   What is the acceleration during this interval?

Answer   (a) Since the acceleration is constant, the average velocity v_{av} is given by

$$v_{av} = \frac{v_1 + v_2}{2} = \frac{10 \text{ ft/sec} + 75 \text{ ft/sec}}{2}$$

$$= 42.5 \text{ ft/sec}$$

(b)   The acceleration a is defined as

$$a = \frac{\Delta v}{\Delta t} = \frac{v_2 - v_1}{\Delta t} = \frac{(75 - 10) \text{ ft/sec}}{5 \text{ sec}}$$

$$= \frac{65 \text{ ft/sec}}{5 \text{ sec}} = 13 \text{ ft/sec}^2$$

REFERENCES

1. (T)   Feynman, Chapter 8, pages 8-1 to 8-4. Once again Feynman points out in an illuminating way the ideas behind the mathematical formalisms of motion. Conceptual difficulties are brought out and examined with great insight.

2. (T)   Lehrman and Swartz, Chapter 6, pages 133 to 145. This is a standard treatment of motion, but there is included a section using the idea of terminal velocity to determine drag forces.

3. (T)   PSSC, Chapter 11, pages 169 to 189, and Chapter 13, Sections 13.1 through 13.4, pages 218 to 225. These sections contain some very good detailed graphical analyses of motion, and some good stroboscopic pictures of moving pucks.

4.   Resnick and Halliday, Chapter 3, pages 32 to 51; Chapter 5, pages 79 to 103; Chapter 16, Sections 16-1 through 16-5, pages 382 to 379. Linear motion, force and Newton's laws, and gravity are treated in an advanced manner.

5. (T)   Shamos, Chapter 6, pages 75 to 92. Further history.

6.   Stevenson and Moore, Chapter 4, Sections 4-1 through 4-4, pages 49 to 58. Graphical analysis of one-dimensional motion.

CHAPTER 9

ENERGY

The approach to the conservation of energy principle adopted in this treatment is different from that used in many introductory textbooks. Our position is that energy is a concept invented by the human mind, and the rules by which numerical values are assigned to the various kinds of energy of a body or a system of bodies are established by mutual agreement among scientists. From this point of view, the conservation of energy is not a law that can be proved, but is true by construction. Such an invention would be valueless if it were necessary to construct new rules for each new event in order to preserve its validity. The remarkable feature of the concept is that only a small number of rules are needed, and all known phenomena can be described as transfers of energy either from one form to another, from one body to another, or both. Our claim thus is that energy is not a necessary concept but simply an "intermediate helping function" to facilitate problem solving. This point of view implies that problems in mechanics could be solved using Newton's laws alone; therefore, we need to justify our use of this new concept of energy.

An indirect justification is that although the energy concept was invented for mechanics, it has been found to be equally useful in other areas such as quantum mechanics, relativity, thermodynamics, electromagnetic theory, etc. In fact, it is now a commonplace concept, but the type of problem for which it was first invented is not commonplace.

So, to return to mechanics, certain quantities, certain relationships, turn out to provide simple ways of solving specific types of mechanical problems. Momentum is a quantity that remains constant during any interaction between bodies, and momentum conservation is a particularly useful concept for the solution of collision or scattering problems. Other concepts are equally useful in other cases. The sum of the kinetic and potential energies remains constant under certain conditions. This will be useful in our discussions leading to a model for ions in crystals. Kinetic energy itself is a *constant of the motion* in some situations; this is important to our development of a model for gases in Chapter 10.

Section 9-1 WORK

Work is defined here as the product of the unbalanced force acting on a body and the distance the body moves while the force acts.

Section 9-2 KINETIC ENERGY

It is shown in this section that the increase in kinetic energy of a body is equal to the work done upon it. It is emphasized that the force in the definition given for work is the unbalanced force acting, and thus is the force, according to Newton's second law, equal to mass times acceleration.

This is a conventional noncalculus derivation. It requires somewhat more algebra than our text usually involves, but none of the steps is difficult. Students must have a clear and fairly detailed knowledge of the relationship between force and kinetic energy in order to follow and understand the arguments of the next chapter, in which the kinetic theory of gases is developed. There is, in addition, much beauty and power in the principle of the conservation of energy, and appreciation of it is aided by an understanding of the details. It is important then, that the material of this and the following section be carefully presented and discussed, and that the necessary time be spent to insure that the students gain this understanding.

QUESTIONS

9-1 Refer back to Experiment 8-3. Assume you exerted a force of 1.5 newton with your three rubber bands on the cart loaded with two bricks (a total mass of 4.0 kg), and the cart moved for 2 meters while the force acted. How much work was done on the cart?

Answer   The equation to be solved is $W_{i \to f} = F \Delta s$. The force exerted by the three rubber bands is given as $F = 1.5$ newton; while it acted the cart and bricks moved a distance given as $\Delta s = 2.0$ meter. Therefore

$$W_{i \to f} = 1.5 \text{ newton} \times 2.0 \text{ meter} = 3.0 \text{ newton-meter} = 3.0 \text{ joule}$$

9-2 If the cart in Question 9-1 started from rest, what was its kinetic energy when the force ceased to act?

Answer   We now apply the work-energy theorem, Equation (9-5), to find the increase in kinetic energy:

$$W_{i \to f} = \Delta KE$$

Because the initial velocity is given as zero,

$$\Delta KE = KE_f - KE_i = KE_f - 0 = W_{i \to f} = 3.0 \text{ joule}$$

9-3 If the cart in Question 9-1 started from rest, what would its velocity have been at the moment the force ceased to act?

Answer   Because $KE_f = \frac{1}{2}mv^2_f = 3.0$ joule, and the mass of the cart and bricks was given as $m = 4.0$ kg, we have

$$v_f^2 = \frac{2 \times 3.0 \text{ joule}}{4.0 \text{ kg}} = \frac{1.5 \text{ joule}}{\text{kg}}$$

$$= 1.5 \frac{\text{newton-meter}}{\text{kg}} = 1.5 \frac{(\text{kg-meter/sec}^2) \text{ meter}}{\text{kg}}$$

$$= 1.5 \frac{\text{meter}^2}{\text{sec}^2}$$

and

$$v_f = \sqrt{1.5} \text{ meter/sec}$$

Section 9-3 THE PRINCIPLE OF CONSERVATION OF ENERGY

This principle is presented as something man has invented. All such principles are formulated by man in an attempt to describe the way in which nature behaves. They are meaningful descriptions only insofar as they contribute to the analysis and the further prediction of the behavior of nature. All of the great conservation principles are useful constructs because they enable us to do this. The conservation of energy is a particularly useful concept for the description of the interactions between particles. We have developed the principle in this manner as a means of acquainting the students not only with it, but also with the basic nature of all physical law.

Section 9-4 POTENTIAL ENERGY

In this section we develop the concept of potential energy as a form of energy which can be stored in a system, and which depends only on the relative positions of the parts of the system. We emphasize throughout the development that our purpose is to preserve the principle of the conservation of energy. Without introducing mathematical arguments, we arrive at a method for calculating the potential energy that is applicable to any frictionless mechanical system.

The carriage-spring system used in the text is not a simple one (examination of Figure 9-3 shows that the potential energy is a complicated function of position, and that the spring does not follow Hooke's law). It was selected as an example in order to emphasize the concept of potential energy. It is true that an expression for the potential energy can be obtained by evaluating $F\Delta s$, but F is a complicated function of position and the evaluation would require an integration of

$$\int_0^{\Delta s} F(s)\, d_s$$

For the students in this course we believe that our verbal approach will lead to a better understanding of the concept of potential energy than would a rigorous mathematical development.

QUESTIONS

9-4   At which position is the velocity of each carriage at a maximum? At which position is the velocity at a minimum?

Answer   The velocity is greatest at the midpoint of the motion of each carriage. This is shown by the fact that the spacings in the stroboscopic picture are maximum at the midpoint. The velocity is least at the endpoints of the motion of each carriage.

9-5   At which position is the kinetic energy at a maximum? at a minimum?

Answer   From the results of Question 9-4 and the definition of kinetic energy, the KE is maximum at the midpoint and minimum at the endpoints. A similar question can be asked about the potential energy; it is greatest at the endpoints and least at the midpoint of the motion.

Section 9-5 THERMAL ENERGY

A bar is placed across the carriages, producing friction and thus reducing the mechanical energy of the system. In conventional treatments the loss of mechanical energy is accounted for by computing the work done against the frictional force. Forces that involve the loss of mechanical energy are called non-conservative forces, and work done against them depends on the path rather than just the initial and final positions. Rather than use this procedure we relate the loss in mechanical energy to the increase in temperature, and so establish another form of energy, thermal energy, which enables us to preserve the conservation of energy principle when forces of friction are present. The rules for the calculation of thermal energy are not developed, but the basis for them is provided by the experiments of Chapter 2.

Section 9-6 IN SUPPORT OF THE PRINCIPLE OF CONSERVATION OF ENERGY

In this section the utility of the principle of conservation of energy is illustrated by its application to a variety of systems. The final example is that of the system composed of the earth and a movable object. The energy of this system is shown to be the sum of the kinetic energy and the potential energy; the latter is a function of the height of the object above the surface of the earth.

QUESTION

9-6   How much work must you do on a 1.0-kg block to lift it from the floor onto a table top 1.0 meter high? How much has the gravitational potential energy of the Earth-block system increased? Has the energy of the Universe changed? Why?

Answer   The energy of the Earth-block system is increased since they are moved farther apart. This increase in potential energy is due to work done by you as an agent external to that system. You must exert a force equal to the weight. (A slightly larger force must be applied momentarily to start the block moving upward, a slightly smaller force must be applied momentarily in order to stop it.) Thus

$$\text{Force} = \text{weight} = mg = 1.0 \text{ kg} \times 9.8 \text{ meter/sec}^2 = 9.8 \text{ newton}$$

This force must act through a distance of 1.0 meter. By an extension of the definition of work given in Equation (9-1), we can write

Work done by an external agent =

(Force exerted by external agent) × (distance through which force acts)

$$= 9.8 \text{ newton} \times 1.0 \text{ meter/sec}^2$$

$$= 9.8 \text{ joule}$$

The gravitational potential energy of the Earth-block system is thus increased by 9.8 joule. This is the work done by you as the external agent; your total energy has decreased by this same amount. Thus the total change in the universe (Earth-block-you system) is zero.

Experiment 9-1   Conservation of Mechanical Energy

This experiment is important because it provides an opportunity for the students to relate abstract ideas about energy to real objects. The experiment shows the extent to which mechanical energy is conserved. Kinetic energy is seen to increase when potential energy decreases, and vice versa. On closer examination, however, it is found that the total mechanical energy is not strictly conserved. It decreases noticeably. Then the question of interest is whether or not we can find one or more additional forms of energy to account for the loss of mechanical energy.

Equipment Needed (per 3 students)	*Cat. Number*
1 Timer Kit (Note a)	68876
1 C-clamp or masking tape (Note a)	68829
1 battery box	68814
4 batteries	68813
heavy string or twine (Note b)	—
1 heavy object for pendulum bob (Note b) (hammer)	68840
1 support mechanism (Note b)	—
1 ruler or meter stick	68849

Laboratory Notes

(a)   The timer is that used in Experiments 8-2 and 8-3 and requires a roll of paper tape and carbon-paper discs. The timer must be mounted so the tape moves freely horizontally. It should be clamped to the table top using the C-clamp, or fastened to the floor with masking tape.

(b)   The pendulum should consist of a heavy object (at least 200 grams) which is compact and symmetrical (to facilitate location of its center of mass), attached to a string about a meter long. The pendulum should be supported as rigidly as possible. A vertical heavy rod attached to the table with a bench clamp and carrying at its upper end a cross bar which is 1 meter above the table top is satisfactory. Instead, the pendulum string may be attached to a rigid light fixture and its length adjusted so that the bob clears the table top. A third alternative is to clamp a horizontal rod to the table top and adjust the length of the string so that the bob just clears the floor.

When the students compare the initial potential energy *(mgh)* with the kinetic energy ($\frac{1}{2}mv^2$) at the bottom of the swing, they will probably find that the latter is 10-20% lower than the former. To illustrate the application of the conservation of energy principle, the discussion of the experiment should be concerned with investigation of the kinds of energy that were developed. Friction is present as the tape slides through the timer, as the bob moves through the air, and as the string slips on its support. Students should be able to see that thermal energy was produced in each case and that they have actually measured this thermal energy in the manner outlined in Section 9-4.

The difference between the measured values of the potential and kinetic energies is also affected by the imprecision of the calibration of the timer, and by the approximations involved in determining the maximum speed. An example of this is the fact that we wish to measure the maximum instantaneous velocity and in reality must measure an average velocity over some time interval that includes the time at which the instantaneous velocity is maximum. One way to minimize this error is to calculate the average velocity for each time interval between successive ticks of the timer and plot these as a function of time. The envelope of this bar graph should look roughly like a sine wave. When the envelope is sketched in carefully, the maximum of the curve is the desired velocity. It is certain that with reasonable care these errors will be small compared to the effect of friction.

QUESTIONS

Note that for Questions 9-7 to 9-11, the required answers will be qualitative because measurements have not yet been made. These questions have been included to help the students get a qualitative sense of what is happening; they should be discussed before the experiment is performed.

9-7   Where does the pendulum appear to have the greatest speed?
       Answer   Near the bottom of the swing; i.e., point *B*.

9-8   Notice the dimension *h*. How can you change *h*?
       Answer   Change the angle of the pendulum.

9-9   Start the pendulum in a number of different positions so that *h* is different each time. How does the speed of the pendulum, as it passes point *B*, appear to vary as *h* is varied?
       Answer   The speed increases as *h* increases. At this point, the functional relationship should not be used, but the qualitative result should be obvious, especially if extreme values of *h* are used.

9-10   We have defined kinetic energy as $(\frac{1}{2})mv^2$. Where in its swing do you think the pendulum has the greatest kinetic energy?
       Answer   From Question 9-7, we know that KE is greatest at the bottom of the swing; i.e., at point *B*.

9-11 Can you detect a relationship between maximum kinetic energy of the pendulum and the height h? (Don't try to be quantitative — you haven't made any measurements yet.)

Answer   From Questions 9-9 and 9-10, the maximum KE increases with increases in h.

Note that Questions 9-12 and 9-13 are for discussion following the experiment, and that the latter provides a means for summarizing it.

9-12 If you used the same h each time, how did the three measured speeds compare? The difference between the highest and lowest speed measured is what percent of the average speed? Why is this of interest?

Answer   The comparison of the measured speeds for three trials with identical initial conditions (as nearly as can be arranged) provides a check on the reliability of the apparatus and the procedure for measurement and calculation. It gives a measure of the statistical error of the experiment. The discrepancy between the highest and the lowest speeds expressed as a percent of the average speed is a quantitative measure of this error. It is likely to be about 5%. See the discussion of the experiment given above.

9-13 Do your measurements convince you that, in this experiment, mechanical energy is conserved? (They might not.)

Answer   Except for the less discerning students, this experiment will not provide convincing evidence that mechanical energy is conserved. If one assumes that there is a more general form of energy conservation, then he is led to search for other forms of energy, such as thermal energy. The decrease in the total mechanical energy is a measure of the thermal energy generated.

9-14 A superball rolls off the top step of the basement stairs and bounces down the stairs to the basement floor. How fast will it be going when it hits the basement floor if the basement is 9 ft below the first floor? The acceleration of gravity g is 32 ft/sec^2. A superball is very elastic and loses very little energy when it bounces. (*Hint:* Consider the potential energy with which the ball begins and ends its trip. Consider its kinetic energy at the same points in time.)

Answer   The bouncing on each step is irrelevant to the solution of the problem; we can consider the total energy at the start to equal the total energy at the end. That is

$$PE_i + KE_i = PE_f + KE_f$$

$$mgy + 0 = m \times (32 \text{ ft/sec}^2) \times 9 \text{ ft} = 0 + \frac{1}{2} mv_f^2$$

$$m \times 288 \text{ ft}^2/\text{sec}^2 = \frac{1}{2} mv_f^2$$

Cancelling the mass across the equation,

$$288 \text{ ft}^2/\text{sec}^2 = \frac{1}{2} v_f^2$$

so

$$v_f^2 = 576 \text{ ft}^2/\text{sec}^2$$

and

$$v_f = \sqrt{576} \text{ ft/sec} = 24 \text{ ft/sec}$$

ADDITIONAL QUESTIONS AND PROBLEMS

9-15 (a) Describe and discuss the sequence of events which occur when a swimmer jumps onto a diving board and bounces. Include the words *work, potential energy, kinetic energy, speed, force,* etc., in your discussion to indicate that you understand what these terms mean. (b) Even if no thermal energy is generated in the diving board, will the swimmer bounce up to a height equal to his original height? Explain your answer.

Answer   (a) The diving board is analogous to the spring in our original discussion of energy. The discussion might be a combination of the spring discussion and the discussion concerning gravitational energy. (b) The swimmer will not bounce up to the original height because some of his original energy will be given to the diving board.

9-16   If a ball is dropped, it will always bounce and rise to a height less than its original height. If a large rock is dropped into a pail of water, however, drops of water may rise to heights greater than that from which the rock was dropped. Compare and contrast the two situations in light of the energy relations involved.

Answer   Because some of the initial energy is converted into thermal energy during the collision of the ball with the floor, the maximum height to which the ball rebounds is less than the initial height. The principle of conservation of energy makes clear that when the rock splashes in the water, the total kinetic energy of all the water droplets must be less than the initial energy of the rock. However, individual drops may acquire appreciably more than the average kinetic energy, which can result in an initial upward velocity great enough to carry them higher than the initial height of the rock.

9-17   One of the characteristics of traveling *waves* is that they can carry energy from one region to another. Consider some type of wave that is familiar to you, such as a water wave. Show how both kinetic and potential energy enter into this wave, and how there is a transfer of kinetic energy into potential energy, and vice versa, and how energy is carried from one region to another.

Answer   The wind, or other energy source, disturbs the surface of the water and creates waves. These waves involve displacements of water masses from their equilibrium positions; some portions are raised against the force of gravity. These raised masses have potential energy due to the work done by the wind in lifting them. As the water in the crests flows back under the influence of gravity, its potential energy is converted to kinetic energy in a manner similar to a swinging pendulum. Because water is an incompressible fluid, the water moving down pushes the water beneath it aside. As with the pendulum, the water moving down moves past its equilibrium position, creating a trough where there was a crest. The water moving sideways pushes the water nearby up, creating a crest where there was a trough. Although the details are complex, this produces alternating troughs and crests, and the horizontal motion results in a transmission of the disturbance. Because the frictional losses in water are relatively small, the waves will continue to oscillate up and down and to spread horizontally for some time. Clearly, wherever the disturbance travels, the oscillating masses of water carry energy, and thus energy is transferred to other objects in the path of the waves.

REFERENCES

1. (T)   Feynman, Chapter 4, pages 4-1 to 4-8. Feynman describes the invention of energy to help organize mechanics. It is such a good job that the PSNS staff has taken over the idea for its own use. The analysis is not identical, but the fundamental principle is the same.

2.   Feynman, Chapter 14, Sections 14-1 through 14-4, pages 14-1 to 14-7. A discussion of work, constrained motion, and conservative and nonconservative forces.

3.   Resnick and Halliday, Chapter 7, Sections 7-1 through 7-6, pages 131 to 145; Chapter 8, Sections 8-1 through 8-8, pages 150 to 171; Chapter 22, Sections 22-1, 22-5 through 22-7, pages 545 to 547, 554 to 561. Also, optionally, Chapter 15, pages 342 to 375. Chapters 7 and 8 are standard but more advanced and general treatments of work, energy, and conservation. Chapter 22 is about heat, another form of energy. Thermodynamic processes are described; the differences of these processes from conservative processes are illustrated. The optional Chapter 15 describes

another kind of motion where the concept of energy is very useful. An example used is the oscillating spring; it is handled in a more general way than our treatment of the same problem.

4.   Stevenson and Moore, Chapter 8, Sections 8.1 through 8.5, pages 167 to 178. An intermediate treatment of kinetic and potential energy.

5.   Feinberg, C., and M. Goldhaber, "The Conservation Laws", *Scientific American,* October 1963, pages 36ff. Many extensions of the conservation ideas from a fairly sophisticated point of view. The limitations of the conservation laws are shown.

CHAPTER 10

THE KINETIC THEORY OF GASES

Section 10-1 MOLECULES AND GAS PRESSURE

This section is devoted to an intuitive discussion of pressure. The word was used in Chapter 7 in connection with the volume versus temperature experiment (Experiment 7-4), but since the pressure was held constant there, no thorough treatment of the concept was necessary. In this section we reintroduce the word and try to develop an understanding of it and its physical origin.

Static pressure as exemplified by atmospheric pressure is considered first, and the relationship between it and force is clearly brought out. This is done by means of a simple thought experiment closely connected with everyday experience. It is quickly made evident, however, that this approach will not lead to an understanding of the basic process by which a gas exerts pressure on the walls of its container. To do this one needs to look at the structure of gases, and the model developed in Chapter 7 is taken as the starting point.

In that model a gas is imagined to consist of many small particles, each moving continuously and colliding with the walls of the container. The forces exerted on the walls during these collisions are now proposed as the cause of the measurable pressure.

Section 10-2 MOLECULES, TEMPERATURE, AND PRESSURE

Experiment 10-1 The Relation Between the Temperature and Pressure of a Gas (A Demonstration)

This experiment is easy to perform and works well. It would be a good demonstration given by a group of students who could take responsibility for measuring and analyzing results for the class.

Equipment Needed	Cat. Number
1 pressure-temperature apparatus (Note a)	68842
pan, polyethylene	68895
coffee can, 2-lb. size	—
4 alcohol burners	68810
2 burner stands	68810
thermometer, −10 to +360°C	68874

Laboratory Notes

(a) The experiment can be performed in a very short time if one has prepared in advance separate containers filled with water at room temperature, boiling water, ice water, and a dry ice-alcohol slush. The copper bulb should be immersed in each bath until the pressure reading is steady. If it is not possible to immerse the entire bulb, it must be rotated to bring all parts of the bulb to the bath temperature. The temperature of the gas in the bulb can be measured by immersing the thermometer

142   The Kinetic Theory of Gases

in the bath until a constant reading is obtained. In the case of the dry ice-alcohol bath, the temperature cannot be measured by an ordinary thermometer, but the correct value (-78°C) is given in the text.

The four points obtained should be plotted on a graph, either on the blackboard by one student or on paper by each student individually. The pressure gage is calibrated in pounds per square inch; this is a suitable pressure unit for the pressure axis in this plot even though it is not a standard mks unit. The temperature axis should be marked off in Celsius degrees. When the four points are plotted they should lie on a straight line. The extrapolation of this line to zero pressure should pass through a temperature near -273° C, just as did a similar plot in the volume versus temperature graph in Experiment 7-4.

Results may not be very good unless you can supply the mixture of dry ice and alcohol. The other three temperatures are closely bunched compared to the interval of extrapolation.

An interesting point can be made if you can supply a container of liquid nitrogen (-196°C) and if the gas in the bulb is either air or oxygen. In this case the gas should liquefy and the resulting data will fall far off the extrapolated straight line representing the other data.

Still another possibility is to pump the air out of the bulb and fill it with some other gas. The students can then observe that the pressure of a gas at a given temperature and volume is independent of the gas used—a result consistent with the predictions of our particle model.

QUESTIONS

10-1 Based on your experimental results, explain why there are more tire blowouts on the superhighways in July than in December.

Answer   An automobile tire, which heats when the car is moving because of the constant flexing of the cords and the friction with the roads, will not be cooled as much in July as it would in December. The volume of the air within the tire is roughly constant; it is determined by the size of the tire casing, which changes very little once a certain low pressure is exceeded. The results of our experiment indicate that for a given volume of air in the tire, the pressure will be larger when the temperature is high. The higher temperature in summer will then lead to greater pressures once the car has been driven awhile. These pressures may produce forces greater than the tire is able to withstand.

10-2 When the apparatus was completely evaporated, we observed a zero pressure reading. After studying your graph, can you suggest a temperature at which a zero pressure reading might be expected when there is gas in the tube?

Answer   If the experiment has been performed carefully, the straight line through the data points can be extrapolated to zero pressure and will cross the temperature axis at -273°C (plus or minus five or ten degrees caused by experimental error). One might therefore expect to observe zero pressure as the temperature approaches -273°C. It is important to point out, however, that all gases liquefy before they reach temperatures in this range. Helium remains a gas down to -269°C at atmospheric pressure, so it could be used to explore much of the low-temperature range and should reach very low pressures before liquefying.

10-3 How is the temperature referred to in Question 10-2 related to the temperature found in Experiment 7-4?

Answer   Experiment 7-4 showed that at constant pressure the volume of a gas is directly proportional to the Celsius temperature plus 273°. Experiment 10-1 shows that at constant volume the pressure of a gas is directly proportional to the Celsius temperature plus 273°. Thus, -273°C is the temperature at which the product of pressure and volume becomes zero, if the gas behaves consistently down that low.

We can now redefine the zero of the temperature scale. The results of Experiments 7-4 and 10-1 can be summarized by saying that the product of pressure and volume for a gas varies linearly with the Celsius temperature. Since this product goes to zero at $-273°C$, a new temperature scale defined so as to add 273 degrees to the Celsius reading will yield a scale (called absolute) for which PV is proportional to T. We next examine our model to see if we can explain the experimental results.

When a cool gas is placed in a hot container, the gas warms and the container cools, and these changes continue until the temperatures equalize. By discussing a thought experiment involving many air pucks colliding on a smooth table, we establish that the average kinetic energies of randomly colliding objects also equalize. These two verifiable results suggest a connection between the mean kinetic energy of the gas particles and the temperature of the gas.

Earlier a theoretical model was developed for the interactions between the molecules of a gas and their container. An implication of the model is that pressure is directly proportional to the average kinetic energy of the particles. Two experiments taken together verify this prediction.

The results of the pressure-temperature experiment (Experiment 10-1) indicate that pressure is directly proportional to absolute temperature. The relationship between the mean kinetic energy of the particles and the temperature of the gas can be demonstrated by a study of Brownian motion. This phenomenon can be demonstrated easily by using a microscope to observe smoke particles suspended in a small chamber built for the purpose (e.g., Cenco 717270). The large smoke particles will be seen to dance around randomly.

For the purposes of this discussion, we might picture the contents of the viewing chamber as a mixture of two gases. One, air, is made up of ordinary submicroscopic gas particles. The other is made up of the extraordinarily large (for a gas) smoke particles. The observed dancing of the smoke particles is evidence of collisions involving exchanges of kinetic energy between the smoke particles and particles of the gas. Thus, regardless of their relative values prior to mixing, the average kinetic energies of both types of particles will be equal soon afterward.

The relation between temperature and kinetic energy can be studied visually by following the motions of the smoke particles. The temperature of the smoke-particle gas is varied by varying the temperature of the mixture and waiting for thermal equilibration. Raising the temperature leads to visibly increased agitation in the dance of the smoke particles. Lowering the temperature leads to reduced agitation. Quantitative measurements would show that the average kinetic energy of the visible particles is proportional to the temperature. This result together with the results of Experiment 10-1 agrees with the theoretical prediction based on our model. This agreement gives us confidence in the usefulness of our model.

QUESTIONS

10-4   Suppose that the gas in a space vehicle is maintained at a pressure of 10 psi (pounds per square inch) and the temperature is $290°$ K (about $63°$ F). What will the pressure become if the temperature is increased to $310°$ K?

Answer   Since we have established in Experiment 10-1 that pressure is proportional to the absolute (or Kelvin) temperature, we can find the final pressure by proportions.

$$P_2 = P_1 \frac{T_2}{T_1} = 10 \text{ psi} \times \frac{310 °K}{290 °K} = 10.7 = 11 \text{ psi}$$

10-5   Suppose the pressure reading in the space vehicle of Question 10-4 was obtained by a gage that compared the pressure on the inside of the vehicle with that on the outside (essentially zero in outer space). What would that pressure gage read if the vehicle were brought back to the surface of the Earth, where the air pressure is approximately 15 psi?

Answer   Gage pressure is the pressure of the gas in the cabin minus the outdoor atmospheric pressure. If the pressure in the cabin is 10 psi and that outside is 15 psi, the gage will read

$$10 - 15 = -5 \text{ psi}$$

10-6 A balloon expands as it rises in the air. This is also true of bubbles rising in beer or soda. Discuss the effects of pressure and temperature in both cases.

Answer   As the balloon rises, the atmospheric pressure surrounding it decreases, and as the bubble rises, the pressure of the liquid surrounding it decreases. However, as the balloon rises, the temperature surrounding it also decreases, which tends to cool the balloon and make it smaller. The net effect is a slight lessening of its tendency to increase in volume as it rises, and the effect occurs all along its path. For the soda bubble, however, the temperature surrounding the bubble remains essentially the same all along its path, so the increase in volume is entirely the result of the decrease in pressure.

10-7 Some liquid sits in an open pan. As you know, the liquid will evaporate (at a rate depending on the surrounding humidity and temperature). Does the liquid become cooler, hotter, or remain at the same temperature? Try to write an explanation for each of the three alternatives. On the basis of these explanations, which would you choose to be correct?

Answer   The initial temperature of the liquid is a measure of the average kinetic energy of the particles comprising it. If the liquid is to become cooler by evaporation, the average kinetic energy of the remaining molecules must be reduced. This can happen only if the molecules that escape have greater than average energy. (If you remove the highest numbers from a numerical list, the average of those remaining becomes less.) If the liquid is to become warmer by evaporation, the average kinetic energy of the remaining molecules must be increased. This can occur only if those that escape have a smaller than average kinetic energy. If the liquid remains at the same temperature during evaporation, the average kinetic energy of the molecules must also remain constant. This requires that the escaping molecules have the same distribution of energies as those remaining. That is, the chance of escaping must be independent of the kinetic energy. One would expect the probability of escape to increase with increasing kinetic energy, and thus that the temperature of the remaining liquid would decrease.

10-8 Now is the time to turn back to Question 1-11 and answer that question again, but this time use the results of your further studies.

Answer   Part (a) of this question has been answered above as part of the answer to Question 10-1. Part (b) is not answerable by the students on the basis of any further studies in this course.

ADDITIONAL QUESTIONS AND PROBLEMS

10-9 One of the assumptions we made concerning gases is that the motion of the gas particles is equally likely in all directions (hence the force and the pressure are equal on all six sides of a cubical container). Suppose we have a cubical container filled with a gas at a high pressure. If now we cut a hole in one of the sides, the gas will rush out of the hole. (a) What will happen to the pressure? (b) What will happen to the force on each side of the cube? (c) How will the forces on each side of the cube compare with each other? (d) What will happen to the cubical container? (e) What have we made? (f) What will happen to the temperature of the gas in the container?

Answer   (a) Pressure decreases. (b) Force on each side decreases. (c) Since the area of the side which contains the hole is now less than the other five sides, the force on this side is less than the force on the other sides. (d) Since there is now a *net* unbalanced force on the container (there is more force on the side away from the hole than the side containing the hole), the container will be accelerated away from the direction of the hole. (e) We have made a rocket. (f) Since pressure is proportional to temperature, and the pressure drops, the temperature drops.

REFERENCES

1.   Andrews and Kokes, Chapter 7, pages 149 to 171. Standard gas laws and elementary kinetic theory of gases.

2. (T) Baez, Chapter 29, pages 365 to 377. The kinetic theory of gases from a qualitative point of view.

3. (T) Christiansen and Garrett, Chapter 9, Section 9-1, pages 118 to 119; Chapter 11, Section 11-3, pages 153 to 154. Some interesting bits. The second reference more properly belongs to Chapter 9.

4.   Resnick and Halliday, Chapter 23, Sections 23-1 through 23-5, pages 571 to 582. A more advanced description of kinetic theory.

5.   Stevenson and Moore, Chapter 13, Section 13.1 through 13.3, pages 288 to 301. An intermediate description of part of kinetic theory.

CHAPTER 11

BONDING FORCES WITHIN A CRYSTAL

We have already given some evidence in Chapters 5 and 6 that solids are made up of small particles in a relatively fixed and regular spatial array. There must be forces acting to hold the particles in this array, and this chapter is devoted to establishing some of the essential properties of these bonding forces. No assumptions are made about the nature of the particles involved, and the only characteristics assigned to the forces are those which can be readily derived or verified in terms of macroscopic observations. The crystal chosen as the focus of the discussion is sodium chloride, which has been examined previously in Chapter 5.

In the introduction to the chapter we ask such fundamental questions as: Why do solids hold together? Why are they rigid? Why do they hold their shape? A class discussion of these questions can be lively, and should leave the students with some understanding of why they are fundamental even though they are not yet answered.

Section 11-1 STRENGTH OF A CRYSTAL

We point out here that the observed resistance of solids to being stretched or compressed requires that the bonding forces be both attractive and repulsive. Students find it hard to understand the need for the repulsive force; they appear to have a vague idea of the particles in a crystal simply coming together until they touch. However, even the hardest substances can be compressed by the application of sufficient force; they can also be pulled apart if subjected to sufficient tension. This implies that matter has a sub-structure which can be altered by subjecting it to sufficient stress. This conclusion is borne out by extensive research, and we can now say with confidence that the force of attraction between the constituent particles of matter becomes vanishingly small at large distances, whereas at very small separations a powerful repulsive force dominates. The average separation between atoms in a solid is that distance at which the two forces balance one another — the distance for which work is required either to separate them farther or to bring them closer together. Clearly then their equilibrium separations can be described as positions of minimum potential energy. We will make use of this description in Chapter 15.

Section 11-2 ON UNDERSTANDING

No elaboration needed.

Section 11-3 REQUIREMENTS FOR THE BONDING FORCES

Three conditions to be met by the sought-after bonding force are discussed in the textbook. The first is the essential property that the force must exhibit both attraction and repulsion. The second is that, hopefully, it will be a previously known and relatively common kind of force. Third, it should be universal in the sense that the same kind of force should be responsible for the bonding in all matter.

The hope that the bonding force in solids will prove to be a previously well-known type of force is a consequence of one of the basic tenets of science: the infinite variety of natural phenomena can be understood and explained on the basis of a limited number of laws and principles. To explain each new effect by hypothesizing a corresponding new cause is no explanation at all. We seek to formulate our explanations in a sufficiently general manner that they will apply to many things, and will help to show the underlying unity of much which at first sight seems diverse.

An estimate of the magnitude of the force required to hold crystals together is needed to evaluate the various known forces for the job. We begin our discussion by calculating the minimum force required to keep a particle from being pulled off the bottom of a sodium chloride crystal by the Earth's gravitation. The calculation involved yields an order of magnitude result. It is desirable to go through it rather carefully, since it provides one of the basic criteria for establishing which type of force is involved, and since it is a typical scientific procedure with which few students are familiar.

To perform an order of magnitude calculation it is necessary to use power of ten notation. If this has not yet been reviewed, now is a good time to do it. A short description appears in Appendix A of the text.

Section 11-4 KINDS OF FORCES

Most people rarely attempt to consider forces in detail. Some might say that glue holds paper together because glue is sticky, but do we inquire into what is meant by being sticky? We say that the force of the golf club drives the ball down the fairway without having any real idea of how it does. We say that something is held back by the force of friction without understanding the mechanism of friction. This section calls attention to the meaning of forces, and singles out gravitational, electrical, and magnetic forces to investigate as the possible source of the crystal bonding force we are looking for.

Students can undoubtedly think of additional examples of forces (see Question 11-1), and there may indeed be others as yet unknown. Each of the three we have selected for study, however, is of very general applicability, governing a multitude of diverse interactions. And most important, the effects of each may be separately identified and separately studied.

QUESTION

11-1 Think of situations that involve force: grasping a book between one's fingers, the attraction of an iron nail to a magnet, the orbiting of a satellite, and the sticking of adhesive tape. Classify these and other examples that you think of under the following headings: gravitational, magnetic, electrical, uncertain. Forces in the last category might be examples of the kind of forces we are trying to explain.

Answer

Situation	Gravitational	Electrical	Magnetic	Uncertain
Grasping book between fingers				x
Attraction of iron nail to a magnet			x	
Orbiting of a satellite	x			
Sticking of adhesive tape				x

Situation	Gravitational	Electrical	Magnetic	Uncertain
Hair attracted to comb		x		
Wind blowing tree over				x
Hammer striking nail				x
Bullet striking metal plate				x
Exhaust driving rocket				x
Firecracker exploding				x

Section 11-5 GRAVITATIONAL FORCES EXAMINED

The purpose of this section is to convince the student that the gravitational force is too weak to hold a crystal together. He can sense the force of gravity between himself and the Earth, and he knows that it is a fairly large force. He must be reminded then that the Earth has a large mass and that it is the large mass which causes the large force. The gravitational attraction between two small bodies, on the other hand, is difficult to measure, although it can be done. The PSSC film "Forces", for instance, shows the gravitational attraction between a box of sand and a bottle of water.

In calculating the gravitational force of attraction between the particles in the string isolated from the sodium chloride crystal, we are forced to draw on information derived in later chapters of the textbook.

QUESTIONS

11-2 When we calculated the gravitational force on the bottom particle of the vertical chain, we considered only the force between that particle and the one above it. Should we have considered the other particles in the string? For simplicity let us assume that each particle in the string has a mass $m = 6 \times 10^{-26}$kg, and that the distance between the centers of adjacent particles is $r = 3 \times 10^{-10}$ meter. What is the gravitational force between the bottom particle and the second one above it? the third one?

Answer   Using Newton's law of gravitation

$$F = G \frac{m_1 m_2}{r^2}$$

The force of attraction between the first two particles is

$$F = 7 \times 10^{-11} \frac{\text{newton (meter)}^2}{\text{kg}^2} \times \frac{(6 \times 10^{-26} \text{ kg})^2}{(3 \times 10^{-10} \text{ meter})^2} = 3 \times 10^{-42} \text{ newton}$$

The only variable factor in the calculation of the force between any two of these particles is the distance separating them. If the distance between the first two is r, then that between the first and the third is $2r$, the first and the fourth is $3r$, etc. Therefore the force between the first and the third particle must be $\frac{1}{4}$ that between the first two; between the first and fourth, $\frac{1}{9}$; etc. Thus, the force between the first and third particle is

$$F = \frac{1}{4} (3 \times 10^{-42}) \text{ newton} = 0.7 \times 10^{-42} \text{ newton}$$

and the force between the bottom particle and the fourth one above it is

$$F = \frac{1}{9} (4 \times 10^{-42}) \text{ newton} = 0.3 \times 10^{-42} \text{ newton}$$

11-3 If there are six particles in the vertical string, what is the total gravitational force acting on the bottom particle? What fractional part of this force is exerted by the particle immediately adjacent to the bottom one?

Answer   With six particles, five are attracting the bottom one. The distances between the bottom one and the others will be $r, 2r, 3r, 4r, 5r$. The forces will be such that

$$F_{total} = Gm_1 m_2 \frac{1}{r^2}\left(1 + \frac{1}{4} + \frac{1}{9} + \frac{1}{16} + \frac{1}{25}\right)$$ where r is the distance between the first two particles. From Question 11-2, this is

$$F_{total} = 3 \times 10^{-42}\left[1 + .25 + .11 + .062 + .04\right]\text{ newton}$$

$$= 3 \times 10^{-42}\,(1.45)\text{ newton}$$

$$= 4.4 \times 10^{-42}\text{ newton}$$

The force between the first and second particles is nearly 70% of the total force:

$$(3 \times 10^{-42} \times 10^2)\,/\,(4.4 \times 10^{-42}).$$

Section 11-6 MAGNETIC FORCES EXAMINED

This section consists of a few questions in which we ask students to decide whether or not magnetism can account for the bonding force within crystals. We expect them to conclude that it cannot, because their observations will indicate that magnetic forces affect only certain substances, mostly those with iron in them.

The questions we ask are all based on observations, but we have not included any experiments on magnetism. For our present purposes their thinking needs only to be channeled by questioning. The way we develop our study of solids does not require an understanding of magnetism; this is the only place where we do any more than mention it, and then only to dispose of it as quickly as possible.

QUESTIONS

11-4 Do magnets exert both repulsive and attractive forces? (A bar magnet and a compass can be used to provide sufficient observations for an answer.)

Answer   Yes. We can summarize our observations by saying that a given end of one magnet will be attracted by one end and repelled by the other end of another magnet.

11-5 Do nearly all objects respond to magnetic forces? Are particles of sugar, salt, and wood affected by a magnet?

Answer   A few materials are strongly attracted by magnets; those we call ferromagnetic of which iron is a common example. On the other hand nearly all substances are very slightly affected by a magnet, although the effect is much too small to measure easily.

11-6 (a)   Is the magnetic force between a small magnet and a nail great enough to support the nail?
      (b)   Is the magnetic force between a nail and a magnet weaker or stronger than the gravitational force between them?

Answer (a)   Yes, unless the magnet is quite weak.
      (b)   It is apparent that the magnetic force between a nail and a magnet can be many times stronger than the gravitational force between them, because if the magnet were to be demagnetized it would not pick up the nail.

11-7 On the basis of the observations required to answer these questions, decide whether or not the magnetic force is a good candidate for the bonding force.

Answer   The magnetic force is not a good candidate for the bonding force because it does not have a strong effect on enough materials.

Section 11-7 ELECTRICAL FORCES EXAMINED

This is a long section containing three experiments and considerable comment. The experiments are designed to provide a basis for reaching and understanding the conclusions which constitute most of the final section of the chapter. There we have summarized what we need to know about electric charges to understand atoms and the structure of solids. Experiments 11-1 and 11-2 may be used as take-home experiments, but 11-3 is a little tricky and is more effective if done in the laboratory. These experiments should establish that (1) electrical forces affect nearly all materials; (2) they are much stronger than gravitational forces; (3) they act at a distance; (4) there are two kinds of charge resulting in either attractive or repulsive forces; (5) charges move in some materials and not in others.

One of the problems students often have is that of understanding electric charge. They can relate gravitational forces to the Earth and perhaps extend them to all matter, and they can relate magnetic forces to a magnet, but their experience does not enable them to relate electrical forces to anything. There is no easy solution for this problem, but Experiments 11-1 and 11-2 may be of some help. In discussing these experiments it is essential, however, to resist the urge to make use of any model of atomic structure. If students use such models, it would probably be well to point out that it is for the purpose of developing a satisfactory model that we are performing these experiments.

Experiment 11-1 Introduction to Electrical Forces

The concept of electric charge is introduced by the students' observing the following:
1. Rubbing a plastic strip with a paper towel, cloth, or plastic wiper gives it the ability to attract small bits of many common materials.
2. Objects of diverse types are attracted by a rubbed strip. The test for the presence of electric charge is the ability of a rubbed object to attract a bit of paper. Consequently, this is essentially our definition of electric charge.

Equipment Needed
(per student)

	Cat. Number
1 plastic strip, vinyl or cellulose acetate (Note a)	68901
3 paper towels (Note b)	—
A variety of materials, each in the form of a small bit or piece:	—
salt, sugar, thread, powdered coffee, tea leaves, pepper,	
aluminum foil, paper, etc.	

General Precautions

Contamination of the surface of the plastic strip due to handling or to high humidity produces a conducting film which can completely spoil this experiment. Such a film may be removed by washing the plastic strip in soap and water and then rinsing it in alcohol. We suggest that the strips be cleaned in this manner before they are given to the students and that you caution them not to handle the end of the strip on which they plan to develop charges. Failure to take these precautions may lead to frustration and failure of the experiments.

Laboratory Notes

(a)   A plastic ruler may be substituted for the plastic strip. Although one of the observational points to be made is that an unrubbed plastic strip will not attract bits of paper, it sometimes happens that it will already be charged before rubbing. Eliminating this charge can be a nuisance, but either of the following two methods will usually work:
  (1)   pass the strip *quickly* through the flame of an alcohol burner (be sure the strips are not highly flammable);
  (2)   rub the charged surfaces on a metal pipe or other metal object which is grounded.
(b)   Paper towels are cheap, so encourage the students to use a new towel after every few charging operations. If the towel is used too often, it becomes permeated with perspiration and loses its ability to establish an electric charge on the plastic strip.

When you perform this experiment, remember that atmospheric conditions greatly affect the results. On a very humid day, you might be unable to pick up paper with a rubbed strip. A sensitive test for the presence of a charge on the strip is to pass the strip close to the hair on your arm. If you do not feel the hair stand on end, very little charge has accumulated on the strip.

A class discussion of this experiment can well be centered around Questions 11-8 through 11-11. A useful procedure would be to repeat appropriate parts of the experiment as the discussion warrants. Students might want to support their argument by performing such demonstrations themselves. It is worth noting during this discussion that the experiment permitted the students to detect forces; the existence of electric charges was inferred.

QUESTIONS

11-8   What evidence do you have that rubbing the plastic strip gives it an ability to exert a force?
  Answer   Before the strip was rubbed, it did not pick up bits of paper; after being rubbed, it did.

11-9   Does the rubbed plastic exert a force on a bit of paper even if it does not touch the paper?
  Answer   When the rubbed plastic is brought close to the paper, the paper begins to move and then literally jumps up to meet the plastic. This motion requires a force, but does not require contact since the paper moves before the strip touches it.

11-10   Are any classes of materials unaffected by the electrical force?
  Answer   No. If you have small enough bits of any material placed on a piece of dry paper, you will almost certainly be able to show a force of attraction. Whether they are conductors or non-conductors appears to be of little importance, unless they rest on a metal surface.

11-11   Is the force exerted by the plastic on the bit of paper as great as the gravitational force exerted by the Earth on the paper? What evidence do you have for your answer?
  Answer   In order for the bit of paper to be picked up by the plastic, the force between the plastic and the paper must exceed the gravitational force between the paper and the Earth. That the paper does get picked up is the required evidence.

Experiment 11-2 An Investigation of Types of Electric Charges

This experiment establishes both the repulsive and the attractive characteristics of electrical forces as well as the existence of two kinds of electric charges.

Equipment Needed
(per student)

	Cat. Number
1 container (Note a)	68853
3 polyethylene bags (Note b)	68853
2 plastic balls, 5/8 inch in diameter, graphite coated (Note c)	68901
2 nylon monofilament threads (Note d)	68901
1 cellulose acetate strip (Note e)	68901
1 tube, quick-drying model cement (Note d)	68901
1 razor blade, single edged (Note d)	68589
cement, Model A	68578
graphite in alcohol	68531

General Precautions

The same precautions as described in Experiment 11-1 must be observed here.

Laboratory Notes

(a)   If this experiment is to be done at home, all materials needed by each student should be placed in a bag or container (not the plastic bag used as a wiper) to guard against contamination of the acetate strip and polyethylene bags. The plastic balls — with nylon thread attached — should be packed carefully to avoid damaging the balls or threads.

(b)   Any of the standard brands of plastic food bags or transparent sandwich wrappers made of polyethylene can be used as long as they are both clean and dry. A polyethylene wiper retains the charge so that it will noticeably attract a ball which has been charged by contact with the strip that it has rubbed. This makes it preferable to the more usual cloth or fur wiper. If a bag is used, it can be worn as a glove while rubbing the acetate strip.

(c)   Plastic balls already coated with graphite are available, or they may be prepared by coating the $\frac{3}{4}$-inch plastic balls used in Experiment 15-2 with the graphite-in-alcohol suspension used in Experiment 4-1. Before attaching the nylon monofilament, however, remove any bumps or protrusions on the surface of the ball, since the charge will leak away very rapidly from such points. These plastic balls should be saved; they will be used again in Experiment 11-3.

(d)   To attach the nylon filament to the plastic ball, put a drop of cement on each ball. Then, keeping the filament taut, touch a part near one end to the drop and allow it to harden. Cut off the short protruding end of the filament close to the hardened drop of cement. The glue and razor blades need be distributed only if the students are to attach the filaments themselves. Nylon monofilament was chosen because it is a very poor conductor, but even it will develop a conducting film from excessive handling. Ordinary cotton thread will not work, since it allows the charge to leak away rapidly. The use of a conducting thread and excessive humidity are the commonest reasons for failure of this experiment.

(e) The acetate strip is used with the polyethylene bag because both become strongly charged when rubbed together.

QUESTIONS

11-12 What does this investigation show about the forces between the charged objects concerning (a) attraction and repulsion, and (b) the size of the force?

Answer   Electrical forces can be either repulsive or attractive. When the rubbed strip is brought close to the uncharged plastic ball, the ball is attracted to the strip. Soon after the ball touches the strip, it jumps away and is thereafter repelled by the strip. It is also noticed that after the two balls have been in contact with the rubbed strip they repel each other. On the other hand, the plastic bag, which is also charged (as indicated by its ability to pick up a bit of supposedly uncharged paper), attracts these balls which repel each other.

The force of attraction between the strip and a piece of paper is strong enough to pick up the paper. Therefore, the electrical force of attraction between these objects is many times greater than the gravitational force of attraction between them. This observation makes the electrical force a candidate for the bonding force in solid matter.

11-13 What evidence do you have for the existence of two kinds of charge?

Answer   When the plastic strip is rubbed with the wiper and then touched to one of the plastic balls, the strip and the ball repel each other. The plastic wiper, however, attracts the charged ball. We are led to conclude that the strip and the wiper acquire different kinds of electrical charges because one attracts the charged ball and the other repels it.

11-14 In 1734 the French physicist Charles Dufay published a record of experimental work that led to the statement, "Like charges repel, unlike charges attract." Do your results confirm or refute this statement?

Answer   Our results confirm this statement. If a rubbed plastic strip touches a ball, it presumably gives that ball some of its charge. The ball is repelled by the plastic strip. Since they each have the same charge, like charges do repel. On the other hand, the plastic wiper that was used to rub the plastic strip will attract that same ball. Since the ball and the wiper presumably have opposite charges, unlike charges do attract.

The conclusion that the plastic strip and wiper take on opposite electric charges when rubbed together suggests that a conservation principle might apply to electric charges. Similar experiments led Benjamin Franklin to draw that conclusion — perhaps more on intuition than on observation. To establish a conservation principle, in the sense we use it, many refined observations must be made of electric charges. Such measurements have been made, and the principle of conservation of electric charge is now well established.

The open-ended questions about the origin or separation of charge when the plastic strip and wiper are rubbed together can lead to some interesting discussions. The main point of such discussions should be observational evidence for either the creation or separation of charges during the rubbing; speculation based on an atomic model is not appropriate at this time.

Should students press the argument about the creation of charges, it will interest them to know that charges can indeed be created. Massless particles, photons, can be changed into charged particles, and, since charge is conserved, two charged particles must be created during each such reaction: one positive and one negative. Because two charged particles are created, the process is called pair production. Conversely, two oppositely charged particles can change into photons; the process is called pair annihilation.

QUESTIONS

11-15 What is the magnitude of the force exerted by a 10 - coulomb charge on a 2 - coulomb charge when they are separated by 0.005 meter?

Answer   Substitute in Coulomb's law: Q_1 = 10 coulomb, Q_2 = 2 coulomb, $r = 5 \times 10^{-3}$ meter,

and $k = 9 \times 10^9 \dfrac{\text{newton (meter)}^2}{\text{(coulomb)}^2}$

$$F = k\frac{Q_1 Q_2}{r^2} = 9 \times 10^9 \frac{\text{newton (meter)}^2}{\text{(coulomb)}^2} \frac{10\text{ coulomb} \times 2\text{ coulomb}}{(5 \times 10^{-3}\text{ meter})^2}$$

$$F = 7 \times 10^{15}\text{ newton}$$

11-16 If the bottom particle of our sodium chloride chain is assumed to be a positively charged sodium ion, what kind of charge must the second particle have in order that the force be attractive?

Answer   The charge must be negative, since oppositely charged objects attract each other.

To calculate the electrical force of attraction between the sodium and chlorine particles of the imaginary string, we must know the charge of each particle. Although we cannot experimentally determine all the data needed for the calculation in this course, we do describe Millikan's oil-drop experiment for determining the electronic charge.

That the electrical force of attraction acting upward on the bottom particle of the string does exceed the weight of that particle is not proof that the bonding force in solids is electrical. The observation that electrical forces are both attractive and repulsive is supporting evidence, and we conclude that, of the three types of force considered, electrical forces are the only possible source of the bonding forces in crystals. More convincing evidence for this must wait until Chapter 15.

QUESTIONS

11-17 How much electrical force do the rest of the ions in the salt string exert on the bottom ion? To approximate this, proceed by answering the following questions in order.

(a)   What is the sign of the charge on the third particle from the bottom? the fourth?

Answer   Since adjacent particles must have opposite charges, the third particle has the same charge as the bottom one; it is positive. The fourth particle must then be negative.

(b)   How does the separation of particles 1 and 3 (Figure 11-4) compare with the separation of particles 1 and 2?

Answer   The distance between particles 1 and 3 is twice that between adjacent particles. Hence it is $2 \times 3 \times 10^{-10}$ meter.

(c)   Using the rule $F \propto 1/r^2$, find the ratio of the electrical force between particles 1 and 3 to that between 1 and 2?

Answer   The ratio of the forces must equal the inverse ratio of the squares of the distances. Consequently,

$$\frac{F_{13}}{F_{12}} = \frac{r_{12}^2}{r_{13}^2}$$

$$\frac{F_{13}}{F_{12}} = \frac{(3 \times 10^{-10}\text{ meter})^2}{(2 \times 3 \times 10^{-10}\text{ meter})^2} = \frac{1}{4}$$

(d)   Is the force between particles 1 and 3 attractive or repulsive?

Answer   It is repulsive.

(e)   Repeat Questions (b) through (d) for particles 1 and 4, 1 and 5, and 1 and 6.

Answer   The data are tabulated below; a repulsive force is considered positive.

Pair of Particles	Separation of Particles in Meters	Relative Force	Absolute Force in Newtons
1 and 2	$r = 3 \times 10^{-10}$	-1	-2.6×10^{-9}
1 and 3	$2r$	$1/4$	0.6×10^{-9}
1 and 4	$3r$	$-1/9$	-0.3×10^{-9}
1 and 4	$4r$	$1/16$	0.2×10^{-9}
1 and 6	$5r$	$-1/25$	-0.1×10^{-9}

(f)   Is the net force exerted on particle 1 by particles 3, 4, 5, and 6 attractive, or repulsive?

Answer   The purpose of this question is to separate out the force between the bottom particle and its nearest neighbor from that between the bottom particle and the more distant particles. The forces between particles 3, 4, 5, and 6, and particle 1 (omitting particle 2) are

attractive: -0.3×10^{-9} newton -0.1×10^{-9} newton $= -0.4 \times 10^{-9}$ newton

repulsive: $+0.6 \times 10^{-9}$ newton $+0.2 \times 10^{-9}$ newton $= +0.8 \times 10^{-9}$ newton

The net force exerted by these particles on particle 1 is, therefore

net force $= (-0.4 \times 10^{-9} + 0.8 \times 10^{-9})$ newton $= + 0.4 \times 10^{-9}$ newton

The net force of the more distant particles is repulsive.

(g)   Is the magnitude of the net force calculated in Question (f) more nearly 20, 50, or 100% of the electrical attraction between 1 and 2?

Answer   The magnitude of the attractive force between particles 1 and 2 is 2.6×10^{-9} newton; the force calculated in (f) is 0.4×10^{-9} newton. Therefore, the force of repulsion by particles 3, 4, 5, and 6, is only about 20% the force of attraction between particles 1 and 2.

11-18   The only valid test to determine whether an object has a charge is to see whether it is repelled by another suitably charged object. Justify this statement.

Answer   We have seen that charged objects will attract uncharged objects. Hence, if a charged ball is attracted by an object being tested, we cannot tell if the object being tested has the opposite charge or is neutral. If, however, the charged ball is repelled by the test object, we are sure that the two have like charges.

Section 11-8 BEHAVIOR OF CHARGE IN MATERIAL

Electrical conductivity becomes one of the important meeting grounds of physics and chemistry. It is used in this course to investigate matter and eventually leads to the identification of the ion and the model of ionic bonding.

To introduce conductivity we ask a rather fundamental question: "How can a charged object attract an uncharged object?" Making a model of what happens not only deals with this problem (which the students may well have raised during Experiment 11-1), but it leads into the subject of conductivity, and equally important, it gives some insight into covalent bonding, discussed in Chapter 16.

Two models are introduced to describe how a charged object attracts an uncharged one. One model involves movable charged particles; the other involves neutral particles containing charges. Both models account for attraction by a charged strip: the first by a migration of charges, the second by an orientation or distortion of the particle. As we see later, the movable-charge model applies to conductors, the neutral-particle model to nonconductors.

It may occur to students that there is a range of conductivities lying between perfect conductors and complete nonconductors. The proposed models are much too simple to account for the conductivity of all materials.

Experiment 11-3 An Investigation of Transfer of Electrical Charge through Various Materials

---

This experiment consists of a series of simple steps and leading questions designed to help students determine empirically the relative conductivities of various materials. Whether it is performed in the laboratory or at home, it is important to go through the experiment as a demonstration during the discussion of the questions. The experiment is a simple one, but it may turn out to be difficult to perform. As with all electrostatic experiments, weather greatly affects the results. In high humidity, many substances absorb or adsorb enough moisture to become conductors. Cleanliness is also very important. If, however, you test only clean objects and the day is not too humid, you should find that metals are the only good conductors. The test should be repeated several times for each material.

Equipment Needed	
(per student)	*Cat. Number*
1 container, to take materials home	68853
1 plastic ball, graphite coated	68901
1 cellulose acetate strip	68901
3 polyethylene bags (or paper towels)	68853
1 styrofoam cup (Note a)	68824

Assorted materials, such as:

    glass stirring rod 68867, wooden stick 68562, chalk, spatula 68864,

    aluminum foil, pencil lead, paper clip, refill for ball-point pen

General Precautions

The precautions with regard to cleanliness described for Experiments 11-1 and 11-2 are even more important in this experiment especially if it is to be performed on a humid day. All plastic, glass, and metal samples should be washed in soap and water and then rinsed in alcohol. A surface film of moisture on any nonconductor will cause it to behave like a conductor.

Laboratory Notes

If this experiment is performed in the laboratory, the pegboard, rotated to stand upon its side, is an effective support for the ball on the nylon thread; if this is done as a take-home experiment, the students must use their ingenuity. The styrofoam cups used in Chapter 2 make an excellent insulating stand. The lip of the cup should be notched to prevent the material being tested from rolling off. Only very clean glass beakers are satisfactory. After they are used several times, they are no longer clean.

Electrical conductivity is an interesting property of matter and it has a wide range of values. The students will find that their materials fall into two groups: conductors and nonconductors. The experimental techniques used will not permit further subdivision.

QUESTIONS

11-19 In general, to what class of materials do the good conductors belong? Which model developed at the beginning of this section works better for conductors? for nonconductors?
Answer   The conductors are metals. Of those materials mentioned in the textbook, pencil lead is the only nonmental likely to conduct. According to our model, conductors have charges that are free to move, nonconductors contain charges that are bound and may be slightly displaced, but that cannot move far.

11-20 Why do you suppose that such materials as clean glass, hard rubber, and plastic are used to build up an electric charge by rubbing?
Answer   The objects mentioned are nonconductors. Since it was possible to discharge objects by touching them with the finger, one cannot hold a conductor in the hand, rub it, and expect it to become charged. One must use an object from which the charge cannot leak rapidly.

Section 11-9 A REVIEW AND EXTENSION

We close the chapter with a series of summarizing statements and a group of questions, none of which is answered. Class discussion is needed to ensure student consideration of them and the related experimental evidence. Encourage the students to think about what might happen to the individual particles of an object as it is charged, but do not choose a model or answer the questions. When we arrive at an atomic model in Chapter 13, we will have the information needed to begin to understand the behavior of electric charge.

QUESTIONS

11-21 Which of these seven statements can you justify by Experiments 11-1, 11-2, and 11-3?
Answer   (1) There are two kinds of charge. This follows from the observation that the same charged ball is attracted by one charged strip and repelled by another charged strip.
(2) There is a force of attraction between oppositely charged objects and a force of repulsion between similarly charged objects. This follows from the observation that balls or other objects to which we have done the same thing in the same way — rubbed them with the same material, touched them with the same rubbed strip — repel each other. Essential also is the observation that different objects — such as the two different pieces of plastic which we rub together, or hard rubber and glass rubbed with cloth — behave differently toward the same charged ball, one attracting it and the other repelling it.
(3) The size of the electric force between two charged objects is described by Coulomb's law:

$F = k \dfrac{Q_1 Q_2}{r^2}$. This statement is not justified by our observations. By rubbing a strip a little, then much more, it is sometimes possible to show that the forces depend on the amount of rubbing, which is assumed to be related to the charge accumulated. If the rubbed strip is brought close to an uncharged ball, it is readily seen that the force depends on the separation of the objects. It is not possible, however, to verify in this way that the force follows an inverse square law. The best we can say is that our observations do not contradict Coulomb's law.

(4) Electric charges move easily through one class of materials (good conductors), move with difficulty through another class of materials (poor conductors), and move negligibly through a third class of materials (nonconductors). The character of conductors and of nonconductors was established by Experiment 11-3; whether a material was a good or a poor conductor was not established.
(5) A charged body attracts uncharged objects. This statement follows from the observation that a rubbed plastic strip attracts bits of paper and other objects.
(6) Electric charge is conserved. Any change in positive charge is balanced by an equal change in negative charge.

The students' observations are not sufficient to verify this. The only relevant observation is the behavior of the charged balls in Experiment 11-2 when the plastic bag is brought close to them. The plastic strip and the plastic bag with which the strip is rubbed acquire opposite charges during the rubbing process. We have not shown that these charges are of equal magnitude.
(7) An object may become charged by bringing it into close contact with a different kind of matter. Close contact at many points can most easily be accomplished by rubbing one substance with another.

That rubbing two objects together sometimes causes both objects to become charged is undoubtedly a correct observation. We say *sometimes* because no substance can be charged by being rubbed by all other substances. These experiments did not tell us anything, however, about the mechanism producing the charges.

QUESTIONS

11-22 If you hold two masses, m_1 = 3.0 kg and m_2 = 2.0 kg, at a distance of 2.0 meter from each other, with what force (in newtons) will they attract each other? What mass has a weight on Earth equal to the force you just calculated?

Answer
$$F = \frac{Gm_1m_2}{r^2}$$

$$= 6.7 \times 10^{-11} \frac{\text{newton (meter)}^2}{\text{kg}^2} \times \frac{3.0 \text{ kg} \times 2.0 \text{ kg}}{(2.0 \text{ meter})^2}$$

$$= 1.0 \times 10^{-10} \text{ newton}$$

What mass will have this weight near the Earth's surface?

Weight = mass x acceleration due to gravity

$$w = mg$$

$$\text{and } m = \frac{w}{g} = \frac{1.0 \times 10^{-10} \text{ newton}}{9.8 \text{ meter/sec}} = 1.0 \times 10^{-11} \text{ kg}$$

11-23 The Earth has a mass of 6×10^{24} kg; the Moon has a mass of 7×10^{22} kg, and its distance from the Earth is 4×10^8 meter. What gravitational force do the Earth and Moon exert on each other?

Answer
$$F = 7 \times 10^{-11} \frac{\text{newton (meter)}^2}{\text{kg}^2} \times \frac{6 \times 10^{24} \text{ kg} \cdot 7 \times 10^{22} \text{ kg}}{(4 \times 10^8 \text{ meter})^2}$$

$$= 2 \times 10^{20} \text{ newton}$$

11-24 In what ways have you observed the effects of electrical charges outside the class room?
Answer   Answers to this question will vary from person to person. Among the commonly mentioned electrical effects are lightning, sparks produced when hair is combed, shocks felt when a door knob is touched after walking across a wool or synthetic carpet, shocks felt when opening a car door.

11-25 If you hold a plastic rod with a negative charge of 1.0×10^{-6} coulomb (one microcoulomb) in one hand and in the other hand you hold a glass rod with a positive charge of 1.0×10^{-6} coulomb, with what force will they attract each other? The distance between the charges is 2.0 meter.

Answer $F = k \dfrac{Q_1 Q_2}{r^2}$, where $k = 9 \times 10^9$ newton (meter)^2/(coulomb)^2

$$F = 9 \times 10^9 \text{ newton (meter)}^2/\text{(coulomb)}^2 \ \frac{(-1) \times 10^{-6} \text{ coulomb} \times 1 \times 10^{-6} \text{ coulomb}}{(2.0 \text{ meter})^2}$$

$$= -2 \times 10^{-3} \text{ newton (an attractive force)}$$

11-26 It was stated in the textbook that to explain the strength of a crystal, the bonding force between the ions of the crystal must be both attractive and repulsive. Assuming that the bonding force is electrical in nature and that each ion is composed only of a single charge, can the force between two ions be both one of attraction and one of repulsion?

Answer   A qualified no. In terms of what we have studied so far there is no way for two point charges both to attract and to repel each other. If the charges are like they repel, if unlike they attract.

REFERENCES

1. (T)   Baez, page 457, Table 36.1. An interesting bit of information. The students may find it interesting to try to verify the entries in the table.

2. (T)   Feynman, Chapter 7, pages 7-1 to 7-11. A further discussion of gravity, particularly in the astronomical realm.

3. (T)   Lehrman and Swartz, Chapter 13, pages 335 to 344. A standard treatment. The textbook questions may help lead the students along.

4. (T)   PSSC, Chapter 23, Sections 23-1 through 23-3, pages 420 to 423; Chapter 24, Section 24-1, 24-2, pages 438 to 441. A treatment similar to ours.

5. Resnick and Halliday, Chapter 26, pages 647 to 660. A standard treatment of charge and matter.

6. (T)   Shamos, Chapter 5, pages 59 through 66. Still more history.

CHAPTER 12

ELECTRIC CHARGES IN MOTION

This chapter provides a transition between the idea of electrostatic bonding in a crystal as discussed in Chapter 11, and the details of the structure of matter, the subject of the remaining chapters.

The experiments in this chapter are written essentially in a dialogue form. Questions make up one-half of the dialogue; the student's responses the other half. The experiments should be conducted with the book in one hand, so to speak. If the student proceeds through the experiment following closely both the steps and the questions, he will be much more apt to understand the subject than if he tries to perform the experiment by skipping the questions and proceeding from one step to the next.

Electric current, the motion of electric charge, is a far more easily measured and observed quantity than is charge itself. For this reason, most experimental investigations of the electrical properties of matter involve current rather than charge. Our general procedure in Chapter 12 is to show intuitively the connection between electrostatic forces and electric charges in motion. We first discuss a thought experiment involving a transfer of charges. From this we develop the concepts of potential difference, the flow of charge, and conductance. We then determine, qualitatively, the conductance of a number of substances in solid, liquid, and dissolved form. We discuss conductance rather than resistance because it seems to fit better into the sequence of ideas we wish to consider. It is, of course, simply the reciprocal of resistance, and there is no harm in pointing this out to students if they ask; however, it is not important to the understanding of our subject.

The concepts of current, potential difference, and conductance are introduced only because they are useful in later chapters. It is not our intention to deal with electric circuits except insofar as the concepts involved bear upon the main stem of the course: the nature of solids. Discussions of Ohm's and Kirchoff's laws and their application to electric circuits are not at all useful to our purposes; they should be avoided, even though they are traditionally included in physical science courses.

Section 12-1 THE MICROSCOPIC AND THE MACROSCOPIC VIEW OF ELECTRIC CHARGE

Our purpose in this course is to investigate the microscopic structure of solid matter, but our principal information is obtained through macroscopic observation. The resultant frequent shifting of point of view may leave students somewhat confused. In this section we attempt to chart our path through the chapter so that they will know what to expect.

Section 12-2 AN ELECTRIC CIRCUIT

This section is devoted almost entirely to two experiments and a number of closely connected questions. Its purpose is to relate work done on electric charges (gain in potential) and work done by them (loss in potential, i.e., potential drop) to their motion through an electric circuit.

160

Experiment 12-1 Production of a Flow of Electric Charges

This is an imaginary or thought experiment. It is concerned with the way in which electrostatic charges are given energy by separating them, and how they then dissipate this energy in a conductor. Since one cannot see charge, and since the amounts involved in ordinary demonstrations of electrostatics are too small to be measured with anything but the most sensitive instruments, little would be gained by actually performing the experiment. As a thought experiment, it is illustrative of a type of reasoning common to scientific work.

QUESTIONS

12-1   According to Coulomb's law, given in Chapter 11, how do the charged strip and wiper interact with each other? On what factors does this interaction depend? Did you exert a force to separate the strip and the wiper? Must you exert a force to hold them apart?
    Answer   Each of the many small charges developed on the strip attracts each of the many small charges of opposite sign developed on the wiper. There are, therefore, many pairs of opposite charges attracting each other, and the force of attraction of each pair is described by Coulomb's law. The factors on which this interaction depend are the amount of charge in each pair and their separation. The students had to exert a force to separate the charged strip from the charged wiper, and they had to exert a force to hold them apart. Neither force is great enough to be noticed, however.

12-2   Review the concepts of work done by an external agent, as discussed in Section 9-4. According to these concepts, what did you do in separating the strip and the wiper from each other? How would you calculate this quantity?
    Answer   Since the force was exerted on the strip and the wiper in separating them, work was done on the wiper-strip system. The amount of work done could, in principle, be calculated by measuring the force and the distance through which they are separated. This is not a practical approach, however, because the force is too small to measure.

12-3   Using the potential energy concept from Chapter 9, how can you describe the effect of separation on the wiper and strip? On what quantities would you expect potential energy to depend?
    Answer   The wiper and strip have been given potential energy by having been separated against the force of attraction. The magnitude of the potential energy depends on the magnitude of the charges, their distribution on the bodies, and the distance between the bodies.

12-4   What makes the charge move through the metal?
    Answer   We have found that metals are conductors, that is, materials in which charges are free to move. When unlike charges are placed on opposite ends of the metal, they will move because of the mutual repulsion of the similar charges on the same end and the attraction of the unlike charges on the other end.

12-5   By thinking about what happens when there is an electric current in an electric iron or in an electric light bulb, make a guess as to what happens to the electrical potential energy of the charges as they move through the metal.
    Answer   When the charges pass through the metallic conductor and recombine with their opposites, their potential energy disappears. It is reasonable, on the basis of the observed effect of electric current in an iron or light bulb, to assume that this energy is somehow converted into heat during the process.

12-6   What is the relationship between the amount of work you, the external agent, did on the wiper-strip system, and the change in energy of that system? What form of energy is involved?
    Answer   Since the wiper and the plastic strip are each electrically neutral in this step, no force need

be exerted to hold them apart; hence no work is done on or by the system during the process. The only form of energy that might be involved is kinetic energy and that only if the wiper and strip are accelerated and not brought to rest.

12-7 In this continuous process, electrical potential energy, heat, and work done by an external agent are all involved. Where is each produced and what transformations occur between them?
Answer   Work is done by the person separating the charged bodies; it appears as the electrical potential energy of the separated charges. We have hypothesized that this electrical potential energy is converted into heat as the charges move through the conductor to recombine.

12-8 Try to design a system in which steps 1 to 4 can be done continuously. Perhaps your instructor can show you such a system.
Answer   Conventional electrostatic devices are the Wimshurst machine and the van de Graaff generator; either can be used to demonstrate the principles being discussed. As far as student designs are concerned, any means for more or less continuously separating and collecting electric charge is suitable.

Experiment 12-2 A Simple Electric Circuit

Although this experiment can certainly be performed in the laboratory, it is particularly suitable for take-home or chair-arm use. It is the study of a simple circuit composed of one or two batteries, a flashlight bulb to indicate current, and a length of bare wire. By interconnecting these elements in different ways, enough information is obtained to serve as a basis for the discussion of Section 12-3, in which current and potential difference are quantitatively defined.

Regardless of where the experiment is initially performed, it should, if possible, be repeated in class during the discussion of the questions, since the subsequent development of the concepts of potential difference, current, and conductivity are built on it. The questions are framed in such a way that no model of the charge carriers is needed, nor should one be used. Electrons have not yet been introduced, so the discussions should be limited to macroscopic observables. Several microscopic models consistent with these observations will be introduced at the end of this chapter; a suitable one is selected in Chapter 13.

Equipment Needed (per 2 students)	*Cat. Number*
1 flashlight bulb, 2 volt (Note a)	68846
2 magnifiers (Note b)	68847
2 flashlight batteries	68813
1 bulb socket with leads attached (Note c)	68814
8-inch stainless-steel wire, bare (Note d)	68516
Plastic electrical tape (Note e)	68556

Optional

Several flashlight bulbs with glass bulb broken away (Note a)

Several 120-volt, 60-watt bulbs with glass broken away (Note a)

Laboratory Notes

(a) It is rather difficult to see the internal structure of the small flashlight bulb by looking through the glass. Therefore, after the students have made their preliminary observations, it would be well to supply them with the same type of bulb, but with the glass broken away. To allow them to see the inner structure even more clearly, you might want to provide several standard household bulbs, also with the glass broken away.

    The glass of a light bulb wrapped in a towel may be cracked without danger of it flying around; however, the violent inrush of air often damages the filament-support wires and tears the filament away. A better way to remove the glass is to wrap the bulb with a towel in such a way as to leave a small part of its neck adjacent to the base exposed. Abrade this exposed glass firmly but gently with the edge of a triangular file or tubing scorer until it breaks through. This will allow air to enter without damage to the filament or support structure. After the air has been admitted, notch the rest of the way around the neck of the bulb and crack it off.

(b) The hand magnifiers listed as part of the equipment of this course do not magnify quite enough for this experiment. They are, however, made so that they can be set one on top of the other to increase the magnification.

(c) The socket is to be used later with the battery box and comes with patch cords attached. These cords are approximately 12 inches long, and their free ends each have an alligator clip attached.

    A third patch cord with an alligator clip soldered to each end is included, but it is not needed in this experiment.

(d) The bare wire is long enough to span two batteries, and when connected in series with the batteries it will become warm but not hot enough to inflict a burn.

(e) Even with four hands available it is sometimes difficult to make all the connections. Stick a 2-inch piece of electrical plastic tape on each battery. The bare wire should be placed on the appropriate battery terminal and held in place with the tape.

QUESTIONS

12-9 Is there a continuous conducting (metallic) path between the two metal parts on the outside of the base of the bulb? Sketch or describe this path.

    Answer   There is a continuous conducting path from the metal button on the bottom of the bulb through one of the heavy support wires, through the filament, and out through the other support wire to the other metal part of the base. Obviously, the order may be reversed (see Figure RB 12-1).

12-10 Describe the two separate conductors on the outside of the battery. One supplies charges like those on the plastic strip of Experiment 12-1 and the other supplies charges like those on the wiper. Does the battery indicate which conductor supplies which charge?

    Answer   The small button on the top of the battery is the positive terminal; the base is the negative terminal. There are no labels on the terminals of these batteries; one must learn and remember which terminal is positive.

Figure RB 12-1

12-11   Do you suppose that the battery actually makes the charges? What made the charges in Experiment 12-1? Could the charges actually have been present all along and been sorted out by some process?

Answer   The battery supplies energy to the charges but does not produce them. Chemical changes within the battery cause the charges to separate, which is analogous to their mechanical separation in Experiment 12-1. It is important for students to realize that electrical charges are not produced in any electrical process, even though some such processes are capable of separating positive and negative charges from each other. This is a corollary of the conservation of electric charge, which was discussed in Chapter 11.

12-12   Is there a complete conducting path for the charges through the whole circuit? Sketch the form of the circuit you have assembled using lines to represent wires, the symbol [B+] for the battery, and —⋀⋀— for the light bulb.

Answer   The complete path for the charges may be represented as shown in Figure RB 12-1. There is no need to insist on conventional diagrams or symbols.

12-13   Does it matter which side of the bulb is connected to which end of the battery? Try reversing the connections and see.

Answer   No. The functioning of light bulbs is independent of the direction of the current through them.

12-14   If the circuit is complete, what is happening in the filament to cause it to get hot? Compare your answer with that to Question 12-5.

Answer   Most of the potential energy gained by the charge carriers in passing through the battery is transformed into heat energy as they pass through the filament.

12-15   In the circuit you have drawn, which part serves the same function as the wiping and separation of charges in Experiment 12-1 (Steps 1 and 2)? What is happening to the charges in this part of the circuit?

Answer   The battery serves as the energy-supplying mechanism in that positive and negative charges are separated as a result of chemical changes within it. (This is essentially a definition for one kind of chemical change; we will study it in Chapter 14.) This separation is equivalent to the increase of electrical potential energy by the mechanical separation of charges in Experiment 12-1.

12-16   Which part of the circuit is analogous to the metallic conductor of Experiment 12-1 (Step 3)? What is happening to the charges in this part of the circuit.

Answer   In this circuit the connecting wires and the filament of the bulb, that is, everything external to the battery, correspond to the metallic conductor of Experiment 12-1. The charges lose their energy in passing through these parts, but primarily in the filament.

12-17   Answer Question 12-12 for this new arrangement.

Answer

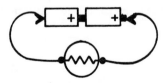

Figure RB 12-2

12-18   Why does the bulb glow more brightly when two batteries are used instead of one?

Answer   With two batteries the charges acquire twice as much energy as with one, and they therefore have twice as much to give up in the filament.

12-19   Why does not the bulb light in this circuit? Are any charges flowing? Is there any force on the charges? Do the charges on one side of the battery combination differ in any way from those on the other side of the combination?

Answer   The two batteries in this experiment are the same or nearly so, that is, they have the same tendency to separate charges and in the same direction. When the batteries are oppositely directed, therefore, these tendencies cancel out.

12-20   Where does the heat come from?

Answer   The wire will become warm because the electrical potential energy generated in the battery is converted to heat in the wire.

12-21   If the brightness of the bulb is a measure of the charge per second passing through it, what observation can you make about the charge per second passing through each of the three places?

Answer   The amount of charge per unit time passing through each of the three points (see Figure RB 12-3) must be the same since the lamp is equally bright at all three locations.

12-22   Now what can you deduce about the way in which charges accumulate at any place in a circuit?

Answer   Charges do not accumulate at any place in a closed circuit.

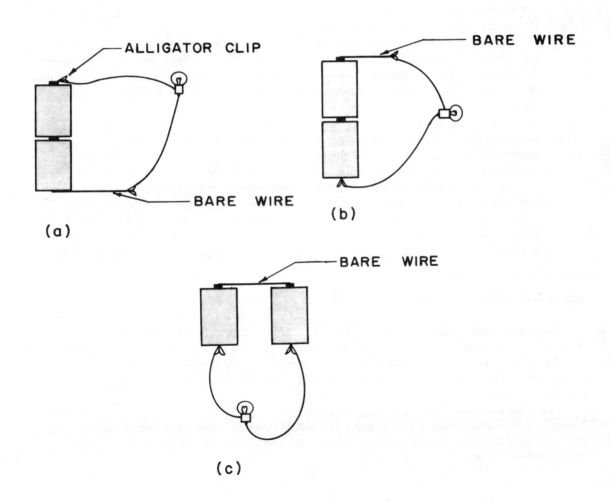

Figure RB 12-3

12-23   Suggest an experiment to demonstrate that whatever flows in the circuit of Experiment 12-2 also flows through the conductor in Step 3 of Experiment 12-1.

Answer   Although the discussions of Experiment 12-1 and Experiment 12-2 are based on the assumption that the charges dealt with in electrostatic experiments are the same thing as those which flow in the electric circuits, we have not proven it. Students may see this, and the point here is to bring this lack of proof out in the open and attempt to devise experiments which will establish the connection between electrostatics and current electricity. In electrostatics one deals with very high potentials and very small charges, and in current electricity one has large charges and relatively small potentials. Experiments to establish the connection must bridge this gap. There are several possibilities:

(a) Compare the spark between the pointer of a Wimshurst machine in which electrostatic charges are separated mechanically with the spark that jumps when wires connected to the terminals of a 90-volt battery are brought close together. The two sparks are very similar so it is reasonable to assume that they are due to the same thing: the motion of electric charges through the air between the points.

(b) Use two small graphite-coated styrofoam balls or very lightweight balls of aluminum foil. Charge one with a plastic strip and the other with the wiper. One has a net positive charge and the other a net negative charge. Both will pick up bits of paper and they will attract each other, so the charges are opposite. Connect the balls by a wire and both will lose their charge.

With the two balls separated, connect one to the positive terminal and the other to the negative terminal of a 300-400 volt battery. (Use caution. Voltages of this magnitude can cause painful and perhaps dangerous shock.) When they are disconnected from the battery they have opposite charges just as when they were charged electrostatically, and they will exhibit the same attractions.

Finally, charge one ball with either the strip or the wiper and the other ball with either the positive or the negative terminal of the battery so that the balls repel each other in the same manner that they did when only the strip and wiper were used, or when only the battery was used.

(c) Show that a fluorescent tube will glow in the same way when it is excited by static electricity as when it is in a fixture and connected to the house current. If a Wimshurst machine or a small van de Graaff generator is available, connect a wire from one generator terminal to one end of the tube, and another wire from the other end of the tube back to the other generator terminal. The charge produced by rubbing a plastic bag and a plastic strip or ruler together will also work, although it may be necessary to darken the room somewhat for the glow to be clearly visible.

Section 12-3 ELECTRIC CURRENT AND POTENTIAL DIFFERENCE

After Experiments 12-1 and 12-2, one should be able to understand the concepts of current and potential difference without difficulty. The definitions and symbols we have used are the standard ones, with the possible exception of our continuous use of subscripts on the symbol for potential difference: $V_{a \to b}$. We use these symbols to emphasize that this represents the difference between the potential at point a and at point b, not the potential at a single point.

The basic idea, that charges gain energy in a battery or generator and lose energy in a light bulb or a heater, or even in a conductor, is all that is required with the simple circuits we will use during the course. A discussion of the sign conventions might well cause confusion and would certainly be an unnecessary digression from the main theme.

QUESTIONS

12-24   If a positive charge flows from a to b in Figure 12-2, what sort of electrical equipment must there be between a and b if $W_{a \to b}$ is positive? if $W_{a \to b}$ is negative?
Answer   (a) $W_{a \to b}$ is positive, work is being done on the charges; therefore there must be a battery or generator between the two points.
(b) $W_{a \to b}$ is negative, the charges are doing work on the circuit, so that there is an element between the two points which converts electrical potential energy into some other form of energy, such as heat or mechanical energy.

   Note that exactly the same answer would apply even if the question specified the flow of a negative charge from a to b. The definitions given in the text for electrical work and electrical potential energy are fundamental ones, and are independent of the sign of the charge and of the direction of its motion.

12-25   Justify the circuit statements (a,b,c, and d) in terms of your observations in Experiment 12-2.
(a) The bulb lights up only when the circuit is completed, that is, when the bulb is inserted into the socket and the socket is connected correctly to the battery.
(b) The bulb was equally bright when inserted at each of the three places in the circuit.
(c) When the bulb was placed in the circuit, energy was emitted in form of light. When the bare wire was placed in the circuit, heat was given off. Were the light left on, the battery would wear out and the light would cease to glow. The only possible conclusion is that the battery supplies the electrical potential energy and the charge carriers convert that energy into some other form in the various parts of the circuit.
(d) When two batteries were placed in the same direction in the circuit, the bulb radiated more energy (it was brighter) than when only one was used. When two batteries were placed in the circuit in opposite directions, the bulb did not light at all. When the batteries were in the same direction, the potential energy given the charge carriers by one battery added to the energy given by the other battery. When the batteries opposed each other, the tendency of each battery to supply energy by moving charge in one direction was cancelled by the opposing tendency of the other.

12-26   Comment on the statement, "The batteries in a flashlight are the source of the charges that flow through the bulb."
Answer   A battery is not a source of charges; the models developed in this and the previous chapter indicate that there are many charges present in any piece of matter. The battery is the source of the energy of the charges. It is the source of current only in the sense that it causes the charges to move and the flow of charges constitutes a current.

12-27   What is the function of a 110-volt electric outlet in your home? How does it differ from a 220-volt outlet?
Answer   The electrical outlets in a home are sources of electrical potential energy, and the magnitude of the potential energy per unit charge available at a 220-volt outlet is twice that available per unit charge at a 110-volt outlet.

Section 12-4 ENERGY AND POWER IN AN ELECTRIC CIRCUIT

   Work and energy were discussed in a mechanical context in Chapter 9. The discussion in this chapter serves both to reinforce that earlier discussion and to extend the energy concept to charges in electric circuits. This will be important to our study of the structure of matter. The concept of electrical power is not essential to our work, and it is introduced mainly because students often describe various appliances, particularly light bulbs, in terms of their power ratings. Although it is not essential to our study of solids, the concept is also a useful one, for it relates electrical energy, potential difference, current, and conductance, and these are important to the mainstem of this course.

QUESTION

12-28   A light bulb has printed on it the statement "60 watts, 120 volts." Assuming that the bulb is
being used as it was designed to be used, what do these two numbers tell you about the following:
(a) the difference of potential across the bulb
(b) the potential energy lost by each coulomb of charge as it passes through the bulb
(c) the current in the bulb
(d) the number of coulombs passing through the bulb each second.
Answer   (a) The potential difference is obviously 120 volts.
(b) From Equation 12-2 we have

$$W_{a\to b} = (V_{a\to b})\,Q \;=\; (120\text{ volt})\,(1.0\text{ coulomb})$$

$$=\; (120\text{ joule/coulomb})\,(1.0\text{ coulomb})$$

$$=\; 120\text{ joule}$$

(c) Dividing both sides of Equation 12-5 by $V_{a\to b}$, we obtain

$$I \;=\; \frac{P_{a\to b}}{V_{a\to b}} \;=\; \frac{60\text{ watt}}{120\text{ volt}} \;=\; \frac{60\,(\text{joule/sec})}{120\,(\text{joule/coulomb})}$$

$$=\; 0.5\;\frac{\text{coulomb}}{\text{sec}} \;=\; 0.5\text{ amp}$$

(d) According to Equation 12-1,

$$Q = It \;=\; (0.5\text{ amp}) \times (1.0\text{ sec}) \;=\; 0.5\,(\text{amp})\,(\text{sec})$$

$$=\; 0.5\,(\text{coulomb/sec})\,(\text{sec})$$

$$=\; 0.5\text{ coulomb}$$

Question 12-28 is a straightforward application of the definitions discussed. It would be very desirable, therefore, to go over it in detail in class to be sure that the definitions and the principles relating
them are clear to everyone. It would be an unfortunate distortion of the purposes of the course, however, to emphasize problem solving *per se.*

Section 12-5 WHAT DETERMINES THE CURRENT IN A CONDUCTOR?

In this section we examine conductance by performing an experiment with a simple circuit. Students
can clearly observe that the current through a circuit depends on the kind and amount of conducting material in it. We make this a quantitative relationship by defining the conductance of a conductor as the ratio
of the current through the conductor to the potential difference across it. Our defining equation (Equation 12-6) is essentially Ohm's law in an unusual form. We write it in terms of conductance rather than
resistance because conductance is a property more clearly related to the motion of charge carriers within
matter. As our development of the subject proceeds we will use this definition as a means of helping to
relate macroscopic observations of conduction to a microscopic model of charge carriers. We are interested
in a way of determining conductance to help us study the structure of matter, not as a means of making
calculations involving electrical circuits. The accompanying problems are for the purpose of strengthening
the students' understanding of the concept, not to mislead them into thinking that they know how to

solve circuit problems. To develop such a facility would require considerable time and would contribute little to their understanding of the rest of the course.

Experiment 12-3 Using an Electrical Circuit to Study Materials

Part A   Metallic Conductors

This experiment is intended for in-lab performance, but Parts A and B are sufficiently separate and different that Part A could well be performed as a chair-arm experiment. In either case, class discussion of the step-by-step results of Part A is desirable to be sure that the students are prepared for Part B. The discussion should make use of the concept of conductance and the circuit statements given at the end of Section 12-3.

A light bulb is used in both parts of Experiment 12-3 as a means of estimating the current through a circuit. The brightness of an incandescent bulb is approximately proportional to the power dissipated in it, which, in turn, is proportional to the current squared. The situation is further complicated by the fact that the conductance of such a bulb changes significantly in precisely the temperature range where its brightness most noticeably changes with changing current. The bulb does not, therefore, give a linearly proportional indication of the current through it. An ammeter could be used, but its use would require considerable explanation and discussion to be understood and would constitute an unnecessary refinement of the experiment. All that is required is an indication of relative conductance, and for this the bulb serves very well.

Equipment Needed (per 2 students)	Cat. Number
1 pegboard and two small clamps (Note a)	68852-68532
1 Battery Box Kit	68814
1 cardboard box (Note b)	68814
4 batteries	68813
4 rubber bands, to keep batteries in box	68814
5 paper fasteners	68814
1 spring, to keep batteries in contact with each other	68814
patch cords and bulb socket (Note c)	68814
2-volt bulb	68846
2 ft copper wire, No. 28 (Note d)	68561
2 ft nichrome resistance wire, No. 28	68561
4 inch, plastic electrical tape	68556

Laboratory Notes

(a)   The apparatus should be connected by the students according to the diagram given in Figure 12-3. Each piece of equipment is to be attached to a pegboard. The two small clamps serve as mechanical supports for the connections at points B and C. These clamps should be inserted in the top row of holes, each clamp about 7 inches from the vertical edges of the pegboard.

(b)   This is a die-cut piece of cardboard from which the battery box can be constructed. The fold-lines are embossed in the cardboard as shown in Figure RB 12-4.

Bend strips A and B up at a 90° angle to form a long trough. Close one end by folding the three C pieces together so that they form a triple-thick layer. The three holes should coincide. Insert a brass paper fastener through them from the inside; bend its two legs over on the outside to keep it in place.

The opposite end is closed in a similar manner, except that the half-inch wire spring in the battery box kit is slipped over the fastener before it is inserted in the three holes of the D tabs. This spring supplies the tension required to keep the four batteries in firm contact with each other. The two brass paper fasteners, one at each end of the box, serve to make the electrical connections to the batteries.

It will facilitate the performance of this experiment, and a number of later experiments as well, if the battery box is mounted in a vertical position against the pegboard. Stand the box on its end with spring end up and with the bottom of the trough-like box against the pegboard (see Figure 14-1). Make three marks on the box to coincide with pegboard holes so that one hole is at the top of the vertical box, one at the middle, and the third at the bottom. Force a paper fastener through each marked position. The fastener heads should be inside the box. Now insert the batteries in the box and hold them in place with the rubber bands.

The loaded battery box can now be placed vertically against the left-hand edge of the pegboard. The three fasteners protruding from the back of the box should be guided into the appropriate pegboard holes and the fastener legs bent over to hold the battery box firmly against the pegboard.

(c)   The bulb socket has a clip that fits over the pegboard. Attach the socket at the top of the right-hand corner of the board.

Remember that there are small clamps at positions B and C. Each end of the wire being tested is folded over a clamp and held in position by an alligator clip. Students often worry about the two small pegboard clamps being made of metal, and therefore, being part of the circuit. You might ask them, then, to consider whether or not the common support for the two metal clamps, the pegboard, would conduct current between them.

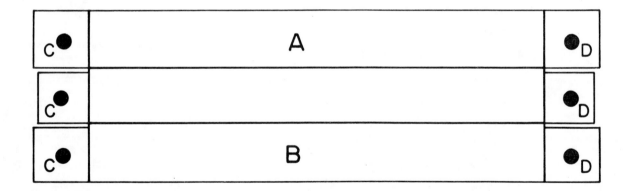

Figure RB 12-4

(d)   The copper wire and high resistance wire can be purchased in spools.

QUESTIONS

12-29   Compare the brightness of the bulb in Steps 1 and 2. Does inserting the copper wire into the circuit noticeably influence the current through the bulb?
Answer   There is no noticeable difference in the brightness of the bulb with the copper wire in the circuit. This observation should lead the student to conclude that copper wire has a high conductance.

12-30   Is as much energy per unit time transformed in the light bulb in Step 3 as in Steps 1 and 2? How could you measure the amount of heat given off by either wire? Can you use the same technique to measure the total amount of energy given off by the bulb?
Answer   The lamp is considerably brighter in Steps 1 and 2 than in Step 3, so the rate of dissipation of energy by the bulb in Steps 1 and 2 must be greater than in Step 3.
    The student can measure the amount of heat given off by either wire by using the simple calorimeter that was used in Experiment 2-7 to detect the heat given off during crystallization. To measure the total energy given off by the bulb, however, he will somehow have to take the light into account, which would not be detected by the styrofoam calorimeter. For that matter, the total energy emission of the light bulb is too small to be measured with such a calorimeter.

12-31   Compare the current in the circuit in Steps 1, 2, and 3.
Answer   The copper wire has such a high conductance compared to the filament of the bulb that doubling its length has little effect on the current through the circuit, so that the first two currents are not noticeably different. The heater wire, however, does significantly reduce the current through the circuit.

12-32   How does changing the length of wire affect the current in the bulb?
Answer   Decreasing the amount of poorly conducting wire in the circuit increases the current through it, as shown by the increased brightness of the bulb.

12-33   Suppose that the light bulb and connectors were removed and that first the copper wire, then the whole nichrome wire, and finally half the nichrome wire were connected directly from *A* to *F*. Estimate the relative current in each step.
Answer   With only the copper wire between the terminals, the battery will drive a very large current through the circuit. With the whole length of nichrome wire in the circuit, the current is low; with half of it, the current is approximately twice as great. (It would be exactly twice as great if it were not for the internal resistance of the battery.)

12-34   What physical properties would cause the two bulbs to carry different currents when connected to 120 volts? (Experiment 12-2, Step 1, and Experiment 12-3, Part A, might suggest an answer.)
Answer   The lengths of the filaments might be different; the diameters of the filament wires could be different; and they could be made of materials of different conductivity.

12-35   How does the conductance of a piece of copper wire compare with the conductance of a similar piece of nichrome wire (see Question 12-33)?
Answer   A copper wire will have a much higher conductance than a nichrome wire of the same size.

12-36   Find the conductance of the 120-watt bulb. How does it compare with that of the 60-watt bulb?
Answer   It is shown in Section 12-5 that the current through a 120-watt bulb connected across 120 volts is 1.0 amp. Therefore, by Equation 12-6,

$$C_{a \to b} = I/V_{a \to b} = \frac{1.0 \text{ amp}}{120 \text{ volt}} = 8.3 \times 10^{-3} \text{ mho}$$

which is twice that for a 60-watt bulb.

12-37   Two wires having the same dimensions but made of different materials have conductances of 0.10 mho and 1.0 mho. A difference of potential of 10 volts is applied to their ends. Compare the current and the power developed in the two wires.

Answer   From Equation 12-6, $I = (C_{a \to b})(V_{a \to b})$.

For wire A, $I = (0.1 \text{ mho}) \times (10 \text{ volt}) = 1.0 \text{ amp}$.

For wire B, $I = (1.0 \text{ mho}) \times (10 \text{ volt}) = 10 \text{ amp}$.

From Equation 12-5, $P_{a \to b} = V_{a \to b} \, I$, so that for wire A,

$$P_{a \to b} = 10 \text{ volt} \times 1.0 \text{ amp} = 10 \text{ watt},$$

whereas, for wire B,

$$P = 10 \text{ volt} \times 10 \text{ amp} = 100 \text{ watt}$$

Section 12-6 THE CONDUCTIVITY OF MATERIALS

This section is devoted almost entirely to Experiment 12-3, Part B.

Experiment 12-3 Using an Electric Circuit to Study Materials

Part B Relative Conductivities of Materials

In addition to the equipment used in Part A of this experiment, this part requires a simple conductivity cell which the students construct as the first step. The principal goal of the experiment is to show not only that the conductivity of materials varies greatly, but also that their conductivity often depends on their state.

Equipment Needed (per 2 students)	*Cat. Number*
pegboard, battery box and batteries, bulb and socket, and patch cords used in Part A (Note a)	(see Part A)
1 pegboard clamps, small (Note a)	68532
4 wood splints	68562
2 stainless steel wires, No. 18, 11 cm long (Note b)	68561
1 ruler	—
4 strips, transparent or electrical tape, 2 in. long	68556
10 test tubes, 13 × 100 mm (Note c)	68906
1 large paper clip	—

Equipment Needed (per 2 students)	Cat. Number
1 alcohol burner and fuel	68810 - 68515
9 paper weighing cups (Note d)	68823
2 pairs, safety goggles	68838
1 beaker, 250 ml (used as a test tube rack)	68815
1 spatula	68864
1 box, matches	68539
1 cup, distilled water	—

Approximately 1 teaspoon of each of the following: sodium chloride (68566), sodium acetate (68548), zinc (68564), zinc chloride (68563), tin (68558), sugar (68554), iodine (68533), *para*-dichlorobenzene (68542), and paraffin (68543).

Laboratory Notes

(a) Remove the two small clamps from the pegboard setup used in Part A. One of the clamps is to be replaced, but first it should be checked to see that the jaws are close enough to grip the small, 13 x 100-mm test tube. If the jaws are too wide, use a pair of pliers to squeeze them slightly at the two back corners, as described previously.

(b) It is important that each stainless steel wire be bent into an L shape, with one arm 9 cm long and the other 2 cm long.

(c) If at all possible, each pair of students should be given 10 test tubes. Working with less than this number will cause them to spend appreciable time washing and drying test tubes.

(d) Paper weighing cups appear to be the most efficient means of distributing the chemicals. Since many of the substances used have the same general physical appearance, it would be wise to label each cup with the name or symbol of the substance it contains.

In performing this experiment, the students should make certain that enough of the material being tested is placed in the test tube to touch the wires but not enough to touch the wooden sticks. The amount of material between the wires should be nearly the same for each substance.

When the student has his test tube in the clamp and makes the connections at points *B* and *C* (see Figure 12-4), it is possible for the alligator clips to touch the pegboard clamp and make a complete circuit that bypasses the material being tested. This problem can be eliminated by keeping the top of the test tube about one inch above the clamp.

The continuity check described in the textbook should also be made as each material is tested.

Some nonconductors, such as zinc chloride, sodium acetate, and sodium chloride become fairly good conductors when melted or when dissolved in water, but in this experiment it is not possible to melt sodium chloride. The experiment indicates the need for a model to account for conduction by charge carriers. It also provides information for later discussions of the differences between ionic and other types of bonding.

Questions 12-38, 39, 40, and 41 can be used as a basis for a discussion of the main points of the experiment. We earlier formed a particle model to account for the changes of state. If at least some of these particles which are free to move about in the liquid state also have electric charges, this would relate the electrical conductivity of a liquid to its fluidity. This still does not answer the questions of how the particles become charged and why some liquids conduct and others do not. These questions will be answered later. Another question arises as the result of our preliminary particle model for conduction. Why does a water solution of a substance such as sodium acetate conduct even though both water by itself and the substance by itself are nonconductors? A tenable hypothesis is that in water the sodium acetate separates into mobile particles, perhaps the same ones into which it separates in the molten state. In addition, if some of these particles are charged, as we have assumed them to be in the melt, the conductivity of the solution is understandable. This hypothesis cannot be tested immediately, nor can many of the questions it raises regarding nonconducting solutions be answered without further study. We will, however, come back to the matter.

QUESTIONS

12-38   Which substances are conductors in the solid state? What other properties do they have in common?

Answer   Zinc and tin are the only materials tested that conducted in the solid state. Both are metals, as are the connecting wires, and the nichrome and copper wires used in Part A of Experiment 12-3.

12-39   Are any of the substances that are nonconductors in the solid state conductors when they are melted?

Answer   Zinc chloride and sodium acetate are nonconductors in the solid state but conductors when molten.

12-40   Do all liquids conduct electricity? Do gases conduct electricity? Does a charge move through them under any special circumstances?

Answer   Not all liquids conduct electricity. Gases do not normally conduct electricity, but charges do move through them under special conditions as in a spark, neon sign, lightning, etc.

12-41   If neither pure water nor pure solid salt conduct electricity, what model can you suggest that is consistent with the fact that a solution of salt in water does conduct electricity?

Answer   If the student was led into the particle model of matter in answering Question 12-30, it is hoped that in answering this question he will refine that model a bit. He would then say that the charged particles in solid salt are not free to move, but apparently when salt is dissolved in water, the charged particles become mobile and so the solution conducts electricity.

Section 12-7 A PRELIMINARY MICROSCOPIC MODEL OF CONDUCTION IN SOLIDS

The material in this chapter is summarized in this section and, using the results of the experiment performed, a model for the conductivity of solids is developed but not completed. Nothing definite is suggested about either the kinds of particles, or the signs or magnitudes of the charges they might bear, although reference is made to the discussion of atoms in Chapter 13. The section includes the following demonstration experiment, which is intended to point out by analogy some of the characteristics of the motion of charged particles through solids.

Experiment 12-4 A Mechanical Analog to Conduction in Solids (*A Demonstration*)

It is recommended that this experiment be performed as a demonstration either by the instructor or a group of students, and that it be accompanied by extensive discussion based on Questions 12-42 through 12-49. Such a discussion should serve to emphasize the important points of this chapter, and to relate them to the previous and the following chapters.

Equipment Needed (per class)	*Cat. Number*
1 Mechanical Analog to Conduction Kit, consisting of:	68893
1 board, 5 in. wide and 36 in. long	
2 wooden strips, to form side boundaries	
1 package, nails	
1 paper grid, to be placed on the board to indicate where the nails are to be driven in	
10 marbles (used in Experiment 2-5), or	68848
10 metal balls	68812
1 clock	68821

Although this demonstration is just an analog, we feel that it is a useful one to help the students visualize a model of the conduction of electricity through metals. The nature of the analogy is brought out by Questions 12-42 through 12-49, which can serve as an excellent basis for discussion.

The analogy will be even better if, after performing Step 3 using the ten marbles suggested, you repeat it using fifty or more. As the demonstration is outlined above, the attention of the students is focused on the motion of individual marbles; the addition of a much larger number of marbles would direct their attention to the flow of marbles *en masse*. It could be pointed out that the number of marbles per second times the mass of a marble gives the rate of transfer of mass down the plane. In the same manner the number of charge carriers per second times the charge on each carrier gives the current.

One important aspect of the analogy not brought out by the questions is the similarity between the force acting on a marble on the incline due to gravity and the force acting on a charge carrier in a conductor due to the electric field produced by the battery. Just as a marble starts to roll again after it stops, so a charge carrier, after a collision, will again accelerate because of the electric field.

QUESTIONS

12-42   The marbles do not move when the board is horizontal. What can you say about the resultant force acting on each marble? What is the analogous situation for the charged particles we have postulated to exist in a solid conductor?

Answer   The force exerted by the board is equal and opposite to the force exerted by the earth, so the resultant force on each marble is zero. The analogous situation with charged particles in a conductor exists when the net electrical force on the charged particles is zero, that is, when there is no potential difference across the ends of the conductor.

12-43   Describe the motion of the marbles. Does the speed remain constant? Does it increase uniformly? Is the speed ever zero? Is there a maximum speed that the marbles never exceed? On what factors does the speed of the marbles depend?

Answer   The description of the motion of the marbles should be in the student's own words. The speed varies considerably as the marbles accelerate down the board, bounce off a nail, and accelerate down the board again; the acceleration is constant except at the instant of collision. The speed of a marble will be zero at the moment of impact during any collision in which it bounces back along exactly the same direction from which it came. It will also be zero momentarily any time it reverses direction and comes back down after having bounced straight up the incline. There appears to be a maximum speed which the marbles never exceed; it depends on the maximum distance a marble can travel between collisions. The average speed of the marble depends on the size of the marbles, the spacing and size of the nails, and the tilt of the board. In an analogous way, the speed of the charged particles in a metal depends on the size of these moving particles, the size and spacing of the fixed particles of the metal, and the potential difference across that section of wire.

12-44   Suppose that this experiment had been performed by using a board without nails. On the basis of your experience, describe the speeds of the marbles in this case. How would the final speed of a marble depend on the height at which it started? What changes take place in the energy of a marble? (If you cannot answer these questions, borrow a marble and use a book instead of the board.)

Answer   Without any nails to impede their motion, the marbles would accelerate at a constant rate; their final speed would depend on the height from which they started rolling, that is, on their initial potential energy. As they roll down the incline their potential energy is converted into kinetic energy.

12-45   Describe the energy transformations that take place as the marble rolls down the board.

Answer   The initial potential energy of the marbles is converted to kinetic energy as they accelerate down the board. Each time they hit a nail some of that kinetic energy is converted to thermal energy in the nails and marbles.

12-46   In a conductor the fixed particles are analogous to the nails. When a charged particle moves through the conductor and strikes the bound particles, what energy transfer takes place? How would you expect to observe macroscopically the effect of this energy transfer? Does this agree with any macroscopic observations you have made?

Answer   When the charged particles strike the bound particles, they give some of their kinetic energy to those bound particles. The bound particles then oscillate faster about their average positions. The more rapid oscillation of the bound particles is detected macroscopically as an increase in the temperature of the conductor. The students observed that the nichrome wire was heated, as was the filament in the bulb.

12-47   In terms of energy, what was done to the marbles to get them to the top of the board? Who did it? How does the amount of energy per marble depend on the height? on the mass of a marble?

Answer   The marbles were given potential energy by lifting them to the top of the board. The operator gave them that energy. The amount of energy is proportional to the height of the top of the board and to the mass of each marble.

12-48   In terms of the circuit of Figure 12-3, what was done to the charged particles that was analogous to lifting the marbles? What part of the circuit accomplished this? On what factors does the energy given to each charged particle depend?

Answer   The energy the charged particles acquired from the battery is analogous to the potential energy given the marbles. The source of this energy is the battery. The amount of energy given each charged particle depends on the number of batteries in the circuit and on the particular chemicals which supply that energy. It also depends on the charge on each particle.

12-49   According to Equation 12-5, the rate at which energy in a conductor is dissipated in the form of heat is equal to the product of the difference of potential across the conductor and the current through the conductor. What are the corresponding factors in the mechanical analog for the rate at which energy is absorbed by the nails?

Answer   The difference of potential corresponds to the elevation of the board, and the current is analogous to the mass of marbles rolling down the board per second.

12-50   Each month the electric company sends us a bill reporting that we have used a certain number of *kilowatt-hours* (kwh). Take these words apart (for example kilo means 1000, etc.) and use Table 12-1 to find out the physical quantity which a kwh measures. This physical quantity is usually expressed in a different unit. How many of these units does 1 kwh equal? It will help you to know that 1 hour is equal to 3600 seconds.

Answer   A kilowatt-hour is

$$(1000 \text{ watt}) \times (1.0 \text{ hr}) =$$

$$(1000 \text{ joule/sec}) \times (3600 \text{ sec}) = 3.6 \times 10^6 \text{ joule}$$

12-51   When an electric stove is in operation the current in the heating element is 10 amp and the difference of potential across it is 220 volts.
(a) How many coulombs pass through the stove in one minute?
(b) How much potential energy is lost by each coulomb in the heating element?
(c) How much potential energy is lost each minute by the charges flowing through the heating element?
(d) What should the label on the stove state as the power of the heating element?

Answer   (a) From Equation 12-1,

$$Q = I \times t = (10 \text{ amp}) (60 \text{ sec})$$

$$= 600 \text{ (amp) (sec)}$$

$$= 600 \text{ (coulomb/sec) (sec)}$$

$$= 600 \text{ coulomb}$$

(b) From Equation 12-2,

$$W_{a \to b} = V_{a \to b} \, Q$$

$$= (220 \text{ volt}) (1.0 \text{ coulomb})$$

$$= (220 \text{ joule/coulomb}) (1.0 \text{ coulomb})$$

$$= 220 \text{ joule}$$

(c) Using the results of Part (a),

$$W_{a \to b} = V_{a \to b} \, Q = (220 \text{ volt}) (600 \text{ coulomb})$$

$$= 13 \times 10^4 \text{ joule}$$

(d) Use Equation 12-4 to obtain

$$P_{a \to b} = \frac{W_{a \to b}}{t} = \frac{13 \times 10^4 \text{ joule}}{60 \text{ sec}} = 2200 \text{ watt}$$

Or use Equation 12-5 to obtain

$$P_{a \to b} = V_{a \to b} \, I = (220 \text{ volt}) (10 \text{ amp})$$

$$= 2200 \text{ (joule/coulomb) (coulomb/sec)}$$

$$= 2200 \text{ joule/sec}$$

$$= 2200 \text{ watt}$$

12-52   Suppose that further experiments on the conductivity of metals demonstrated that the moving particles in a metallic circuit carry a negative charge rather than a positive charge as we assumed in describing the energy changes in the circuit of Figure 12-3. If the moving charge is negative, in which direction does it move through the battery box? Will it have more potential energy at A or at F? Trace the path of the charge through the rest of the circuit and describe the energy changes.
Answer   A negative charge would move through the battery box in the opposite direction from that in which a positive charge would move. It would, however, gain exactly as much energy in passing through as would an equal positive charge, and it would lose exactly as much of its energy in each part of the external circuit as would a positive one.

12-53   If you were asked to measure the conductance of a metal rod, what measurements would you make? What additional measurements would be required if you wished to determine the conductivity of the metal?
Answer   Since conductance is defined as

$$C_{a \to b} = I/V_{a \to b}$$

we must determine both the current and the potential difference. Conductivity is defined as the conductance between opposite faces of a sample in the form of a unit cube. In addition to the current and potential difference, then, we would need to know the dimensions of the sample.

12-54   It was observed in a conductivity experiment similar to that of Experiment 12-3, Part B, that the current was 0.2 amp when the difference of potential across the cell was 40 volts. What was the conductance of the cell? At what rate was electrical energy used in the cell?
Answer   By Equation 12-6,

$$C_{a \to b} = I/V_{a \to b} = \frac{0.2\,\text{amp}}{40\,\text{volt}} = 0.005\,\text{mho}$$

By Equation 12-5,

$$P_{a \to b} = V_{a \to b}\,I = (40\,\text{volt})\,(0.2\,\text{amp})$$

$$= 8\,\text{watt}$$

ADDITIONAL QUESTIONS AND PROBLEMS

12-55   Do charges flow through or on the surface of a conductor? Design an experiment to test your answer.
Answer   Under ordinary circumstances charges flow through a conductor. This could be checked experimentally by making measurements on several conductors of the same metal and having the same cross-sectional area, but with differing cross-sectional shapes. The differing shapes would ensure that their surface areas would all be different. It would be found that their conductances would be equal, which means that it is the cross-sectional area which is the determining factor and not the surface area.

12-56   How could you demonstrate that the law of conservation of energy applies to an electrical circuit?
Answer   We must show that the thermal energy produced in the circuit is equal to the electrical energy furnished to the circuit. What is needed is a simple calorimeter (an insulated container of water in which the circuit can be immersed). Then a determination of the amount of water present and a knowledge of its temperature rise would enable us to calculate the heat loss and

compare it with the electrical input. This is the same principle as was illustrated in the cooling-curve experiment of Chapter 2, although no actual calculations were made there concerning the heat loss.

12-57 List properties of a substance which might affect its electrical conductance.
  Answer Its state (solid, liquid, gas), crystallinity, temperature, size, shape, purity, pressure, etc.

REFERENCES

1. (T) PSSC, Chapter 25, Sections 25-2 through 25-5, pages 467 to 473. Electrolytic current and cells.

2. Resnick and Halliday, Chapter 29, Section 29-1, pages 708 to 711; Chapter 31, Sections 31-1 and 31-5, pages 770 to 773, 783 to 785. Definitions and short descriptions of some parameters of electrical conduction.

3. Sienko and Plane, Chapter 8, Section 8.4, pages 180 to 183; Chapter 13, Sections 13.1, 13.2, pages 288 to 294. Electrolytic conduction and electrolysis. This reference should be returned to following our Chapter 14.

MODELS OF ATOMS

Our aim in this course has been to obtain a better understanding of solid matter. In our attempt to reach this objective we have observed various properties of matter in its solid, liquid, and gaseous states, and in each case we have asked a question, "What must matter be like in order to have the properties we have observed?" or "Can you formulate a model which will account for the observed properties of the bulk material?"

After the profusion of models which we have advanced, it is time to take stock to see how they are related, and to see whether they can be combined or made compatible. To do that, it is worthwhile to recall briefly the models we have developed and the context in which we have developed them. In Chapter 5, in connection with the salol experiment and the home-grown crystals, we thought of small particles in the melt or in the solution coming together in some regular fashion. Further study led us to a model of a crystal as being made up of small structural units. In Chapter 6 we saw that these units could be studied using x rays, but only if we considered them as regular fixed arrangements of scattering centers, which we represented as points. In Chapter 7 we considered solids, liquids, and gases, and formulated a model which described matter as made up of particles which interact in ways that depend on the state. In Chapter 10 we considered the particles in a gas and found that they behave as small hard solid spheres. In Chapter 11 we again considered crystals and proposed a model involving small particles held together by forces which arise because the particles have electric charges. In Chapter 12 we investigated the conduction of electricity in various materials. Our model in this case involved mobile, charged particles. In a solid conductor the charge carriers were free to move between the fixed particles making up the solid; it appeared that all of the particles in a liquid conductor might be charged and free to move.

All the models we have advanced involve particles of various kinds interacting in various ways. The students, on the basis of previous contacts with science, may give the names atoms, ions, molecules, or electrons to some of them. At this stage it is appropriate that we turn our attention to these particles and attempt to refine our models by such considerations as whether or not all of the particles might be different forms of the same particle, or whether they might have an internal structure that could account for the differences in their behavior.

If we are to determine the nature of these particles, it is evident that we must resort to a different procedure than that which we have been following. We have hypothesized the existence of the particles on the basis of simple experiments. If we wish to investigate their structure, we must move even farther from common experience toward a greater degree of abstraction and to more sophisticated experiments. Limitations imposed by equipment requirements and by the students' lack of training will prevent our exclusive use of the laboratory approach; we must become increasingly dependent on simplified descriptions of crucial experiments and the analysis of their results. This dependence on the experimental results of others is typical of the work of most scientists. Since we are trying to acquaint the students with how a scientist goes about his business, it is reasonable for us to show this same dependence. Thus we begin our attempt to determine the structure of particles knowing that we must place greater reliance on the literature of science, and recognizing that the students may have increasing difficulty as our models become more complex.

Section 13-1 THE BEGINNINGS

Each model we have developed to explain a property of matter has been a particle model. In this we are influenced, at least subconsciously, by a long history of particle theories of matter. The development of these theories from 600 BC to the work of J.J. Thomson is briefly summarized in this section to acquaint the students with the long search for understanding of the nature of matter. The history of these ideas is a fascinating study of man's effort to understand things on a scale far smaller than that provided by his senses. This history is well described by Mason in *Main Currents of Scientific Thought* and by Toulmin and Goodfield in *The Architecture of Matter,* but we will limit our comments here to the contributions of Boyle and Dalton.

At intervals from 600 BC to the seventeenth century, there was considerable speculation about the elemental substances of which all matter is composed. In the period 600 to 300 BC, some Greek scholars suggested that all matter was derived from a single, or a very few, elemental substances. Such suggestions were a consequence of the view that the only way to understand the world was in terms of the changing relations and arrangements of unchanging fundamental entities. Chemical elements in the modern sense were recognized by Boyle in 1661, even though at that time only about twenty had been identified. He recognized them as being the basic substances from which all other materials are formed.

In the first decade of the nineteenth century, Dalton put forward the ideas that the atoms of any one element are identical, that the atoms of different elements are different, and that the substances making up the world are formed by different combinations of these atoms. He became interested in the combining weights (or masses) of certain elements, particularly carbon, hydrogen, oxygen, and nitrogen. He noticed, for example, that eight grams of oxygen combine with one gram of hydrogen to form water, and that the ratio of about eight to one was highly reproducible. The combining proportions are not random. This could be explained by assuming that the elements hydrogen and oxygen are composed of atoms which combine to form molecules of water. If the mass of an oxygen atom is eight times as large as the mass of a hydrogen atom, and if all water molecules contain one atom of hydrogen and one atom of oxygen, then this hypothesis would explain the apparent necessity of an eight to one ratio in the masses of the elements as measured experimentally. Dalton used the symbols H, O, and HO to represent atoms of hydrogen, atoms of oxygen, and molecules of water, respectively. He could describe the formation of water by the "chemical equation", $H + O \rightarrow HO$. This formulation of a reaction was an important step forward, but there was a major difficulty: the molecular compositions derived from weight data could not be reconciled with molecular compositions derived from other kinds of data. The discrepancy came about because the molecular composition determined from weight data depended on the assumption that one atom of hydrogen combined with one atom of oxygen to form a molecule of water.

In 1808 Gay-Lussac found that when gases combine, the volumes of the combining gases bear a simple numerical ratio to each other. When Avogadro proposed that equal volumes of gases of the same temperature and pressure contain the same number of molecules, it became possible to see connections between volume ratios, chemical reactions, chemical equations, and atoms and molecules. But although Avogadro advanced his suggestions in 1811, it was not until 1860 that the relationships were clarified. The delay came about because there was no known mechanism for explaining how atoms were held together in a molecule.

The force holding atoms together in a molecule was finally recognized as having an electrical nature, as a result of the electrolysis experiments of Davy and Faraday. These studies of the relationship between electricity and matter took a new turn with the discovery of electrons by J. J. Thomson in 1897, as a result of his experiments on cathode rays.

It is desirable to demonstrate the properties of cathode rays to students. These rays are created whenever high voltages are applied between electrodes in evacuated tubes. The rays themselves are invisible, but their properties can be readily demonstrated visually. The following demonstrations can be performed in less than a half hour of class time. The tubes and other specialized equipment are available from commercial scientific supply houses.

A.   The Nature of Electrical Discharges in Gases

Equipment Needed

Discharge tube

Induction coil

Reversing switch

Stopcock

6-volt battery

Vacuum pump

In performing this demonstration it is necessary to have the room dark. Connect the equipment as shown in Figure RB 13-1 and set the stopcock to a nearly closed position. Close the reversing switch and adjust the induction coil so that it operates, as indicated by the vibrations of the contact. Turn on the vacuum pump and observe the discharge as the pressure is reduced. There will first be spark-like streamers between the two electrodes. These streamers spread out to fill the whole tube with a pinkish glow, characteristic of air. If the pressure is sufficiently low the pink glow moves away from the cathode, and the glow itself breaks up into bright disc-shaped regions. As the pressure is further lowered the cathode dark space continues to grow and fills nearly the whole tube. Under these conditions of extremely low pressure, we observe a bright greenish glow on the inner surface of the glass at the anode end of the tube. This glow is due to fluorescence of the glass as it is struck by cathode rays.

It is inadvisable to attempt to explain the striations in the tube or to account for the gaseous discharge phenomena since they are extremely complicated.

B.   Charge Carried by Cathode Rays

Equipment Needed

Perrin tube

Electroscope

Bar magnet

Plastic strips and wipers used in Experiment 11-3

Induction coil

Reversing switch

6-volt battery used in previous demonstration

The Perrin tube should be connected to the induction coil, reversing switch, and battery, as shown in Figure RB 13-2. The electroscope lead should be connected to the center post of the electroscope; the ground lead should be connected to a good ground (water pipe or gas line).

The tube has been permanently evacuated to a pressure lower than that of the previous demonstration. The smaller bulb is the source of cathode rays which proceed from the cathode A. The rays travel in straight lines and move into the larger tube where they produce a fluorescent spot on the glass opposite the entrance to the bulb.

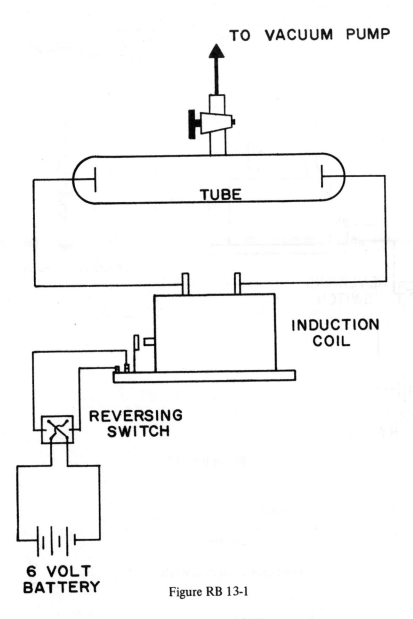

Figure RB 13-1

The beam of cathode rays can be deflected by a strong bar magnet held near the tube. The deflection comes about because the charged particles of the cathode rays experience a force when in a magnetic field; it is conclusive proof that cathode rays consist of charged particles. A consideration of the direction of motion of the rays, the direction of the magnetic field, and the direction of deflection establishes that their charge is negative. Such an analysis is not possible in this course, however, since we have not considered the properties of magnetic fields.

The nature of the charge can also be established if the cathode rays are deflected into the cup connected to the electroscope. The leaves of the electroscope will gradually diverge as the charge accumulates. A glass rod rubbed with silk has a positive charge (by definition). If such a charged rod is brought near the electroscope, the leaves will collapse, indicating that the charge deposited by the rays is negative.

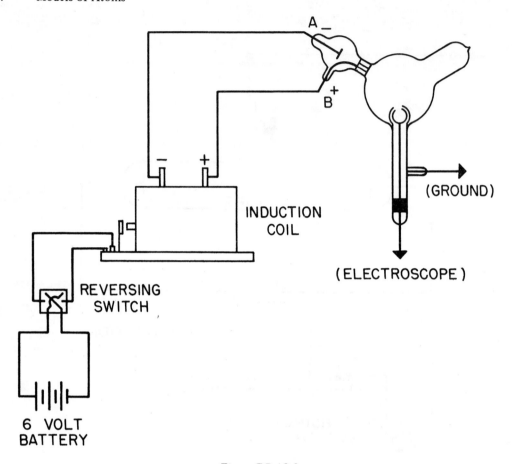

Figure RB 13-2

C.   Direction of Motion of Cathode Rays

Equipment Needed

Maltese cross cathode ray tube

Induction coil

Reversing switch

6-volt battery

Bar magnet used in previous demonstration

Refer to the text and to text Figure 13-2 for a description and discussion of the demonstration. This tube may also be used to demonstrate the deflection of cathode rays by a bar magnet.

D.   *Momentum of Cathode Rays*

Equipment Needed

Cathode ray tube containing paddle wheel

Induction coil

Reversing switch

6-volt battery used in previous demonstrations

This tube is evacuated to a very low pressure and contains a light-weight paddle wheel which is free to roll on parallel tracks. When the induction coil is started, the cathode rays strike the uppermost vane of the wheel and transfer their momentum to it, causing it to roll. Reversing the direction of the cathode rays reverses the direction of motion of the wheel. This is a demonstration that the particles comprising cathode rays have momentum, which may be interpreted as saying that they also have mass. But photons, which have no rest mass, also have momentum, so this experiment is not a conclusive proof that cathode rays consist of particles having mass. When the experiment demonstrating their charge and this experiment demonstrating their momentum are combined, however, we can conclude that cathode rays consist of particles carrying a negative charge.

J. J. Thomson determined the ratio of charge to mass for cathode-ray particles by measuring the deflection of the beam in electric and magnetic fields at right angles to each other, but an analysis of the experiment would be out of place here.

QUESTIONS

13-1 If the charge of the electron is $e = 1.6 \times 10^{-19}$ coulomb, and the charge-to-mass ratio is $e/m = 1.8 \times 10^{11}$ coulomb/kg, what is the mass of the electron?

Answer

$$\frac{e}{m} = 1.8 \times 10^{11} \text{ coulomb/kg}$$

$$m = \frac{e}{1.8 \times 10^{11} \text{ coulomb/kg}}$$

$$= \frac{1.6 \times 10^{-19} \text{ coulomb}}{1.8 \times 10^{11} \text{ coulomb/kg}}$$

$$= 9 \times 10^{-31} \text{ kg}$$

13-2 The charge-to-mass ratio of a beam of hydrogen ions is 9.5×10^{7} coulomb/kg. If we assume that the charge on the electron is equal to that on the hydrogen ion, what is the mass of the hydrogen ion? What is the ratio of the mass of the hydrogen ion to the mass of the electron?

Answer

$$\frac{e}{M} = 9.5 \times 10^{7} \text{ coulomb/kg}$$

$$M = \frac{e}{9.5 \times 10^7 \text{ coulomb/kg}}$$

$$= \frac{1.6 \times 10^{-19} \text{ coulomb}}{9.5 \times 10^7 \text{ coulomb/kg}}$$

$$= 0.17 \times 10^{-26} \text{ kg} = 1.7 \times 10^{-27} \text{ kg}$$

The ratio of the mass of the hydrogen ion M to the mass of the electron m is thus

$$\frac{M}{m} = \frac{1.7 \times 10^{-27} \text{ kg}}{9 \times 10^{-31} \text{ kg}} = 0.19 \times 10^4 = 1900$$

13-3 A hydrogen atom is composed of a hydrogen ion and an electron. What is the mass of a hydrogen atom?

Answer   The mass of the hydrogen atom is equal to the sum of the masses of the hydrogen ion and the electron

$$\text{mass of hydrogen atom} = m + M$$

$$\text{mass} = 9 \times 10^{-31} \text{ kg} + 1.7 \times 10^{-27} \text{ kg}$$

To find this sum, the exponents of ten must be the same, therefore

$$\text{mass of hydrogen atom} = (1.7 \times 10^{-27} + 0.0009 \times 10^{-27}) \text{ kg}$$

The mass of the electron is so much smaller than the mass of the ion that the two cannot be meaningfully added together unless the mass of the hydrogen ion is known to at least five significant figures. Therefore the mass of the atom is essentially the same at the mass of the ion, 1.7×10^{-27} kg.

Section 13-2 RUTHERFORD'S SCATTERING EXPERIMENT

In the decade which followed Thomson's identification of the electron and his deduction that it is part of the atom, there was much speculation about the nature and structure of the atom. The atom was generally assumed to be neutral; if it contained electrons it must also contain positive charge. The problem was to determine the nature of the positive part. The mass of the atom was known to be large compared to that of an electron, so the positively charged part was assumed to make up most of the mass. Thomson proposed that the positive portion, being most massive, occupied all the volume of the atom and that the electrons were imbedded in the positive material.

This was the generally accepted model at the time of the Rutherford-Geiger-Marsden scattering experiment, which is the subject of this section. Since the scattering experiment was performed using alpha particles, the first part of the section is devoted to a discussion of radioactivity so that the students may have some understanding of the nature of alpha particles. The emphasis should thus be on the products of radioactive decay, rather than on the nuclear reactions involved.

QUESTIONS

13-4 What kind of a charge, positive or negative, does the alpha particle have?

Answer   Alpha particles are positively charged, since they are attracted toward the negative plate.

13-5 Gamma rays are not deflected by charged plates. Does it necessarily follow that they are like x rays?
Answer   No indeed. Sound waves are not deflected by charged plates. Many more characteristics of gamma rays must be found to be similar to those of x rays before gamma rays can be considered part of the electromagnetic spectrum.

Geiger and Marsden's source of alpha particles in their first experiment was radon, $^{222}_{86}$Rn (atomic number 86, atomic mass 222), confined in a conical glass tube with a thin mica window at the large end. The alpha particles escaped from the tube only through the mica window since they could not pass through the thicker glass. Radon and two of its daughter elements emit alpha particles of three different energies. To simplify the analysis of their second experiment, Geiger and Marsden used $^{224}_{83}$Bi, which emits alpha particles of but a single energy. The daughter elements of $^{224}_{83}$Bi emit only beta particles. Although both alpha and beta particles produce scintillations it is possible to distinguish between those produced by one and those produced by the other and thus to count only the alpha particle scintillations.

The Rutherford-Geiger-Marsden scattering experiments are discussed without any reference to the nature of the interaction between the alpha particle and the gold atom. This interaction is treated as though it were the collision between a marble and a billiard ball, a collision between two hard spheres of different masses. Unfortunately, this impression of the interaction is reinforced by Experiment 13-1, *Determining the Size of an Object by Collision Probabilities.* The students should realize that the marble experiments involved actual contact and so provided a means of measuring size, whereas the alpha particle experiments involve action-at-a-distance forces and so provide only an estimate of the largest possible size of the nucleus. The scattering experiment proved that we can consider the nucleus as being massive compared to the alpha particle, with very small dimensions compared to the whole atom. In fact, the scattering observed by Rutherford could be explained by treating the nucleus as a point charge which is the center of a Coulombic repulsion. These conclusions eliminated the Thomson model which assumed a much larger and more tenuous positive portion of the atom.

The justification for our conclusions about the mass and charge distribution within the atom may be made somewhat clearer through a consideration of Figure RB 13-3. There we depict some of the scattering trajectories one might find when an alpha particle approaches a region of positive charge. We will make no quantitative restrictions on the size of that region, but it will simplify our analysis if we discuss two rather different sizes concurrently. Let us regard the large shaded region of the figure as being about equivalent in size to the spacing of atoms in crystals, that is, about 2 or 3 Å in diameter; let the central spot be many times smaller. We will further assume the positive charge to be uniformly distributed throughout the volume we are discussing, whichever one it happens to be at the moment. Thus the larger volume is a relatively diffuse charge distribution, the smaller volume a relatively dense one, but the total charge is the same in either case.

As long as the positive charge is uniformly distributed throughout a spherical volume, the repulsive force between it and an alpha particle is given by Coulomb's law. Calculations made on this well-established basis predict the degree to which an alpha particle will be deflected; qualitatively, the nearer its original path approaches the positively charged sphere, the larger its deflection. Compare paths AA and BB in the figure for an illustration of this relationship. Much more important, however, these same calculations say that you can tell nothing about the size of the sphere from the amount of deflection, provided that the alpha particle path does not pass through any portion of the charged region. In other words, paths AA and BB of the figure are unaffected by whether the charge is considered to be spread throughout the volume of the larger sphere, or whether it is thought of as being concentrated in the much smaller central volume.

The character of the scattering changes radically, however, for paths which penetrate the charge distribution. Consider paths CC and DD, for example. They are appreciably less deflected than AA and BB because an alpha particle inside the charge distribution is repelled away from the center only by that portion of the charge between it and the center; not all of the charge distribution now contributes to the deflecting force. The difference between the two situations becomes clear when we consider paths CC′ and DD′, which represent the scattering of alpha particles incident along the same initial paths, but approaching

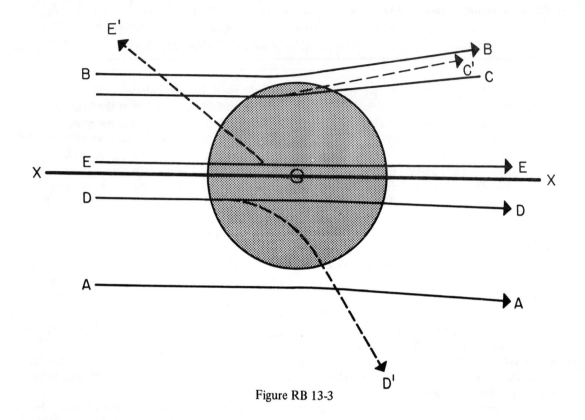

Figure RB 13-3

a small concentrated region of charge. Since the distances of the alpha-particle paths from the center of the charge are now small, the magnitude of the scattering force is very large. An even more extreme case is illustrated by paths EE and EE'.

Clearly, it is extremely improbable that an alpha particle would be deflected through more than a small angle by the large and diffuse charge distribution we have postulated for the first of our examples. Equally clearly, some *back scattering* would be expected from a compact, concentrated charge distribution. These two conclusions are borne out by theoretical calculations as well. But further, such theoretical calculations can be used to predict the statistical distribution of alpha particles in terms of the maximum size of the charge distribution. The relationship which can be derived cannot tell us the actual size of the nucleus; it can simply say that, given an empirical scattering pattern, the scattering centers can be no larger than a certain size. Rutherford was able to show without doubt that the scattering observed by Geiger and Marsden in his laboratory could only have come about if the positively charged scattering centers in the atom were much smaller and more dense than had previously been imagined; these nuclei of charge within the atoms could not have been larger than about 10^{-14} meter.

Experiment 13-1   Determining the Size of an Object from Collision Probabilities

---

The simplicity of this experiment makes it especially suitable for a take-home assignment. Its purpose is to let the student learn from his own experience that diameters of objects can be determined from scattering experiments. It is not a substitute for, nor does it duplicate, Rutherford scattering. The radius of a target marble obtained by the scattering experiment is surprisingly close to the radius obtained by using the meter stick.

The three most common mistakes made by students performing this experiment are:

1.   Allowing several marbles to overlap.
2.   Not rolling the bombarding marble randomly (students tend to aim).
3.   Not rolling the bombarding marble parallel to the sides of the target area.

Refer to the answer to Question 13-6 for some typical student results.

Equipment Needed (per 2 students)	*Cat. Number*
9 black marbles (Note a)	68848
1 white marble	68848
books, boards, etc., to form three-sided enclosure	
1 masonite board, 15 X 60 cm	
1 ruler or meter stick	

Laboratory Note

(a)   These are the same marbles used in Experiment 2-5.

The results obtained by different groups of students can be added and analyzed collectively if they all use the same number of target marbles and the same width of opening to their target enclosures. For example, the discrepancy between values of the diameters obtained by the two different methods is about 5%, so it might be of interest to plot both sets of data obtained by the whole class. One set will yield a graph of the distribution of the diameters obtained using the meter stick, the other is the set of diameters obtained by rolling. These can be bar graphs, where the height of each bar indicates the number of students (or groups of students) who obtained a particular diameter such as 1.39 cm, or the number of students whose results fell within a certain range of diameters such as 1.37 cm to 1.39 cm. The resulting curves should each resemble a bell-shaped curve, although with a small class there will not be enough data to obtain a good Gaussian distribution. The curve from the marble-rolling data will probably indicate a wider spread of values than the one using data from meter-stick measurements. A comparison of these two sets of data should lead into a brief discussion of experimental error, but a detailed statistical analysis would be out of place in this course.

A number of questions are given in the text to focus attention on particular aspects of the marble-rolling experiment. Some differences between that experiment and the alpha-particle scattering experiment are considered in Question 13-9.

QUESTIONS

13-6 What is the numerical difference between the radius of a target marble as determined by Equation 13-1 and as measured by using a meter stick? What percent of the radius measured by the meter stick is this numerical difference?

Answer   Actual experimental results are given for 503 rolls, but the results for 200 or 300 rolls are nearly as good.

The total number of rolls $T = 503$

The number of hits	$H = 303$
The width of the opening	$d = 35.2$ cm
The number of target marbles	$N = 8$

$$(R + r) = \frac{Hd}{2\,NT} = \frac{(35.2)\,(303)}{(2)\,(8)\,(503)} = 1.32 \text{ cm}$$

The diameter of these same marbles was measured by the meter stick as 1.39 cm. Consequently, the numerical difference is 0.07 cm.

$$\text{Percent difference} = \frac{0.07 \text{ cm} \times 100}{1.39 \text{ cm}} = 5\%$$

13-7   Which method do you think yields the better result?
Answer   The measurement by the meter stick is apt to be more reliable.

13-8   List as many reasons (sources of error) as you can to explain why the radii found by the two different methods are not exactly the same.
Answer   1.   Statistically too few rolls
        2.   Lack of randomness in rolling
        3.   Overlapping of target marbles
        4.   Inability to line up rows of marbles with divisions on meter stick
        5.   Marbles not perfectly spherical
These sources of random error are inherent in the methods used; personal errors also enter in.

13-9   In what ways does the situation in this experiment differ from that where alpha particles were used to bombard the gold foil target?
Answer   There are many ways; we will list some of them.
1.   The target marbles and the bombarding marble have the same mass. The gold atoms have a mass nearly 50 times that of an alpha particle.
2.   In one case the data concern the magnitude of the scattering or deflection. In the other, all collisions count the same; the information desired is simply hits and misses.
3.   One is hard-sphere scattering, the other is action-at-a-distance scattering.

13-10   Would the probability that a collision will take place increase or decrease if some of the target marbles were too close together to let the bombarding marble go through? Explain the reason for your answer.
Answer   The probability that a collision takes place would decrease if the target marbles were too close together to permit the bombarding marble to go through. The probability of collision depends on the total target size. If the center of the bombarding marble passes within the target size of one marble it will suffer a collision. If two targets overlap, only one hit would be counted. The ratio of the effective target size to the opening of the target area is decreased.

13-11   What is the total range of possible results for the probability of scoring a hit?
Answer   The probability P of scoring a hit is defined as

$$P = \frac{H}{T}$$

If no hits are scored $H = 0$ and $P = 0$. If a hit is scored with each throw $H = T$ and $P = 1$.

13-12   If a gold atom has a diameter of 2.8 Å, how many layers of gold atoms are needed to make a foil 1.1×10^{-5} cm thick?
Answer   The diameter D of a gold atom should be converted from Ångstroms to centimeters

$$D = 2.8 \text{ Å} \left(\frac{10^{-8} \text{ cm}}{1 \text{ Å}} \right) = 2.8 \times 10^{-8} \text{ cm}$$

Therefore the number of layers N must be

$$N = \frac{1.1 \times 10^{-5} \text{ cm}}{2.8 \times 10^{-8} \text{ cm}} = 0.39 \times 10^3 = 390$$

13-13   The mathematical theory Rutherford developed did not permit him to state for sure whether the nucleus of an atom is positive or negative. What evidence supports the idea that the nucleus is positively charged?

Answer   Rutherford scattering cannot determine the charge on the nucleus because the alpha particle will travel along a hyperbolic path no matter what the charge on the nucleus. In Figure RB 13-4 (a) the alpha particle is deflected by a positively charged nucleus; in (b) it is deflected by a negatively charged nucleus.

The Rutherford scattering experiment showed the nucleus to be massive compared to the alpha particle, the electron was known not to be. The nucleus, then, could not be made of electrons. The atom was known to contain negatively charged electrons, and it was also known to be neutral. The nucleus must therefore be positive.

13-14   Compute the density of the gold nucleus assuming its diameter is 2×10^{-12} cm and its mass is 3.3×10^{-22} grams. Assume the nucleus is a sphere with a volume of $(4/3)\pi r^3$. Compare the density of the nucleus and the density of water.

Answer

$$\text{Volume} = \frac{4}{3} \pi r^3 = \left(\frac{4}{3} \right) (3) \, r^3$$

$$V = \frac{4(3)(1 \times 10^{-12})^3 \text{ cm}^3}{3}$$

$$= 4 \times 10^{-36} \text{ cm}^3$$

$$\text{Density of gold nucleus} = \frac{\text{mass}}{\text{volume}}$$

$$D = \frac{3.3 \times 10^{-22}}{4 \times 10^{-36}} = 0.8 \times 10^{+14} \text{ g/cm}^3$$

(a)   (b)

Figure RB 13-4

$$\text{Density of water} = 1.0 \text{ g/cm}^3$$

Section 13-3 ATOMIC MASS

Although the common term for a relative atomic mass is *atomic weight,* the PSNS staff has chosen to be part of the growing trend to use the term *atomic mass.* No matter what term is used, atomic weight or atomic mass, it refers to the relative masses of the atoms. This relative mass is a pure number, that is, one without dimensions; it is a ratio of two numbers each with the same dimension.

Experiment 13-2 Determination of the Atomic Mass of Magnesium

---

Equipment Needed (per 2 students)	Cat. Number
2 pairs, safety goggles	68838
1 box, matches	68539
1 Bunsen burner (Note a)	—
1 Coors crucible, No. 00	68825
1 crucible lid, Coors, No. 240	68825
1 triangle, 2-inch wire, with pipe stem	68907
1 burner tripod, or ring and ring stand	68878
1 iron tongs, approximately 9 in. long	68905
1 balance	68831
2 paper weighing cups	68823
1 set, beads for balance (Note b)	68831
1 piece, magnesium ribbon, about 20 cm long	68537
1 pair, forceps	68833

Laboratory Notes

(a) We must use a Bunsen burner to obtain reliable results in this experiment. If Bunsen burners or LP gas burners are not available, it would probably be best to skip this experiment.

(b) Note that we are only concerned with relative masses and, therefore, use the bead as our unit mass.

The purpose of this experiment is to make clear the concept of atomic masses. It also illustrates the care and tedium that goes into quantitative work. This is the first quantitative chemical experiment in the course, and requires more care than almost any other experiment. The students should read all of the instructions given in the text carefully before coming to the lab to perform the experiment. They should also carefully adjust and calibrate their equal-arm balances.

Since this experiment requires a higher temperature than the alcohol burner can provide, it is necessary to use a Bunsen burner. It may be helpful to explain some of the features of the flame. Of particular interest is the observation that the tip of the bright blue cone is the hottest part of the flame. The student should also be warned not to heat the crucible too rapidly at first. Gentle heating to a high temperature will prevent crucibles from cracking. But once the crucible and its contents are hot, it should be heated by the hottest part of the flame.

QUESTIONS

13-15   If you spilled some magnesium oxide before determining the mass of the crucible and its contents after heating, would the atomic mass of magnesium that you determined be too high or too low? Justify your answer.
Answer   Too high. The reaction can be simply stated:

magnesium + oxygen → magnesium oxide

The student measures the mass of the magnesium and of the magnesium oxide. The difference between these two is the mass of the oxygen:

(mass of oxygen) = (mass of magnesium oxide) - (mass of magnesium)

If the mass of the magnesium oxide is too low because some of it was lost before its mass was determined, the mass of the oxygen will also be too low. Since the material was lost after the magnesium was oxidized, the original mass of magnesium was not altered.

The atomic mass of magnesium is determined by the proportion

$$\frac{\text{atomic mass magnesium}}{16} = \frac{\text{mass of magnesium}}{\text{mass of oxygen}} \qquad \text{(RB 13-1)}$$

Consequently, since the original mass of magnesium is unaltered but the mass of oxygen is too small, the ratio on the right side of RB 13-1 is higher than it would be had no magnesium oxide been lost. If the ratio on the right is too high, then so is the ratio on the left. But the atomic mass of oxygen, 16, is being used as a comparison, so its value is constant. Therefore the numerator of the left ratio, the atomic mass of magnesium, must be too high.

13-16   List possible sources of error in this experiment.
Answer   Strictly speaking, insensitivity of the balance is the most important source of error; the following causes of inaccuracy are due to carelessness or poor technique and should be classed as mistakes, not errors.
1.   The equal-arm balance was not calibrated carefully enough.
2.   The determinations of mass may have been done carelessly.
3.   The magnesium ribbon may not have been heated long enough. It may take as long as 45 minutes.
4.   If the lid of the crucible is lifted too high, some of the magnesium oxide may go up in smoke and be lost.

13-17   Suppose the original strip of magnesium contained some impurities that did not react with oxygen and were not driven off during the heating process. Would the atomic mass of magnesium be too high or too low? Justify your answer.
Answer   Too high. The terms on the right side of Equation RB-1 are experimentally determined. The mass of magnesium is too high by the mass of the impurities. The mass of oxygen is too low since the impurities consume no oxygen in the ignition. The ratio on the right, and left, is high. The result for the atomic mass of magnesium will be too high.

There is a brief discussion in the textbook about the concept of atomic number and the periodic variation of atomic properties with atomic number. The periodic table lists the elements in the order of increasing atomic mass. The atomic numbers are the serial numbers in this listing assigning the number 1 to hydrogen, the lightest element. To account for the properties of the elements, physical and chemical, it was found possible to arrange the elements in groups and periods. When it became possible to determine the charge on the atomic nucleus, it was found that the charge on the nucleus of an atom corresponds to this serial number, the atomic number, of the periodic table. The charge on the nucleus equals the number of electrons in the atom. The arrangement of these electrons provides the structure of the atom which in turn is related to the properties of the atom. The relationship between the atomic number and the properties of an element is an outstanding example of the intimate relationship between the structure and properties of matter.

QUESTIONS

In class discussions of these questions, it is instructive to point out where each of the elements mentioned is located on a periodic table.

13-18   What is the difference between the atomic numbers of: (a) helium and neon; (b) neon and argon; (c) fluorine and chlorine?
Answer   (a) 10 - 2 = 8; (b) 18 - 10 = 8; (c) 17 - 9 = 8. (Note: Notice locations of these elements on the periodic table.)

13-19   What is the difference between the atomic numbers of: (a) chlorine and bromine; (b) bromine and iodine; (c) argon and krypton?
Answer   (a) 35 - 17 = 18; (b) 53 - 35 = 18; (c) 36 - 18 = 18. (Note: Notice locations of these elements on the periodic table.)

13-20   Use the periodic table to find at least two places where the sequence of atomic numbers is different from a sequence based on increasing atomic mass.
Answer   Cobalt and nickel, atomic numbers 28 and 29, have atomic masses of 58.9 and 58.7, respectively. Tellurium and iodine, atomic numbers 52 and 53, have atomic masses of 127.6 and 126.9, respectively. Thorium and protactinium, atomic numbers 90 and 91, have atomic masses of 232.05 and 231, respectively. The parentheses about the 231 in the periodic table mean that this element does not occur to any appreciable extent in nature. The most stable isotope of this element has atomic mass 231; its half life is only about 30,000 years.

Section 13-4 SPECTRA AND ENERGY LEVELS

The most important clues as to the nature of the atom, in addition to the chemical clues, were in atomic spectra. As early as 1860, Bunsen and Kirchoff were able to say that gases of atoms and molecules absorb and emit light at certain discrete wavelengths, in contrast to the absorption and emission at all wavelengths by solids. The spectra of gases were used as fingerprints to identify the atoms and molecules present, and it was possible to discover new atoms (cesium, the rare earths, some of the rare gases) by means of spectroscopic observation.

Experiment 13-3 Observations of Various Spectra

Equipment Needed (per 3 students)	*Cat. Number*
3 spectroscopes, cardboard tube type (Note a)	68865
1 lamp, straight line filament (Note b)	68863

Equipment Needed (per 3 students)	*Cat. Number*
2 ceramic sockets, wired (Note b)	68863
1 neon glow lamp (Note c)	68851
1 uncoated fluorescent lamp and fixture (Note d)	68892
1 coated fluorescent lamp and fixture	68891
cellophane paper, 3 pieces each of	
red, 2 in. ✕ 2 in.	68822
blue, 2 in. ✕ 2 in.	68822

Laboratory Notes

(a)   These spectroscopes were used in the experiment in Section 6-2.

(b)   This is the lamp and socket that was used in the experiments in Chapter 4.

(c)   The neon glow lamp also fits into the ceramic socket and operates on 110 volts a.c. The intensity of the neon lamp is such that the students should place the spectroscope slit directly against the glass bulb of the lamp.

(d)   The uncoated fluorescent lamp and fixture are available as a unit. Observation of the light emitted by this lamp can be compared with the light from the fluorescent lamps used in many classrooms.

QUESTIONS

13-21   Describe the source.

Answer   1. An incandescent light bulb is a glowing filament of wire.

2.   A neon sign or glow lamp is a gaseous discharge tube filled with neon gas. Of course, many "neon" signs are filled with other gases or coated with fluorescent material for color effects.

3.   If possible, you should show the students other gaseous discharge tubes to demonstrate that line spectra differ from one element to another.

4.   A fluorescent light is a gaseous discharge tube which is coated on the inside with a fluorescent material. The ultraviolet light emitted by the gaseous discharge causes the fluorescent coating to glow.

5.   Candles are made of paraffin, a substance made up of carbon and hydrogen. The combustion products, with an adequate supply of oxygen, would be carbon dioxide and water. In air, however, the combustion is incomplete, and some of the carbon is heated to incandescence without actually being burned (it can be collected as soot or lamp black on a cool surface).

13-22   Where does the light source gets its energy?

Answer   1. The incandescent light draws its energy from the electrons passing through the filament. The electrons lose energy as they pass through the poorly conducting filament, and it becomes hot.

2.   The neon gas emits light because the electrons passing through collide with and excite the atoms of neon. As those atoms return to a lower energy level they emit light.

3.   The same as (2) above, except for gases other than neon.

4.   A fluorescent light emits light as a result of gaseous discharge. The light so emitted causes the coating on the inside of the tube to fluoresce.

5. Incandescent carbon is the source of the light given off by candles; its energy comes from the heat of combustion.

13-23 Describe the spectrum observed and give the sequence of colors and their relative intensities.

Answer   1. A continuous spectrum from the red through the orange, yellow, green, blue to the violet. The yellow region is the most intense and the intensity decreases toward the red and toward the violet.

2. The neon spectrum consists of many, many bright lines in the red and orange region of the spectrum.

3. The answer to this question depends on which gaseous discharge tubes you show the class.

4. Light from a fluorescent tube consists of the bright-line spectrum of mercury superimposed on the more or less continuous spectrum of the fluorescent coating.

5. The incandescent carbon of a candle flame emits a continuous spectrum containing rather more red and yellow than green and blue light.

13-24 What is the predominant color (or colors) in the spectrum, and how does this compare with the color of the source when viewed without the diffraction grating?

Answer   1. Incandescent light:
   a. Spectrum: All colors are present.
   b. Without grating: all the colors blend to give a yellowish white light.

2. Neon:
   a. Spectrum: red
   b. Without grating: red

3. It depends on the spectra used.

4. Fluorescent light:
   a. Spectrum: Nearly continuous, with a superimposed bright-line spectrum.
   b. Without grating: nearly white

5. Candle flame:
   a. Spectrum: red, orange, and yellow
   b. Without grating: yellow color

The reason for discussing discrete, bright-line spectra is to indicate to the student that they are a primary source of information about the energy levels within the atom. An electron transition from one level to another lower level produces a *photon* with a particular amount of energy. This energy is first of all the difference between the energies of the atom in the two states, before and after, and at the same time it is related to the frequency of the light emitted. By studying the frequencies (or wavelengths) of the spectral lines produced by a given element, we can construct energy-level diagrams for that element.

It is difficult to develop analogies to illuminate our basic ideas about the actual process by which atoms and molecules absorb and emit energy. The processes and the rules which govern them are so far from the realm of human experience that an analogy which fits any one aspect will almost certainly imply other consequences which are known to be incorrect. This is, unfortunately, the case with almost all of atomic and nuclear science, at least.

With this reminder before us, however, it may be useful to present one or two analogies to the emission and absorption of energy by atoms, analogies which cannot be extended beyond their initial limits without danger of serious error.

The means by which scientists were able to infer something of the structure and of the processes of change within the atom from primarily spectroscopic data is baffling to the untrained student. We can perhaps relate the inference of discrete energy levels within the atom, made on the basis of the characteristic, discrete energies it radiates, to the following situation. Assume that we could tell, from the intensity of the sound made by an unseen falling object when it hits the ground, just how far the object had fallen. Since energy and height are directly related, this is equivalent to saying we could determine the energy of the object from the sound it makes when it hits. A careful listener could in this way determine the relative heights above the ground of the windows in a building if someone were to drop things from them.

The hypotheses about energy levels based on emission data were, of course, in accord with those based on the absorption of energy, also a discrete process characteristic of each type of atom. Our analogy can be extended to include this approach by considering another way in which a blindfolded observer could discover something about the height of the windows above the ground. If he were to throw pebbles upward against the face of the building, many would simply bounce and come back down with the same energy as that with which they had been thrown upward. Some, however, would not come back down. They would be the ones throw upward with just the right energy to go through one of the open windows; they would have been "absorbed" by the building.

Section 13-5 REMOVING ELECTRONS FROM ATOMS

The conceptual ideas of this section are clear and should be easily understood by the students. The only puzzling aspect of the subject is likely to be the question of how the energy needed to ionize an atom is given to it. There are various ways, of course, but a very common and easily visualized one involves bombarding the vapor of the element being investigated with electrons and determining the minimum voltage needed to accelerate these electrons sufficiently to cause ionization. This also illustrates clearly the utility of the electron volt as an energy unit.

The use of ionization energies of not only the first electron but of succeeding electrons is a very effective way of establishing the shell model of the atom. Table 13-3 of the text is of prime importance and should be considered in great detail by the class. As is indicated by the blank spaces in the table, not all of the values are known.

QUESTIONS

13-25 The energy required to remove the electron from a hydrogen atom is 13.6 eV. How many joules is this?
Answer   The conversion factor from electron volts to joules is given as

$$1 \text{ eV} = 1.6 \times 10^{-19} \text{ joule}$$

Therefore the amount of energy E in joules is:

$$E = 13.6 \text{ eV} \frac{1.6 \times 10^{-19} \text{ joule}}{1 \text{ eV}}$$

$$= 22 \times 10^{-19} \text{ joule}$$

13-26 Plot the data of Table 13-2 with atomic numbers along the abscissa and ionization energy along the ordinate. What is the difference between the atomic numbers of successive peaks? Compare this answer with your answer to Question 13-18.
Answer   The peaks occur at atomic numbers 2, 10, and 18 (see Figure RB 13-5). The differences between these numbers are 8 and 8. This is the same difference as was obtained in Question 13-18.

13-27 Chemical families have been mentioned. In which family (list the members) do the members have high ionization energies? In which family do the members have low ionization energies?
Answer   High ionization energies: helium, neon, argon. Low ionization energies: lithium, sodium, potassium.

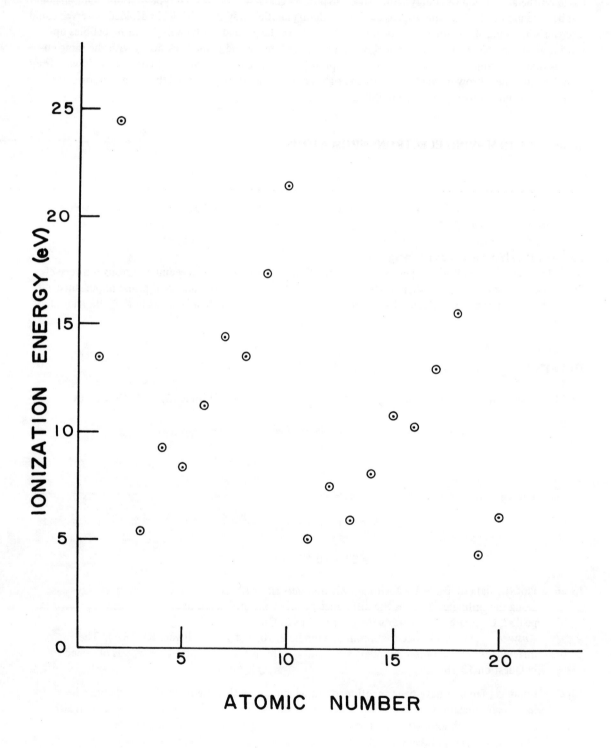

Figure RB 13-5

Section 13-6 THE SHELL MODEL AND CLOUD MODEL OF THE ATOM

Table 13-1 is our evidence for the shell model of the atom. The important feature of the model is the classification of atomic electrons into groups on the basis of energy. These groups came to be known as shells when they were visualized as collections of electrons traveling in circular orbits of about the same radius but in different planes, that is, moving in a spherical shell about the nucleus. The pictorial connotations of the term "shell" are no longer considered in serious discussions about atomic structure, but the classification of electrons into shells on the basis of energy is still very important.

The chemical behavior of atoms is determined by a few electrons, those with the highest energy, which are in the outermost shell. It has been possible to discover rules which can be used to predict the number of electrons in each shell for each kind of atom, and hence it is possible to predict the number of electrons in the shell of highest energy (the *valence shell*). That is the information which is needed to understand why the various atoms form particular ions and molecules. If we want to understand the shapes of molecules, then we need more details about the distribution of the valence electrons in space.

A model for the electron which provides the information about the spatial distribution of the electrons required for an understanding of molecular structure is the cloud model. Each electron in an atom is pictured as a motionless cloud with a characteristic shape and size. Electrons in higher energy shells have larger clouds which are concentrated farther from the nucleus. The clouds for the various electrons in an atom overlap somewhat and crowd together to form one large cloud of negative charge around the nucleus. The electrons which play active roles in the formation of ions and molecules have clouds which are concentrated in the outer regions of the atomic cloud and do not significantly overlap the clouds of other electrons. This is the picture of the atom which is used in Chapter 16 to build up models for molecules. The details of the cloud picture are not required for the development of models for ions, which are the particles of interest in Chapters 14 and 15, so we do not develop the cloud model in detail at this stage of the course. It is sufficient to be able to visualize the electron as a more or less spherical cloud around the nucleus, so that we can think of ions as nuclei surrounded by spherical clouds of negative charge.

QUESTION

13-28   What do scientists mean when they speak of a model? What function does a model serve in science?
Answer   A model is a mental picture of some action or phenomenon which scientists wish to understand, yet which they cannot actually see. This mental picture may, in part, be described by mathematics. Its function is to serve as a hypothesis, an idea, which may be studied and compared with experimental observations. The model should suggest new experiments which will act as a test for the value of the model. If the outcome of these new experiments can be successfully predicted from the model, the model becomes more valuable. If the outcome is contrary to predictions made from the model, it must either be altered or discarded.

13-29   What evidence did Thomson have for the existence of electrons as constituent parts of all atoms?
Answer   The charge-to-mass ratio for electrons in cathode-ray beams is constant (for electrons whose speed does not approach that of light). The charge-to-mass ratio does not depend on the gas in the tube or on the metal of which the cathode is made.

13-30   How many electrons does the sodium atom have? If one electron is removed from each sodium atom, is it still sodium?
Answer   The sodium atom has 11 electrons. If one electron is removed the sodium atom becomes a sodium ion. The chemical properties of the sodium ion differ considerably from those of the sodium atom.

13-31   How was it decided that hydrongen should be element number 1?
Answer   In 1830 Dalton prepared a table of the relative masses (then called weights) of the atoms. He assigned the number 1 to hydrogen, the lightest known element. In 1867 Mendeleev arranged the

200   Models of Atoms

elements in order of their atomic masses and noted the periodic relation between the properties of the elements and their atomic masses. He placed hydrogen in the number one position. Since no element of lower atomic mass than hydrogen has been discovered, hydrogen is still element number one. It is hoped that the student will realize the fundamental nature of this position number when he learns that the atomic number of an element is the charge on the nucleus of an atom and that the nucleus of the hydrogen atom has unit positive charge.

13-32 An electron "falls through" 50 volts. What is its kinetic energy? Express your answer in joules and in electron volts.

Answer $KE = QV$

$Q = 1.6 \times 10^{-19}$ coulomb

$V = 50$ volt

$KE = (1.6 \times 10^{-19} \text{ coulomb})(50 \text{ volt})$

$= 80 \times 10^{-19}$ joule $= 8.0 \times 10^{-18}$ joule

Or

$KE = (1 \text{ electron})(50 \text{ volt}) = 50 \text{ eV}$

13-33 Consider the hypothesis, "The charge carriers responsible for conduction in metals are electrons." What evidence has been presented in Chapter 13 in support of this hypothesis?
Answer Metals such as lithium, beryllium, sodium, magnesium, aluminum, potassium, calcium (see Table 13-2) all have low ionization energies. This means that electrons can be stripped off the atoms of metals rather easily. Once the electron is stripped off, it is much more easily accelerated than the ion it leaves behind, for the mass of the electron is much less than the mass of any metal ion. This evidence is indirect.

REFERENCES

1. Andrews and Kokes, pages 17 to 20; Chapter 3, pages 31 to 62. A brief discussion of atomic structure.

2. (T) Baez, Chapter 48, Sections 48-1 through 48-3, pages 603 to 609. This is a standard treatment, but there are some nicely diagrammed pictures.

3. (T) Chem Study, Chapter 15, Sections 15-1 through 15-1.4, pages 252 to 260. The "notched beam" idea given here is an everyday, simple analogy to energy levels in atomic spectra. The analogy is not exact, but hopefully the use of a greatly different phenomenon having the same type of quantum effect will help to illustrate the principle.

4. (T) Greenstone, *et al.,* insert facing page 84; third page of insert between pages 548 and 549. Good photographs of spectra colors.

5. (T) Lehrman and Swartz, Chapter 21, pages 565 to 569. Again a standard treatment, but the text questions may help lead the student along.

6. Mason, *Main Currents of Scientific Thought,* Development of ideas about the nature of matter.

7. Resnick and Halliday, Chapter 47, pages 1173 to 1197. A more advanced and comprehensive description of light and quantum physics, including the hydrogen atom.

8.   Stevenson and Moore, Chapter 9, Sections 9.1 through 9.6, pages 201 to 212. An intermediate treatment of quantum ideas.

9.   Toulmin and Goodfield, *The Architecture of Matter,* Same as Reference 6.

CHAPTER 14

IONS

By the end of Chapter 13 students have been provided with an electron shell model for atoms, based largely on ionization potentials. This model is now applied specifically to explanations of the formation and behavior of ions. The nature of ionic crystals will be considered in Chapter 15; bonding other than ionic is not discussed until Chapter 16.

Section 14-1 A LOOK BACK AND A LOOK FORWARD

The first experiment in Chapter 14 is an extension of earlier conductivity experiments. This time, however, the emphasis is not on conductivity but on electrolysis. Accordingly, in the first part of Section 14-1 we recall some pertinent things which have already been learned and which will aid us in making this transition.

We have tentatively adopted the hypothesis that the nature of the bonding in crystals of sodium chloride is electrical. It is important that this hypothesis be kept in mind since it motivates the investigations and discussions of Chapters 14 and 15. In this chapter we are looking for additional evidence both to support the hypothesis and to enable us to extend our understanding of the nature of the bonding in sodium chloride. We do this by investigating the conductivity of melts and solutions.

Section 14-2 IONS IN MELTS

This section is devoted entirely to the procedure for performing Experiment 14-1 and to a discussion of the results.

Experiment 14-1 The Effect of an Electric Current on Lead Chloride

---

Since our hypothesis was stated specifically for sodium chloride we would like to use that material here, but it melts at too high a temperature for convenient use in our experiment. We have, therefore, chosen to use lead chloride which melts at a lower temperature. To reduce the melting point still further we are using a mixture consisting of 10% sodium chloride and 90% lead chloride. We make no attempt to explain why the melting point of a mixture is less than that of either of its constituents; however, this phenomenon was previously observed in Experiment 7-2B.

In the electrolysis of the molten mixture of lead chloride and sodium chloride, students should observe: (1) a brown substance diffusing into the liquid from the positive electrode, and (2) a liquid which forms in the loop of the other electrode and solidifies with a metallic appearance when removed from the melt. We will consider the two electrode reactions separately.

Negative Electrode

The liquid collected is lead. The evidence which enables students to conclude that it is lead is that it looks like lead, and that it does not act like sodium. It is soft, gray, and unreactive. If a large enough drop of metal is collected, it might be well to suggest testing it for electrical conductivity.

The metal is not sodium. Sodium reacts violently with water and corrodes readily in air. Students may not be familiar with the reactivity of sodium and the temptation may be great to demonstrate it. We caution against this, however, because it is dangerous. We will infer later that there are sodium ions present in the melt and to make a strong case against sodium here can only contribute to lack of faith in the inference.

Equations for possible reactions at the negative electrode are

$$Pb^{+2} + 2e^- \rightarrow Pb$$

$$Na^+ + e^- \rightarrow Na$$

The energy required for the sodium reaction is much greater than that required for the lead reaction. Consequently, the lead is plated out in preference to the sodium.

Positive Electrode

The main observations students can make at this electrode are that a brown material diffuses into the liquid and that tiny bubbles of gas appear on the electrode. Chlorine is the only gas one would expect to come out of this melt; it can be identified by its pungent odor and its greenish yellow color. We do not recommend, however, that students try to smell the gas in the vicinity of the mouth of a U-tube full of molten salt, and the bubbles are so small that the color of the gas is not evident. In spite of the difficulty in identifying it, we conclude that chlorine is produced at the positive electrode and we infer that chlorine ions were present in the melt. The brown material in the liquid remains a bit mysterious; it is probably largely chlorine dissolved in the liquid, together with some more complex substances from the binding material in the carbon rod. The equation for the reaction taking place at the electrode is

$$2Cl^- \rightarrow Cl_2 + 2e^-$$

At the end of this section the inference is drawn that there were lead and chlorine ions in solid lead chloride. This is quite important since it will support our later conclusion that there are sodium and chlorine ions in table salt crystals. As is pointed out, however, we still do not have strong evidence for this.

If satisfactory results are to be obtained in this experiment, a Bunsen burner must be used. A small propane torch could be substituted, but an alcohol burner will not work. In the absence of sufficient, appropriate burners for individual lab work, the experiment should be done as a demonstration.

Equipment Needed (per 2 students)	Cat. Number
2 pairs, safety glasses	68838
1 pegboard	68852
1 asbestos sheet, 6 in. × 6 in. (Note a)	68532
1 buret clamp (Note b)	68532
1 Bunsen burner	—
1 battery pack (including patch cords, lamp, and socket)	68814
4 flashlight batteries, 1.5 volt	68813

Equipment Needed
(per 2 students)   *Cat. Number*

6 paper fasteners (Note c)	68532
1 U-tube (Note d)	68908
1 carbon rod (Note e)	68886
20 cm, copper wire, No. 22, bare (Note f)	68561
50 grams, lead chloride (Note g)	68534
5 grams, sodium chloride (Note g)	68566
1 pair, needle-nose pliers	68854

Laboratory Notes

(a)   The asbestos sheet should be attached to the pegboard with several of the paper fasteners. It is important that the asbestos sheet be used and that the U-tube be mounted as near the edge of the pegboard as possible. Instruct the students to keep the tip of the inner blue cone of the flame touching the U-tube. This is the hottest part of the flame. The flame should be kept moving up and down on each arm of the tube and back and forth from the front to the back of the tube; it should never be directed toward the pegboard.

(b)   This is the modified clamp that has the threaded end pointed. This was done so the clamp could be screwed into any hole in the pegboard. The clamp jaws are covered with asbestos. The jaws come close enough together to insure a reasonable grip on the glass U-tube.

(c)   Three paper fasteners are to be used to attach the battery box to the pegboard, as outlined in Experiment 12-3. The remaining fasteners are to secure the asbestos sheet to the board, as mentioned earlier.

(d)   The U-tubes have been specially made of 11-mm O.D. hard glass tubing with an arm length of about 10 cm and an inner distance between arms of approximately 1.5 cm.

(e)   The carbon rod is approximately 1/8 inch in diameter and must be at least 4 inches long; it should be connected to the positive terminal of the batteries.

(f)   Needle-nose pliers are needed to make a small loop at one end of the wire. Lead will be electrolytically deposited here, and the small loop will hold a large drop of the liquid metal when the copper electrode is lifted from the U-tube. If held momentarily above the melt, the drop of lead will quickly harden.

(g)   The chemical mixture used contains about 10% sodium chloride. The reason for this is that the melting point of pure lead chloride (501 °C) is too high for the Bunsen flame. By adding the sodium chloride, a mixture is obtained that does melt. Ideally both chemicals should be in powder form or in very fine crystals. This permits one to obtain a more homogeneous mixture which is less difficult to melt.

QUESTIONS

14-1 What did the glowing light bulb indicate?
  Answer The glowing light bulb indicated that the mixture of lead and sodium chlorides conducted a current.

14-2 On which electrode did bubbles of gas appear?

Answer   Bubbles of gas appeared on the carbon rod, which was the positive electrode.

14-3 What could the gas be that formed the bubbles?

Answer   Since lead and sodium are known to be metals, the most likely gas is chlorine.

14-4 Why do you suppose the melt in one arm of the U-tube turned light brown? Which electrode was in this arm?

Answer   Chlorine was given off at the carbon electrode, which was positive. Some of the chlorine probably either reacted at the carbon electrode or dissolved in the melt to cause the brown color.

14-5 Did the appearance of either electrode change? Describe what you saw.

Answer   The copper wire electrode changed. It became coated with a dull gray metal.

Section 14-3 INTRODUCTION TO THE USE OF CHEMICAL EQUATIONS

Chemical symbols and formulas have been used earlier; for example, the formula H_2O was used to represent water. Now it is time to explain such symbols in some detail.

The chemical formula for a substance (including both elements and compounds) expresses, in symbols, its composition. Care must be taken to distinguish among the formulas as follows. Most elemental gases at STP are diatomic: $H_2, O_2, N_2, F_2, Cl_2, Br_2, I_2$. This is explained later in the textbook, but it means that a molecule of each such gas consists of two atoms, and that a mole of the gas consists of two moles of atoms. The formula of a molecular compound, for example, H_2O and CH_4 (methane), describes the number of each kind of atom in a molecule. The formula CH_4 represents a molecule of methane. It consists of one atom of carbon and four atoms of hydrogen. This formula also represents a mole of methane. A mole of CH_4 consists of one mole (6.02×10^{23} atoms) of carbon and four moles of hydrogen atoms combined in such a way as to form one mole of methane gas (6.02×10^{23} molecules).

The commonly used formula for table salt NaCl, however, is not strictly in keeping with these ideas. Individual sodium ions and chlorine ions do not join with one another to form stable pairs in the solid state. The forces between them are such that they tend to associate in groups containing many, but equal numbers, of each. When a sodium chloride crystal is melted or dissolved, the ions tend to separate again into individual units. Thus the NaCl formula merely represents the fact that in a crystal, the ratio of sodium ions to chlorine ions is 1 : 1. The same interpretation can be attached to the formula for any ionic compound. For example, the formula $CuBr_2$ describes a material which contains twice as many bromine as copper ions.

The burning of magnesium is described by the symbolic expression

$$Mg + O_2 \rightarrow MgO$$

As an expression, this simply states that magnesium (Mg) combines with oxygen (O_2) to yield ($\rightarrow$) magnesium oxide (MgO). To make the expression quantitative it must be balanced. The subscripts are fixed; therefore, balancing is done by introducing coefficients:

$$2Mg + O_2 \rightarrow 2MgO$$

The equation now reads, "Two moles of magnesium react with one mole of oxygen to yield two moles of magnesium oxide."

The balancing of equations of this kind is based on the conservation of atoms. The number of atoms of each element must be the same on both sides of the arrow. To balance an expression such as

$$N_2 + H_2 \rightarrow NH_3$$

we might begin by saying that only half of the nitrogen atoms on the left are accounted for on the right, and write

$$\tfrac{1}{2}N_2 + H_2 \rightarrow NH_3$$

Then we might observe that 1½ of the H_2 molecule would also account for the total of 3 hydrogen atoms on the right and write

$$\tfrac{1}{2}N_2 + \tfrac{3}{2}H_2 \rightarrow NH_3$$

This expression is now a balanced equation. If the formulas are to represent molecules, however, one must now get rid of all fractions by doubling all coefficients:

$$N_2 + 3H_2 \rightarrow 2NH_3$$

The equations

$$2Cl^- \rightarrow Cl_2 + 2e^-$$

and

$$Pb^{+2} + 2e^- \rightarrow Pb$$

are balanced since the number of atoms is the same on both sides. Note that such equations need also to be balanced electrically in order to describe the conservation of charge.

QUESTIONS

14-6 The equation for the combination of hydrogen and oxygen to form water is: $2H_2 + O_2 \rightarrow 2H_2O$. List all the information which you obtain by inspecting this equation.

Answer   Two moles (or two molecules) of hydrogen combine with one mole (or one molecule) of oxygen to form two moles (or two molecules) of water.

Note that although the number of atoms is conserved, the number of molecules is not. Each hydrogen and oxygen molecule contains two atoms; a water molecule contains two atoms of hydrogen and one of oxygen.

14-7 Magnesium reacts at high temperatures with the nitrogen of the air, forming magnesium nitride Mg_3N_2. Write an equation for the reaction of magnesium with nitrogen.

Answer $3Mg + N_2 \rightarrow Mg_3N_2$.

Section 14-4 IONS IN SOLUTION

The preliminary demonstration in this section is essential. The goal is to observe that copper ions in solution seem to produce a color and that some deposit on the negative electrode as copper atoms. Similarly, the negative ions migrate to the positive electrode where they are liberated as gas molecules.

Experiment 14-2 Migration of Ions

What is observed in the experiment is a change in color, from colorless to the characteristic blue of hydrated copper ions, as these ions migrate into the liquid around the negative electrode. Somewhat later a change in color, from colorless to brown will be observed in the liquid around the positive electrode. In addition, some copper is plated on the negative electrode and some gaseous bromine is formed (and may be detected by its odor) at the positive electrode.

The electrically caused migration of colors suggests that there were charged particles, ions, in the gel. The electrode reactions are

$$Cu^{+2} + 2e^- \rightarrow Cu$$

and

$$2Br^- \rightarrow Br_2 + 2e^-$$

Equipment Needed (per demonstration team)	*Cat. Number*
1 alcohol (or Bunsen) burner	68810
2 pairs, safety glasses	68838
1 pegboard	68852
1 buret clamp, modified	68532
2 battery packs	68814
8 flashlight batteries	68813
1 U-tube (Note a)	68909
2 carbon rods (Note b)	68886
1 balance	68831
2 beakers, 250 ml (Note c)	68815
1 stirring rod	68867
10 grams, cupric bromide (Note d)	68523
100 ml nitric acid, 2% (Note e)	68541
1 pkg, unflavored gelatin	68530

Laboratory Notes

(a) The U-tube is larger than the one used in Experiment 14-1. It is made from 2-cm O.D. hard glass, and has an arm length of approximately 6 in. with 2-3 in. between the arms.

(b) The rods are the same type as used in Experiment 14-1. Clean them carefully, however, before reusing them in this demonstration.

(c) The two beakers are used to prepare the gelatin and the cupric bromide solutions.

(d) Cupric bromide can be obtained in 10-gram vials; one vial should be enough for several demonstrations.

(e) The nitric acid can be obtained as a 2% solution; one would then use it without further dilution. If additional 2% nitric acid is required, it can be prepared according to the instructions which follow.

Preparation of Solutions (Time: about 20 minutes)

1. The gel: Heat 25 ml of water to boiling, turn off the source of heat, and place 1.2 grams of unflavored gelatin into the water with constant stirring. When it has dissolved proceed to the next part while the gelatin cools. If you prefer, you may use 0.175 gram of agar in 25 ml of hot water. When the copper bromide solution is added, it will gel without refrigeration.

    Dissolve about 2.5 grams of copper (cupric) bromide in 25 ml of cold water. This should result in a greenish blue solution.

    Check the temperature of the gelatin. When it is 35 to 40°C pour the solution of copper (cupric) bromide into it while stirring.

    Pour this mixture into a U-tube until each arm is filled to an inch or two past the curved portion. Place the U-tube in a beaker and then in a refrigerator so that the gelatin will stiffen. This may require at least one-half hour in the refrigerator. It can be left in the refrigerator until it is needed for use.

2. The 2% nitric acid: Pour 5 ml of concentrated nitric acid into 50 ml of water while stirring. (A rule of safety is always to pour the heavier liquid into the lighter liquid.) Let this mixture cool. It can be kept until needed if it is prepared ahead of time.

Preparation for Demonstrations

1. Mount the U-tube on a pegboard. Slowly pour the cool 2% solution of nitric acid on top of the gel mixture in the U-tube. Pour until there is about 1 in. of clear nitric acid above the blue gel mixture.
2. Place a carbon electrode into the clear solution of nitric acid in each arm of the U-tube so that the bottom of the carbon rod is about 1/2 in. from the gel.
3. A 12-volt d.c. source is needed for this electrolysis. To obtain this connect two battery packs in series.

Demonstration

Connect the carbon electrodes in the U-tube in series with the two battery packs. There will then be approximately 12 volts potential difference between them. When this is done you will probably observe some small gas bubbles at each electrode. These are hydrogen and oxygen.

QUESTION

14-8 Explain what you have observed.

Answer   Hydrated copper ions, which are blue, are attracted to the negative electrode. Some of these ions are neutralized by losing their charge at the negative electrode, and are deposited as copper atoms.

Bromine ions, which are colorless, are attracted to the positive electrode where they are neutralized and become bromine atoms. The atoms immediately form bromine molecules. Most of the bromine molecules dissolve in the clear solution causing it to turn light brown.

Section 14-5 ELECTROLYSIS OF SOLUTIONS

We have previously found ions in a melt and in a gel. Now we ask whether they are present in water solutions, specifically, solutions of lead nitrate and of sodium chloride.

Experiment 14-3

Part A Electrolysis of Lead Nitrate

In the electrolysis of lead nitrate, we observe that lead plates out at the negative electrode and a color-less gas is produced at the positive electrode. The appearance of metallic lead is to be regarded as evidence for the exitence of lead ions, which, with their positive charge, move to the negative electrode. The color-less gas is actually oxygen. The electrode reactions and their corresponding electrode potentials are

$$2e^- + Pb^{+2} \rightarrow Pb \qquad \text{(-0.13 volt)}$$

$$2H_2O \rightarrow O_2 + 4H^+ + 4e^- \text{ (-1.23 volt)}$$

Part B Electrolysis of Sodium Chloride

In the electrolysis of a solution of sodium chloride, we might expect to find sodium plating out at the negative electrode and chlorine at the positive electrode:

$$Na^+ + e^- \rightarrow Na \qquad \text{(-2.71 volt)}$$

$$2Cl^- \rightarrow Cl_2 + 2e^- \qquad \text{(-1.36 volt)}$$

The electrode reaction for the production of chlorine does take place, as evidenced by the appearance of Cl_2 gas at the electrode. The electrode reaction for the production of sodium does not occur, however; it cannot compete with the production of hydrogen according to the electrode reaction

$$\tfrac{1}{2}H_2O + e^- \rightarrow \tfrac{1}{2}H_2 + OH^- \text{ (-0.83 volt)}$$

Thus hydrogen gas is evolved at the negative electrode.

If the students do not get a small pop when they place a lighted match over the mouth of the U-tube which contains the copper wire, cover the mouth of the tube with a small piece of cardboard. Make a slit in the cardboard to straddle the copper wire. Permit the current to pass through the solution for about 5 minutes; then lift one edge of the cardboard and quickly apply a lighted match to the mouth of the tube.

Chlorine gas is identified by means of a potassium iodide-starch paper test. This test depends on the fact that free iodine turns starch blue (deep blue — nearly black). Chlorine replaces the iodine ions, form-ing chlorine ions and free iodine, and the iodine then reacts with the starch. The reactions are

$$Cl_2 + 2I^- \rightarrow I_2 + 2Cl^-$$

$$I_2 + \text{starch} \rightarrow \text{blue product}$$

The potassium iodide paper must be wet when used.

Note in this section a heavy dependence on the idea that when two reactions are possible the one that will occur is the one which either (1) *requires* the lesser amount of energy or (2) *produces* the larger amount of energy.

Equipment Needed (per 2 students)	*Cat. Number*
2 pairs, safety glasses	68838
1 pegboard	68852
1 buret clamp	68532
1 battery pack (including patch cords, lamp, and socket)	68814
4 flashlight batteries, 1.5 volt	68813
3 paper fasteners	68532
1 U-tube, small	68908
1 carbon rod	68986
1 copper wire, 10 cm, No. 22, bare	68561
10 ml, lead nitrate solution (Note a)	68535
10 ml, sodium chloride solution (Note a)	68566
1 box, safety matches	68539
1 vial, potassium iodide-starch paper	68552

Laboratory Note

(a)   Each pair of students will need about 10 ml of each chemical solution. To prepare sufficient lead nitrate solution for a lab section of 24 students, dissolve 36 grams of $Pb(NO_3)_2$ in 120 ml of water.

The same amount of sodium chloride solution is made by adding 12 grams of NaCl to 120 ml of water. Salt dissolves very slowly so occasional stirring helps. Since the solubility of sodium chloride changes very little with a change in temperature, no advantage is gained by heating the solution.

QUESTIONS

14-9   Did you notice any difference between the solution in the negative (copper wire) electrode side and that in the positive (carbon rod) electrode side in Part A? in Part B?
Answer   In Part A there was no visible change in the solution in either arm of the U-tube, although there were reactions at the electrodes. In Part B the solution around the positive carbon rod turned to a yellowish-green color.

14-10   Was the product formed at the copper electrode the same for the lead nitrate solution as for the lead chloride melt?
Answer   Yes. The copper electrodes were coated with lead in both cases.

14-11   In Parts A and B, at which electrodes did you observe an evolution of gas?
Answer   In Part A gas is given off at the positive electrode. The gas is oxygen, although the student has no way to identify it. In Part B gas is given off at both electrodes. Hydrogen is liberated at the negative electrode whereas chlorine is liberated at the positive electrode.

14-12 Look at the diagram in Figure 14-2 and trace the path of the current from the battery through the bulb and back to the battery.
Answer   Starting at the negative end of the battery the current passes through the clip lead, the wire filament of the bulb, electrode W, the melt, electrode R, and back to the battery.

14-13 The symbol for a lead ion is Pb^{+2}. The addition of two electrons converts the lead ion to a lead atom. Write an equation to show the reaction.
Answer
$$Pb^{+2} + 2e^- \rightarrow Pb$$

14-14 The expression $H_2O + e^- \rightarrow H_2 + (OH)^-$ represents the reaction at one of the electrodes. Write it as a balanced equation.
Answer
$$2H_2O + 2e^- \rightarrow H_2 + 2(OH)^-$$

14-15 Identify the carriers by means of which the charges are conducted through the various parts of the circuit, excluding the battery, in the electrolysis of the sodium chloride solution.
Answer   The carriers of the charges in the metal wires and the filament of the light bulb are mobile electrons. The charges are carried through the sodium chloride solution by the Na^+ and Cl^- ions. There are initially small concentrations of H^+ and $(OH)^-$ which make a negligible contribution to the current.

Section 14-6 CHEMICAL PROPERTIES OF IONS AND ATOMS

The examples of sodium and chlorine in the textbook indicate that a loss or gain of one or two electrons per atom results in the production of totally different substances: ions, for example, sodium ions and chlorine ions.

Section 14-7 BEHAVIOR OF IONS

We turn in this section to a more careful and systematic consideration of the behavior of ions. We finally accept the hypothesis that Na^+ and Cl^- ions make up crystalline sodium chloride, a topic to which we will return in Chapter 15.

Section 14-8 REPLACEMENT OF IONS

Almost all of this section is devoted to Experiment 14-4 and a discussion of the results.

Experiment 14-4 Replacement of Ions

Equipment Needed (per student)	Cat. Number
3 paper cups, plastic lined (Note a)	68896
6 paper cups, 1 oz (Note a)	68897
3 grams, lead nitrate crystals (Note b)	68535
3 grams, copper nitrate crystals (Note b)	68525

Equipment Needed (per student)	*Cat. Number*
3 grams, silver nitrate crystals (Note b)	68547
3 paper envelopes, or (Note c)	68528
3 paper weighing cups (Note c)	68823
1 plastic bag and tie wrap	68853
1 piece, steel wool	68902
3 pieces, lead wire or strips	68843
3 silver dimes (Note d)	–
3 pennies	–
3 wooden stir sticks (Note e)	68562

Laboratory Notes

(a)   These paper cups have a capacity of 6 oz and are to be used to prepare each solution. They should be filled one-third to one-half full of water, although the amount is not really critical.

   The cups should have plastic linings since the solution may remain in them for some time and they must not leak. For this reason, styrofoam cups are normally not satisfactory. The smaller cups are to be used to divide each solution into three portions. Do not use aluminum or iron cups. These cups will dissolve by reacting with the silver and copper salts.

(b)   For economic reasons, 1 lb each of lead nitrate and copper nitrate should be purchased. The silver nitrate, however, should be purchased in 4-oz bottles. This amount is to supply 25 students.

(c)   The paper envelopes are to be used if the experiment is to be a take-home. These envelopes are the type doctors use to dispense medicine (1 in. × 2 in.). After the chemicals have been placed in the envelopes, the ends should be folded twice and sealed with a stapler. If the experiment is done during the regular laboratory period, it would be more convenient to distribute the chemicals in the paper weighing cups. There would be no problem about filling the cups ahead of time since all three substances are stable in air. There might be a small amount of discoloration, but this would not affect the results. The plastic bag is to be used to carry everything home, in case this is a take-home experiment.

(d)   Since dimes are rarely silver these days, it is recommended that small pieces of silver foil (obtainable from any laboratory supply house) be substituted.

(e)   These are the sticks supplied for the destructive distillation of wood. The students use them to facilitate the preparation of the three solutions. If your supply is short and you give each student only one stick, be sure to have him rinse it after each use.

   The expected results of this Experiment are summarized in Table RB 14-1; for best results, use distilled water and metals with uncontaminated surfaces.

   If any of these results are not observed within a reasonable time (the lead replacements are likely to occur slowly), allow the solutions to stand for a while – until the next class meeting, perhaps. Again the reactions are presented as competitions for electrons. The possible changes are expressed in the equations immediately following Table RB 14-1.

Table RB 14-1

Metal	Solution		
	Lead Nitrate	Copper Nitrate	Silver Nitrate
Lead	no reaction	reddish deposit of copper	black deposit of silver
Copper	no reaction	no reaction	black deposit of silver
Silver	no reaction	no reaction	no reaction

$$Pb \rightleftharpoons Pb^{+2} + 2e^- \quad (0.13 \text{ volt})$$

$$Cu \rightleftharpoons Cu^{+2} + 2e^- \quad (-0.34 \text{ volt})$$

$$Ag \rightleftharpoons Ag^+ + e^- \quad (-0.80 \text{ volt})$$

Thus we would expect a replacement series to be: Pb replaces Cu replaces Ag.

The reaction couples which occur are

$$1. \ Pb \rightarrow Pb^{+2} + 2e^-$$

$$Cu^{+2} + 2e^- \rightarrow Cu$$

$$2. \ Pb \rightarrow Pb^{+2} + 2e^-$$

$$2Ag^+ + 2e^- \rightarrow 2Ag$$

$$3. \ Cu \rightarrow Cu^{+2} + 2e^-$$

$$2Ag^+ + 2e^- \rightarrow 2Ag$$

Caution regarding the "electron-acquisition competition list": the list which the students establish here is based purely on their own experiments and may or may not coincide with tables of electromotive series in references. Such tables are based on data collected under standard conditions which are not the same as those in the student experiments.

QUESTIONS

14-16 Which of the metals (lead, silver, and copper) was coated with another metal when it was taken from the lead nitrate solution? the silver nitrate solution? the copper nitrate solution?
Answer   None of the metals are coated when taken from the lead nitrate solution; lead and copper are both coated with black silver when taken from the silver nitrate solution. Lead is coated with copper when in copper nitrate, but silver is not.

14-17 Which of the solutions changed color?
Answer   When lead was submerged in copper sulfate, the blue color decreased in intensity as the blue copper ions changed to copper atoms. The silver nitrate containing the copper metal became pale blue as the copper atoms changed to copper ions.

14-18   Give a reason for any color change in the solutions.
         Answer   Any color change is due to copper atoms changing to copper ions or vice versa.

14-19   If a piece of iron were placed in a silver nitrate solution, do you think it would become coated with silver?
         Answer   The iron wire would become coated with silver (see Question 14-40).

Section 14-9 COMBINATION

This section is devoted to Experiment 14-5 and to a discussion of the results

---

Experiment 14-5 Combining Zinc and Iodine (A Demonstration)

So far all our experiments in this chapter have consisted of taking apart ionic substances. A very logical question is, "Can you put elements together and have them form ions?" The reaction chosen to illustrate that this can be done is that of zinc and iodine. This experiment is best done as a demonstration since it involves the production of rather large amounts of iodine vapor. It is easily performed, however, so it is suitable as a demonstration to be done by students. Sufficient directions to do the experiment are given in the textbook.

The reaction is quick and violent when water is added to the mixed zinc and iodine. Considerable heat is evolved, and the result is that much of the iodine is vaporized. The solid product does not look like crystalline zinc iodide; it is a dark mess. After standing, however, visible zinc iodide crystals do form. The equations for the combination of zinc and iodine are:

$$Zn \rightarrow Zn^{+2} + 2e^-$$

$$I_2 + 2e^- \rightarrow 2I^-$$

The student performing the demonstration should indicate to his classmates any changes which they cannot observe, such as the evolution of heat.

It is mentioned in the textbook that the energy of attraction between the ions in a crystal can be calculated. This energy, which is called the lattice energy of the crystal, cannot be measured directly, for there is no convenient way to separate the ions in a crystal to distances where they no longer exert coulombic forces on each other. The lattice energy can be determined indirectly from experimental data in the following way.

The lattice energy is the energy produced when the separated ions are brought together to form a crystal, for example,

$$Na^+(g) + Cl^-(g) \rightarrow NaCl(s)$$

Here we use (g) to identify a gas and (s) to identify a solid. Although this process can not be carried out directly, it can be carried out in several steps for which the energies can be measured:

$Na^+(g) \rightarrow Na(g)$	+118.5 kcal/mole
$Na(g) \rightarrow Na(s)$	+25.9 kcal/mole
$Cl^-(g) \rightarrow 1/2\ Cl_2(g)$	-58.1 kcal/mole
$Na(s) + 1/2\ Cl_2(g) \rightarrow NaCl(s)$	+98.2 kcal/mole

$Na^+(g) + Cl^-(g) \rightarrow NaCl(s)$	+184.5 kcal/mole

The energies given above are all treated as energies *produced*. If they were treated as energies *required*, then the signs would be reversed. You will note above that when you add the first four chemical equations and the associated energies you arrive at the defining equation for lattice energy, and the value of the lattice energy for solid sodium chloride, 184.5 kcal/mole.

As described in these notes, this demonstration is not dangerous. The instructions should be followed closely, however, since it is possible to produce copious quantities of iodine vapor at the start of the reaction. This vapor is an irritant and is toxic.

Equipment Needed (per demonstration)	Cat. Number
3.2 grams, iodine, powdered (Note a)	68841
0.8 grams, zinc, powdered (Note a)	68841
1 test tube, 25 × 150 mm (Note b)	68873
1 cork stopper, loose fitting	68859
1 pegboard and clamp	68852
1 medicine dropper	68845
1 beaker, 400 ml	68884
1 spatula	68864
1 mortar and pestle	—
1 pair, safety glasses	68838

Laboratory Notes

(a) Vials containing the proper amounts of powdered zinc and iodine already mixed together are available. If these are used, you need only to pour the contents of one vial into the test tube, and everything is ready to go. If you prepare your own mixture, be sure to follow carefully the instructions given below.

Grind 3.2 grams of iodine crystals in a mortar until the particle size is small. Do not inhale the vapor of the iodine. Pour the powdered iodine onto a square of paper. Add 0.8 gram of powdered zinc and mix thoroughly by tumbling, or with a spatula. Pour the mixture into a 6-in. test tube. The reaction occurs rapidly only if the zinc and iodine are of small particle size, are well mixed, and a small amount of water is present.

(b) The test tube is to be used with the small pegboard clamp. The cork must fit properly.

The following notes outline the procedure for demonstrating the reaction and offer suggestions on how to dispose of the chemicals after the reaction has occurred.

With the test tube held in a clamp, and with a loosely fitting stopper ready, cautiously drop 2 or 3 drops of water onto the mixture. Place the cork in the test tube to prevent the escape of iodine vapor. The reaction is visible as a sudden surge of iodine vapor, and the test tube becomes hot. The contents of the test tube, when the reaction subsides, will be a dark-colored semisolid. After standing for several hours this mixture usually begins to crystallize, forming colorless crystals of zinc iodide.

If crystallization does not begin, cautiously add about 1 ml of water to the test tube and let the contents stand until the dark color of iodine has disappeared. Then decant the clear liquid into a separate, small beaker or evaporating dish and allow it to stand in a warm place until the water evaporates and crystallization begins.

The reason that the decantation step may be necessary is that the reaction is often incomplete, leaving both zinc and iodine unreacted. After standing in the presence of water, the reaction can go to completion. If zinc remains, it must be separated by decantation. Some zinc hydroxide may also be formed as a white flocculent precipitate which is also separated in the decantation step.

The reaction takes place very slowly without water. Apparently the water functions to give some hydrogen iodide by reaction with iodine, and this may serve to initiate the reaction on the surface of the zinc.

QUESTIONS

14-20   Was there a chemical reaction? What visible evidence supports your conclusion?
Answer   Yes. The evidence was the formation of heat and the formation of a new substance.

14-21   Was energy liberated? What evidence do you have for your answer?
Answer   Energy was liberated as shown by the evolution of heat.

14-22   What caused the purple color?
Answer   The purple color was caused by the sublimation of some of the iodine.

14-23   Can you guess what the product of the reaction might be?
Answer   A logical guess is that the product is zinc iodide.

14-24   How might one decompose the product formed during this demonstration? Would an energy change be a part of that reaction?
Answer   Zinc iodide can be decomposed electrolytically or by heating to a high temperature. Energy must be supplied to decompose zinc iodide.

14-25   Write an equation for the process of forming a zinc ion from a zinc atom.
Answer
$$Zn \rightarrow Zn^{+2} + 2e^-$$

14-26   Write an equation for the process of forming an iodine ion from an iodine atom.
Answer
$$I + e^- \rightarrow I^-$$

14-27   Modify the equation you wrote as an answer to Question 14-26 to take account of the fact that the iodine molecule has two atoms.
Answer
$$I_2 + 2e^- \rightarrow 2I^-$$

14-28   Combine the two equations (from Questions 14-25 and 14-27) by addition to obtain an equation for the overall reaction.
Answer
$$Zn \rightarrow Zn^{+2} + 2e^-$$
$$I_2 + 2e^- \rightarrow 2I^-$$
$$\overline{Zn + I_2 \rightarrow Zn^{+2} + 2I^-}$$

14-29   What is the ratio of zinc ions to iodine ions in zinc iodide? What is the ratio of magnesium ions to chlorine ions in magnesium chloride? Write the formulas for these compounds. (*Hint:* compounds are neutral.)
Answer   The ratio of zinc ions to iodine ions in zinc iodide is 1 : 2. The ratio of magnesium ions to chlorine ions in magnesium chloride is also 1 : 2.

Zinc iodide: ZnI_2

Magnesium chloride: $MgCl_2$

14-30   What do you predict will be the behavior of oxygen (atomic number 8) with respect to a gain or loss of electrons? Write an equation to show this.

Answer   The second electron shell needs two electrons to reach a stable configuration of eight, therefore

$$O + 2e^- \rightarrow O^{-2}$$

or more properly

$$O_2 + 4e^- \rightarrow 2O^{-2}$$

14-31   Write a reaction for the formation of magnesium ions (atomic number 12) and combine this with the oxygen reaction (Question 14-30) to obtain the equation for the reaction of magnesium with oxygen.

Answer

$$Mg \rightarrow Mg^{+2} + 2e^-$$

$$\frac{O + 2e^- \rightarrow O^{-2}}{Mg + O \rightarrow Mg^{+2} + O^{-2} \ (\text{or } Mg^{+2} \ O^{-2})}$$

14-32   Is the formula for magnesium oxide, which was given without evidence in Experiment 13-2, consistent with our model of the electron transfer for formation of chemical compounds?

Answer   It is consistent since magnesium needs to lose two electrons to reach a stable configuration and oxygen needs to gain two electrons. The two electrons transfer from the magnesium to the oxygen.

14-33   What happened to the wire made of lead in copper nitrate? Can you interpret this in terms of electron transfers? Both the lead and the copper ions have a charge of +2 in these reactions.

Answer   Each lead atom gave up two electrons and each copper ion gained two electrons in the nitrate solution.

14-34   Write an equation for each of the two electron-transfer ionic reactions of Question 14-33. Multiply each by some number so that the number of electrons lost in one reaction will be equal to the number of electrons gained in the other reaction.

Answer

$$Pb \rightarrow Pb^{+2} + 2e^-$$

$$\frac{Cu^{+2} + 2e^- \rightarrow Cu}{Pb + Cu^{+2} \rightarrow Pb^{+2} + Cu}$$

Section 14-10 OXIDATION AND REDUCTION

This is a historical treatment of the definitions of oxidation and reduction. The *-ous* and *-ic* endings are of small importance because the recent trend is to identify specific oxidation states as follows: cuprous ion Cu^+ is now referred to as copper (I) ion; and cupric ion Cu^{+2} is now referred to as copper (II) ion. What is more important is the idea that an oxidation does not take place without a simultaneous reduction, and vice versa; that is, electrons are conserved.

Section 14-11 CELLS

This section involves the construction of a simple cell and the testing of its operation.

Experiment 14-6 An Electric Current by Electron Transfer

The experimental cell involves the following reactions:

$$Mg \rightarrow Mg^{+2} + 2e^- \qquad \text{(+2.37 volts)}$$

$$\frac{Cu^{+2} + 2e^- \rightarrow Cu \qquad \text{(+0.34 volts)}}{Mg + Cu^{+2} \rightarrow Mg^{+2} + Cu \qquad \text{(+2.71 volts)}}$$

Magnesium is being used as one of the electrodes to obtain enough potential difference to light a low-current flashlight bulb. An open-circuit potential of 2.71 volts is obtained when a magnesium-copper couple is used in an electrolyte of one molar concentration. Zinc, which is more commonly used with copper in a couple, will give only 1.1 volts.

$$Zn \rightarrow Zn^{+2} + 2e^- \qquad \text{(0.76 volts)}$$

$$\frac{Cu^{+2} + 2e \rightarrow Cu \qquad \text{(0.34 volts)}}{Zn + Cu^{+2} \rightarrow Zn^{+2} + Cu \qquad \text{(1.10 volts)}}$$

The electrons released by magnesium are given off to the wire and flow to the carbon rod where they are accepted by Cu^{+2} ions to form copper metal. (The electrons accepted by Cu^{+2} are not necessarily the same ones yielded up by Mg.) As a result three things happen: (1) the magnesium rod slowly dissolves, (2) copper is plated on the carbon rod, and (3) an electric current exists in the external circuit (i.e., through the bulb).

Equipment Needed
(per 2 students)

	Cat. Number
1 beaker, 400 ml	68884
1 porous battery cup (Note a)	68883
1 socket and connecting wires from battery box kits	68814
1 light bulb, 60 ma (Note b)	68814
1 carbon rod, 3-4 in. long	68886
1 piece, magnesium ribbon, 3-4 in. long (Note b)	68537
100 ml, magnesium sulfate solution, 1 M (Note c)	68538
200 ml, copper sulfate solution, 1 M (Note d)	68526
1 pegboard and clamps	68852
1 piece, steel wool	68902

Laboratory Notes

(a)   The porous cup is 40 mm in diameter and 90 mm high. It is helpful to soak it overnight in a saturated solution of magnesium sulfate before it is used in this experiment; this allows the conducting solution to penetrate into the walls of the cup.

(b) A low-current bulb must be used. If it does not light when connected into the apparatus, the most probable trouble is a thin oxide coating on the magnesium ribbon. Take a new piece of ribbon, scrape it carefully and then quickly place it in the magnesium sulfate solution. When you attach the alligator clip to the top of the ribbon, move the jaws around slightly so that they make good electrical connection with it.

(c) The concentration of the solutions is not really critical. Add 25 grams of $MgSO_4$ to 100 ml of water and stir to dissolve. This will produce the proper amount of solution per pair of lab students. If technical grade chemicals are used, there may be a little undissolved material. This presents no problem.

(d) To prepare the copper sulfate solution, place 200 ml of water in a beaker and add 50 grams of copper sulfate. After this has dissolved, put the presoaked, porous battery cup in the beaker.

Magnesium was chosen as one of the electrodes because it has a high oxidation potential in solution, +2.37 volts. This is necessary in order that the output of the cell be sufficient to light the bulb. The carbon rod plainly shows the metallic copper being deposited upon it. Once the carbon becomes plated with copper, the electrode behaves as a copper electrode. The oxidation potential of copper is -0.34 volt. This coupled with magnesium will give a voltage for the cell of 2.71 volts in 1 molar solutions. The copper sulfate and magnesium sulfate solutions should contain about 25 grams per 100 ml water.

Bubbles of gas will be observed escaping from the magnesium ribbon submerged in the magnesium solution. The gas is hydrogen which is produced by the action of magnesium in a water solution. The magnesium becomes negatively charged during the cell reaction, and some of the water molecules are reduced to form hydrogen.

QUESTIONS

14-35 Why did the bulb light up?
Answer Charge passed through it.

14-36 What is the source of the energy?
Answer The chemical reactions.

14-37 Write half-reaction equations to describe what is happening at each electrode.
Answer
$$Mg \rightarrow Mg^{+2} + 2e^-$$
$$Cu^{+2} + 2e^- \rightarrow Cu$$

14-38 In which direction are the electrons flowing through the wire; from magnesium to carbon or from carbon to magnesium?
Answer The electrons flow from the magnesium to the carbon rod.

14-39 Why does one electrode appear to have partially dissolved while the other one has a deposit on it?
Answer The more active metal loses its electrons to form ions and goes into solution. The less active metal ions in the solution gain the electrons and are deposited as metal atoms.

QUESTIONS

14-40 Following is an electron-acquisition competition list such as you constructed earlier in this chapter.

Element	Symbol
Lithium	Li
Potassium	K
Sodium	Na
Magnesium	Mg
Zinc	Zn
Chromium	Cr
Iron	Fe
Cobalt	Co
Nickel	Ni
Tin	Sn
Hydrogen	H
Copper	Cu
Silver	Ag

Name two elements which will react with water to form hydrogen at room temperature. Name two elements which will not so react.

Answer   Lithium, potassium, and sodium will readily react with water to form hydrogen. Copper and silver definitely will not.

14-41   You observed a gas escaping from the magnesium electrode in Experiment 14-6. What is this gas? How can you prove this experimentally?

Answer   The gas escaping from the magnesium electrode is hydrogen. The gas could be collected and tested with a lighted splinter.

14-42   In an electrolysis experiment, at which electrode does oxidation take place? At which electrode does reduction take place?

Answer   Oxidation takes place at the positive electrode, reduction at the negative.

14-43   Two chemical reactions you have seen or investigated yourself are the reaction of zinc with iodine and the reaction of a sodium chloride solution with silver nitrate. Does either or both of these reactions involve oxidation and reduction? Explain.

Answer   The reaction between zinc and iodine is an oxidation-reduction reaction. A zinc atom loses two electrons (oxidation). Two atoms of iodine gain two electrons (reduction). The reaction between sodium chloride and silver nitrate does not involve oxidation and reduction. There is only an exchange of ions between the two compounds as shown by the equation:
$NaCl + AgNO_3 \rightarrow AgCl \downarrow + NaNO_3$. All of these compounds are ionic, including the precipitate.

14-44   Cobalt is a metallic element resembling iron. It is used in small amounts with iron in making some kinds of steel. Like iron, it combines with oxygen to form two different oxides, CoO and Co_2O_3. Give the names of these two oxides, and write an equation for the reaction of oxygen with cobalt to form each.

Answer CoO cobaltous oxide or cobalt (II) oxide.

$$2Co + O_2 \rightarrow 2CoO$$

Co_2O_3 cobaltic oxide or cobalt (III) oxide

$$4Co + 3O_2 \rightarrow 2Co_2O_3$$

14-45 If electric charges were passed through a water solution of cupric chloride $CuCl_2$, what would be deposited at each of the electrodes?

Answer In a solution of $CuCl_2$ there are four substances which could be deposited at the electrodes. Either copper or hydrogen could be deposited at the negative electrode. Since less energy is needed to deposit copper than is needed to liberate hydrogen, the copper will be deposited first. If the charges were to pass through the solution long enough, the concentration of copper ions would become low enough so that hydrogen would be liberated from the water molecules. Chlorine will be given off at the positive electrode in preference to oxygen as long as there are sufficient chlorine ions.

ADDITIONAL QUESTIONS AND PROBLEMS

14-46 In the experiment on passing electric charges through a melted mixture of lead chloride and sodium chloride, a slight yellowing was observed when the mixture was first melted. What could have been the product of decomposition that caused this yellow color? Write an equation (and balance it) describing the reaction which produced this substance.

Answer The yellowing in melted lead chloride is probably the result of dissolved chlorine produced by thermal decomposition. The reactions are

$$Pb^{+2} + 2e^- \rightarrow Pb$$

$$2Cl^- \rightarrow Cl_2 + 2e^-$$

The lead, no doubt, remains molten (and there is not very much of it anyway).

14-47 If a solution of sulfuric acid (H_2SO_4) in water were electrolyzed and a gas were observed forming at the *positive* electrode, what gas could this be?

(a) hydrogen   (b) oxygen
(c) an oxide of sulfur   (d) either a or b
(e) either b or c

Answer Answer (e). By reasoning used in the textbook, the possible products include any gases which could be formed from the reactants under the prevailing conditions. Thus oxygen could come from the water of the $SO_4^=$, and SO_2 or SO_3 could come from the $SO_4^=$. Hydrogen gas could be formed, of course, but not at the positive electrode.

14-48 Write in symbols the expression, "Aluminum reacts with chlorine and yields aluminum chloride." (*Hint:* Try to tell from a table, such as Table 13-4, the number of chlorine atoms that will combine with one aluminum atom.) Balance the expression you wrote.

Answer $2Al + 3Cl_2 \rightarrow 2AlCl_3$

14-49 Write an equation which describes the change of an aluminum atom to an Al^{+3} ion.

Answer $Al \rightarrow Al^{+3} + 3e^-$

14-50 If the formula $CuSO_4 \cdot 5H_2O$ represents the common hydrated form of copper sulfate, (a) how many moles of $SO_4^=$ ions are represented? (b) how many moles of water? (c) how many moles of oxygen atoms?

Answer (a) 1 mole of $SO_4^=$ (b) 5 moles of H_2O (c) 9 moles of (oxygen) atoms (4 moles in $SO_4^=$ and 5 in $5H_2O$)

14-51   For a certain oxidation-reduction reaction the equations are

$$A \rightarrow A^{+2} + 2e^-$$

$$B^{+3} + 3e^- \rightarrow B$$

This means that: (a) A plates out at the positive electrode; (b) A plates out at the negative electrode; (c) B plates out at the positive electrode; (d) B plates out at the negative electrode; (e) Both A and B remain in solution.

Answer   Answer (d). Plating results from ions changing to atoms. The metal ions are positive and therefore will plate out at the negative electrode.

REFERENCES

1. (T)   *Chem Study,* Chapter 12, Section 12-1, pages 199 to 207.   Electrolytic cells.

2. (T)   Greenstone, *et al.,* Chapter 7, pages 115 to 121; Chapter 13, pages 201 to 208. The first reference is just for building skills. The second concerns particle dynamics in solutions.

3. (T)   PSSC, Chapter 25, Sections 25-2, 25-3, pages 467 to 471. Our Chapter 12 reference again — "Here it is again" — a new look in the light of new knowledge and skills.

4.   Sienko and Plane. Same reference as in our Chapter 12.

CHAPTER 15

THE NATURE OF AN IONIC SOLID

In this chapter we complete the development of a model for crystals and we use the model to explain some aspects of crystal behavior. The chapter can be treated as a climax in our search for a reliable model for crystals.

It has been established in earlier chapters that some crystals are composed of charged particles which exert electrical forces on each other. These are the forces that hold the crystal together. We have developed a model for the charged particles themselves, and we have studied their behavior when they act more or less as individuals. In a crystal the particles have a collective behavior that depends partly on the nature of the particles and partly on their orderly arrangement in the crystal. In this chapter we build up a model for the orderly arrangement, and then we consider what happens to the arrangement when the crystal melts or dissolves.

Section 15-1 PRELIMINARY STEPS IN DETERMINING THE STRUCTURE OF A CRYSTAL

It is impossible to determine the positions of the almost uncountable number of ions in an ionic crystal from a few pieces of experimental data without introducing a grand assumption. We assume that a crystal is built up from identical bits called unit cells; a unit cell is so small that it contains only a few ions. Thus, the problem of determining the crystal structure is reduced to that of locating a few ions in the simple geometric array of the unit cell.

This section is an attempt to determine the shape and composition of the unit cell. We assume that its shape is the same as the shape of an observable crystal if the latter can be prepared in such a way as to have no flaws. The identification of the types of ions present (qualitative chemical analysis) and the determination of the relative numbers of each type (quantitative analysis) is discussed from a macroscopic viewpoint, and we assume that the results can be carried over to the unit cell.

Several crystals are mentioned in this section but two are singled out for special attention, namely, NaCl and CsCl. This selection is important, for it is maintained in subsequent sections.

QUESTION

15-1 In experiments 7-2 and 12-3 Part B we used the following crystalline materials: copper bromide, iodine, lead chloride, lead nitrate, naphthalene, *para*-dichlorobenzene, sodium acetate, sodium chloride, sugar, and zinc chloride. Which of these substances are ionic crystals? What property do the ionic crystals have that enables you to distinguish them from nonionic crystals? To refresh your memory you may wish to refer to the properties of these materials as you observed them in these experiments.

Answer Materials that are good conductors in the melted or dissolved state are ionic materials, whereas those with poor conductivity are nonionic.

224   The Nature of an Ionic Solid

The properties of the materials listed above are summarized in the following table:

Material	State	Experiment	Conductivity	Bonding
Sodium chloride	solution	12-2	good	ionic
Sodium acetate	solution	12-2	good	ionic
Zinc chloride	melt	12-2	good	ionic
Sugar	melt, solution	12-2	none	nonionic
Iodine	crystal	12-2	none	nonionic
para-Dichlorobenzene	melt	12-2	none	nonionic
Naphthalene	melt	7-2	not tested	nonionic
Lead chloride	melt	14-1	good	ionic
Copper bromide	gel	14-2	good	ionic
Lead nitrate	solution	14-3	good	ionic

Experiment 15-1 Crystals of Sodium Chloride and Cesium Chloride

---

This should be a take-home experiment. The discussion (half an hour, perhaps) could be based on Questions 15-2 to 15-6.

The students will probably be able to grow cubic crystals of NaCl, but they may be disturbed by the results they get with CsCl. After the evaporation of the water, the CsCl will be left as a frostlike pattern of needles, some of which are joined at 90 degrees. If the students watch carefully they will observe that NaCl starts to crystallize as a cube whereas CsCl starts as a small cross. Evidently, different crystals can have different structures. To identify the appropriate structure, it is necessary to have more information.

Equipment Needed
(per student)   *Cat. Number*

2 glass vials, 5 ml, with plastic tops (Note a)   68880

0.3 grams, sodium chloride (Note b)   68566

0.3 grams, cesium chloride (Note b)   68521

2 glass microscope slides   68850

1 plastic pill box (Note c)   68866

1 glass stirring rod   68867

1 magnifier   68847

1 plastic bag (Note d)   68853

2 straight pins (per class)   68871

Equipment Needed (per student)	Cat. Number
1 china marking pencil	—
1 graduated cylinder, 50 ml	68836
1 beaker, 250 ml	68815

Laboratory Notes

(a)   These glass vials should have a 5-ml capacity and should have plastic caps that screw on and off readily.

(b)   Solutions of NaCl and CsCl should be prepared ahead of time. Dissolve 9 grams of NaCl in 75 ml of water for each 25 students. Fill 25 vials half full of the solution, screw the caps on tightly, and identify the vials by marking them with a china marking pencil. Repeat the preceding process with CsCl.

(c)   This is the plastic box used in Experiment 5-2. (Remove and save the glass beads.) The two sides of the box have identical dimensions; one side should be used for NaCl, the other side for CsCl. Place identifying marks on the top and bottom of the box before opening it.

(d)   If this is to be done as a take-home experiment, all the "per student" items should be packed in this plastic bag for ease in carrying.

Experimental Results

The NaCl solution yields reasonable cubic crystals both on the microscope slide and in the pill box. The CsCl solution will not yield crystals which appear to be cubes in either case. The students should not know this in advance. Care must be exercised to turn this apparently fruitless experiment into a useful experience by using the negative result to predict something about the structure of CsCl. The students may be requested to bring their crystals to class. An overhead projector can be used to show the crystals of NaCl and CsCl.

QUESTIONS

15-2   For each of the two materials:
   (a)   What is the form of the first crystal you saw?
   (b)   Describe the pattern of growth of the first crystal.
   (c)   Describe the appearance of the materials left on the microscope slides after all the water evaporated, noting any significant difference between NaCl and CsCl.

Answer   (a) For NaCl the smallest observable crystal is cubic. For CsCl the smallest observable crystal has the form of a small cross.

(b)   For NaCl the growth occurs on the sides of the square and to a lesser extent on the bottom and top. For CsCl the growth occurs at the ends of the arms and to a much lesser extent as a thickening of the arms. The intersecting arms of a number of crystals form a lacy pattern.

(c)   The water evaporates from the microscope slide, leaving a group of NaCl crystals in the center and much smaller crystals around the edges where the water first disappears. The water of the CsCl solution evaporates from the microscope slide leaving a lacy frostlike pattern in the center and a white powder around the edge. The pattern appears to consist of intersecting sets of parallel lines.

15-3 Describe the shape of the crystals you have grown. Classify them according to geometrical form. By looking at them, can you guess the shape of the smallest possible crystal?
Answer   The NaCl crystals appear to be cubic and we would expect the smallest possible such crystal to be cubic; CsCl forms intersecting needles and we probably would not guess that the smallest possible CsCl crystal is cubic.

15-4 Did the NaCl crystals break or cleave in the same way as the rock salt you used in Experiment 5-3? Do they appear to have the same structure as the rock salt crystals?
Answer   The small NaCl crystals can be cleaved or broken with a pin point. They will break along planes parallel to the sides of the squares. The fragments are cubic with smooth faces. That the cleavage is similar to that of rock salt is an indication that the structure is similar to that of rock salt.

15-5 Could you cleave the cesium chloride crystals? Were they too small to cleave or is it possible that they do not have cleavage planes?
Answer   It is not possible to cleave CsCl crystals. The needle-like structures can be broken but the ends are not regular and are not cleavage planes. The students may not be able to see this; their crystals may be too small to break. CsCl crystals have no cleavage planes, but the students may not be able to convince themselves of this.

15-6 From the appearance of the crystals and their cleavage properties, what have you deduced about the structure of NaCl? about the structure of CsCl?
Answer   All the evidence for crystal shape, growth pattern, and cleavage implies a cubic structure for the unit cell of NaCl. No evidence was found for the structure of CsCl except that it cannot be the same as that of NaCl.

15-7 Use the data given for cesium chloride and the method used for sodium chloride to calculate the relative number of cesium ions and chlorine ions in cesium chloride.
Answer   In CsCl 78.9% is Cs^+ and 21.1% is Cl^-. Thus in 100 grams of CsCl there are

$$100 \text{ g} \times 0.789 = 78.9 \text{ g of } Cs^+ \text{ ions}$$

$$100 \text{ g} \times 0.211 = 21.1 \text{ g of } Cl^- \text{ ions}$$

The mass of a Cs^+ ion is

$$132.9 \times 1.7 \times 10^{-24} \text{ g} = 2.3 \times 10^{-22} \text{ g}$$

The mass of a Cl^- ion is

$$35.5 \times 1.7 \times 10^{-24} \text{ g} = 6.0 \times 10^{-23} \text{ g}$$

Therefore the number of Cs^+ and Cl^- in 100 g of cesium chloride is:

$$\text{Number of } Cs^+ \text{ ions} = \frac{78.9 \text{ g}}{2.3 \times 10^{-22} \text{ g}} = 3.4 \times 10^{23}$$

$$\text{Number of } Cl^- \text{ ions} = \frac{21.1 \text{ g}}{6.0 \times 10^{-23} \text{ g}} = 3.5 \times 10^{23}$$

The difference between the 3.4 and 3.5 is rounding-off error.

15-8 For water, 11.1% of the mass is due to hydrogen atoms and 88.9% is due to oxygen atoms. Use the method just outlined and the atomic masses from the periodic table to show that there are twice as many hydrogen atoms as oxygen atoms in any sample of water.

Answer   In 100 grams of water there are 11.1 grams of hydrogen and 88.9 grams of oxygen. The atomic mass of hydrogen = 1.0. The atomic mass of oxygen = 16.0.

The mass of the hydrogen atom is

$$1.0 \times 1.7 \times 10^{-24} \text{ g} = 1.7 \times 10^{-24} \text{ g}$$

The mass of the oxygen atom is

$$16.0 \times 1.7 \times 10^{-24} \text{ g} = 2.7 \times 10^{-23} \text{ g}$$

Therefore the number of hydrogen atoms in 100 grams of water is:

$$\text{number of hydrogen atoms} = \frac{11.1 \text{ g}}{1.7 \times 10^{-24} \text{ g}} = 6.5 \times 10^{24}$$

$$\text{number of oxygen atoms} = \frac{88.9 \text{ g}}{2.7 \times 10^{-23} \text{ g}} = 3.3 \times 10^{24}$$

Consequently there are two atoms of hydrogen to every atom of oxygen in the water molecule.

15-9 Sodium chloride and cesium chloride crystals each contain two kinds of ions. As we have just seen there are equal numbers of the two kinds of ions in any sample of either crystal. Suggest a regular, repetitive, three-dimensional arrangement containing equal numbers of the two kinds of ions. Try to think of more than one such arrangement. The shape of sodium chloride crystals suggests that you limit the possible arrangements to those which would form cubes.

Answer   There are a number of possibilities, but the students may have trouble thinking of any more than the simple cubic structure. This question is asked to encourage the student to think of cubic structures to prepare him for later sections. Many of the arrangements which he may produce, however, do not occur in crystals. The ions of an ionic crystal are arranged such that any ion's nearest neighbors have opposite charge. This restriction was implied in the discussion of bonding forces in Chapter 11 and should be brought in to class discussion of this question. Two kinds of structures which do occur in nature are shown in Figures 15-7 and 15-10.

Section 15-2 USE OF X-RAY DIFFRACTION IN DETERMINING THE STRUCTURE OF A CRYSTAL

The method described is the Bragg diffraction method, which is used primarily with single crystals. No attention is given to other methods (powder and Laue patterns) which can be applied to powders or to random collections of small crystals.

When looking at Figure 15-1, the student may wonder why the x rays do not simply pass through the holes in the crystal. He may also wonder why the process is called diffraction and pictured as reflection. It may be helpful to point out that the ions are not actually small dots as suggested by Figure 15-1. The dots there are used to locate the positively charged nuclei, which are surrounded by approximately spherical electron clouds. X rays can penetrate through many layers of ions; in so doing they lose energy to the clouds of electrons. The electrons then reradiate this energy in all directions in the form of x rays of the same wavelength as they have absorbed. We summarize this process by saying that each ion scatters some of the incident radiation. This scattering takes place in all directions, but it is only in a certain few directions that constructive interference can occur. The conditions which determine these directions were outlined in Section RB 6-5. It is only by considering scattering that it is possible to account for the different intensities of the diffracted beams. This is described in Part 5 of Section 15-2.

The student will find that this section of the chapter requires patient attention to details in the figures. The objective is to relate experimental data to crystal structure so that guesses about the structure can be tested against the data. The data are presented in the form of graphs, such as those of Figures 15-3 and 15-6, which show the intensity of x rays reflected at various angles. Bragg showed how to interpret this information in terms of models of crystal structure. The heights of the peaks are related to the number and types of ions in a set of parallel planes. The locations of the peaks are related to the distances between planes. It is true that the interpretations are based on assumptions about the orderly array of the ions in planes and the repetition of simple arrangements involving only a few ions, but the interpretations make sense, and the model derived in this way is successful in explaining other properties of crystals.

QUESTIONS

15-10 In a hypothetical Bragg diffraction experiment such as that shown in Figure 15-2, a maximum intensity of the diffracted beam is found when the angle γ between it and the incident beam is $168°$. What is the angle θ between the incident beam and the layers of ions?

Answer   Referring to Figure 15-2, we see that

$$\gamma = 168°$$
$$\text{but } \gamma + 2\theta = 180°$$
$$\text{so } 2\theta = 180° - 168° = 12°$$
$$\theta = 6°$$

15-11 X rays having a wavelength of 1.5×10^{-10} meter are diffracted by a crystal for which the spacing of one set of layers of ions is 4.12×10^{-10} meter. What are all the values of $\sin \theta$ less than 1 for which there is a diffracted beam of x rays from these layers?

Answer   From the Bragg equation,

$$\sin \theta = \frac{n\lambda}{2d} = n \cdot \frac{\lambda}{2d} = n \, \frac{1.5 \times 10^{-10} \text{ meter}}{2 \times 4.12 \times 10^{-10} \text{ meter}}$$

$$= n \times \frac{1.5}{8.24} = n \times 0.18$$

Substituting 1, 2, 3, 4, and 5 for n, we have

$$n = 1, \sin \theta_1 = 0.18 \quad \theta_1 = 10°$$
$$n = 2, \sin \theta_2 = 0.36 \quad \theta_2 = 21°$$
$$n = 3, \sin \theta_3 = 0.54 \quad \theta_3 = 33°$$
$$n = 4, \sin \theta_4 = 0.72 \quad \theta_4 = 46°$$
$$n = 5, \sin \theta_5 = 0.90 \quad \theta_5 = 64°$$

The students, of course, are expected to find $\sin \theta$, not θ.

15-12 We know that sodium chloride has a cubic structure and that along one edge of such a cube Na^+ ions and Cl^- ions alternate, and are 2.81 Å apart. (a) How far apart are the Na^+ ions? (b) The unit cell is cube-shaped and the arrangement of ions is the same along every edge. What are the dimensions of the unit cell? (c) What is the volume of the unit cell?

Answer   The Na^+ ions are 5.62 Å apart and so are the Cl^- ions. Thus a Na^+ ion must be moved 5.62 Å to reach the position of the next Na^+ ion, so the unit cell must be 5.62 Å on an edge. The volume is $(5.62 Å)^3 = 1.78 \times 10^{-22} cm^3$.

15-13 Potassium chloride has the same structure as sodium chloride.
(a) Which of the three ions K^+, Na^+, and Cl^- has the most electrons? the least?
(b) When oriented correctly, a sodium chloride crystal yields an x-ray diffraction pattern with weaker peaks for $n = 1, 3, 5, \ldots$ similar to those in Figure 15-6. If a potassium chloride crystal were oriented in the same direction as the sodium chloride crystal, would it too yield weaker peaks for values of $n = 1, 3, 5, \ldots$?
(c) Justify your answer in part (b).

Answer   (a) A sodium atom has 11 electrons and a Na^+ ion has 10. A potassium atom has 19 electrons and a K^+ ion has 18. A chlorine atom has 17 electrons and a Cl^- ion has 18.
(b) and (c) Since K^+ and Cl^- ions both have the same number of electrons, they both scatter x rays equally well. Therefore, the waves scattered from adjacent parallel planes in the KCl crystal are always equal in amplitude, regardless of the orientation of the planes within the crystal. Since the waves are also 180° out of phase, they will cancel one another, and the diffraction pattern from KCl will have alternate peaks missing. The missing peaks will be those corresponding to $n = 1, 3, 5, \ldots$, etc., (see Figure 15-6).

The planes parallel to the cube faces of the NaCl crystal are made up of equal numbers of Na^+ and Cl^- ions alternating with each other. Nevertheless, each of these planes is identical to every other one, and we again find that all peaks corresponding to odd n are missing from their diffraction pattern. It is possible, however, to find directions in NaCl in which planes made up exclusively of Na^+ ions alternate with planes made up exclusively of Cl^- ions; they are the planes making equal angles with all of the cube edges of the NaCl crystal. Since Na^+ and Cl^- ions have quite different numbers of electrons, their scattering powers are quite different, and the waves scattered from successive planes in these sets, even though opposite in phase, are not equal in amplitude. Therefore, the diffraction patterns from these planes consist of alternating peaks, as shown in Figure 15-6.

Section 15-3 THE STRUCTURE OF CESIUM CHLORIDE

At this point in the chapter the problem of determining the crystal structure has been reduced to that of determining the structure of the unit cell from x-ray diffraction patterns, together with a knowledge of the relative number of ions of each type present.

Experiment 15-2 Construction of a Model of Cesium Chloride

This experiment can be carried out conveniently at home. If time does not permit the construction of both CsCl and NaCl models, it may be desirable to have half of the class build the open model of CsCl and the packing model of NaCl while the other half builds the open model of NaCl and the packing model of CsCl. Perhaps several models could be put together to make one large model which would facilitate identification of the planes. This can be done by rotating the model and sighting along the planes.

The students can bring their models to class for a discussion of the structure. The discussion could be based on Questions 15-14, 15, and 16. The planes parallel to the faces of the model would give a diffraction pattern with alternating peaks (see Figure 15-6). Planes containing two of the diagonals of a unit cell would give a pattern like the one shown in Figure 15-3.

Equipment Needed
(per student)   *Cat. Number*

A. Open Model

12 polystyrene balls, 1-in. diameter ⎫	68887
6 polystyrene balls, 3/4-in. diameter ⎬ (Note a)	68887
35 toothpicks, round, wooden	68887
1 push pin (Note b)	68887
1 plastic bag to transport loose materials	68853

B. Packing Model

27 polystyrene balls, 1-in. diameter	68887
8 polystyrene balls, 3/4-in. diameter	68887
1 tube, polystyrene cement	68578
1 plastic bag to transport loose materials	68853

Laboratory Notes

(a)   The larger balls are used to represent chloride ions (Cl^-); the smaller balls are used to represent cesium ions (Cs^+).

(b)   This pin has a very large head on it which can be gripped readily. It is also known as a map pin.

QUESTIONS

15-14   Examine the diagram in Figure 15-8(a) and the open model of the CsCl crystal, and justify the statement that a unit cell composed of eight Cl^- ions at the corners of a cube with a Cs^+ ion at the center is equivalent to a unit cell composed of eight Cs^+ ions at the corners of a cube with a Cl^- ion at the center. In combining a large number of unit cells to form a model of a crystal, does it matter which of the two unit cells you use as long as you use the same one?
Answer   There is the equivalent of one Cs^+ and one Cl^- ion per unit cell in either case. This calculation is indicated in Question 15-15.

15-15   (a) If one uses the model of the unit cell shown in Figure 15-8(b), how many Cl^- ions are in each unit cell? how many Cs^+ ions? (b) In a large crystal composed of many unit cells, in how many of them does each Cl^- ion participate? In how many unit cells does each Cs^+ ion participate? How do these statements agree with the calculation you made in Question 15-7? If they do not agree, can you make them compatible?

Answer   (a) There are eight Cl⁻ ions and one Cs⁺ ion in each unit cell. (b) Each Cl⁻ ion partici-pates in eight unit cells, each Cs⁺ ion in one.

Thus $\dfrac{1}{8}$ x 8 Cl⁻ ions = 1 Cl⁻ ion per unit cell

and   1 x 1 Cs⁺ ion   = 1 Cs⁺ ion per unit cell

The ratio of Cl⁻ ions to Cs⁺ ions per unit cell is 1 to 1, which is the same result as was calculated in Question 15-7.

15-16   We have just seen that x-ray diffraction studies indicate that the unit cell of CsCl is a cube. Does this model correspond to the appearance of the crystals you grew in Experiment 15-1?
Answer   Experiment 15-1 provided no evidence of any cubic structure for CsCl. The crystals were not cubic in appearance, and there was no cleavage.

Section 15-4 THE STRUCTURE OF SODIUM CHLORIDE

The students may already be familiar with the structure of sodium chloride. This structure was guessed in Chapter 5, assumed in Chapter 11, and partially derived in Experiment 15-1. In this section the verification of the structure by x-ray diffraction is described. The unit cell shown in Figure 15-10(a) may be confusing, particularly in comparison with the simpler CsCl unit cell. It may be helpful to emphasize that the unit cell must be identified in such a way that adjacent cells are the same. If any one of the eight equal cubes making up the cell in Figure 15-10(a) is selected, the adjacent cubes would have different ions at corresponding corners. It is also helpful to notice that a unit cell is identified (and classified) by looking at one type of ion only, as if the other type were not present.

Experiment 15-3 Construction of a Model of Sodium Chloride

If time does not permit the construction of both CsCl and NaCl models, it may be desirable to have half of the class build the open model of CsCl and the packing model of NaCl while the other half builds the open model of NaCl and the packing model of CsCl. Perhaps several models could be put together to make one large model which would facilitate identification of the planes. This can be done by rotating the model and sighting along the planes.

This experiment can also be carried out conveniently at home.

Equipment Needed (per student)		*Cat. Number*
A. Open Model		
14 polystyrene balls, 1-in. diameter		68862
13 polystyrene balls, ½-in. diameter	(Note a)	68862
14 toothpicks, round, wooden		68862
1 plastic bag, to transport loose materials		68853

Equipment Needed
(per student)   *Cat. Number*

B. Packing Model

63 polystyrene balls, 1-in. diameter	68862
62 polystyrene balls, 1/2-in. diameter	68862
1 tube, polystyrene cement	68578
1 plastic bag, to transport loose material	68853
4 strips, foamed polystyrene, 5 in. long x 1½ in. wide x 1 in. thick	68862

—or—

8 wooden blocks, 1/2 x 1/2 x 1/4-in. (Note b)   —

Laboratory Notes

(a)   The larger balls are used to represent chloride ions (Cl^-), whereas the small balls are used to represent sodium ions (Na^+).

(b)   Either the foamed polystyrene or the wooden blocks are required to support the balls while they are being cemented.

QUESTIONS

15-17   Consider the unit cell shown in Figure 15-11(a) and the open model you constructed. How many Cl^- ions are present in this unit cell? how many Na^+ ions? If these numbers are different could you construct an equivalent unit cell in which the numbers of Cl^- ions and Na^+ ions are interchanged?

Answer   From Figure 15-11 there are two layers like (a) and one like (b) per unit cell.

2 (a) layers with 5 Cl^- and 4 Na^+ each give	10 Cl^- and 8 Na^+
1 (b) layer with 4 Cl^- and 5 Na^+ each give	4 Cl^- and 5 Na^+
Total	14 Cl^- and 13 Na^+

A unit cell with Na^+ ions at the corners and Cl^- ions adjacent to each corner would have 14 Na^+ and 13 Cl^- ions.

15-18   Again consider the unit cell shown in Figure 15-11(a), but this time as if it were part of a large crystal. (a) In how many unit cells does each of the following ions participate: a Cl^- at the corner; a Cl^- ion at the center of a face; a Cl^- ion inside the unit cell; a Na^+ ion along an edge; a Na^+ ion inside the unit cell? (b) In Section 15-1 it was found that there are equal numbers of Na^+ and Cl^- ions in a sample of NaCl. Does this agree with your answer to Question 15-17? If not use the first part of this question to eliminate the discrepancy.

Answer Type of Ion	No. in Unit Cell	No. of Cells Participated in	Equivalent No.
Cl⁻ at corner	8	8	$1/8 \times 8 = 1$
Cl⁻ in center of face	6	2	$1/2 \times 6 = 3$
Cl⁻ inside cell	0	1	$1 \times 0 = 0$
Na⁺ along edge	12	4	$1/4 \times 12 = 3$
Na⁺ inside cube	1	1	$1 \times 1 = 1$

There are thus the equivalent of 4 Cl⁻ and 4 Na⁺ ions in each unit cell. These equal numbers agree with the calculations of Section 15-1.

15-19 We have just seen that x-ray diffraction studies indicate that the unit cell of NaCl is cubic. Does this model correspond to the crystals you grew in Experiment 15-1?
Answer The cubical shape of the crystals grown in Experiment 15-1 and the cleavage of the crystals into smaller cubes both point toward cubic unit cells.

Section 15-5 SIZES OF IONS

The student will probably have little difficulty seeing that the interionic distance can be regarded as a sum of ionic radii, so that if one radius were known then the other could be found. It may be desirable to point out that such radii are not as definite as they might appear to be; the electron clouds can be squeezed a little more in one crystal than in another.

The student may have difficulty accepting the argument based on Figure 15-14 to determine the absolute size of one ion, namely, the iodine ion. Rightly so. The argument is based on an assumption. It is assumed *a priori* that the lithium ion is so small that the iodine ions touch each other in the LiI crystal. It is known from other data that the assumption is valid, but here the argument is only an idea, subject to further testing.

QUESTIONS

15-20 List the positive ions of Table 15-2 in order of increasing size. Do the same for the negative ions.
Answer Positive ions in order of increasing size: lithium, sodium, potassium, rubidium, cesium. Negative ions in order of increasing size: fluorine, chlorine, bromine, iodine.

15-21 How much larger is the chlorine ion than the fluorine ion? the potassium ion than the sodium ion? Do you get more than one answer for these differences? If you do, what does this tell you about the assumption that the ion size is the same for similar compounds?
Answer From Table 15-2:
Difference between chlorine and fluorine ions in Å

in LiF and LiCl,	$2.57 - 2.01 = 0.56$	
in NaF and NaCl,	$2.81 - 2.31 = 0.50$	
in KF and KCl,	$3.14 - 2.67 = 0.47$	
in RbF and RbCl,	$3.29 - 2.82 = 0.47$	
From tables of ionic radii,	$1.81 - 1.33 = 0.45$	

234   The Nature of an Ionic Solid

Difference between potassium and sodium ions in Å

in KF and NaF,   2.67 - 2.31 = 0.36

in KCl and NaCl,   3.14 - 2.81 = 0.34

in KBr and NaBr,   3.29 - 2.97 = 0.32

in KI and NaI,   3.58 - 3.23 = 0.35

From tables of ionic radii,   1.33 - 0.97 = 0.36

The assumption that the radius of a particular type of ion is constant, independent of the other types of ions in the crystal, is a fairly good one judging by these data; it appears to be better for the positive ions than for the negative ions.

15-22   In Chapter 13 we described Rutherford's scattering experiment to determine the size of the nucleus. Why cannot a similar experiment be performed to determine the size of an ion?
Answer   Appreciable scattering of a heavy, charged particle can occur only from compact, dense scattering centers. The ion is large and diffuse (compared to the nucleus), so it will not cause scattering that can be analyzed easily.

Section 15-6 THE MASS OF AN ATOM AND AVOGADRO'S NUMBER

This section needs no amplification.

QUESTIONS

15-23   As a rough verification of these values, calculate the mass of the hydrogen atom from the mass of the chlorine ion and its atomic mass; from the mass of the cesium ion and its atomic mass.

Answer   (mass of H atom) = $\dfrac{\text{atomic mass of H}}{\text{atomic mass of Cl}}$ x (mass of Cl^- ion)

$$= \frac{1.0}{35.5} (0.61 \times 10^{-22} \text{ g}) = 1.7 \times 10^{-24} \text{ g}$$

(mass of H atom) = $\dfrac{\text{atomic mass of H}}{\text{atomic mass of Cs}}$ x (mass of Cs^+ ion)

$$= \frac{1.0}{133} (2.3 \times 10^{-22} \text{ g}) = 1.7 \times 10^{-24} \text{ g}$$

Good agreement to two significant figures.

15-24   Potassium bromide has a cubic structure like that of sodium chloride. The density is 2.8 g/cm^3 and the unit cell is 6.6 Å (6.6 x 10^{-8} cm) on each side. Find the masses of the potassium and bromine ions.
Answer   Step 1   Size of unit cell = $(6.6 \times 10^{-8} \text{ cm})^3 = 2.9 \times 10^{-22} \text{ cm}^3$

Step 2   Mass of a unit cell = $(2.8 \text{ g/cm}^3)(2.9 \times 10^{-22} \text{ cm}^3) = 8.1 \times 10^{-22} \text{ g}$

Step 3   Per cent of mass due to potassium and to bromine:

Atomic mass of potassium = 39.1

Atomic mass of bromine   = 79.9

$$\text{Per cent mass of potassium} = \frac{39.1 \times 100}{39.1 + 79.9} = 32.9\%$$

$$\text{Per cent mass of bromine} = \frac{79.9 \times 100}{39.1 + 79.9} = 67.1\%$$

Step 4   Mass per unit cell due to potassium = $0.329 \times 8.1 \times 10^{-22} = 2.7 \times 10^{-22}$ g

Mass per unit cell due to bromine   = $0.671 \times 8.1 \times 10^{-22}$ g $= 5.4 \times 10^{-22}$ g

Step 5   Each unit cell contains four potassium and four bromine ions so:

$$\text{Mass of each potassium ion} = \frac{2.7 \times 10^{-22} \text{ g}}{4} = 6.8 \times 10^{-23} \text{ g}$$

$$\text{Mass of each bromine ion} = \frac{5.4 \times 10^{-22} \text{ g}}{4} = 13.5 \times 10^{-23} \text{ g}$$

These masses could have been calculated from the atomic mass of each atom and the mass of the hydrogen as was done in Question 15-8.

15-25   Use the results of Question 15-24 to find the number of potassium atoms in 39.1 grams of potassium, the number of bromine atoms in 79.9 grams of bromine.

Answer   From Question 15-24, the mass of a potassium atom is 6.8×10^{-23} gram and the mass of a bromine atom is 13.5×10^{-23} gram. The number of potassium atoms in 39.1 grams is

$$39.1/6.8 \times 10^{-23} = 5.8 \times 10^{23}$$

The number of bromine atoms in 79.9 grams is

$$79.9/13.5 \times 10^{-23} = 5.9 \times 10^{23}$$

The differences between these values and the accepted value for Avogadro's number is caused by rounding-off error.

Section 15-7 CRYSTAL FORCES AND POTENTIAL WELLS

The forces in a crystal are complicated. The ions are actually held apart by the repulsive forces between touching electron clouds, even though the ions have opposite overall charges. In view of the complexity of the forces, it is desirable to describe the crystal in terms of potential energy. We can take this approach because we do not want precise calculations of the trajectories of the ions. What we do want is a conceptual understanding of the structure and behavior of a crystal, and this can be achieved more easily through potential energy considerations than through a description of the forces. This is done in the text in terms of the oscillations of a carriage on an air track; several graphs are presented to show different aspects of the potential energy-displacement relationship for the carriage and for an ion in a crystal.

The relation between the force which causes motion and the corresponding potential energy is developed in the discussion associated with Figure 15-15. For those interested, the mathematical analysis of that discussion can be developed as follows. Let the position of the carriage along the horizontal axis passing through the point c' be denoted by x. The potential energy $U = U(x)$ is a function of position as shown in Figure 15-15. We take $x = 0$ and $U = 0$ at the point c'. This choice of the location of $U = 0$ is arbitrary. The force F is related to U by

$$F = -\frac{dU}{dx}$$

Thus the magnitude of the force is the magnitude of the slope of the graph of U versus x. The steeper the hill, the greater the force. At any point where the graph has a minimum (or maximum), the slope is zero and the forces are balanced, leaving no net force.

We have defined the relation between potential energy and force, but this does not express the relation between potential energy and motion. Potential energy is worthy of recognition because it is related in a simple way to both force and motion, and it can act as an intermediate in the derivation of one from the other. The relation to motion is expressed by the statement that the sum

$$E = \frac{1}{2}mv^2 + U$$

is constant in time. (The prediction of change is assisted by finding quantities which do not change, and the total energy E is one of the most useful constants of motion.) To see that E is constant in time, we use Newton's second law in the form $F = ma$ to derive

$$\frac{dE}{dt} = m\frac{dv}{dt}v + \frac{dU}{dx}\frac{dx}{dt} = (ma - F)v = 0$$

where $v = dx/dt$ is the velocity and $a = dv/dt$ is the acceleration. Since E is constant, its value can be calculated from initial data (x, v) at $t = 0$. Thus the foregoing equation relating E to v and x becomes an equation for predicting motion without reference to acceleration. If we draw a horizontal line at the level of E on the U versus x graph, we can represent the kinetic energy at each point as the difference between the E level and the U level. In other words, the kinetic energy at any point x is the length of a vertical line between the U curve and the E line. We can readily see how the kinetic energy varies during the motion. In particular, we can see how the energy determines whether or not the particle is trapped or free. Furthermore, since the average kinetic energy for a collection of particles is proportional to the absolute temperature of the collection, we can see that the temperature determines the condition of the collection. At low temperatures, most of the particles are trapped in deep wells, as in a solid. At higher temperatures, the particles are trapped in the shallower wells of the liquid. At still higher temperatures, most of the particles are not trapped at all; the substance becomes a gas. Whether a well is deep or shallow depends on the extent to which neighboring particles are trapped, so we can see qualitatively why liquid wells are shallower than the crystalline wells.

QUESTIONS

15-26   Energy is required to melt NaCl, but energy is given out by NaCl dissolving in water. Explain.
Answer   The potential wells for the ions are shallower in melted NaCl than in crystalline NaCl because of the greater order in the crystal. Each ion in a crystal is surrounded by nearest neighbors of opposite charge. In the melt the orderliness is lost and ions of like charge can approach each other. Since the potential wells in the crystal are deeper than those in a melt, it requires energy to melt the crystal.

The situation is different in the aqueous solution, where each ion is surrounded by water molecules not present in the melt (see Figure 15-22). The water molecules, which are dipoles, become oriented around the ion in such a way as to isolate it from the effects of other ions. An ion surrounded by water molecules in this way is said to be hydrated. If the hydration deepens the liquid wells so much that they are deeper than the crystal wells, then the potential energy of an ion in the liquid is lower than that in the crystal. This is evidently the case for NaCl in water, because energy is given off during the process of dissolving it.

15-27 Reconsider Experiment 2-2. Explain why the sodium carbonate solution was warm while the ammonium chloride solution was cold.

Answer Since the temperature rises when sodium carbonate dissolves in water, the potential wells for the ions must be deeper in the solution than they are in the crystal. Since the temperature falls when ammonium chloride dissolves, the potential wells must be shallower in the solution than they are in the crystal. This is the desired "explanation."

The explanation can be enlarged by adding the following. The sodium ions are much smaller than the ammonium ions, and hence the sodium ions can draw the neighboring water molecules into a tighter array, which deepens the wells for the ions. The chloride and carbonate ions can be neglected because negative ions generally do not hydrate as much as positive ions. The positive ions attract the negative part of the surrounding water molecules, which is concentrated on the oxygen atoms. The negative ions attract the positive part of the water molecules, which is not concentrated in one location.

In terms of energy transformations, we can say that if a temperature change occurs when we dissolve one substance in another, there must be a corresponding change in the kinetic energy of the particles involved. If the mixture becomes warm, the average kinetic energy of the particles has increased proportionally; if it cools, the kinetic energy of the system has decreased to the same extent. But the mere process of dissolving one thing in another does not involve the addition of energy. The total energy of the system remains essentially constant; any apparent change in its energy must be a redistribution of its internal energy. If its kinetic energy goes up, its potential energy must decrease by the same amount. We describe this situation by saying that the constituent ions are in deeper potential wells. If the kinetic energy goes down, the potential energy goes up, and the potential wells are then said to be shallower.

QUESTION

15-28 Why does it require more energy to vaporize a crystal than to melt it?

Answer To melt a solid, enough energy must be added to convert the crystal wells to the shallower liquid wells. To vaporize a solid, enough additional energy must be supplied to convert the shallow liquid wells to the almost nonexistent vapor wells. That is, to vaporize a substance its potential wells must first be converted to shallower liquid wells, and then eliminated.

Experiment 15-4 Water in an Electric Field

This is particularly appropriate as a take-home experiment.

Equipment Needed (per student)	*Cat. Number*
acetate plastic strip	68901
cotton cloth	68901
vinyl plastic strip	68901
wool cloth	68901

Laboratory Note

These materials were used in Experiments 11-2 and 11-3. A positive charge is produced on an acetate strip when it is rubbed with cotton cloth, and a negative charge is produced on a vinyl strip when it is rubbed with wool.

QUESTION

15-29   How does the deflection of the stream of water depend on the charge on the rod?
Answer   The water is deflected toward the rod, whatever its charge because the charge on the rod orients the water molecules so that the portions with opposite charge are closer to it. Consequently they are attracted.

Section 15-8 MELTING AND DISSOLVING – EQUILIBRIUM

The previous section dealt largely with the energetics of melting and dissolving, although we did not go into the detailed mechanisms for these processes. The sharpness of a melting point or a solubility cannot be explained solely in terms of the depths of potential energy wells, however. It is necessary to consider competing mechanisms, and the history of the collection of particles. These points are illustrated by analogy in this section.

Section 15-9 ENTROPY

The concept of entropy which is introduced in this section is a statistical entropy which behaves like the entropy of thermodynamics. The statistical entropy as defined in the text is the number of states with a particular distribution which is commonly denoted by W. The statistical entropy S is usually defined, however, as

$$S = k \ln W$$

where k is a constant. In any case, entropy is a simple property: it is just a number – a number of states. For our purposes, we may think of the entropy of a crystal as the number of ways of distributing the energy among the ions of the crystal.

Entropy has other meanings than we have chosen not to consider. Their interpretation can be both subtle and difficult, so it would be best to ignore them completely in discussing this material.

QUESTION

15-30   What are the possible states and distributions for three coins? Find the entropy of each distribution.
Answer   The possible states are HHH, HHT, HTH, THH, HTT, THT, TTH, TTT. The corresponding distributions (for each state) can be described by 3 heads, 2 heads, 2 heads, 2 heads, 1 head, 1 head, 1 head, no heads. Thus the entropy of three heads is 1, the entropy of two heads is 3, the entropy of one head is 3, and the entropy of no heads is 1.

Experiment 15-5 The Law of Entropy

This experiment, which could be a take-home experiment, seems silly before it is tried, but it is quite impressive. The equipment for the experiment is simple: a hundred coins and any box or platter which can hold the coins while being gently shaken in such a way as to flip only a few of the coins. The counting may take some time, but the results are interesting and convincing. Furthermore, this is not a crude analogy to illustrate the law of entropy; it is a full-fledged application of the law. The main difficulty lies in the recognition that few heads and many tails (or vice versa) represent a distribution of low entropy whereas nearly half heads or tails represents a state of high entropy.

Equipment Needed
(per student or per demonstration)

100 coins (i.e., pennies) or washers with one face marked

1 box or flat-bottomed container

No PSNS equipment is available for this experiment.

Laboratory Note

It should be pointed out that the coins will not remain nicely laid out during the flipping but will pile up in a haphazard manner. In spite of that, the number of heads can be counted by sorting. The results of the experiment do not depend on the way in which the coins pile up. The experiment can be repeated with 10 coins, 50 coins, etc. It may be desirable to have several teams dealing with various numbers of coins, and then to compare the results in a discussion.

QUESTIONS

15-31 Look at a pencil. What are you taking for granted about its history when you identify it as a particular thing? How do you know it will not suddenly rise into the air or separate into two parts flying in opposite directions?
Answer   There are many ways of expressing an answer. One may say that he assumes that the pencil has been a pencil for some time. It is not a sudden, accidental aggregation of molecules, all of which could now be moving away from each other. Thus the collection of molecules has been aged in a bound condition without enough energy to fly apart.

The pencil will not suddenly rise into the air because the pencil is sufficiently aged so that the molecular velocities are distributed randomly: just as many molecules are moving downward as upward. For the pencil to separate into two parts it would be necessary to have the molecular velocities in the two parts so well organized that the velocities in one part are directed in one direction while the velocities in the other part are directed in the opposite direction. This kind of organization is very unlikely because of the aging.

15-32 What will happen when you puncture a filled balloon? How can you be so sure?
Answer   Gas will escape from the hole. Since the gas is aged in the sense that many collisions have occurred in the balloon recently, we are assured that the velocities are randomly distributed and about half of the particles at the site of the puncture are aimed outward.

15-33   Predict what will happen if you drop a crystal of potassium permanganate into a glass of water. Refer to your notes for Experiment 1-3. Can the reverse process be observed? if not, why not?

Answer   As the potassium permanganate dissolves to form a purple cloud, it spreads out until it becomes more or less uniformly distributed throughout the water. This is due to the fact that the ion velocities in the dissolving crystal are distributed unevenly; there are always some ions aimed outwards. The reverse process can be imagined, but it will not be observed. To observe that, one would need to prepare a solution in which all the ions were directed toward a particular position, but any practical method of preparation would produce a solution that is too aged to have such an unusual distribution of ion velocities. Of course you could take a motion picture of the dissolving crystals and then run it backwards during projection. Aging, as we have used it here, is that which determines the direction of time; it is the process which enables us to tell that the motion picture is being run backwards.

15-34   The entropy of a crystal is reduced when the crystal is cooled by removing heat. Why doesn't this contradict the law of entropy?

Answer   The more energy a crystal has, the more ways there are to divide up the energy among the ions, and hence the greater the entropy. If heat is removed from a crystal, this reduces the energy, and hence it reduces the entropy. On the other hand, the only way to remove heat from a crystal is to have the crystal in contact with a colder body. Thus the energy lost by the crystal passes into the colder body and becomes available there for distribution among the particles. The entropy of the colder body is increased. The law of entropy does not say that entropy cannot decrease, but it says that if it does decrease in one material, it must increase by at least the same amount in another material so that the total entropy for both materials does not decrease.

The students will have difficulty with this question. If a student says that the entropy does decrease in the crystal but it must increase in another material, that is certainly a good answer. The student may wonder how we know that the entropy increase in one material must be at least as large as the entropy decrease in the other so that the total entropy does not decrease. One way to look at this question is to notice that in the system as a whole, the crystal together with the colder body, there is an unusual concentration of energy in one part of the system.

15-35   What factors other than the distance between positive and negative ions might affect the attractive forces in crystals? Are these other factors the same in sodium fluoride, sodium chloride, sodium bromide, and sodium iodide? Are they the same in magnesium oxide and sodium chloride? in cesium chloride and sodium chloride?

Answer   The other important factors are the charges on the ions and the sizes of the ions. In the sequence NaF, NaCl, NaBr, NaI, the charges are the same in all cases, but the size of the negative ion increases. Comparing MgO and NaCl, we find similar sizes for the positive ions and similar sizes for the negative ions, but the ion charges are different (two units of charge for each ion in MgO and one unit for each ion in NaCl). In CsCl and NaCl the ion charges are the same, but the cesium ion is larger than the sodium ion.

15-36   An iron object can be plated with chromium metal by an electrolytic process, that is, by a process in which electric current is involved with a chemical reaction. Without using a reference book, suggest the essential details of a process by which steel automobile bumpers can be chrome plated.

Answer   The iron bumper acts as the negative electrode with an excess of electrons which can be given up to chromium ions:

chromium ions + electrons → chromium metal (plated on bumper electrode)

15-37   With a sufficiently powerful microscope, would you expect to be able to see the individual sodium and chlorine ions in a sodium chloride crystal and thus determine their position?

Answer   No. The wavelength of visible light is very long compared to the size of an ion, whereas for significant interaction to occur, the wavelength must be at least as small as the object to be illuminated (see RB Section 4-3).

15-38   If a mixture of sodium chloride and potassium chloride is dissolved in water, and the water is then permitted to evaporate slowly, sodium chloride crystals will form. Is it likely that some potassium ions will be found in place of some sodium ions in these crystals? If the original mixture was composed of sodium chloride and cesium chloride, would you expect cesium ions to be found in place of sodium ions? Explain your answers.

Answer   Some potassium ions could sneak into the sodium chloride structure, for potassium forms the same type of crystal structure with the chlorine ion as does sodium. Cesium ions would be less welcome in the sodium chloride structure. They are so much larger than the sodium ions that they tend to form a different crystal structure with chlorine ions.

15-39   Magnesium oxide crystals have the sodium chloride structure, that is, the pattern of arrangement of magnesium ions and oxide ions is like that of sodium ions and chlorine ions. But the magnesium ions have a charge of +2 and the oxygen ions a charge of -2. What prediction can you make about the melting point of magnesium oxide compared with sodium chloride? What can you predict about the relative solubilities of the two substances in water?

Answer   Since the ions in MgO have a greater charge than the ions in NaCl, the nearest neighbors of opposite charge are attracted more strongly to each other and the potential energy wells in the crystal are deeper. This means that a higher temperature (kinetic energy) is required to get enough ions out of their potential wells so that the crystal can participate in the competitions of melting and dissolving. We expect MgO to have a higher melting point and a lower solubility (at a particular temperature). However, the strong forces of attraction between ions which make the solid hard to melt are the same forces which lead to greater hydration in solution, so the prediction is not infallible.

15-40   Any ionic crystal dissolves to some extent in water. Some crystals dissolve to a great extent, and others to a small extent. Why?

Answer   Some ions find deeper potential energy wells in the solution than they have in the crystal. This favors trapping in the solution and leads to greater solubility. Other ions, particularly if they are larger, find shallower wells in solution, and the solubility is small. In the solution smaller ions can surround themselves more tightly with a cage of water molecules which produces a deep well. There are other factors which help to determine the solubility: the charges on the ions have an effect, as indicated in the notes above on Question 15-39; some crystal structures are more difficult to build than others, which favors the destruction process and leads to greater solubility.

15-41   The entropy of any crystal would be increased if the crystal were vaporized. Why don't all crystals vaporize?

Answer   They will vaporize if they have enough energy. The law of entropy does not say that every substance takes the form of maximum entropy, but that every substance takes the form of greatest entropy which is allowed by the available energy.

15-42   If the molecules in the air in your room were all moving toward one wall, that wall would be blown out and you would be left sitting in a vacuum. Is such a catastrophe impossible? improbable? Why?

Answer   The catastrophe is possible but very improbable because the molecules are moving in all directions, not in one direction. The molecules were not recently placed in the room with selected directions, but they are molecules in an atmosphere that has aged enough to allow the molecules to take on a random distribution of velocities.

REFERENCES

1.   Andrews and Kokes, Chapter 5, pages 79 to 111. A preview of chemical bonding of several types. Chapter 8, pages 188 to 194, 196 to 206. Crystal structure, ionic crystals. Chapter 20, pages 329 to 341. Entropy and probability.

2. (T) Campbell, pages 80 to 90. A very good but relatively simple introduction to the ideas of entropy. This uses the chemist's view of entropy.

3. (T) Christiansen and Garrett, Chapter 19, pages 310 to 324. Standard treatment, but nicely collected ideas of ions.

4.   Resnick and Halliday, Chapter 25, pages 619 to 642. Entropy and the second law, from a more advanced view, and from a physicist's view.

5. (T) Sienko and Plane, Chapter 6, Sections 6.1 through 6.4, pages 131 to 142. Good diagrams of crystal structures.

6.   Stevenson and Moore, Chapter 12, pages 257 to 271; Chapter 13, Sections 13.4 and 13.5, pages 301 to 305. Chapter 12 gives a short introduction to randomness and probability; the Chapter 13 sections introduce entropy by statistics. Quite brief, but it is nicely done.

7. (T) Wood, pages 10 to 12, pages 18 to 24. Discussions concerning crystal structure. Other parts of this book can be read with profit.

8.   Germer, L. H., "The Structure of Crystal Surfaces," *Scientific American,* March, 1965, pages 32 ff. This article is written by one of the people responsible for the Davisson-Germer experiment. Just as in this famous experiment, electron diffraction is used to determine crystal structure.

CHAPTER 16

MOLECULES.

Having "discovered" ions and investigated some of their properties, and having used them in explaining the structure of salt crystals, we are led to ask whether all substances are like this. In this chapter, we look back to our conductivity experiments and recall that a very common substance, water, was practically a nonconductor. We then postulate that water is not ionic but, rather, is composed of molecules — each an H_2O unit. This brings up two questions: "What is the nature of the bonds that hold the atoms together in water molecules?" and, "What kind of bond holds one water molecule to another in liquid water or, better yet, in ice?"

Section 16-1 AN ATTEMPT TO ELECTROLYZE WATER

This section is devoted almost entirely to a demonstration experiment on the electrolysis of water.

Experiment 16-1 Electrolysis of Water (A Demonatration)

Although the purpose here is to electrolyze water, we actually use a dilute solution of sodium sulfate. The salt makes the solution conducting; water itself is a very poor conductor.

Hydrogen gas and oxygen gas are collected in the ratio of 2 volumes to 1 volume. Students are told that if an experiment were done to determine the amount of sodium sulfate after electrolysis, it would be found unchanged; for example, by evaporating to complete dryness the solution remaining after electrolysis, an amount of sodium sulfate equal to that initially added would be recovered. Thus the electrolysis products must have come from water. This is interpreted as leading to the conclusion that the bonds in H_2O molecules are electrical.

The equations for the electrode processes are

$$2H_2O \quad \rightarrow O_2 + 4H^+ + 4e^- \text{ (positive electrode)}$$

$$4H_2O + 4e^- \rightarrow 2H_2 + 4OH^- \text{ (negative electrode)}$$

We note from the equations that two molecules of hydrogen and one molecule of oxygen are produced; thus, considering Avogardo's hypothesis we are not surprised that two volumes of hydrogen are produced for each volume of oxygen.

Equipment Needed
(per demonstration)   *Cat. Number*

1 electrolysis apparatus, Hoffman type (Note a)	68830
2 battery packs (Note b)	68814
8 batteries, 1½-volt	68813
1 milliammeter and rheostat box (Note c)	68894
250 ml, sodium sulfate solution (Note d)	68551
1 clock, with sweep second hand	68821
matches	68539
3 wooden splints	68562
2 test tubes, 25 x 100 mm	68873
4 electrical connecting wires	68814

Laboratory Notes

(a)   This is the standard Hoffman apparatus which is available from any scientific apparatus company. It comes as a complete unit including the ironware, special clamps, the eudiometers (gas collection tubes), and the electrodes.

(b)   These are the PSNS student battery packs of 6 volts each. The rate at which the gas is evolved depends on the electrode voltage. If it is desired to decrease the required time, the best way is to increase the applied voltage. Three or even four of the 6-volt battery packs may be used in series instead of the two indicated. The freshest batteries available should be used in this experiment.

(c)   This is boxed and wired as a single unit. If you prefer to furnish the component parts separately, the rheostat should be a slide-wire type with a maximum resistance of 10 to 15 ohms, capable of carrying 1 to 2 amperes. The ammeter should have a rating of 0-500 milliamperes at full scale deflection and should be graduated in units of 10 ma.

(d)   For this experiment one needs only about 250 ml of the sodium sulfate solution. Experiment 16-2, however, uses considerably more of the same solution, thus making it convenient to prepare about two liters at one time for both experiments. This can be done by adding 100 grams of anhydrous sodium sulfate to 2,000 ml of water. The matches, splints, and test tubes are used to test the gas collected in each eudiometer.

QUESTIONS

16-1   List the properties of the gas collected over the negative electrode. What is the gas?
Answer   The gas is (should be) colorless, odorless, combustible, and only slightly soluble in water. It is hydrogen.

16-2   List the properties of the gas collected over the positive electrode. What is the gas?
Answer   The gas is colorless, odorless, noncombustible, and only slightly soluble in water. It is oxygen.

16-3   Which gas was liberated in greater volume?
Answer   Hydrogen.

16-4 What was the ratio of the volume of gas collected over the negative electrode to that collected over the positive electrode?

Answer   About two to one.

16-5 Hydrogen has a very low density. Can you suggest a test other than combustibility for it?

Answer   One way to test for hydrogen is to fill a balloon with the gas. Hydrogen is one of the few gases that is lighter than air (less dense than air).

Section 16-2 COMBINING HYDROGEN AND OXYGEN

This section is devoted entirely to a demonstration experiment on the combining volumes of hydrogen and oxygen.

Experiment 16-2 Combining Hydrogen and Oxygen (A Demonstration)

Two volumes of hydrogen and one volume of oxygen combine explosively in the experiment. This verifies previous observation, namely: (1) the 2 to 1 volume ratio is confirmed; (2) whereas it took energy to separate the components of water, energy is given off when they combine.

> *CAUTION:* Some teachers have been tempted to collect more than the 20 cm^3 of gas suggested in the instructions for the experiment. Do not do so! Even with a large safety factor built into the demonstration, it is possible to convert this electrolysis apparatus into a rocket by collecting and exploding too much gas.

Equipment Needed (per demonstration)	*Cat. Number*
1 special electrolysis apparatus (Note a)	68900
2 clamps, large, ring stand (Note b)	68888
2 battery packs	68814
8 batteries, 1½-volt	68813
1 milliammeter and rheostat box	68894
1.5 liter, sodium sulfate solution	68551
4 electrical connecting wires	68814
1 polyethylene pan (Note c)	68895
1 induction coil	68839
10 feet, copper wire, No. 28, bare	68561
safety goggles	68838

Laboratory Notes

(a)   This special electrolysis apparatus consists of the following component parts (see text Figure 16-2):
(1)   Glass ignition tube, pyrex. This tube should be 12 to 16 inches long and should have an O.D. of 2 inches with a wall thickness of 3/16 inch.

(2)   Rubber stopper, two-hole. For the glass tube listed above, a No. 9 or 10 two-hole rubber stopper is appropriate. It is to be wired securely in place in one end of the ignition tube. To do this, first wrap the tube with three or four turns of plastic electrical tape, about 2 or 3 inches below the stopper. The second turn should overlap about three-fourths of the first, etc. (The collected gas will be between the bottom of the rubber stopper and the top of the wrapping tape.)

The wire to be used for securing the stopper should be about No. 22 gage and very flexible. Wrap four or five turns tightly around the tube on top of the plastic tape. (The tape is to prevent the wire from slipping on the glass tube.) The wire must be tightly wrapped and the ends twisted together. The two ends should be long enough so that after the twist they can be passed over the top of the stopper and back down to the wire coil on the side opposite the twist. These ends should be fastened to the coil at this point. If difficulty is experienced in getting the wire ends under the coil, simply put two or three more turns of wire over them and around the glass tube as before. The wire over the stopper must be pulled tight enough so that the stopper will not slip when the gases are exploded.

(3)   Ignition electrodes. Two alternatives are suggested:

Method (1): Two pieces of bare copper wire, preferably of about 28 or 30 gage, are used for electrodes C. They are put through the holes so that they extend about 3/8 inch below the stopper. They are held in place by forcing pieces of glass rod or wooden pegs into the hole along side of each wire; these must fit very tightly. Golf tees work quite well for this purpose. You should insert these electrodes before wiring the stopper in the glass tube and adjust the ends of the two pieces of wire to be close enough together so that the induction coil will cause a spark to jump between them.

Method (2): A machine bolt is anchored securely in each hole of the rubber stopper just discussed. The bolt should be at least 2 inches long and of sufficient diameter to fit tightly in the hole in the stopper. Each bolt should extend about 1/4 inch below the stopper. Before the stopper is wired in the ignition tube, check to see that the induction coil can cause a spark to jump between these electrodes.

(4)   Electrodes, platinum. Each electrode should be 6 to 8 inches long, plastic coated, and bent in the shape of a J. The wire at the end of the long leg of the J is connected to the voltage source. The wire at the end of the short leg of the J is platinum; it is immersed in the solution as shown in Figure 16-2. Position the two electrodes at the bottom, open end of the ignition tube. They should be diagonally across from each other, with the platinum tip inside the tube and the long, insulated portion of the wire outside the tube. The electrodes can then be taped in place using the electrical tape.

(b)   These clamps are used to hold the tube vertically; the iron ring stand for the Hoffman Electrolysis Apparatus (Experiment 16-1) should be used to support it.

(c)   The pan serves as the container for the solution and should be about 4 inches deep and 6 to 8 inches in diameter.

General Instructions

The glass tube must be completely filled and inverted in the sodium sulfate solution in the pan without getting any air into the tube. Fill the tube to overflowing and place a small glass plate over the end. If a piece of glass is not available, a piece of cardboard with a glazed side works fairly well. Hold the plate tightly against the tube opening, invert the tube, and submerge the plate and end of the tube in the solution in the pan. The plate can now be removed. (One hand must be dipped into the sodium sulfate solution, but it is quite harmless.)

Make all connections as shown in Figure 16-2 and let the current continue long enough to collect about 20 cm^3 of gas. A gas depth of 1.5 cm will contain approximately 20 cm^3 of gas.

The two leads from the secondary of an induction coil are now touched to the two electrodes C. A spark should jump between the electrodes and explode the gas. A heavy lucite or glass shield should be held between the performer and the apparatus when this is done. The students should be kept several feet away.

There is very little danger since the explosion is small, and water will be forced out of the bottom of the tube and the tube will not break. It is possible that the stopper might blow out. This is not dangerous and it entertains the students, but the experiment must then be repeated. There should be no gas left in the tube after the explosion.

Section 16-3 COMBINING VOLUMES

Three combining volumes ratios of oxygen and hydrogen are presented. This will help the student to draw a general conclusion about the true combining volume ratio of oxygen with hydrogen.

Section 16-4 AVOGADRO'S HYPOTHESIS

Our earlier discussion of Avogadro's number brought out that the number of particles in a mole is the same for all substances. The present application is to the number of gas molecules in a standard volume (22.4 liters at STP) of hydrogen or oxygen or any other gas.

Section 16-5 DIATOMIC MOLECULES

The reasoning which leads to the idea of diatomic hydrogen and chlorine molecules is very simple. These gases combine in the proportion (hydrogen:chlorine:hydrogen chloride) 1:1:2 by volume. From the combining ratio, then, one molecule of hydrogen and one molecule of chlorine combine to produce two molecules of hydrogen chloride. Since two molecules of hydrogen chloride must contain at least two atoms of hydrogen and two atoms of chlorine, the hydrogen molecule must contain at least two atoms of hydrogen, and the chlorine molecule must contain at least two atoms of chlorine. That is, these two gases must be at least diatomic.

Extending this reasoning, water is formed according to the following reaction:

2 volumes hydrogen + 1 volume oxygen → 2 volumes water (gaseous)

2 molecules hydrogen + 1 molecule oxygen → 2 molecules water

Again, since two water molecules must contain two atoms of oxygen, the oxygen molecule must be diatomic.

For ammonia the proportion of nitrogen:hydrogen:ammonia is 1:3:2.

1 volume nitrogen + 3 volumes hydrogen → 2 volumes ammonia

1 molecule nitrogen + 3 molecules hydrogen → 2 molecules ammonia

Since two molecules of ammonia must contain two atoms of nitrogen, we conclude that the nitrogen molecule must consist of two atoms of nitrogen, and thus is also diatomic.

QUESTION

16-6 Write the chemical equation for the formation of water.

Answer $2H_2 + O_2 \rightarrow 2H_2O$

Section 16-6 BONDS IN MOLECULES

To understand the capacity of atoms to form bonds with each other when they are not ionized, we use the cloud model for the electron. This model is distinct from the particle and wave models associated with electrons in earlier discussions. This is not to imply that the earlier models are less accurate descriptions than the cloud model; they are merely less useful for our present purposes.

At the beginning of the section, the cloud is introduced as a time-averaged representation of the electron position, and we quickly abandon all detailed interpretations and concern ourselves with the cloud as the basic entity. If we think of the electron as a particle and try to translate the results of quantum mechanics into an account of what the particle does, we get a strange picture which does not lend itself easily to intuitive development. Even the probabilistic interpretation of particle behavior has its short-comings: it involves a somewhat vague use of the concept of probability, and it requires conceptual adherence to the impossible geometric particle. These problems may bother the student unnecessarily if they are emphasized or if the particle-probability interpretation is presented as the true or superior model. The wave terminology is no better, even if standing waves are distinguished from propagating waves; the terminology has bothersome connotations. We may as well go over entirely to the motionless charge cloud model. Then intuitive development is easy and accurate. This is not to say that such a commitment is appropriate in all circumstances, but it is appropriate for our description of atoms and molecules. We do not even mention the spin of electrons, for that suggests still another picture to confuse the issue, and it turns out to be unnecessary here.

The objective of this section is to build up the cloud pictures for atoms shown in Figure 16-13. Those pictures can be used to predict the valence (number of covalent bonds the atom will form) of atoms, and the structure (bond angles and lengths) of molecules. Making these predictions requires a few rules, but the rules are simple. First we learn that two electron clouds can merge to occupy the same space if they are pulled together by attraction to positive nuclei. The resulting cloud is dead in the sense that it cannot accept merger with a third electron. Other electron clouds must go elsewhere. The merging of two clouds is possible because the repulsion of the clouds is reduced somewhat by the overlap, as explained in the text book. This gives an advantage to attractive forces between the clouds and nuclei. If two electrons in an atom can occupy different clouds which are equally well attracted to the nucleus, they will do that and remain alive rather than merge to become a dead pair. On the other hand, two electrons in an atom will merge rather than have either one pushed out into a larger cloud that involves less attraction to the nucleus. Two live clouds in different atoms will always merge; they are pulled toward each other by attraction to the nuclei. The dead cloud formed in such a merger is a covalent bond. The formation of molecules is attributed here to the urge to merge.

These rules governing the behavior of clouds are sufficient to explain the valences of atoms if we know the possible variety of cloud shapes for an electron in an atom. In the text we have tried to derive the possible shapes by some guessing, guided by experimental facts that are introduced without supporting experiments. The first electron takes the shape of a sphere centered on the nucleus. This gives the model for the hydrogen atom pictured in Figure 16-13 (and earlier figures). The picture for helium is similar except that the spherical cloud is dead, being occupied by two electrons. This assignment is supported by the inert character of helium. For lithium, we must assign to the third electron a shape which allows the charge to be concentrated outside of the dead inner core, and that can be a larger sphere. For beryllium, there are two electrons in the second shell which do not have to merge because they are concentrated away from the nucleus. They can take the shape of lobes poking out of the core in opposite directions (see Figure 16-13). Similar reasoning applies to boron and carbon, and the pictures are again supported by data on the valences of those elements and the bond angles in their molecules. In the case of nitrogen, however, which shows a valence of three (not five), there must be a new rule introduced to extend the model. Evidently the four lobes of carbon represent the maximum number of lobes that can be equally well attracted to the nucleus. The extra electron of nitrogen must either go into a larger shape concentrated farther from the nucleus or else merge with one of the live electrons in the tetrahedral lobes. The latter choice is taken, evidently, and the valence is cut down to three. Similarly for oxygen, fluorine, and neon. Additional electrons in larger atoms must be concentrated outside of the neon core. They are attracted less strongly to the nucleus, but there is more space in the region outside of the core, and the variety of possible shapes is enriched.

Although it would be undesirable to take it up in class, these cloud pictures are basically derived from wave mechanics as applied to the hydrogen atom. It is assumed in wave mechanics that the state of the electron in a hydrogen atom can be described in terms of a function $\Psi (x, y, z)$, where x, y, and z are the coordinates of the electron position in a coordinate system centered on the nucleus. To say that Ψ describes the state is to say that all measurable properties of the electron can be derived from Ψ. If we ask for the position of the electron, that can be derived by treating $|\Psi|^2$ at (x, y, z) as the magnitude of the probability that the electron is at (x, y, z). This is a strange answer to our question; it becomes more meaningful if we treat the electron as a cloud of charge and say that $-e|\Psi|^2$ is the charge density at (x, y, z). To find an overall picture of the way the charge is distributed in a state described by Ψ, we can look for the shape of the contour surfaces determined by $|\Psi|^2$. A contour surface can be found as follows. Choose a point (x, y, z). Find the value of $|\Psi|^2$ at the point. Identify neighboring points where $|\Psi|^2$ has the same value. Then construct a surface that passes through all of these points. The surface will be a sphere or some other closed surface with a characteristic shape. The function $|\Psi|^2$ has the same value at all points on the surface. Other surfaces with similar shapes can be found inside and outside of our first surface by taking different values of $|\Psi|^2$. This construction of contours is somewhat like showing ground elevation on a map by drawing a set of closed curves. Each represents a particular elevation: each goes around the side of a hill or a valley at a constant altitude.

When the recipe of wave mechanics is used to find the wave function, a set of allowed wave functions (states) is found. These functions (states) are sometimes called orbitals. The word orbital is also used to identify the region of space most probably occupied by the electron in the state determined by a particular wave function, Ψ. There is only one orbital associated with the lowest energy level. The wave function for hydrogen has the form $\Psi = ae^{-br}$, where a and b are constants and $r = \sqrt{x^2 + y^2 + z^2}$ is the distance from the nucleus. The contours of this function are surfaces of constant r, that is, concentric spheres. The charge density $(-e|\Psi|^2)$ decreases exponentially with increasing r. It is convenient to represent the orbital by one of its contours, namely the sphere that contains, say, 95% of the charge cloud. Then we approximate further and think of the spheres as a more or less uniform cloud, and we ignore the little bit that extends out beyond this region.

The helium atom, in its state of lowest energy, can be described approximately by treating both electrons as electrons in hydrogen-like orbitals. In a description in which electron spin is considered explicitly, we would say that the electron clouds can merge when they occupy the same orbital, provided the spins are paired (i.e., spins oppositely directly). It is not possible for a third electron cloud to join the merger because there is no way to pair three different spins. We do not mention spin in the text book, but merely say that the cloud becomes too crowded if a third electron tries to enter.

The quantum mechanical treatment of helium, as described earlier in terms of orbitals, and as described in the text book in terms of clouds, is based on the assumption that the two electrons can be described separately. We say that they each occupy an orbital (cloud) which is like the spherical orbital of lowest energy for the hydrogen atom. Then we say that these electron clouds overlap to form one atomic cloud. This approximation is very good, and it can be refined further and made more precise as needed.

If we try to build up models of larger atoms by the approximation scheme described earlier, however, we run into a new problem. Consider lithium for example. Let us say that the first two electrons are assigned to the lowest-energy, hydrogen-like orbitals described earlier. These are the so-called 1s orbitals. The third electron must go into the next shell, that is, it must be assigned to a hydrogen-like orbital associated with the first excited level of hydrogen. According to quantum mechanics there is an infinite variety of orbitals associated with this energy level. How do we choose the appropriate orbital to the one that will be the best approximation in the sense of agreeing most closely with experiment?

The recipes of quantum mechanics offer some guidance for the selection of orbitals. The infinite variety of second-shell orbitals is not as big as it looks; the orbitals are not independent. In fact, the largest possible number of independent orbitals is four. Given four independent orbitals, all of the others can be regarded as superpositions of the basic four. Nature evidently insists on independent orbitals and permits at most two electrons in any one of them. This empirical restriction, which cannot be derived from more fundamental considerations, is known as the Pauli Exclusion Principle.

If we accept this much of quantum mechanics, we are left with the problem of choosing four independent orbitals. This problem has been considered in some detail ever since the discovery of the quantum mechanical recipe, and a small number of choices have been identified as the best ones for the various predicaments of electrons in atoms and molecules. For the lithium atom, with one electron in the second shell, the best choices are known as the $2s$, $2p_x$, $2p_y$, and $2p_z$ orbitals. The $2s$ orbital corresponds to a spherical cloud centered on the nucleus. This cloud is larger than the $1s$ cloud, and it is concentrated farther from the nucleus than the $1s$ cloud. The $2p$ orbitals have clouds that look like dumbells lying on the x, y, and z axes (i.e., perpendicular to each other). The $2s$ cloud has a slightly lower energy than the $2p$ clouds, and hence the most stable state of the lithium atom is the one in which the third electron is in the $2s$ orbital.

Moving on to beryllium, which has two electrons in the second shell, we are tempted to assign the third and fourth electrons to the $2s$ orbital. Then their clouds would be overlapped, and the atom would be chemically dead. This picture is a good one for an isolated atom. On the other hand, when beryllium atoms interact with each other or with other atoms, the valence electron clouds are distorted in such a way that the selection of independent, second-shell orbitals must be changed if we want to avoid the necessity of correcting the approximation. A better selection is one in which we keep the $2p_y$ and $2p_z$ orbitals (any two $2p$ orbitals) and replace the $2p_x$ and $2s$ by two other orbitals known as sp hybrids. They are superimpositions of the $2s$ and $2p_x$ orbitals, which have slightly lower energy than the other second-shell orbitals. These hybrids each have a large lobe and a small lobe. The large lobes are directed oppositely, and they correspond to the clouds pictured in the text book. These are the clouds that poke out of the beryllium core when other atoms approach for bonding. If there are no other atoms except for other beryllium atoms, the hybrids have to bend and become delocalized, as described later. This example is used in the text book to introduce the idea of delocalization. It should be pointed out, however, that this distortion of the beryllium clouds is so drastic that the molecule is not very stable. In a sample of beryllium vapor, most of the atoms are not paired into molecules. The other hybrid clouds described in the text (for C, N, O, F) are much more stable.

The graphic representations of beryllium bonding in Figures 16-8 and 16-9 may seem quite arbitrary. An alternative possibility is indicated by Question 16-11. Both representations can be made quantitative; they can be used as starting points in the calculation of bond energy. The main idea to be derived from these pictures is that the urge to merge is so great in live electrons on different atoms that the merger will take place even if it means the formation of more than one bond between two atoms. Furthermore, some of these bonds involve electrons which must be regarded as delocalized to some extent; particular electrons are not so tightly bound to particular nuclei. It is possible to regard all of the bonds as equivalent and to regard each of them as partially delocalized. The delocalization idea is expanded in Figure 16-15 to the case of benzene, and expanded further in the next chapter to explain the electrical conductivity of graphite. The extreme case of delocalization occurs in metals; it is the basis of their stability and electrical conductivity.

When delocalization of electron clouds is used to explain stability or electrical conductivity, it is being treated as a matter of electron freedom and mobility. Stability results from the reduced repulsion between dead clouds when some of the clouds are free to move away from others. Mobility results from the fact that delocalized electrons are not so tightly bound to any particular pair of atoms. They can be stimulated into motion by slight perturbations, such as an external electric field. Once the electrons are moving, it may be better to picture them as particles or waves rather than as clouds, but we do not try to develop a transition between models. If a student is concerned about our inconsistency in treating electrons here as clouds which can spread out to fill a metal and treating electrons earlier as balls which are deflected by collisions with nuclei, then he can be told again, perhaps, that different models are often applied to the same objects in explanations of different phenomena. This merely demonstrates the inadequacy of all available models.

Bond polarity is an important concept in this section for two reasons. First, it shows how we can connect our models for ions in previous chapters with our models for molecules in this chapter. Ions are formed as a result of extreme polarity. Once formed, they can be regarded for many purposes as charged particles. It is not necessary to notice any details about their cloud shapes. The ions are chemically dead, since their clouds consist of dead pairs of electrons, and that is why they cannot be squeezed together very much in a crystal. The charge that an ion will have can be predicted by the rules used here to predict valence. The valence of an atom is treated here as the number of live clouds, and those are the clouds that have to be lost or killed to form an ion. Thus the valence is the number of covalent bonds that can be formed, the number of positive units of charge that can be exposed by losing live atomic electrons, and the number of negative units of charge that can be acquired by bringing new electrons to merge with live atomic electrons. We are led to view chemical bonding, whether ionic or covalent, as a consequence of the instability of live clouds and the stability of dead clouds.

The second reason for examining bond polarity is that it helps to explain why materials composed of neutral molecules can form liquids and crystals. The molecules may be neutral overall, but if one part is positive and another part is negative, the positive part of one molecule can be attracted to the negative part of another at close range. The nature of intermolecular forces is considered again in Chapter 17.

QUESTIONS

16-7   Suppose two hydrogen atoms are very close to each other. Do they necessarily form a hydrogen molecule.
Answer   No. It all depends on their energy. If they are moving so fast relative to each other that their relative kinetic energy is as large as indicated in Figure 16-5(c), the forces of attraction will not be strong enough to hold them together, and no molecule will form.

16-8   Why was the spark necessary to initiate the combination of hydrogen and oxygen gas in Experiment 16-2?
Answer   The reaction between hydrogen and oxygen is too slow to be observable under ordinary circumstances. The bonds between the hydrogen atoms in the hydrogen molecule and the oxygen atoms in the oxygen molecule must be broken to form chemically reactive atoms, and considerable energy is required to break up these molecules. The spark supplies the energy needed to dissociate some of the nonreactive molecules into active atoms. The combination of hydrogen and oxygen atoms to form water molecules is sufficiently exoergic to become self sustaining once it has been initiated.

16-9   In what way are bonds in molecules and bonds in ionic crystals alike? How are they different?
Answer   The bonds are alike in the sense that they both represent situations in which particles are trapped in potential wells with insufficient energy to separate. This is a somewhat abstract use of the term "bond," which literally refers to the "glue" between two atoms in a covalent molecule. The bonds are different in the sense that they belong to pairs of particles in molecules and to the entire aggregate in ionic crystals. In addition, the bond in a molecule is due to the merger of charge clouds, whereas the bond in an ionic crystal is due to the attraction and repulsion of charged bodies whose clouds do not overlap appreciably.

16-10   In a gas composed only of lithium atoms, the atoms combine to form diatomic Li_2 molecules. Make a sketch like the one in Figure 16-6 for the formation of Li_2.
Answer   The sketch could be very much like the one in Figure 16-6 with the hydrogen pictures replaced by lithium pictures which are mirror images of the lithium pictures already there.

16-11   Suggest a sequence of pictures to replace Figure 16-9 to show the formation of two identical bonds representing four partially delocalized electrons, rather than one localized and one delocalized electron pair as in Figure 16-9(e).
Answer   The main idea is to start with pictures different from those in Figure 16-8, that is, with the atomic clouds parallel instead of aimed into each other. Both bonds form at the same time instead of first forming one, as in Figure 16-8, and then forming the other, as in Figure 16-9. The bonds formed in this approach tend to look like the two parts of the second bond formed in the other approach (see Figure 16-9) and it may be desirable to show the two parts fatter here to emphasize that each part separately is a whole bond rather than half of a bond (Figure RB 16-1).

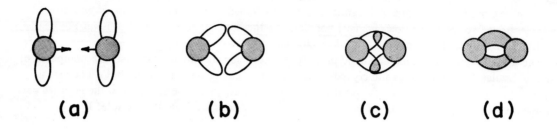

(a)   **(b)**   **(c)**   **(d)**

Experiment 16-3 Model for Carbon Bonding (A Demonstration)

Equipment Needed (per demonstration)	*Cat. Number*
4 rubber balloons (Note a)	68517

Laboratory Note

Balloons with a general teardrop shape are best for this experiment. After the inflated balloons have been tied together, they should be placed on a flat surface and arranged so that all four are in the same plane.

When this configuration is bounced about, the balloons will quickly fall into a tetrahedral arrangement. The experiment can be enlarged with profit by repeating with two- and three-balloon tie-ups. Two balloons will seek opposite directions and three balloons will seek the trigonal orientations of the boron clouds.

QUESTIONS

16-12   Sketch a tetrahedron or use a model for a tetrahedron to convince yourself that there can only be one type of molecule CH_2Cl_2 if the bonding is tetrahedral.

Answer   Conviction may come when it is noticed that each vertex of a tetrahedron is equidistant from all of the other vertices. Another way is to draw or construct two apparently different structures and notice that one can be rotated into the other. This is not the case for Figure 16-11.

16-13   Explain why helium and neon are chemically inactive.

Answer   All of the electron clouds in the atom are dead. They have no urge to merge.

16-14   Count the number of live electron clouds in each of the atoms in Figure 16-13 and write formulas for the molecule formed by each atom with hydrogen.

Answer

Atom	*No. of live clouds*	*Molecular formula*
H	1	H_2
He	0	none
Li	1	LiH
Be	2	BeH_2

Atom	No. of live clouds	Molecular formula
B	3	BH_3
C	4	CH_4
N	3	NH_3
O	2	OH_2 (or H_2O)
F	1	FH (or HF)
Ne	0	none

16-15   Predict the number of bonds in each of the diatomic molecules N_2, O_2, and F_2. Sketch cloud pictures to show the electron delocalization of bonding electrons in N_2 and O_2.
Answer

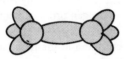

F_2 OR F—F (ONE BOND)
EACH ATOM HAS A CORE
AND THREE DEAD CLOUDS

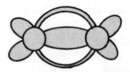

O_2 OR O=O (TWO BONDS)
EACH ATOM HAS A CORE
AND TWO DEAD CLOUDS

N_2 OR N≡N (THREE BONDS)
EACH ATOM HAS A CORE
AND ONE DEAD CLOUD

16-16   Table 16-2 shows that H_2, F_2, and O_2 melt at much lower temperatures than HF and H_2O which in turn melt at much lower temperatures than LiF. Explain why there should be such a sharp division of these compounds into three classes.
Answer   The molecules HF and H_2O are polar whereas the molecules H_2, F_2, and O_2 are not. The polar molecules can form crystals in which they are lined up with parts of opposite charge facing each other. They are attracted to each other more strongly than the nonpolar molecules. They form deeper potential wells in the crystal, and it takes more kinetic energy (higher temperature) to break up the order of their crystal structure. In the case of LiF, the polarization of the bond is carried to the extreme: ions are formed, and the ions can form much deeper crystal wells than neutral molecules because each one can be completely surrounded by ions of opposite charge. (In the case of HF and H_2O, the intermolecular forces are strengthened by hydrogen bonding, which is discussed in Chapter 17.)

QUESTIONS

16-17   If we had a porous cup or barrier separating the two electrodes in Experiment 16-2, would we have a way of making sodium hydroxide and sulfuric acid? Explain.

Answer   This question forces us to review the details of what happens in the electrolysis process. If there is no barrier or porous cup, water is decomposed at both electrodes. At the negative electrode, hydrogen gas is released and hydroxyl ions are produced. At the positive electrode, oxygen gas is released and hydrogen ions are produced. The hydrogen and hydroxyl ions produced at the electrodes migrate together and combine to form water molecules, leaving the sodium and sulfate ions unchanged. This process is not altered by the presence of a porous cup which permits ion migration. If the electrodes were separated by an impenetrable barrier, the hydrogen and hydroxyl ions would be kept apart, but since there is no ion migration there can be no electrolysis, no production of hydrogen and hydroxyl ions. The answer to the question is no.

16-18   Refer to the data collected in Experiment 16-1. From the current and the time, calculate the total charge that was transferred in the electrolysis. Calculate the number of grams of hydrogen that were produced by this charge transfer, and calculate from this the volume of hydrogen that was produced. How did the experimentally measured amount of hydrogen produced compare with this calculated amount?

Answer   The total charge transferred is the product of the current and the time (see Section 11-3). If the current is expressed in amperes and the time in seconds, the product is the charge in coulombs. Dividing the electron charge into the number of coulombs transferred, we find the number of electrons transferred. Dividing that by Avogadro's number, we find the number of moles of hydrogen atoms (or twice the number of moles of molecules) produced. Since a mole of hydrogen atoms has a mass of 1.0 gram, the number of moles of hydrogen atoms is equal to the number of grams of hydrogen gas produced. Half of this number is the number of moles of molecules, and that multiplied by 22.4 gives the number of liters of gas (at STP).

16-19   Substances other than sodium sulfate can be used to make water conduct electricity when it is being decomposed by electrolysis. Name several. What properties do they have in common?

Answer   Sodium nitrate, sodium carbonate, potassium sulfate. They are ionic crystals which dissolve to form solutions containing ions, none of which are discharged at the electrodes.

16-20   Your lungs hold about 4 liters (roughly a gallon) of air. If 6.02×10^{23} molecules are present in 22.4 liters of air, how many molecules can your lungs hold? (Give only an order of magnitude answer.)

Answer   Your lungs hold 4 liters, which is $(4/22.4) (6.02 \times 10^{23})$ or about 10^{23} molecules. A precise calculation is not worthwhile; the point to be made is that there are many molecules in a familiar quantity of gas.

16-21   When water is decomposed by electrolysis, the volume of hydrogen produced is twice the volume of oxygen. The density of hydrogen is about 0.09 gram per liter; the density of oxygen is about 1.43 grams per liter. What is the mass ratio of the gases formed when water is electrolyzed?

Answer   The mass of a particular quantity of gas is the product of the volume and density. The ratio of the masses is the product of the ratio of the volumes and the ratio of the densities: $(2/1) (0.090/1.4) = 0.13$.

16-22   Use Avogadro's hypothesis and the densities in Question 16-21 to calculate the relative mass of molecules of oxygen and hydrogen.

Answer   According to Avogadro's hypothesis, equal volumes of two gases contain the same number of molecules. Thus a liter of hydrogen contains the same number of molecules as a liter of oxygen. The ratio of the molecular masses should be the same as the ratio of the liter masses, which is $(1.43)/(0.09) = 16$.

16-23   The compound ammonium chloride (NH_4Cl) is bonded both ionically and covalently. Explain how this is possible and suggest a possible structure for the compound.

Answer   The crystal is composed of NH_4^+ ions and Cl^- ions. These ions are bound together ionically. They form a structure like that of sodium chloride or cesium chloride. On the other hand, each NH_4^+ ion contains several atoms that are held together covalently. In fact, this ion is similar to the CH_4 molecule. The nitrogen core has four tetrahedral bonds sticking out to the four hydrogen atoms.

16-24   Some of the formulas that follow represent molecules that have been prepared experimentally. Guess which ones. In any case, indicate which atoms are bonded to each other, and suggest a likely shape for the molecule.

$$CCl_4, O_2F, OF_2, HCN, CBNF, PSNS$$

Answer   First we notice the number of bonds (i.e., the valence of each atom) that each atom must form to become chemically dead. Then we notice which formulas allow each atom to become dead by forming the number of bonds determined by the valence. These are the formulas for compounds that are stable enough to be prepared experimentally. For CCl_4, we have valences of 4 and 1 for carbon and chlorine respectively, and these valences can be satisfied by four bonds that join the four chlorine atoms to the carbon atom. Since the live clouds on carbon are directed toward the verticles of a tetrahedron, we expect the CCl_4 molecule to be tetrahedral in shape.

For O_2F we have two oxygen atoms, each with a valence of 2, and one fluorine atom with a valence of 1. Clearly we must have the fluorine atom bonded to an oxygen atom, and this combination can form one bond (from the oxygen atom) to another atom. That will not satisfy the valence of the other oxygen atom. Such a molecule probably does not persist long enough to be detected.

In OF_2 the one oxygen atom can be bonded to both fluorine atoms. This satisfies the valences of all of the atoms. Such a molecule is probably among those which have been prepared. Since oxygen has two live clouds separated by a nearly tetrahedral angle (also, nearly a right angle), the bonding would be nearly tetrahedral (or nearly right angular).

In HCN we have three atoms with valences of 1, 4, and 3, respectively. By joining the hydrogen and the nitrogen to the carbon, $H - C \equiv N$, we satisfy the valences. The molecule is linear as seen by the formula.

In $CBNF$ it does not seem to be possible to find a way of connecting the atoms to satisfy the valences. This would not be a stable molecule.

$PSNS$ seems to be possible on the basis of valence consideration, but there is no evidence that this compound exists in nature. If it did, it might look like this:

$$\begin{array}{c} P = N \\ | \quad | \\ S - S \end{array}$$

REFERENCES

1.   Andrews and Kokes, Chapter 5, pages 79 to 111, especially pages 91 ff. This discusses bonding in molecules in a somewhat more formal way than our treatment.

2. (T)   CBA, Chapter 7, pages 229 to 278; Summary, pages 450 to 455; Chapter 11, Sections 11-1 and 11-4 through 11-13, pages 456 to 458 and 464 to 478. These sections contain a large amount concerning bonding. The use of these references illustrates nicely the necessity to read something in total at first for general understanding, then to return periodically for items which give a more specific understanding.

3. (T) *Chem Study,* Chapter 16, pages 274 to 297. More about bonding and molecular shapes.

4. (T) Christiansen and Garrett, Chapter 7, Sections 7-1 through 7-3, pages 81 to 85. Early atomic theory.

5. (T) Greenstone, *et al,* pages 98 to 100. Simple descriptions of bonding.

6. Stevenson and Moore, Chapter 10, Sections 10.1 and 10.4, pages 228 to 232, 234 to 238. A physicist's view of bonding — including a discussion of van der Waals' forces.

CHAPTER 17

NONIONIC MATERIALS

Most of the solids encountered in everyday experience are not ionic crystals. We have stressed them in the textbook, not because they predominate over other types, but because, in the development of models, the connections between experiments and concepts are more direct for ionic crystals than for other types of solids. In this chapter we look at a variety of other types. Each substance we consider represents a group of nonionic compounds of which the one discussed is typical. Although all bonding forces are electrical in nature, it is convenient to make a distinction between covalent bonding, which involves an overlapping of electron clouds, and weaker forces, where electrical attraction between oppositely charged particles occurs at longer range. A brief discussion of this distinction follows.

If two atoms have live electron clouds which overlap to form a covalent bond, the force which holds the two atoms together is the strongest of all the forces considered in the text.

A somewhat different situation exists for particles which have no live clouds and therefore cannot form covalent bonds. Such particles can, however, exert weaker forces on each other, forces whose magnitude is determined by the distribution of electrical charge throughout the space occupied by the particles. Atoms of nonionic solids can be held together by both types of forces. Atoms within a molecule are held together by strong forces. The molecules are held together by weaker forces.

It is possible for covalent bonding to extend indefinitely far in one direction forming a very long chain which can be regarded as a huge molecule. A crystal can be formed by a large number of these molecular chains held together by weaker forces. Some polymers (Section 17-12) are crystals of this type.

The diamond typifies materials in which the atoms are held together exclusively by covalent bonds. Iodine is quite different. A molecule of iodine is composed of two atoms of iodine bound together by a covalent bond. But the molecules of iodine are held together in an iodine crystal by weak forces; in iodine, it is the interaction between induced dipoles that binds the molecules to each other.

The distribution of charge in a particle, such as an iodine molecule, can be described formally in terms of electrical *multipoles*, that is, *monopoles, dipoles, quadrupoles, octapoles,* and so forth. A particle which has an overall net charge can be represented as a monopole, either positive plus or negative minus. Clearly, what we have referred to as ions are monopoles, and ionic bonding can be said to be due to monopole forces. A molecule which is neutral or uncharged overall may, nevertheless, have a nonuniform charge distribution which is effectively positive in one region and negative in another (a dipole). As was brought out in Chapter 16, water molecules are examples of this sort of permanent polarization. Except for what we have called covalent bonding, nearly all of the bonding between atoms, ions, and molecules can be described, to a good approximation, as being due to monopole and dipole forces.

Multipoles, especially dipoles, do not have to be permanent to be effective in exerting binding forces, however. The motions of the electrons about atoms and molecules, or the momentary pulsations of the electron clouds, can cause corresponding momentary fluctuations in the charge distribution. Although such changes are only temporary, it is quite possible that when the proper combination of atoms or molecules is present, the fluctuating charge distributions, the *momentary dipoles,* exert on the average a net attractive force on one another. These are called van der Waals forces.

The attraction between the iodine molecules is explained in terms of momentary dipoles experiencing van der Waals forces. These forces are also the ones which hold many other crystals together: crystals composed of dead atoms such as He, Ne, and A; crystals of dead diatomic molecules such as H_2, O_2, N_2, and I_2; crystals of dead, symmetric, polyatomic molecules, such as CH_4 and CCl_4. The pictures in Figures 17-7 and 17-8 are especially appropriate for the dead atoms, somewhat less appropriate for molecules such as CH_4, and still less appropriate for symmetric molecules such as I_2. (A molecule of I_2 is not a sphere but a spherical representation does convey the idea of a particle with no permanent dipole, which is why it is commonly used in the description of van der Waals forces.)

Another example of a bonding force should be mentioned here: the hydrogen bond. The hydrogen bond is more than a dipole-dipole attraction. It is true that hydrogen-bonded molecules have dipoles, and the dipoles attract each other, but the force of the attraction is too large to be explained in terms of dipoles. For example, two molecules with O-H groups will be attracted to each other because of the dipoles associated with the polar O-H bonds. The hydrogen part of one bond will be attracted to the oxygen part of the other. There is more to the story, however. The oxygen atom in an O-H group attracts the bonding cloud so strongly that the tiny proton is left somewhat naked and exposed on the outer fringe of the bonding cloud. The proton in one O-H bond can come so close to the electron cloud of the oxygen atom in another O-H bond that it can distort that cloud and cause a small amount of overlap between the dead clouds associated with the two O-H groups. A force involving the overlapping of electron clouds comes into play. This force is ten times smaller than the force associated with an ordinary covalent bond, but it is twice as strong as the strongest dipole forces.

Hydrogen bonding cannot develop between molecules unless the molecules contain hydrogen atoms which are attached to highly electronegative atoms (e.g., oxygen, fluorine, and nitrogen). In methane CH_4, for example, the bonding clouds are not drawn so tightly toward the carbon atom that the hydrogen atoms are left exposed on the outer fringes of the clouds. The hydrogen atoms are deeply submerged. On the other hand, in CH_2Cl_2 there is some hydrogen bonding between molecules; the chlorine atoms pull the electron cloud away from carbon, causing the carbon atom to pull harder on the bonding clouds that contain protons.

We will leave a discussion of the metallic bond until we take up Sections 17-6, 7, and 8. It is no less important than the types we have been considering, but metals are sufficiently different from other solids (e.g., they are the only ones which conduct electricity well) that it is appropriate to take them up separately.

The variety of classifications we have set up for the binding forces in solids may be confusing, particularly when we recognize, as we must, that all such forces are ultimately electrical in nature. If we were to restrict ourselves to a particle description of nature, wherein we considered only the charged electrons and the oppositely charged nuclei, the only forces involved would be coulombic. In this description of matter the forces are simple, but the resulting structures and motions tend to become complex. Furthermore, such a model would include details unnecessary to our present purposes; it also would tend to obscure some simplifying and unifying characteristics. It is not inaccurate, but it is cumbersome and inconvenient. On the other hand, since a nucleus and the associated electrons persist as a unit through many transformations, it is convenient to consider them as an aggregate: an atom. When we take this view we find it useful to make an arbitrary distinction between covalent bonds, ionic bonds (electrostatic monopoles), induced dipole bonds (van der Waals forces), hydrogen bonds, and metallic bonds. Although the details of each may be quite complicated, they are useful labels for some very general sets of properties which enable us to compare and contrast otherwise diverse appearing substances; they serve as important unifying concepts.

Section 17-1 THE STRUCTURE OF DIAMOND

Our survey of nonionic crystals begins with a crystal in which the forces are relatively simple. There is only one type of bond between the atoms, the covalent bond. There is no distinction between intramolecular and intermolecular forces. The crystal can be regarded as a collection of atoms held together by interatomic forces only, or as a single molecule with intramolecular forces only.

The textbook tries to lead the student to infer the nature of the bonding from given experimental facts. It is important to start with speculations about the possible structures allowed by the model for carbon atoms developed in Chapter 16. Carbon has live electrons, so it has to form covalent bonds. If the only atoms present are carbon atoms, carbon must be bonded to carbon. The bonding can be tetrahedral in three dimensions, as in methane (CH_4), or it can be trigonal in two dimensions, as in benzene (C_6H_6). Either way, the bonding cannot be terminated to form small molecules if the only atoms present are carbon atoms. A collection of carbon atoms must form huge, macroscopic molecules.

A speculation of this type, together with the given data, can make the conclusions drawn in the text at least plausible, if not forceful.

QUESTIONS

17-1 Describe in terms of positions of atoms what you think may happen when diamond is heated above 3500° C.

Answer Diamond vaporizes above 3500° C. The atoms acquire such a large amount of energy that they break their bonds and move away from their lattice positions at high velocity.

17-2 Explain why diamond is a poor conductor of electricity.

Answer Diamond is a substance in which the atoms of carbon are held together by strong covalent bonds. There are no delocalized electrons available to carry a charge, therefore little electrical conduction is possible.

17-3 A diamond cleaves smoothly along four planes which are at right angles to the four covalent-bond directions. Can you suggest why this should be so?

Answer A plane passing at right angles to a covalent bond direction would intercept only one of the four bonds of each carbon atom (see Figure 17-1a). The forces bonding the atoms together would be equal in each of these orientations of the plane. Any other orientation of the plane would intersect more bonds per atom.

Section 17-2 OTHER CARBON COMPOUNDS

A crystal composed of carbon and other elements does not have to contain huge molecules. The remarkable ability of carbon to bond to carbon can be killed by terminating the bonding with atoms of other elements. Then the crystal can be held together by weak intermolecular forces between molecules, which in turn are held together by strong intramolecular forces.

The possible variety of molecules is illustrated by starting with methane (CH_4) and substituting other atoms (chlorine) for hydrogen atoms. Methane itself is so symmetrical that it has no permanent dipole, but the substituted molecules, except for CCl_4, do; Experiment 17-1 offers a way to test for them. It may be desirable to review Experiment 15-4 and to point out that water was deflected there because water molecules do have dipoles.

Some of the other carbon molecules mentioned in the text also have dipoles. For example, although ethane has no dipole, propane, butane, and pentane do. This can be seen by sketching a picture of propane and putting plus at each hydrogen and minus at each carbon. The carbon atoms draw the bonding clouds toward themselves so that each bond has its own dipole. The bond dipoles cancel each other in ethane, but not in propane. It is difficult to visualize the molecular structures well enough to see the dipoles, and the text does not pursue the question for these molecules. In fact, the role of permanent dipole forces in determining crystal stability and structure is soft pedaled throughout the chapter. Permanent dipole forces are omitted in Table 17-1 because permanent dipole-dipole interactions are weak compared to the other forces considered in hydrocarbons.

Experiment 17-1 Electrical Properties of Two Fluids

Equipment Needed (per 12 students)	*Cat. Number*
2 burets, 25 ml (Note a)	68885
1 pint, carbon tetrachloride, reagent (Note b)	68520
1 pint, dichloromethane, reagent (Note b)	68527
2 beakers, 250 ml	68815
2 pegboards (Note c)	68852
4 pegboard clamps, small	68532
4 acetate plastic strips (Note d)	68901
4 cotton cloths	68901
4 vinyl plastic strips	68901
4 wool cloths	68901

Laboratory Notes

(a) To economize, it is suggested that only two burets be provided for 12 students, especially since the time required to do the experiment is minimal. A soft glass buret is adequate and the calibration is not important, but each buret should have a glass or teflon stopcock.

One buret should always be used to contain the carbon tetrachloride. Similarly the other buret should always be used to contain dichloromethane. In using the burets the stopcocks should be adjusted so that the liquids flow in the finest possible continuous stream.

(b) Reagent grade pure chemicals are necessary for this experiment. Separate beakers are used to catch each liquid which is then used again.

Carbon tetrachloride and dichloromethane vapors are both hazardous to health; there should be plenty of fresh air ventilation in the room when this experiment is being done. Discard chemicals by washing them down the drain with large amounts of water.

(c) A pegboard is used as a buret support. Two small clamps will secure the buret to it.

(d) The cotton and wool cloths and the plastic strips are the electrostatic materials used in Experiments 11-2 and 15-4. A positive charge is produced when the acetate strip is rubbed with cotton cloth, and a negative charge is produced when the vinyl strip is rubbed with wool.

QUESTIONS

17-4 How many different compounds with the molecular formula $C_2H_4Cl_2$ are possible? Draw diagrams representing their structure.

Answer   Two different compounds are possible:

1, 2 Dichloroethane   1, 1 Dichloroethane

Since rotation around the carbon-carbon bond is possible, any other location of the chlorine atoms would duplicate one of the two structures shown.

17-5 Knowing that carbon forms four covalent bonds, hydrogen one, and oxygen two, draw all the possible isomers for C_2H_6O.

Answer C_2H_6O may be arranged in two ways:

$$
\begin{array}{cc}
\text{H} \quad \text{H} & \text{H} \qquad \text{H} \\
| \quad\; | & |\qquad\quad | \\
\text{H - C - C - OH} & \text{H - C - O - C - H} \\
| \quad\; | & |\qquad\quad | \\
\text{H} \quad \text{H} & \text{H} \qquad \text{H}
\end{array}
$$

Ethyl alcohol   Dimethyl ether

Section 17-3 GRAPHITE

After the digression in Section 17-2 to consider small carbon molecules, we return to the case of crystals composed entirely of carbon atoms. If carbon atoms do not bond tetrahedrally, as in diamond, they bond to form two-dimensional sheets, as in graphite. The atoms in each sheet are held to each other by strong covalent bonds, but the sheets are held to each other by weak forces of another type.

This model for graphite is quite successful in explaining some of the properties of the crystal. For example, it should be difficult to pull a sheet apart but easy to slide one sheet over another; this is found to be true. Note, however, that since the graphite in pencil lead does not exist in large sheets but in small sheets oriented in all directions, the spreading of the graphite in pencils is not evidence for the sheet model. To really test the model it is necessary to work with a single crystal.

The electrical properties of graphite offer a better test of the model. A single crystal permits the passage of electrons in one direction better than in another direction. This can be explained in terms of the delocalization of bonding electrons in the sheets. The delocalized electron clouds can be visualized by starting with benzene, as described in Chapter 16. The graphite sheet is a collection of rings similar to benzene rings, bonded to each other. The delocalized clouds on each ring merge to form large, highly delocalized clouds that lie above and below the sheet containing the rings. These clouds can be moved easily along the sheets, which is what happens when electricity is conducted in a direction parallel to the sheets.

QUESTION

17-6 Graphite is used as a lubricant at temperatures high enough to destroy an ordinary oil or grease. Suggest how it may function as a lubricant.

Answer   The forces which hold the sheets of carbon atoms together in graphite are quite weak. When graphite is placed between two surfaces, one of which is moving with respect to the other, one sheet of carbon atoms would be expected to glide easily across another. This is only part of the story, however, because minute amounts of moisture must also be present for graphite to function as a lubricant. If these trace amounts of moisture are removed either by heating to sufficiently high temperatures or by reducing the pressure sufficiently, graphite becomes a very abrasive material.

Section 17-4 LOOSELY BONDED CRYSTALS

In this section we come to grips with the weak forces that have been more or less ignored in previous work. The iodine molecule, whose atoms are held together by a strong chemical bond, has no live clouds, is not charged, and has no permanent charge separation. It is somewhat surprising then that iodine molecules can form crystals stable at room temperature. The explanation, as was pointed out earlier, lies in a type of force which is new to the students: van der Waals, a force between induced dipoles.

QUESTION

17-7 Would you expect methane CH_4 and tetrachloromethane CCl_4 to have similar melting points? Explain.
Answer CH_4 would be expected to have a lower melting point than CCl_4. CH_4 molecules are both lighter and smaller than CCl_4 molecules. The van der Waals forces are stronger between the larger molecules.

Section 17-5 HYDROGEN BONDING

Here we encounter a special force that comes into play in only a relatively small number of materials, but these materials are quite important. It is hydrogen bonding that makes water a liquid instead of a gas at ordinary temperatures, and causes water to freeze at a much higher temperature than might be expected. For example, hydrogen sulfide (H_2S), with larger, heavier molecules, is a vapor at ordinary temperatures; it has no appreciable hydrogen bonding. It is also hydrogen bonding that draws and holds amino acids to the RNA template in the synthesis of proteins, which are essential for life. The amino acids are held in a coded order while they form chemical bonds with each other, and when the protein is completed, hydrogen bonds are broken and the protein falls away.

QUESTIONS

17-8   Would you expect hydrogen fluoride HF and fluorine F_2 to have similar melting points? Explain.
Answer   Permanent dipole forces and hydrogen bonding both exist between the molecules of HF, but only van der Waals forces exist between the F_2 molecules. HF would have a higher melting point.

17-9   What observation can you recall from everyday experience concerning the relative densities of ice and water? Is our discussion of the structural differences between ice and water consistent with this experience?
Answer   Ice always forms on the surface of water; therefore ice must be less dense. Water molecules are more closely packed in water than in ice, which causes water to be more dense than ice. Water molecules are held in place in ice by hydrogen bonding. When ice melts some of the hydrogen bonds are broken and some crowding takes place.

17-10   Water has an unusually high boiling point for such a small molecule, as well as an unusually high melting point. How is this explained?
Answer   The high boiling and melting points of water are caused by the strong hydrogen bonding between the water molecules. Each molecule is attracted to four others through hydrogen bonding.

Sections 17-6, 7, 8 METALS

It was suggested in Chapter 16 that the bonding in metals represents the extreme case of electron delocalization. When the atoms are brought together so closely that the live electron clouds must be shared with many neighboring atoms, the live clouds merge to form one huge dead cloud that fills the entire space occupied by the metal. As the atoms come together, the overlapping of the merging clouds reduces the repulsive forces between atoms so that attractive forces are stronger and the potential energy becomes negative. As the atoms draw still closer, they reach a configuration in which repulsive forces have been revived to a level where they balance attractive forces. Further compression leads to more repulsion than attraction, and the potential energy increases. There is a particular configuration of lowest potential energy, and that is the stable, crystalline configuration for the metal. The individual atoms become ions trapped in potential wells which are due to the released, delocalized, and merged electron clouds.

The model described here is slightly different from the one developed in the textbook. There the delocalized electrons are described more as particles roaming freely through the crystal than as a cloud pervading the crystal. The particle model is better in the explanation of an electric current as a stream of electrons that move through the crystal and suffer collisions with ions. The cloud model is better in the sense that it brings the various types of bonding together under one idea. The stability of a metal can be understood more easily in terms of the atomic cores immersed in an electron cloud than in terms of wandering electron particles. Both models are useful and neither model is perfect.

The student is led to a model by a consideration of experimental facts and observations. These do not force him toward any particular model, however, and it may be helpful to suggest a review of electron delocalization as described in Chapter 16. Once a model is proposed, it can be accepted or rejected by the students on the basis of how well it explains the properties of metals in a qualitative way.

The malleability and ductility of metals are compared with the rigidity of diamonds. Both are bonded together by the overlapping of electron clouds, but in diamond the bonding clouds are localized. They cannot be distorted without destroying the bond. The carbon atoms hold each other apart at arms length, so to speak, and in particular directions. The metallic bonding cloud, on the other hand, can be distorted without severing cloud mergers. It is conceivable that a diamond under pressure would collapse into a metal with delocalized bonding electrons, but such pressures have not been reached. It is conceivable, for that matter, that all elements might become metals under high enough pressure. (A more detailed description of the metallic bonding cloud throws some doubt on the possibility of stable mergers for some elements.)

Electrical conductivity in metals is compared with that in graphite. Both have delocalized electron clouds that offer high conductivities, but in graphite the clouds are essentially two-dimensional sheets while in metals the cloud fills the entire space. This difference explains why the conductivity of graphite depends on the direction of current flow while the conductivity in metals is the same in all directions. Diamond is a poor conductor in any direction because the bonding electron clouds are not delocalized.

It might be worthwhile to indicate how much we can understand of the structure and properties of matter on the basis of the cloud model. The structure and properties of ionic crystals are due partly to the repulsion between the dead clouds of ions. The formation of molecules, molecular structures, and the possibility of macromolecules are due to the lowering of potential energy when live clouds merge. The malleability of metals, the ease of spreading of graphite, and the conductivity of both are due to cloud delocalization. Molecular dipoles arise from cloud polarization. Van der Waals forces arise from cloud fluctuations. Hydrogen bonds arise from cloud distortion when a dead cloud encounters the highly concentrated charge of an exposed proton.

Experiment 17-2 Mechanical Properties of Metals

Equipment Needed (per 2 students)	Cat. Number
4 ft, copper wire, No. 22 gage (Note a)	68913
10 in., iron wire, No. 14 gage	68913
1 hammer and anvil (Note b)	68840
1 dowel rod, 1 in. x 14 in.	68890

Laboratory Notes

(a)   The copper wire should be cut and supplied in two different lengths — one 6 in. long and the other 3½ ft long. The shorter section will be hammered on, and the longer section will be attached to the dowel rods and stretched. The wire diameter is not important as long as the students can stretch it. The wire should not have a cloth or plastic coating, but an enamel surface will not interfere with anything.

(b)   The hammer (and anvil) are the dense metal blocks used originally in Experiment 5-3. Each pair of students should be given two of the blocks, one to be used as the hammer and the other as an anvil.

Section 17-9 A COMPARISON OF CRYSTAL BOND TYPES

The classification of forces mentioned in the introductory notes earlier becomes explicit in this section of the textbook. Various types of forces are listed in order of decreasing strength (Table 17-1) as indicated by the heat of sublimation. The forces are referred to as "bond types." The term "bond" is used here in the sense that it applies to any aggregate of particles which holds together over a period of time because the particles do not have enough energy to escape from potential wells. The covalent and metallic bond types are the strongest. The ionic bond type, which comes next, represents monopole forces. The hydrogen bond and the van der Waals bond represent dipole forces.

The covalent bond is the strongest because the bonding clouds are localized. If delocalized bonds are added to localized bonds, as in some of the examples considered in Chapter 16, the overall bonding becomes stronger, but that does not mean that delocalized bonds are strong. In metals all bonds are delocalized; and these are weaker than covalent bonds.

Among the dipole forces, the hydrogen bond is the strongest because it is due to permanent dipole forces strengthened somewhat by the attraction of the strong electronegative element for the proton. Van der Waals bonds are weaker because they are due only to momentary dipoles.

QUESTIONS

17-11   What is meant by the statement, "There are no directed bonds in a metal crystal?"
Answer   A delocalized mobile electron in a metal crystal is not associated with any specific atom and therefore is not directed.

17-12   Suppose a metal has a metallic impurity whose atoms are larger than those of the host metal. What effect will this have on the properties of the metal?
Answer   A metallic impurity whose atoms are larger than the host metal would weaken the structure and the conductivity of the host metal by localizing some of the mobile electrons near the impurity.

Sections 17-10, 11, 12 SULFUR, GLASS, POLYETHYLENE

These sections illustrate the variety of materials that appear to be solid but which may not be crystalline (in the sense of having an orderly array of particles). These materials can form crystals, but they can also be prepared in such a way that considerable aging is required to achieve the crystalline arrangement of particles. The possibility of the materials congealing into amorphous states arises from the complexity of the ions and the molecules, which makes them hard to pack. The attractive forces between the ions and molecules are too weak to cause the rapid organization of neighboring particles needed to produce deep potential wells for trapping. Such materials are too slow in flowing to be regarded as ordinary liquids and too slow in crystallizing to be regarded as solids.

Sulfur is somewhat like carbon in the sense that the atoms tend to bond to each other. This tendency is not nearly as pronounced as in carbon, and even if it were it would not be possible for sulfur to form macroscopic molecules of the type that occur in diamond and graphite; sulfur atoms can only form two covalent bonds to other sulfur atoms, so the sulfur aggregates have to be chains rather than two-dimensional sheets or three-dimensional crystals. Sulfur vapor at high temperatures is composed of atoms, but as the temperature is reduced, molecules containing up to eight atoms are formed. The molecules are chains of atoms and some of the chains close to form rings. At $445°C$, the vapor condenses to form a liquid composed of rings and chains. Some of the chains are longer than the chains in the vapor because of unions formed in the intimacy of the liquid state. As the temperature of the liquid is reduced, S_8 rings begin to predominate over chains because the rings are especially stable (all electron clouds dead and happy with the bond angles). When sulfur freezes(at 10 to $20°$ above the boiling point of water), S_8 rings crystallize out, and they organize themselves into a crystal structure. Several structures are possible, but only one structure is completely stable at a particular temperature. This is a matter of the "survival of the stablest" in the battle where chains are being broken, connected, and ringed. If the liquid is frozen so rapidly that the battles cannot be completed, the solid is a chaotic mass of rings and chains. In any case, the final, stable sulfur crystal contains chemically bonded sulfur organized into S_8 rings. The rings are held to each other by van der Waals forces.

In polyethylene we again have chemical bonding extended to form chains which are held together by weak forces. In this case, however, it is ethylene groups and not atoms that combine to form chains. An ethylene group is a pair of carbon atoms joined together by a double bond (see Figure 17-4). One of the two bonds can be regarded as delocalized and therefore is easily distorted out of shape. When two ethylene molecules approach each other head on, one of the delocalized electrons on each molecule can withdraw from the merger with the other delocalized electron in the same molecule, and delocalized electrons on each of the two molecules can merge to form a localized bond. This produces a molecule twice as long as ethylene which has live electron clouds at both ends. The live ends combine with other ethylene molecules, and the chain grows until the growth is terminated by killing the live ends with the addition of atoms or molecules that only have one live cloud. The finished polymer molecule has no delocalized electrons.

It is possible to prepare polymers in which the finished polymeric molecules do still have delocalized electrons involved in double bonds connecting carbon atoms. These molecules are dead, but they can be brought back to life if double bonds on one molecule draw near to double bonds on another molecule. The delocalized electrons are happily merged on their own molecules, but the possibility of forming new mergers that result in stronger localized bonds is enough to pull the double bonds open and develop new bonds between molecules. This is what happens when rubber is vulcanized.

QUESTIONS

17-13 Give formulas for the compound of sulfur with hydrogen and for the compound of sulfur with sodium.

Answer   Sulfur needs two electrons to complete its outermost shell. Both hydrogen and sodium have only one electron in its outermost shell.

$$S + H_2 \rightarrow H_2S \text{ and } 2Na + S \rightarrow Na_2S$$

17-14 Would you expect hydrogen sulfide to be ionic? Would you expect sodium sulfide to be ionic?

Answer   Sodium sulfide would be expected to be ionic since sodium easily gives up its single electron from the outer shell. Hydrogen sulfide would be expected to be only weakly ionic since the single electron in hydrogen is held more tightly than the outer electron of sodium. Since sulfur and oxygen have the same number of electrons in their outermost shell, H_2O which has been shown to be weakly ionic may be compared with H_2S.

Experiment 17-3 Physical Properties of Sulfur

Equipment Needed (per 2 students)	*Cat. Number*
3 test tubes, 150 x 25 mm	68873
20 grams, sulfur	68555
1 microscope slide, glass	68850
2 magnifiers	68847
1 pegboard and clamps	68852
1 porcelain crucible	68825
1 beaker, 250 ml	68815
1 alcohol burner	68810
1 thermometer, $-10°$ to $+360°$C (Note a)	68874
1 glass stirring rod	68867
2 pairs, safety goggles	68838
1 safety matches	68539
paper towels	—

Laboratory Note

The thermometer suggested here has a range of -10° to 360° C. It need only be calibrated in degrees Celsius. This same thermometer was used in Experiment 2-6.

At ordinary temperatures sulfur exists as rhombic crystals; when heated to 95.6° C it undergoes a slow transition to the monoclinic form. Both forms exist in the solid state as S_8 molecules.

The changes which occur when sulfur is heated are somewhat complicated. When heated carefully it melts at about 115° C to give a yellow liquid. There is some evidence that the melting process breaks some of the S_8 rings to give chains of the composition S_6 and S_4. Between 115° and 160° C there should be little change noted in the fluidity of the liquid sulfur. Between 160° and about 200° C the material becomes more viscous and changes to a brown color. The increased viscosity is probably due to the formation of long chains of sulfur atoms.

Above 200° C the viscosity decreases again as a result of the breaking up of the long chains. At the boiling point, 444.6° C, sulfur is again a mobile liquid. If sulfur at a temperature in the range of 160 to 200° C is cooled rapidly, a soft rubbery material known as plastic sulfur is formed. In this state the long sulfur chains are in the form of coils; the rubbery character is due to the ability of these chains to uncoil and coil again under stress. When left to stand, plastic sulfur slowly reverts to the rhombic form.

Experiment 17-4 A Model of Sulfur

Equipment Needed (per student)	Cat. Number
8 polystyrene spheres, ½-in. diameter	68903
2 push pins	68887
8 wooden toothpicks	68862
1 protractor	—
1 tube quick-drying cement	68578

Experiment 17-5 Experiments with Glass

Part A   Manipulating Glass

Equipment Needed (per 2 students)	Cat. Number
12 in. soft glass tubing, No. 6 or 7	68835
12 in., hard glass tubing, No. 6 or 7	68835
1 tubing scorer	68835
1 alcohol burner	68810

Laboratory Notes

The glass tubing can be identified by looking at the end of the tube. Soft lime glass is faintly greenish and hard glass is distinctly blue.

The sodium ions present in glass impart the yellow color to the flame.

Part B   Testing Conductivity (A Demonstration)

Equipment Needed	Cat. Number
1 a.c. line cord with a regular plug on one end and an insulated battery clip on each of the two wires at the other end	—
2 carbon electrodes (similar to those used in Experiment 14-1)	68886
1 2-in. piece of No. 7 soft glass tubing	68835
200-watt bulb (Note a)	—
line switch	—
Bunsen burner	—

Laboratory Notes

The 200-watt bulb is used to show when current is passing; it also acts as a current limiter. A bulb of less than 200 watts will have too much resistance.

When the switch is turned on before the heating starts, the bulb does not light. When the glass tubing is heated enough to become quite soft the bulb will glow. Glass is composed of compounds which are mostly ionic such as sodium and calcium silicate. When the glass is softened the positive Na^+ and Ca^{+2} ions and the negative silicate ions migrate and carry the charges between the electrodes.

Experiment 17-6 Experiments with Polyethylene

Equipment Needed (per 2 students)	Cat. Number
4 test tubes, 150 x 25 mm	68873
20 grams, polyethylene, granular (Note a)	68899
1 thermometer, -10 to 360°C	68874
1 alcohol burner	68810
1 buret clamp, modified (Note b)	68532
1 battery pack, lamp, lamp socket and connecting wires (see Experiment 16-1) (Note c)	68814
4 batteries, 1½-volt	68813
1 glass stirring rod	68867
safety matches	68539
2 pairs, safety goggles	68838

Laboratory Notes

(a)   The polyethylene suggested for use here should be the branched, low-density, or high-pressure variety, not the linear, high-density, low-pressure type. The latter has an appreciably higher softening point and never becomes fluid, even when heated well above its softening point.

(b)   It is very hard to hold the test tube with a normal test-tube holder or a pegboard clamp since the substances being tested in this experiment become glue-like in consistency. It is difficult to stir these substances without having the test tube slide around. The modified buret clamp used earlier in Experiment 14-1 solves this problem.

(c)   The electrical conductivity of the polyethylene threads may be tested by using the same setup as was used in Experiment 14-1, but replacing the U-tube and electrodes with the threads of polyethylene. The conductivity of the melted polyethylene may be tested by using the same apparatus with two carbon electrodes. The method of Experiment 12-3, Part B may also be used.

QUESTIONS

17-15   Did you expect polyethylene to conduct electricity as a solid? Why?
  Answer   Since polyethylene is a covalent carbon compound it would not be expected to conduct electricity.

17-16   Polyethylene does not have a distinct melting point. Try to predict how this would affect the shape of its cooling curve.

Answer   Since polyethylene does not have a distinct melting point, the shape of its cooling curve would be a gradual slope with no plateaus.

Section 17-13 RUBBER – NETWORK POLYMERS

Experiment 17-7 An Experiment with Rubber

Equipment Needed (per 2 students)	Cat. Number
1 test tube, 150 x 25 mm	68859
15 ml, toluene (Note a)	68559
1 beaker, 250 ml (Note b)	68815
3 rubber bands (and some miscellaneous pieces of rubber)	68859
1 cork stopper, for the test tube (Note c)	68859

Laboratory Hints

(a)   Toluene is both highly flammable and toxic. When used there should be plenty of ventilation and no flames.

(b)   The beaker is used as a test-tube rack.

(c)   Do not try to use a rubber stopper in this experiment.

   The toluene will cause the rubber to become a soft, gummy, sticky substance. Almost all of its elasticity will be lost. Pure rubber will be more affected than synthetic rubber, but samples of pure gum rubber are difficult to find. Rubber tubing, automobile tires, erasers, and some rubber bands are a mixture of both synthetic and natural rubber.

QUESTIONS

17-17   How are the properties of paraffin wax different from those of polyethylene? Paraffin has a structure of hydrocarbon chains like polyethylene, but the chain lengths are only 1/100 to 1/1000 that of the chain lengths in polyethylene. Explain the difference in properties in terms of structure.

Answer   Paraffin wax is softer, has less tensile strength, and a lower melting point than polyethylene. These differences can all be attributed to the difference in the length of chains. The paraffin chains, which are much shorter, will not coil and entangle with each other as much as the longer polyethylene chains.

17-18   Do you think a hardened phenol-formaldehyde resin would melt? Explain.

Answer   One would expect a phenol-formaldehyde resin to melt since it is a long-chain polymer like polyethylene. Phenol-formaldehyde resins are made up of benzene rings linked together in long chains. Once hardened by heat and pressure, however, these resins soften but do not melt. Bakelite is a good example.

17-19   Does stretching rubber cause a change in the entropy of the rubber? Explain.
Answer   Stretching rubber orients the long carbon chains in a more orderly arrangement (see Figure 17-7). Therefore stretching a piece of rubber would cause a decrease in the entropy of the rubber.

17-20   Would a network polymer such as a hardened epoxy resin yield a regular x-ray diffraction pattern? Explain.
Answer   Epoxy resins are made up of long-chain molecules which are cross linked and entangled. No regular pattern is formed.

Section 17-14 MIXTURES

No comments.

Section 17-15 CONCLUSION

The questions raised at the end of the section, with reference to Figure 17-21, are not easily answered, but they can be useful if the student gives them some thought before hearing about possible answers.

Silicon carbide is a mystery unless it is noticed that silicon is just below carbon in the periodic table. A silicon atom is very much like a carbon atom in that it has the same number of live electron clouds but a larger dead atomic core. We may think of a silicon atom as an overstuffed carbon atom. Then we might guess that silicon carbide is like diamond except that half of the carbon atoms are replaced by overstuffed carbon atoms. Actually, there are various ways to put the two different kinds of atoms into the diamond lattice, and hence there are various forms of silicon carbide. In all forms, however, silicon carbide is a crystalline solid like diamond (if we ignore the differences in the sizes of the atoms) and the atoms are held together by localized, covalent bonds. Since the binding forces are localized covalent bonds, silicon carbide undoubtedly has the highest melting point among the materials listed, and it is not an electrical conductor. All crystalline forms melt above $2200°C$.

Potassium fluoride is an ionic crystal. Any compound involving one element which is distinctly metallic (far to the left on the periodic table) and another element which is distinctly nonmetallic (far to the right on the periodic table) is an ionic crystal. The polarization is so extreme that the live electron cloud of the metal atom is torn away and transferred to the nonmetal atom forming ions with dead clouds. Since there are no mobile ions in the solid crystal, and since there are no delocalized electrons, the material is a poor conductor (unless dissolved). The crystal structure is probably something like the structure of NaCl or CsCl.

Iron is a metal. It conducts electricity because of its delocalized electrons. It has a high melting point ($1535°C$) because of the stability of the highly delocalized electron cloud. The structure is a close-packed structure (see Section 17-7 and Experiment 5-2). In the molten state iron does not have an orderly crystalline structure, but it still has the delocalized electron cloud, which makes a good conductor of electricity.

In the compound with six OH groups, the molecules are held together by hydrogen bonds and the material is probably a liquid or solid at ordinary temperatures and pressures. To propose a detailed model is out of the question. Regarding conductivity, however, we can make a good guess: there are no delocalized electrons and there are no ions, therefore this substance would be a nonconductor.

The long chains (d) form a linear polymer with no opportunity for cross linking. Again, there are no ions or delocalized electrons, so the material is probably a nonconductor. The material is likely to be an amorphous solid. The chains are bonded together by the weak van der Waals forces which are relatively strong in this case because of the chlorine atoms. These atoms are dead, but they form polar bonds with carbon and they have large electron clouds that are easily polarized. The structure of the solid would depend on the manner of crystallization.

QUESTIONS

17-21 (a) We know that an atom consists largely of empty space. The nuclei are very small indeed. What keeps the nuclei from coming much closer together than the distance of the sum of the radii of the two atoms? (b) When you push on a table (made of atoms) with your finger (made of atoms), what keeps your finger from sinking into the table?
Answer Repulsion of dead electron clouds.

17-22 Heptane is one of the components in gasoline which causes knocking in automobile engines. It is a straight chain (i.e., unbranched) hydrocarbon and has 7 carbon atoms and 16 hydrogen atoms. Draw the structure of this hydrocarbon and give its formula.
Answer The formula is C_7H_{16}. The structure can be represented in a variety of ways. Three of these are given below.

$$H - \overset{\overset{H}{|}}{\underset{\underset{H}{|}}{C}} - \overset{\overset{H}{|}}{\underset{\underset{H}{|}}{C}} - \overset{\overset{H}{|}}{\underset{\underset{H}{|}}{C}} - \overset{\overset{H}{|}}{\underset{\underset{H}{|}}{C}} - \overset{\overset{H}{|}}{\underset{\underset{H}{|}}{C}} - \overset{\overset{H}{|}}{\underset{\underset{H}{|}}{C}} - \overset{\overset{H}{|}}{\underset{\underset{H}{|}}{C}} - H$$

$$CH_3 \quad CH_2 \quad CH_2 \quad CH_2 \quad CH_2 \quad CH_2 \quad CH_3$$

$$CH_3 \quad (CH_2)_5 \quad CH_3$$

17-23 Draw diagrams of models of the chloromethane (CH_3Cl) and trichloromethane ($CHCl_3$) molecules. Trichloromethane (called chloroform) is a liquid at room temperature. Predict whether it would be deflected by a charged rod as in water. Explain the basis of your prediction.
Answer Both molecules are tetrahedral, similar to methane CH_4. See Figure 17-3. Trichloromethane is slightly polar because of the stronger attraction of the chlorine atoms for electrons as compared to hydrogen atoms. There will be a weak attraction between a charged rod and a fine stream of trichloromethane.

17-24 Suppose the structure of ice were more closely packed than that of water. How would this affect what happens in lakes in the winter? in the summer?
Answer If the molecules of ice were more closely packed than water its density would be greater. As a result the lakes would freeze at the bottom first and probably freeze solid in time. The ice at the bottom of the lake might not melt during the summer.

17-25 If a fish bowl were filled with water and placed outdoors when the temperature was below $0°C$, the bowl would probably break. Why?
Answer When water freezes, its volume increases due to the decrease in density.

17-26 When the whole weight of a person is concentrated on the narrow blade of an ice skate, the open structure of the ice beneath the blade is subjected to a very high pressure. What would you suppose might happen as a result? How is this related to the almost complete lack of friction between the skate blade and the ice?
Answer The pressure of an ice-skate blade on the ice tends to compress the material into its low volume, high-density state. Thus, increased pressure converts low density ice to higher-density water; a thin layer of liquid molecules forms between the skate blade and the ice. The skate blade glides along on this thin layer of water, which offers very little resistance to the skate.

17-27 Consider some substances not mentioned in this chapter. Describe a property of each that gives some clue as to its structure. What is the clue and what does it tell you?
Answer No specific answer can be given for this question.

17-28   Would you expect a diamond to become a conductor at very high pressures? The answer is not known at the present time. If it does become a conductor, what has happened to the bonds? *Answer*   For diamond to become a conductor, some of the strong covalent bonds between the carbon atoms would need to be broken to free some electrons so that they would be mobile. The mobile electrons would need to form a "sea" or delocalized clouds of electrons as with metals to make the diamond conductive.

REFERENCES

1.   Andrews and Kokes, Chapter 5, pages 83 to 111; Chapter 6, pages 114 to 143; Chapter 8, pages 194 to 196. Nonionic bonding.

2. (T)   CBA, same references as for Chapter 16.

3. (T)   Sienko and Plane, Chapter 3, pages 49 to 74. An intermediate description of various bond types.

APPENDIX I
COURSE PLAN

A.   TEACHING THE COURSE

In the preface to this resource book, we listed four threads found throughout all scientific work: the usefulness of mathematics; the necessity to question; the necessity to perform experiments; the need to make models. It is desirable that the course be taught in such a way that these threads become clear to the student. In this section we suggest ways in which this may be accomplished.

Mathematics

We make only limited use of mathematics and the level of difficulty is not high. We assume that the students taking this course will have had high school algebra and that, in general, they dislike mathematics. It is our belief, however, that students should realize the usefulness of mathematics and the immense simplification and precision it brings to the scientific enterprise. Accordingly we have introduced mathematical reasoning in Chapters 4 and 6 in the development of the Bragg equation, and in Chapters 8, 9, and 10 in the development of the concepts of energy and kinetic theory.

We have tried to go about the developments slowly and carefully, and we urge you to go about them in the same way. If you proceed slowly with each mathematical development and allow frequent pauses for discussion, we believe that you can instill in most of your students an understanding of the importance of mathematics in science and an appreciation of its logical beauty.

Questions

To involve the students in the business of science we have done what the scientist does: ask questions of ourselves and nature. Many such questions appear without a number in the body of the text. These are rhetorical in nature, sometimes intended to make the student pause and think about what he is reading, and sometimes used as a means of introducing a new discussion. They are not necessarily questions for which an answer is expected. Many, in fact, do not have an answer. This is intentional because we hope that students will gradually come to realize that science does not have all the answers, even in those areas which are its legitimate concern, and that in all probability it never will have because each time we extend our level of understanding in science, we seem to open up still larger and previously unknown areas for investigation.

We have also included a large number of questions throughout the text which are designed to serve as the basis for classroom discussion. These questions have been set apart from the body of the text and assigned numbers. As many as possible should be assigned to the students and then discussed in class, since they are an integral part of the course. The majority of these numbered questions require a certain amount of thought and reasoning to answer them. Few ask for mere factual answers or call for simple substitution into memorized formulas. The presence of more than a few such traditional questions could undo all of our efforts to develop a scientific attitude and spirit on the part of the student.

It is our experience that the aims of this course will be better met and the students' understanding of science will be better developed if you, as the teacher, assume the role of a guide helping the students to seek answers to questions rather than that of an expert who tells them what the answers are.

You will find that all numbered questions are discussed here in the same section as that in which they appear in the text. At the ends of some chapters of this volume a few additional questions with answers have also been included. These additional questions may serve as a basis for further discussion if you feel that it is desirable.

The parts of a course which become important to students depend largely on the kinds of questions they are asked on examinations. In order to direct the students' study in the desired directions, we urge that you avoid stereotyped factual questions and that you use questions similar to those in the text. RB Appendix II includes a number of questions from which you can draw in preparing examinations. Many of these are suitable for machine scoring.

Experiments

Just as experimentation is essential to the development of science, so the laboratory is an integral part of this course, and the students must be made aware that the experiments are not just a set of exercises to perform. Rather, they are our way of questioning nature to find out how it behaves. Before each experiment the students should know what question is being asked and why. This knowledge can be strengthened by a prelab discussion either in the classroom or in the laboratory. The students should keep these questions in mind as they perform the experiment, and a postlab discussion should be held to verify and interpret the results obtained.

We urge you to require your students to record in a notebook the observations which they make as they perform each experiment. These records may be in the form of notes or numerical data. Upon completion of the experiment they should write down their conclusions and the answers they find to the questions which were asked. Frequently these conclusions will be in the form of answers to questions which are actually stated in the text. It appears that little is gained and much motivation is lost by requiring the students to write formal reports, but we believe that their powers of observation will be strengthened if they are required to record their results. Obviously the notebooks will be effective as teaching tools only if they are collected, examined, and commented on by the instructor.

An equipment list for each experiment accompanies the discussion of the experiment in the resource book; usually some notes are included indicating ways in which it is to be set up and used. In general, we have attempted to keep the equipment as simple as possible. We could have gone in a different direction and, by using more complicated and sophisticated apparatus, made sure that the results were more accurate. But again, we have made our choice intentionally. In the first place, much scientific equipment is too sophisticated for nonscience students to understand or appreciate. It takes on the character of a black box, which, when its knobs and dials are turned the right amount in the proper sequence, will give the result they have been assigned to find. This contributes very little to their knowledge or understanding of science. Second, we want students to know that there is a great deal which can be learned about the world around them using only the simplest equipment. This is of particular importance to those who go into elementary teaching. If they learn that many important questions can be answered using only elementary logic, careful observation, and simple equipment, they will be far better teachers for it.

We have divided our experimental work into four categories. *Chair-arm* experiments are so straightforward and require so little equipment that they can be performed by students during the course of a lecture at their own seats. *Take-home* experiments require no supervision and only a minimum of equipment, but take more time or require additional facilities such as running water, so that they are not suitable as chair-arm experiments. Even what we have called *laboratory* experiments do not (with few exceptions) require the use of a laboratory as it is usually defined. All that is needed is a room with some work tables and a sink in it. We have also included a few demonstration experiments which are so designated, either because more extensive equipment is required or because more classroom discussion is desirable as they are being performed. A conscious effort should be made to involve the students in these demonstrations so that they participate as actively as possible. The number of these demonstration experiments has been kept to a minimum since this is intended to be a course in which the students engage in science rather than just watch it.

To guide you in scheduling these experiments and in planning your experimental work we have included in Section B of this Appendix a list of all of the experiments in the course, with an indication of the preferred, the satisfactory, and the undesirable ways of administering them.

Models

In the development of science the use of mental and mathematical and structural models plays a very significant role. If our students are to understand the nature of science and its development, they must understand the development and use of models. In the text we have made a conscious effort to bring about this understanding. We have tried to do it by example wherever possible, suggesting alternative models and designing tests to determine which is better. We have also asked the student to do it: "What models can you construct which fit your observations?" "What new phenomena can you predict using your models?"

Students may be unhappy with some of the models that we propose. They are usually upset not because the model does not fit their observations, but because it is not the model they were given in high school. In dealing with atomic structure in Chapter 13, for instance, we present the Bohr model which some students will say is wrong. We also present the shell model, the quantum-mechanical model, and the charged cloud model. Which is right? Some are right for some phenomena, others right for other phenomena, but no one model is right for all phenomena. When students understand this, they will have come a long way toward understanding the purpose of models in science.

B.   SCHEDULING THE COURSE

Lecture, Discussion, and Laboratory Schedule

In reading the textbook for this course your first impression may be that it is designed for a class of fifteen to twenty students who meet in a combined classroom and laboratory so that they can move from discussion to experiment or vice versa whenever it appears desirable. There is little question that this is the ideal way to present a science course if students are to get a feel for the business of science, but practical considerations of scheduling and economics usually make it impossible. However, the experience at a number of schools where this course has been taught experimentally demonstrates that it can be effective for larger groups of students if the following conditions are met:

(a)   The duration of the course should be a full school year.
(b)   Frequent laboratory experiences must be provided.
(c)   There must be time for discussion in groups small enough to permit extensive student participation.

These requirements can be perhaps ideally met by a schedule which includes three lecture periods, or two lectures and one recitation period, plus a two-hour laboratory meeting per week throughout the year. A number of variations have been used, however, and any which do not differ radically from the ideal have been quite satisfactory.

Scheduling Experiments

As a guide to help you in planning the experimental work, we include on the following pages a list of all of the experiments described in the text or in this resource book. Following the number, title, and text reference for each experiment, we indicate which methods of conducting it are preferable, which are satisfactory, and which are undesirable. In interpreting these recommendations you should bear in mind that:

A *demonstration experiment* is performed with only one set of equipment for the class, but the students may be called upon to take data or to interpret the results of the experiment.

A *laboratory experiment* is to be performed by students, usually working in pairs. Such an experiment ordinarily requires a prelab and a postlab discussion. Some such experiments require less than a full laboratory period, so two or more may be combined.

A *chair-arm experiment* is to be performed on the arm of the chair during class. The materials may be passed out to the students in plastic bags as they enter the classroom or during the class.

A *take-home experiment* is sufficiently simple that the students can perform it at home. Any required materials may be distributed in plastic bags as the students leave. The results obtained should be discussed and compared at a subsequent class meeting.

You will find it very helpful to secure the services of a student assistant to set up equipment for laboratory meetings and to prepare kits for chair-arm and take-home experiments. With some guidance and the instructions in this resource book, an able undergraduate student should be adequate to do the task. The following table of experiments includes estimates of the time required by such an assistant to prepare each individual set of equipment.

As a final comment on experiments, it might be well to note that students should wear safety goggles at all times in the laboratory when they are heating or mixing substances; in some states this is required by law.

| Experiment | | | Method of Administration (2) | | | | Time for Experiment; Minutes (3) | |
Number (1)	Title	Reference to textbook section	Demonstration	Laboratory	Chair-arm	Take-home	Preparation per set-up	Performance (class time)

(1)   The absence of a number after a dash indicates a recommended demonstration.

(2)   P - Preferred; S - Satisfactory; U - Undesirable

(3)   Preparation times are approximate, and depend in part on the condition and location of equipment.

Number	Title	Ref.	Demonstration	Laboratory	Chair-arm	Take-home	Preparation	Performance
1-1	The salol experiment	1-3	U	S	P	S	2	15
1-2	Solution of powders	1-3	U	S	U	P	5	—
1-3	Formation and dissolving of crystals							
	A. Potassium permanganate	1-3	S	P	P	U	2	15
	B. Metal and Powder	1-3	U	P	P	P	8	—
1-4	Classification of objects	1-5	U	P	S	P	5	30
2-1	Making measurements	2-2	U	P	S	S	15	60
2-2	Observations of dissolving solids	2-4	U	P	S	P	5	10
2-3	A thermal illusion	2-4	U	P	S	P	—	—
2-4	The temperature sensitivity of the hand	2-4	U	P	S	P	—	—
2-5	Heat transfer of different substances	2-5	S	P	U	S	5	30
2-6	Temperature change during cooling	2-5	S	P	U	U	5	45
2-7	A closer look at the plateau	2-5	S	P	U	U	—	15
3-1	Chemical reaction produced by light	3-1	U	S	S	P	5	—
3-2	Colored objects	3-2	U	P	P	P	5	10
3-	Color demonstrations	3-2	P	U	U	U	10	15
3-3	Breaking up white light	3-2	P	S	U	P	—	—
3-	Dispersion by single and double prism	3-2	P	S	U	U	10	10
3-4	Water waves	3-3	U	S	S	P	—	—
3-	Wave machine	3-3	P	S	U	U	10	5
3-	Waves in a ripple tank	3-3	P	S	S	U	10	15
3-5	Waves in a spring	3-3	S	P	U	P	5	30
3-	Pulses in an expanded slinky spring	3-3	P	U	U	U	30	15

Number	Title	Reference to textbook section	Demonstration	Laboratory	Chair-arm	Take-home	Preparation per set-up	Performance (class time)
4-1	Young's double-slit experiment	4-1	S	P	U	U	5	20
4-	Interference of water waves, ripple tank	4-3	P	S	U	U	10	20
4-2	Measuring the wavelength of light	4-3	S	P	U	U	5	60
4-3	Separation of wires in a mesh	4-3	P	S	U	U	5	30
5-	Salol experiment (repeat)	5-1	S	S	P	S	5	—
5-	Harvesting crystals (Experiment 1-2)	5-2	U	S	S	P	—	—
5-1	Salt and sugar	5-2	U	S	U	P	—	—
5-2	Packing of spheres	5-2	S	S	P	S	5	10
5-3	Cleaving crystals	5-4	S	P	P	P	5	10
6-	The grating spectroscope	6-2	S	P	P	U	5	15
7-1	The distillation of wood	7-2	S	P	U	U	10	60
7-2	Effect of heat on various solids							
	A. General observations	7-2	S	P	S	U	10	45
	B. The melting point of a mixture	7-2	S	P	U	U	2	25
7-3	The vaporization of a liquid	7-3	S	P	U	U	5	20
7-	Diffusion demonstrations	7-4						
	1. Ammonia vapor from an open dish		P	U	U	U	5	15
	2. Ammonia and HCl in a glass tube		P	U	U	U	15	10
	3. Ink in water		P	U	U	P	5	10
	4. Potassium permanganate in water		P	U	U	U	5	10
	5. Bromine in vacuum and in air		P	U	U	U	20	15
7-	Brownian motion	7-5	P	S	U	U	—	—
7-4	Effect on a gas of change in temperature	7-6	S	P	U	U	5	120
8-1	Motion on a horizontal surface	8-1	S	P	U	P	—	—
8-	Air pucks	8-1	P	U	U	S	10	10
8-2	Acceleration of falling objects	8-2	S	P	U	U	5	60
8-3	Force and motion	8-3	S	P	U	U	5	60
9-1	Conservation of mechanical energy	9-5	S	P	U	U	5	60
10-1	Temperature and pressure of a gas	10-2	P	S	U	U	10	20
11-1	Introduction to electrical forces	11-7	S	P	P	P	5	10
11-2	Types of electric charges	11-7	S	P	S	P	10	20
11-3	Transfer of charge through materials	11-8	S	P	S	S	10	30
12-1	Production of a flow of charges	12-2	P	U	U	U	—	—
12-2	A simple electric circuit	12-2	S	P	P	P	5	20
12-3	Electric current used to study materials							
	A. Metallic conductors	12-5	S	P	P	P	5	15
	B. Conductivities of materials	12-6	S	P	U	U	10	40
12-4	Mechanical analog to conduction	12-7	P	U	U	U	20	15
13-	Cathode rays	13-1	P	U	U	U	20	10
13-1	Size of an object by collisions	13-2	S	P	U	P	3	60

Number	Title	Reference textbook section	Demonstration	Laboratory	Chair-arm	Take-home	Preparation per set-up	Performance (class time)
13-2	Atomic mass of magnesium	13-3	Sa*	Pa*	U	U	10	60
13-3	Observation of spectra	13-4	S	P	P	U	5	30
14-1	Effect of electric current on $PbCl_2$	14-2	Sa*	Pa*	U	U	5	30
14-2	Migration of ions	14-4	P	S	U	U	25	15
14-3	A. Electrolysis of lead nitrate solution	14-5	S	P	U	U	5	15
	B. Electrolysis of sodium chloride solution	14-5	S	P	U	U	5	15
14-4	Replacement of ions	14-8	S	P	S	P	10	30
14-5	Combining zinc and iodine	14-9	P	S	U	U	20	5
14-6	Current by electron transfer	14-11	S	P	U	U	10	20
15-1	Crystals of NaCl and CsCl							
	A. Growing the crystals	15-1	S	P	U	P	5	20
	B. Examination of the crystals	15-1	S	P	U	P	—	20
15-2	Construction of CsCl model	15-3	U	P	S	P	5	45
15-3	Construction of NaCl model	15-4	U	P	S	P	5	45
15-4	Water in an electric field	15-7	S	P	U	P	5	10
15-5	The law of entropy	15-9	S	P	U	P	—	30
16-1	Electrolysis of water	16-1	P	S	U	U	20	20
16-2	Combining hydrogen and oxygen	16-2	P	S	U	U	15	10
16-3	Model for carbon bonding	16-6	P	S	P	P	5	15
17-1	Electrical properties of two fluids	17-2	P	P	U	U	20	15
17-2	Mechanical properties of metals	17-6	S	P	U	P	5	30
17-3	Physical properties of sulfur	17-10	S	P	U	U	15	45
17-4	A model of sulfur	17-10	S	P	P	P	5	15
17-5	Experiments with glass							
	A. Manipulating glass	17-11	U	P	P	S	5	30
	B. Testing conductivity	17-11	S	S	U	U	10	10
17-6	Experiments with polyethylene	17-12	S	P	U	U	10	30
17-7	An experiment with rubber	17-13	S	P	U	U	5	15

*a — Bunsen burner required

APPENDIX II

ADDITIONAL QUESTIONS AND PROBLEMS

Four different kinds of questions and problems are included in this appendix. Type I: essay questions; Type II: double multiple-choice questions; Type III: simple multiple-choice questions; Type IV: multiple-answer multiple-choice questions.

Type I   ESSAY QUESTIONS

The following are sample questions that may be useful as is, or after appropriate modifications. Some of them might be given to students before an exam so that they will be prepared to write about them (a semi-takehome exam). Others may be given out at the time of the exam; perhaps for these, students should be allowed to use books and notes, or that is, to make out a "crib sheet" to use as they see fit. The purpose of an examination is to see how well students understand a subject and to help them learn more about it. If they gain understanding *during* as well as *before* an exam, all the better.

1.   Make up a question you expected in this exam. Explain very briefly why this question is important with respect to the course.* (What would it teach?)

Comment: You might use this question several times during the course of the year. If students come to expect it, so much the better.— at least they will have thought about reasonable answers. This question gives us a good idea of what the students understand to be the point of it all. Discourage excessively long answers (too hard to grade as well as the fact that long answers usually mean loose thinking), but also make it clear that a trivial question will be graded appropriately.

2.   You are working on a project for the Peace Corps. In the course of your work, you discover that you need to teach your fellow workers essentially what is in our text. Design a very simple demonstration experiment to explain one of the topics we have looked at so far.† (Your experiment cannot be identical to any already used in the text). You must use materials that are readily available, and the experiment must be very simple to use and describe. Describe this experiment very briefly. What does it teach? What principles does it use and illustrate?

Comment: This question may also be used several times. It gives students an opportunity to create an approach independent of ours, and it gives us an insight into their understanding of the material. You may find some unorthodox and ingenious approaches, which is good.

   This is one of the questions you may warn them about in the previous class meeting. To guard against their having their friends do it for them beforehand, do not let them use notes for this one. Have them write it up again during the exam without notes or books.

---

* You may wish to restrict the subject matter of the question (e.g., to light, liquids, forces inside matter, etc.) for a particular exam, but the explanation half of the question is very important.

† Again, to facilitate relative evaluation of answers, you may wish to restrict the subject area more narrowly.

3.   The following objects are found in a laboratory:
     (a)   a ping-pong ball
     (b)   several identical steel balls
     (c)   an assortment of balls of various sizes and materials
     (d)   a spring
     (e)   a source of water
     (f)   several pieces of thin steel rod, all of uniform cross section, but of varying lengths
     (g)   some tops
     (h)   an assortment of paper

Also in the laboratory are to be found all the equipment we have used in our experiments so far, i.e., meter sticks, glassware, thermometers, clocks, burners, etc.

Outline the beginning of an experiment to discover some of the properties of any of these newly found objects or group of objects. It is suggested that you organize your experiment around the questions that would arise. What questions do arise? How do you answer these questions?

Comment: This is a very open-ended question that will help to indicate whether the students have gotten the idea that science is experimental and open-ended in itself. Do not expect that everything they suggest will be significant or even completely logical, but do see if their procedure is well organized. You can use the question again by substituting other available objects.

4.   In a number of our experiments we have used water. List as many of the properties of water we made use of in those experiments as you can. Do not list those properties we have not used. In other words, what have you *observed* about water?

Comment: Do not use this question until Chapter 4 has been completed. Let them get some experience first. This is a pure observation question.

5.   Make a list of the properties of light that we have utilized. Make a list of the properties of waves.

Comment: Again, a pure observation question. If they correlate the two lists, so much the better, but it is not necessary.

6.   You have some unknown powder in a test tube. After you heat it and melt it completely, you decide to run a cooling curve on this liquid. When you do this, you discover that the curve has two plateaus. Which one of the following is a good initial hypothesis as to the reason for this behavior; that is, on which of these hypotheses will you base a further experiment to test your hypothesis? Give your reasons. (Note: there are other possible hypotheses, but we want to look at these first.)
     (a)   Nature is capricious and inscrutable.
     (b)   The remaining heat rises in the test tube so that the top and bottom are at different temperatures.
     (c)   The liquid is a mixture of two substances which do not dissolve in each other.

Comment: (c) is the best initial hypothesis since it very readily leads to further simple experiment to test the hypothesis. So would (b), but two plateaus would require two sharply defined regions with different temperatures. That would be very unlikely and not simple to test for.

7.   Ten grams of a white, crystalline solid were placed on a watch glass. This solid was then left in open air for one day. At the end of that time there was a pool of clear liquid on the watch glass and this liquid was found to weigh 20 grams. State arguments for or against each of the following possibilities as to what happened; suggest experiments to test your conclusions.
     (a)   the solid melted
     (b)   the solid picked up water vapor from the air
     (c)   the solid reacted with oxygen or nitrogen from the air
     (d)   the solid decomposed

282   Appendix II

No

Comment: (a) and (d) are ruled out since they do not account for the increase in weight. (b) and (c) are both possible, but (b) seems better as a first guess as it gives a simpler reason for the formation of a liquid. Experiments could be (1) try adding 10 grams of water to 10 grams of solid; (2) try the experiment in *dry* air; (3) try the experiment in oxygen or nitrogen alone or in some other gas; (4) try the experiment in a closed vessel.

8.   A green box is wrapped with parallel strips of red, green, and clear transparent ribbon. The strips do not overlap. Describe and explain the appearance of the result.

Comment: The red will appear black, and the green and transparent strips will both appear green.

9.   When crystals of iodine are heated, violet (or purple) fumes of gaseous iodine may be seen above them. Using the ideas and terminology of the molecular model of the nature of matter, describe what is occurring here. That is, explain how the heat is used.

10.   Design an experiment you could use to justify Newton's first law to a skeptical friend. Do not use the same experiments we used to justify it to you.

11.   An object slides without friction down a straight inclined plane. The top of the inclined plane is at a height *h* above the floor. Another objects falls straight down from the same height *h*.
   Now it takes longer for the object to slide down the plane, since the acceleration is less than for falling, but this acceleration lasts longer, so it has a longer time and a longer distance to accelerate and increase the speed of the object. What would you say about the final velocities of the two objects? Are they the same, or are they different? Can you justify your answer using a general principle we have examined?

12.   Sometimes, to facilitate peeling a tomato, one plunges it momentarily into boiling water. Try to form a hypothesis for what happens to make the tomato easy to peel.

13.   A very common test for the temperature of a household iron, the kind with which you press your clothes, is to lick your finger and then momentarily touch it to the iron. What information have you gotten if you hear a "sizzle"?

14.   (a) Open your mouth wide and breathe on the back of your hand. (b) Purse your lips and blow on the back of your hand. Describe the difference in sensations which your hand experiences in the two cases. Try to form a hypothesis to explain the difference.

15.   Discuss on a submicroscopic scale the activity that is taking place when a liquid is boiled. Include words such as *energy, force,* and other words in your discussion in a way to indicate that you understand what these words mean.

Comment: There will be many ways in which this is discussed. You should look for a discussion of how energy enters into the liquid, and what this energy does to the forces holding the liquid together.

16.   "Potential energy is always associated with a force." Discuss this statement. Can you think of a situation in which the statement is *not* true? Does this prove or disprove the statement?

Comment: One way to describe potential energy is to call it a measure of the *possibility for a change in motion.* Now to produce a change in motion requires a force so there should not be any situation in which the statement is not true. If someone claims there is such a situation, have them examine it very carefully. The fact that one cannot find an exception does not prove the statement, however.

17.   Two bodies that attract each other electrically may or may not both be charged. Two bodies that repel each other electrically, however, must both be charged. Show how our theory of electricity accounts for both of the above observations.

X

18. Discuss the processes that take place in the circuit shown as charges move through it. Include the words *newton, joule, coulomb, potential energy, kinetic energy,* and *volt* in your discussion in a way to indicate that you understand what these terms mean.

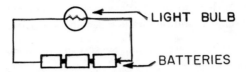

Comment: Notice that most of the terms requested concern energy; you should look for an understanding of when and how energy is gained and lost in the circuit. Don't expect a formal definition for each term, but remember that an improper usage of a term usually means a lack of understanding of its meaning.

19. Discuss the processes that take place in the experiment shown. (If a light bulb is inserted in the circuit, it glows, indicating that charges are flowing through the circuit.) Include the words *ion, charge,* and other terms necessary to your discussion in ways to indicate that you understand what they mean.

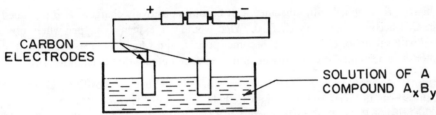

Comment: An electrolysis experiment; again, there will be many ways in which it is discussed. You should look for a discussion of how charges exist, move, where they go, and what the subsequent results are.

20. "Any solid is mostly empty space." Discuss this statement. Describe experiments that can be used to verify this statement.

Comment: The most obvious experiment is the Rutherford experiment. Others can be osmosis experiments (if they are aware of these from previous experience), or the fact that solids are transparent to many things, including light and x rays. Discussion might center on how this fact was discovered, or the implications of the fact, or many other things.

21. If you melt sodium chloride, it will conduct an electric current. As the current goes through the liquid, sodium is deposited on one electrode, and chlorine is released at the other electrode. If you melt ice, however, it will not conduct an electric current. What do these experiments indicate concerning the basic structural units in solid sodium chloride crystals and in solid ice crystals?

Comment: The basic structural units in solid sodium chloride must be charged, those in solid ice must be neutral.

22. Some white powder is dissolved in water and then two similar pieces of metal (electrodes), which are connected to the two terminals of a battery, are dipped into the solution. After a while, one of the metal electrodes turns brownish. State arguments for and against each of the following possibilities for what happened.
     (a) the metal electrode rusted
     (b) electrolysis deposited a brown metal on the metal electrode
     (c) some metal of an electrode changed places with something in the solution.

284   Appendix II

Devise experimental tests to determine which of the three possibilities is correct

Comment: None of the possibilities is ruled out with the evidence given. However, for (a), if one of the metal pieces turns brown the other should also. If (c) is the correct possibility, the reaction should occur without the battery, so an experimental test is to disconnect the battery. If (b) is the correct possibility, increasing the voltage should speed up the reaction.

23. You are given a sample of an unknown crystal. Suggest an experimental test to show whether your unknown is an ionic crystal or not.

Comment: Dissolve the crystal (if it is not soluble in water, try some other solvent). Perform an electrolysis experiment.

24. (a) Describe a model for an ionic solid and use it to account for at least two properties of the solid.
    (b) Describe a model for a solid composed of covalently bonded molecules and use it to account for at least two properties of the solid. What holds such a solid together?

Comment: There may be many different possible models suggested. You should look for some explanation of how the solids are held together, and how the fact that the substances are ionic or covalent enters into the model.

25. If substance B is rubbed with substance A, it becomes positively charged. If B is rubbed with substance C, it becomes negatively charged. What would you expect to happen when substance A is rubbed with substance C; i.e., which becomes positive and which becomes negative. Formulate a hypothesis to account for your answer, and construct a model that exemplifies it.

Comment: A should become negatively charged, C should become positively charged. We could hypothesize about how strongly charges are held to each of the three substances. If we put them into the order A-B-C with A most negative and C most positive and hypothesize that A has the strongest attractive force for negative charges and C the weakest, with B intermediate; then the experimental observations can be accounted for.

26. We live in a universe such that not more than two electron clouds can overlap each other to form a dead cloud. Let us call this the "bi-schizo" universe. Now suppose that there are other possible universes (undetectable by us bi-schizos) in which more than two electron clouds can overlap to bind atoms into molecules. That is, suppose more than two electrons are needed to form a dead cloud.
    (a) In a "tri-schizo" universe (three clouds overlap to form a dead one) what would be the maximum number of electrons in the first shell of an element?
    (b) How many hydrogen atoms would combine to form a hydrogen molecule?
    (c) How many electrons would be in the first shell of oxygen (atomic number 8)?
    (d) How many in the second shell of oxygen?
    (e) Assume nine electrons form dead second shells in a molecule of oxygen (9 electrons = 3 dead clouds with 3 electrons per cloud). Deduce then the formula for the oxygen molecule.

Comment:
    (a) 3 (3 form a dead cloud).
    (b) 3 (one electron from each of the three will combine to produce a dead cloud). So the molecular formula of hydrogen would be H_3.
    (c) 3.
    (d) 5 = 8 - 3.
    (e) O_3. Since each oxygen atom would have two live clouds, three atoms before combination would have 6 live clouds. These 6 live clouds would combine to form two dead clouds of three electrons each.

27. The atoms of the elements germanium, silicon, and carbon have many similarities; an important one is the fact that they all have four electrons in their outermost shell. (a) Suggest a possible structure

16

for the electron clouds surrounding germanium or silicon. (b) Suggest a possible structure for a crystal of germanium or silicon. (c) Would you expect either germanium or silicon to be a good conductor of electricity?

Comment: (a) The most obvious suggestion would be for four live electron clouds pointing in a tetragonal structure similar to carbon. (b) The most obvious suggestion would be a diamond structure, although it is possible that a graphite structure would be suggested. (c) If a diamond structure is suggested, *no;* if a graphite structure is suggested, *yes.*

28. Choose those statements below that you think are correct; give your reasons. Examine the statements very carefully. Several are correct.
    (a) Metals in a gaseous state are good conductors of electricity.
    (b) Metals in a gaseous state are not good conductors of electricity.
    (c) The bonds in water are stronger than the bonds in the molecules of hydrogen and oxygen.
    (d) The bonds in water are weaker than the bonds in the molecules of hydrogen and oxygen.
    (e) If a substance conducts electricity when liquid but not when solid, it is a covalent substance.
    (f) Electron charge clouds are abstract products of the human imagination, hence cannot be used to prove anything of the real world.
    (g) Solid matter is not really "solid."

Comment: (b) and (c) are correct, (f) and (g) can be chosen either way, depending on the interpretation and the reasoning used. Since solid metal conducts because of its delocalized electrons, and since gaseous metal atoms would be electrically neutral and not delocalized, gaseous metals should not be as good conductors as solid metals. Since it requires energy to split water into oxygen and hydrogen, and since energy is given off when oxygen and hydrogen are combined to form water, the water bonds must be stronger. (f) or (g) can be either correct or incorrect (philosophically) — you must judge how good the reasoning is.

29. Pick one of the statements in the previous problem that is incorrect and justify why you think it incorrect. Design an experiment to verify your answer.

Comment: (a), (d), and (e) are incorrect; (f) and (g) again can go either way depending on reasoning.

30. Kinetic energy and potential energy can be considered what we can call a "conjugate pair" (in a purely mechanical system). Solids, liquids, and gases can be considered what we can call a "conjugate triad." Can you think of other such pairs or triads or other multiples?

Comment: Examples (pairs): two complementary angle; two supplementary angles; male and female; north-south; east-west, etc. Examples (triads): plus charge, negative charge, and neutral charge (based on conservation of charge); the angles in a triangle (sum equals 180 degrees), etc. Other multiples can be things like a filled outer electron shell (adds to 8).

Type II   DOUBLE MULTIPLE-CHOICE QUESTIONS

The following questions are considerably more complex than standard multiple choice questions; therefore you should allow more time for each. Because these questions have two parts, and since the correct combination of answers to the two parts is necessary, the time allowed for each should probably be more than twice the time allowed for a standard multiple-choice question.

Instructions: In the following questions, choose the appropriate answer for *both* parts. *Both* parts must be correct for the answer to be considered correct. Answers are underscored

1. Light is best described as
   (a) a wave

(b)   a stream of particles

(c)   having both wave and particle properties

The reason for your answer involves

(1)   experimental evidence

(2)   theoretical consistency

(3)   both experimental evidence and theoretical consistency

2.   If you were to watch salol growing under a microscope, the smallest solid particles you would observe in the liquid would be expected to be

(a)   diamond shaped

(b)   round

(c)   square

(d)   irregular

The reason is that

(1)   the hot liquid eats at the edges and causes irregular or round boundaries

(2)   small things like to form compact shapes – like round raindrops

(3)   the angles between faces of the growing crystals appear to remain constant as they grow, and larger salol crystals are diamond shaped

(4)   salol ought to form square outlines in small crystals, as sodium chloride (salt) does

3.   Weight and mass

(a)   measure the same thing

(b)   are completely unrelated

(c)   are proportional to each other

The reason is that

(1)   the system of units used (e.g., English units or metric units) must be carefully chosen

(2)   the gravitational force on an object depends on the mass of the object

(3)   things do not weigh anything far away from the earth

4.   As the substance solidified in the cooling curve experiment,

(a)   heat energy was absorbed into the solid

(b)   heat was continuously given off

(c)   there was a period of time during which there was no change in its heat content

The experimental evidence for this is that the

(1)   liquid contained more heat than the solid

(2)   temperature did not change

(3)   water or air surrounding the test tube became warmer

5.   In an interference experiment, if the frequency of the light is increased, the angle of constructive interference (reinforcement)

(a)   increases

(b)   decreases

(c)   remains the same

This conclusion is supported by the fact that

(1) $n \lambda = d \sin \theta$

(2)   the frequency is not explicitly stated in the interference equation

(3)   the two quantities are directly proportional to each other

6.   The explanation of x-ray diffraction involves

(a)   the superposition principle

(b)   the phenomenon of interference

(c)   both the superposition principle and the phenomenon of interference

(d)   multiple slits

The reason for your answer is that
- (1)   the x rays have gone between the atoms in a crystal, and these look like slits
- (2)   one is the mathematical basis for the other
- (3)   interference and diffraction are not really different effects

7.   When the salol was heated, liquefied, and then cooled, a seed was needed to crystallize it because
- (a)   the seed cooled it sufficiently to let it solidify
- (b)   it needed something to grow onto
- (c)   the seed was needed to absorb the heat given off

This is related to the reason
- (1)   for the growth of crystals in the jars
- (2)   why liquids have more heat than solids
- (3)   for the fact that heat goes from warmer things to colder things
- (4)   for the characteristic shapes of crystals

8.   If the density of an aluminum block is determined outdoors on a hot day in August, the result will be
- (a)   larger than a room-temperature measurement
- (b)   smaller than a room-temperature measurement
- (c)   the same as a room-temperature measurement

Since
- (1)   the block will increase in volume, but not in mass, on a warm day
- (2)   density is a constant for aluminum
- (3)   the arms of the balance used to weigh it will expand because of the heat

9.   A rowboat made entirely of wood _____ made to sink to the bottom by putting water into it, because _____ .
- (a)   can be
- (b)   cannot be
- (c)   can sometimes be
- (1)   the combination of boat plus water weighs too much
- (2)   the density of the combination of boat plus water can be varied by varying the amount of water added
- (3)   the density of wood is less than the density of water

10.   The fact that x rays give a pattern of_____when they strike a photographic film after passing through a single stationary crystal is taken as conclusive evidence for _____ .
- (a)   intersecting lines
- (b)   dots or spots
- (c)   concentric, diffuse, alternating light and dark circles
- (1)   the repetitive nature of crystalline structure
- (2)   Maxwell's theory of electromagnetic radiation
- (3)   the interference of light

11.   Some crystals _____ easily in certain directions because the _____ between their adjacent layers are smaller in the corresponding directions.
- (a)   cleave
- (b)   transmit light
- (c)   bend
- (1)   angles
- (2)   interference effects
- (3)   distances
- (4)   forces

12. Metals can be_____ more easily than most crystalline solids because _____ .
    (a) polished
    (b) bent
    (c) cast
    (1) metals are noncrystalline
    (2) metals are opaque
    (3) the bonds between metal atoms are nondirectional

13. Water waves _____ light waves since_____ .
    (a) differ fundamentally from
    (b) vibrate at a lower frequency than
    (c) correspond closely to
    (1) they are both subject to interference and bending around obstacles
    (2) water is heavy and it is difficult to make it vibrate rapidly
    (3) both are visible
    (4) their wavelengths are longer

14. Water waves and light waves are both subject to interference effects when they scatter from _____
    structures. Interference effects are seldom noticed with sound waves (with wavelengths about 5
    feet) however, because_____ .
    (a) two-dimensional
    (b) irregularly spaced
    (c) hollow
    (d) regularly spaced
    (1) they are invisible
    (2) appropriate structures are uncommon
    (3) the intensities are usually too low
    (4) their frequency and wavelength are not related in the same way

15. A fundamental difference between sunlight and most artificial light is _____ , _____ .
    (a) the color
    (b) its intensity
    (c) the heat content
    (1) as can sometimes be noted by comparing the appearance of colored clothing as seen under
        first one source and then the other
    (2) as could be shown by comparing the reading on a thermometer near a light bulb with the
        reading on one out in the sunlight
    (3) since overexposure to sunlight causes sunburn

16. The _____ of a steel spring at the Moon's surface would differ from its value on Earth
    because_____ .
    (a) strength
    (b) mass
    (c) weight
    (d) length
    (1) the Moon has no atmosphere
    (2) the gravitational attraction is less there
    (3) it is too far away for the Earth to affect it noticeably

17. Sunglasses come in a variety of colors, including amber, green, and gray. _____ sunglasses
    will change the appearance of objects least, since_____ .
    (a) Amber (yellow-brown)
    (b) Green
    (c) Gray

(1)   green is the predominant color of the landscape
(2)   it would be the most effective color in cutting out the ultraviolet
(3)   black absorbs all colors equally, and gray is a shade of black
(4)   amber is nearest the color of sunlight

18. In some auditoriums or lecture halls, there are regions where sound cannot be heard well, so-called dead spots. This comes about because of _____ . The details are complicated, but the most important overall reason is that_____ .

(a)   too much sound absorbing material in that section
(b)   interference between sounds reflected from different parts of the hall and those coming directly from the speaker
(c)   too many obstructions such as columns, railings, etc., between that section and the speaker.
(1)   the sound coming directly toward a person is much stronger than reflected sound
(2)   the only way sound is lessened is through absorption by a soft substance
(3)   the intensity of the reflected sound is too great in these regions

19. The interference pattern formed by water waves as they come through a series of regularly spaced openings, such as a row of piles, will be most widely spread out when _____ . The equation, $n\lambda = d \sin \phi$, expresses this mathematically, since it states that _____ , and a large value for $\sin \phi$ corresponds to a widely spread out pattern.

(a)   there are many small openings closely spaced
(b)   there are a few large openings spaced far apart
(c)   the openings and the spaces between them are all the same size
(1) $\sin \phi$ is directly proportional to the wavelength
(2) $\sin \phi$ is inversely proportional to d (the space between the center of one opening and the center of the next)
(3)   for a fixed spacing and a fixed wavelength, the order number n depends upon $\sin \phi$

20. The two waves shown below are traveling toward each other.

wave 1   wave 2

One of the following patterns is possible at *some* later time. Which?

(a)
(b)
(c)

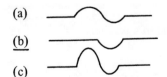

One of the following patterns is *not* possible at *any* later time. Which?

(1)
(2)
(3)

21. If you stretch a spring and then shake one end at an increasing frequency (more and more times per second) _____ . _____ .
    (a)   the velocity of waves along the spring increases
    (b)   the wavelength of the waves decreases
    (c)   the wavelength will remain constant
    (1)   Stretching the spring further and repeating the experiment will prove this
    (2)   The equation, $f\lambda = v$, is a mathematical statement of this experimental result
    (3)   This cannot be checked experimentally; it is a theoretical result
    (4)   We know that wavelength is a constant of the medium

22. The interference equation, $\sin\phi = \dfrac{n\lambda}{d}$, _____ , because _____ .
    (a)   is true only for wave motion
    (b)   is true for motions other than waves
    (c)   is only of limited usefulness
    (1)   once proven, an equation is universally true
    (2)   in the derivation, waves were assumed
    (3)   it doesn't agree very well with experimental results

23. A car is driven with a constant speed along a straight, level road. On coming to a curve in the road, the driver turns the steering wheel. When this happens, the car's *velocity* _____ . This is a consequence of _____ .
    (a)   increases
    (b)   decreases
    (c)   remains the same
    (d)   changes
    (1)   the conservation of energy
    (2)   the definition of velocity
    (3)   how long the steering wheel was turned
    (4)   the fact that one should drive more slowly around curves than on level roads

24. A body moves with a constant acceleration. A velocity-time graph of its motion would be _____ , because _____ .
    (a)   a straight horizontal line
    (b)   a straight sloping line
    (c)   a parabola
    (1)   the rate of change is always the same
    (2)   the distance traveled is $s = \frac{1}{2}at^2$, which is the equation of a parabola
    (3)   the area under the velocity-time graph increases
    (4)   acceleration cannot be obtained from the graph

25. If you quickly compress the gas in a balloon, it will _____ . This can be deduced from the fact that _____ .
    (a)   get hotter
    (b)   get colder
    (c)   stay at the same temperature

    (1)   it was not heated

    (2)   the gas molecules cannot move as far before collisions since the volume is smaller

    (3)   it required energy to compress it

26. If an object is dropped from a height above the Moon's surface, its speed of fall will be _____ . This is due to the fact that _____ .

    (a)   the same as its speed of fall on Earth

    (b)   greater than its speed of fall on Earth

    (c)   less than its speed of fall on Earth

    (1)   the force of gravity is less on the Moon

    (2)   the diameter of the Moon is less than the diameter of the Earth

    (3)   the Moon is so distant

27. An object is on a frictionless table on the surface of the Moon. We find that a horizontal force of 1 newton, acting for 1 second, gives it a velocity of 1 meter per second. If this same experiment were done on Earth, the velocity of the object would be _____ . This is a consequence of _____ .

    (a)   greater than on the Moon

    (b)   less than on the Moon

    (c)   the same as on the Moon

    (1)   Newton's law of gravity

    (2)   the independence of vertical and horizontal forces in frictionless situations

    (3)   the law of the conservation of energy

28. If more salol had been used, and if it had been melted in a spoon or the end of a test tube so that it formed a deeper puddle, there would have been _____ because _____ .

    (a)   no crystals formed

    (b)   diamond shapes in vertical as well as horizontal orientation

    (c)   horizontal layers of thin diamond shaped crystals

    (d)   crystals having a shape different from a diamond would have been formed

    (1)   there wouldn't have been any flat surface to help shape them

    (2)   their natural form is very thin flat diamonds

    (3)   they grow as extensions of the seed, regardless of its orientation

29. The central bright line or fringe in the interference pattern seen through two slits is always _____ the source, because _____ .

    (a)   the same size as

    (b)   one of the colors present in

    (c)   exactly the same color as

    (1)   constructive interference occurs in different directions, which depend on the wavelength

    (2)   the two slits do not have the ability to magnify

    (3)   the central region of the pattern corresponds to constructive interference for all wavelengths

    (4)   to see it, you must be looking directly at the source

30. If you rub a balloon and move it toward an uncharged window, it will first _____ the window.

    (a)   be attracted to

    (b)   be repelled from

    (c)   charge

The reason for this is that

    (1)   charges can flow easily from the balloon to the window

    (2)   charges cannot flow easily from the balloon to the window

    (3)   the balloon charge interacts with the charges in the window

31. A plastic rod is rubbed with a piece of synthetic cloth. After they are separated, the force between the rod and the cloth will be
    (a)   an attraction
    (b)   a repulsion
    (c)   unknown — it depends on the material of the rod and the cloth
    The reason is based on
    (1)   the conservation of energy
    (2)   the conservation of charge
    (3)   the fact that both are synthetic materials

32. In general, which of the following is the best conductor of electricity?
    (a)   a solid metal
    (b)   a solution of salt
    (c)   air
    The reason for this choice is that in this best conductor
    (1)   the charges that are moving are smaller and lighter
    (2)   both positive and negative charges can move
    (3)   the space between the molecules is greater, so less collisions are made between the charges and the molecules

33. Electric current is charges in motion. This is deduced from the fact that
    (a)   a body becomes warmer when it conducts current
    (b)   lightning tends to hit conductors of electricity
    (c)   more current can go through short conductors than long conductors
    Your answer is consistent with the fact that
    (1)   heat is energy and energy is associated with motion
    (2)   metals conduct electricity
    (3)   current is proportional to voltage

34. In an atom, the energy is in the form of
    (a)   potential energy
    (b)   kinetic energy
    (c)   both potential and kinetic energy
    The reason is that
    (1)   the energy is determined only by the positions of the electrons and the nucleus
    (2)   the electrons cannot be stationary or they will fall into the nucleus
    (3)   a change in energy changes both the motion and the location of the electrons

35. Electrolysis must necessarily involve
    (a)   heating of the substance
    (b)   ionic liquids
    (c)   solution in water
    This is deduced from the fact that
    (1)   the material must be free to move
    (2)   electrolysis occurs only at high energies
    (3)   a flow of electric charge is required for electrolysis

36. If you connect a light bulb across a battery and then increase the voltage
    (a)   the light bulb glows less than before
    (b)   the light bulb glows the same as before
    (c)   the light bulb glows brighter than before
    You can support your answer by
    (1)   the fact that the conductivity of the light bulb is constant

(2)   the equation (work) = (voltage) × (charge)
(3)   connecting two light bulbs to the battery

37.   In the electrolysis of $PbCl_2$ the chlorine ion
      (a)   picked up an electron at the negative electrode
      (b)   picked up an electron at the positive electrode
      (c)   gave up an electron at the negative electrode
      (d)   gave up an electron at the positive electrode
      In deducing the answer above, it was necessary to know that
      (1)   chlorine has 7 electrons in its outermost shell
      (2)   chlorine exists as Cl_2
      (3) $PbCl_2$ does not conduct in the solid state

38.   Polar and nonpolar substances differ from each other by
      (a)   their complexities
      (b)   whether the number of atoms are even or odd
      (c)   the symmetries of electric charge distributions
      This can be supported by
      (1)   making a model
      (2)   counting the atoms
      (3)   experiment only

39.   The covalent bond
      (a)   is a fundamental basis for modern biology
      (b)   is a fundamental basis for modern physical science
      (c)   is the universal bond; all other bonds are manifestations of it
      This is because
      (1)   the covalent carbon-carbon bond always occurs in organic chemistry
      (2)   all charges are shared
      (3)   biology is based on physical science

      (Note: We have not discussed this at all, but the answer can be easily deduced. It is included to show that there is a large area of science yet to be considered which *can* be very interesting).

Type III SIMPLE MULTIPLE-CHOICE QUESTIONS

The following are simple multiple choice questions. It is recommended that they *not* be the only kind used; it is very desirable to include some from the other 3 types. Answers are underscored.

1.   The particular color of a ray of light depends on which one of the following properties of the light wave?
      (a)   amplitude
      (b)   wavelength
      (c)   intensity
      (d)   strength
      (e)   velocity

2.   What property of visible light makes it unsuitable for the study of the internal structure of crystals?
      (f)   amplitude
      (g)   wavelength
      (h)   intensity

294   Appendix II

(j)   strength
(k)   velocity

3.   The inertia of a body is most closely related to its
     (a)   mass
     (b)   volume
     (c)   density
     (d)   shape
     (e)   weight

4.   An important distinction between mass and weight is that
     (f)   an object may have weight but no mass
     (g)   weight is a force and mass is not
     (h)   mass is always smaller than weight
     (j)   mass is always greater than weight
     (k)   the weight of an object is always the same

5.   Dr. Max Von Laue was awarded a Nobel Prize for showing that x rays are a form of electromagnetic radiation. The key experimental result which led to this conclusion was the discovery that x rays
     (a)   were able to go through certain types of matter
     (b)   travel at the speed of light
     (c)   had a wavelength
     (d)   were diffracted by a crystal
     (e)   travel in a straight line

6.   A force (F) gives a mass (M) on acceleration (A). The acceleration produced by a force of (2F) on a mass of (½M) would be
     (a)   ¼ A
     (b)   ½ A
     (c)   A
     (d)   2A
     (e)   4A

7.   There are two solid objects, A and B. Object B has a volume twice that of object A. Object A has a mass twice that of object B. The density of object A compared to that of object B would be
     (f)   4 times that of B
     (g)   twice that of B
     (h)   ¼ that of B
     (j)   the same as B
     (k)   ½ that of B

8.   The velocity of an object on which no force is acting is necessarily
     (a)   zero
     (b)   changing
     (c)   constant in magnitude but not in direction
     (d)   constant in direction but not in magnitude
     (e)   constant in magnitude and direction

9.

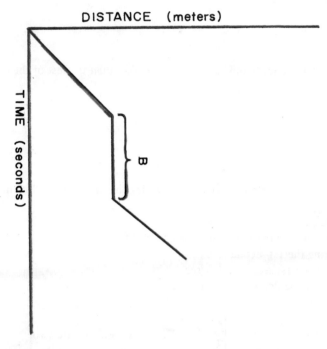

The above graph represents the motion of a certain object. section B of the graph indicates the object in question is

    (f)   moving with constant, nonzero velocity

    (g)   moving with constant, nonzero acceleration

    (h)   moving with a varying velocity

    (j)   moving with a varying acceleration

    (k)   at rest

10.   What would be the wavelength of a light wave whose frequency was found to be 6×10^{15} per sec? The speed of light is 3×10^{10} cm/sec.

    (a) 5×10^{-6} cm

    (b) 2×10^{5} cm

    (c) 1.8×10^{26} cm

    (d) 2×10^{-5} cm

    (e) 0.5×10^{-3} cm

The following two questions are based on the diagrams below which show the appearance of five objects under white light.

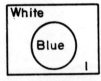 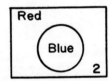 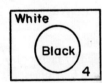 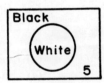

11.   Viewed under a source of red light the circle would appear much lighter than the rest of the object in which of the following?

    (a)   1

    (b)   2

    (c)   3

        (d)   4
        (e)   5

12. Viewed under a source of blue light the circle would appear much darker than the rest of the object in which of the following?

        (f)   1
        (g)   2
        (h)   3
        (j)   4
        (k)   5

13. A body starts from rest and moves with constant acceleration. During the first second of its motion it travels 1 foot. It follows that

        (a)   the acceleration is 1 ft/sec/sec
        (b)   the total distance covered during the first 2 seconds will be 4 ft
        (c)   the average velocity during the 1st second is ½ ft/sec
        (d)   the velocity at the end of the 1st second is 1 ft/sec
        (e)   the distance covered during the 2nd second will be 2 ft

14.

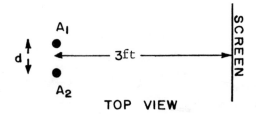

TOP VIEW

A_1 and A_2 are two regular light bulbs having long straight filaments (*Drawing not to scale*).

An experimental setup was assembled as shown in the diagram above. The room which contained the setup was made dark. When the two lights were turned on, the screen was uniformly illuminated with white light. No interference pattern was seen. What is the most likely reason for this result?

        (f)   The two lights do not give out just a single wavelength of light but a wide range of wavelengths
        (g)   The distance (d) between the sources was too small
        (h)   The two lights do not send out light waves in phase (at the same time)
        (j)   The two lights send out light waves with different velocities
        (k)   The distance from the lights to the screen was too long

15. A gas is enclosed in a nonexpandable sealed container. Its temperature is initially 200°K. Later the temperature of the gas is raised to 400°K. As a result of the increase in temperature the kinetic energy of the molecules of the gas would be

        (a)   left unchanged
        (b)   halved
        (c)   doubled
        (d)   increased by factor of $\sqrt{2}$
        (e)   increased four times

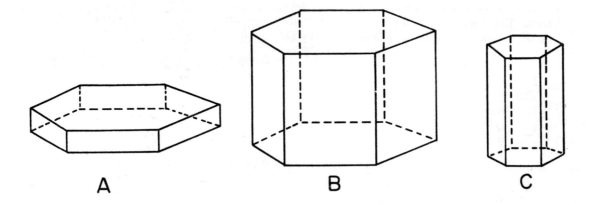

The above crystals are all of the same color and density.

16. From the information given above plus observation of the crystals it is possible to say that
    (a)   all 3 crystals must be composed of the same material
    (b)   each of the 3 crystals is composed of a different material
    (c)   crystals A and B may be composed of the same material but C is composed of a different
          material
    (d)   it is possible that all 3 crystals are composed of the same material
    (e)   crystals B and C are probably composed of the same material but A is composed of a differ-
          ent material

17. From the shape of crystal B it is certain that
    (f)   all crystals of the same material as B must have exactly the same shape as B
    (g)   the molecules making up B must be spherical in shape
    (h)   each molecule of B has the same shape as the crystal
    (j)   the molecules making up B must be cubical in shape
    (k)   any plane parallel to the surface of B will also be parallel to some plane containing the center
          of many molecules

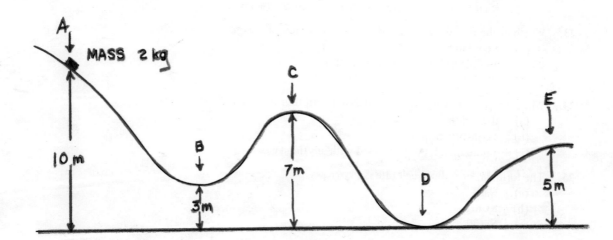

A mass of 2 kg starts from rest at point (A) and moves down a frictionless roller coaster type track. The heights of various points of the track above the bottom horizontal line are measured in meters. Assume that g, the acceleration due to gravity, is 10 m/sec^2.

18. At what point will the mass have its maximum kinetic energy?
  (a) A
  (b) B
  (c) C
  (d) D
  (e) E

19. At what point will the mass have its maximum potential energy?
  (f) A
  (g) B
  (h) C
  (j) D
  (k) E

20. What will be the value of the mass's kinetic energy at point D?
  (a) 20 joules
  (b) zero
  (c) 140 joules
  (d) 200 joules
  (e) 2 joules

21. With what velocity will the mass be moving at point E?
  (f) 0 meter/sec
  (g) 100 meter/sec
  (h) 10 meter/sec
  (j) $\sqrt{200}$ meter/sec
  (k) 20 meter/sec

22. The potential difference, or voltage, between two points is fundamentally defined as
  (a) the work to move a unit charge from one point to the other point
  (b) the current through a wire multiplied by the resistance of the wire
  (c) what keeps the charges moving between the two points

23. Which of the following can be used as a description of *charge*?
  (a) a coulomb
  (b) a fundamental property of matter
  (c) current

24. Which of the following can be used as a description of a chemical *element?*
  (a) the weather
  (b) a constituent part
  (c) a pure metal, not combined with anything else

25. The formula for sodium chlorate is
  (a) NaCl
  (b) $KClO_3$
  (c) $NaClO_3$

26. In the energy level diagram shown, which transition represents an emission of light with the shortest wavelength?

(A) a
(B) b
(C) c
(D) d
(E) e
(F) f

27. If a positively charged rod is brought near an object and is found to attract the object, this proves that the object

    (a) cannot be neutral
    (b) cannot be negatively charged
    (c) cannot be positively charged

28. In the electrolysis of a water solution of copper bromide $CuBr_2$, which of the following is *not* true

    (a) copper ions lose 2 electrons at the cathode
    (b) oxidation takes place at the anode
    (c) each bromide ion loses 1 electron at the anode
    (d) copper ions go to the cathode

29. The fundamental reason that the elements Li, Na, K, Rb, and Cs are in the same group or family in the periodic table is that they all

    (a) are metals
    (b) react with water
    (c) have similar melting points
    (d) have 1 electron in the outermost shell

30. An endothermic reaction is one which absorbs energy. An exothermic reaction is one that gives up energy. The process of forming an ion is

    (a) endothermic
    (b) exothermic
    (c) sometimes one, sometimes the other
    (d) always both
    (e) neither

31. The difference (differences) between the CsCl model and the NaCl model is (are)

    (a) relative orientation of the ions
    (b) the distances between the ions
    (c) the sizes of the ions
    (d) all of the above

Type IV MULTIPLE-ANSWER MULTIPLE-CHOICE QUESTIONS

The following are multiple choice questions, many of which have more than one correct answer. The student should choose as many answers as he thinks correct. You *must* subtract points for incorrect choices, otherwise some shrewd student will mark *all* of the answers and get a perfect score. It should be easy to grade this in a machine — just run the answer sheet into the machine twice, once with the machine set at "correct answers", once with it set at "incorrect answers." Answers are underscored.

Instructions: Choose the correct answers to the following questions. In many of the questions, more than one of the choices is correct. Choose as many of these as you think are correct for each question. Points will be subtracted for incorrect answers, so choose carefully.

1.   All crystals
    (a)   have internal regularity
    (b)   have external regularity
    (c)   have large scale symmetry
    (d)   can be cleaved
    (e)   are made of "building blocks"

2.   Density is a measure of
    (a)   the amount of material in a substance
    (b)   a characteristic property of a substance
    (c)   an arbitrary standard kept in France

3.   The process of solidifying from the molten state
    (a)   is accompanied by a temperature change
    (b)   is almost always a crystallization process
    (c)   is always a process of increasing density

4.   Acceleration is best defined as
    (a)   how much faster it goes
    (b)   the amount of energy used to go faster
    (c)   how much the velocity changes in an interval of time

5.   Salt, sugar, iron, rubies, mica, and ice are examples of solids. Strictly speaking, which of the following are *not* solids?
    (a)   sand
    (b)   graphite
    (c)   glass
    (d)   concrete
    (e)   mercury

6.   Photography involves light shining onto a photographic film. Which of the following questions would be appropriate to ask if you wanted to learn more about the processes involved?
    (a)   Is photography a chemical process?
    (b)   Does the light have to be focused onto the film?
    (c)   Is the presence of air (oxygen) necessary?
    (d)   Is the amount of light significant?
    (e)   Is the color of the light significant?
    (f)   Is the velocity of the light significant?
    (g)   Is energy involved?

[Teacher's Note: Oxygen is *not* necessary, but it is a significant question nevertheless.]

7.   Some of the properties of waves are
    (a)   temperature
    (b)   speed
    (c)   frequency
    (d)   density
    (e)   force
    (f)   reflection

8. Force is best defined as
   (a) what changes the motion of a body
   (b) what keeps a body moving
   (c) the energy used to move a body

9. Beer, vinegar, brass, and steel are examples of solutions. Strictly speaking, which of the following are *not* solutions?
   (a) acid
   (b) tomato juice
   (c) ginger ale or Coca Cola
   (d) the original liquid in the jars in Experiment 1-1, from which the crystals grew
   (e) wood

10. Some of the characteristics of velocity are
    (a) magnitude
    (b) force
    (c) time
    (d) direction
    (e) frequency

11.

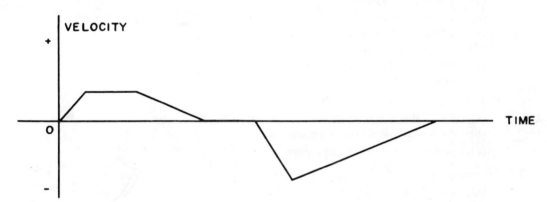

Which of the following statements about the motion of a car are indicated by the accompanying graph?
   (a) the car started up a hill
   (b) the car changed its direction abruptly
   (c) the car started twice
   (d) the car backed up faster than it moved forward
   (e) when the car moved forward, its acceleration was greater than its deceleration
   (f) the car never returned to its original position
   (g) there was a period during which the car had positive velocity and no acceleration
   (h) the average velocity for the whole trip was positive

12. Which of the following properties of matter might be useful to describe the temperature of a uniform body?
    (a) color
    (b) shape
    (c) pressure

(d)   diffraction
(e)   size

13.   The color of light is
      (a)   characterized by wavelength only
      (b)   characterized by frequency only
      (c)   characterized by both wavelength and frequency
      (d)   characterized by interference
      (e)   influenced by the motion of the light source

      [Teacher's Note: The students won't know (e), but it is included to see if they can reason it out.]

14.   Waves are
      (a)   a way to transmit energy
      (b)   sometimes a motion of material bodies
      (c)   always a motion of material bodies
      (d)   never a motion of material bodies
      (e)   related to temperature

15.   Temperature is
      (a)   a measure of kinetic energy
      (b)   a measure of potential energy
      (c)   a measure of total energy
      (d)   unrelated to energy
      (e)   a measurement using an arbitrary standard
      (f)   neither created nor destroyed

16.   Newton's laws are used to
      (a)   define the units of force
      (b)   determine the motion of a body
      (c)   prove the conservation of energy

17.   A stretched spring
      (a)   contains kinetic energy
      (b)   can do work on another body
      (c)   can exert pressure on another body
      (d)   can receive work from another body
      (e)   all of the above

18.   Which of the following are significant questions concerning crystals if we are concerned only with their structure?
      (a)   Is it equally strong in all directions?
      (b)   Does it dissolve in water?
      (c)   How easy is it to melt?
      (d)   Will it oxidize? (burn?)
      (e)   How many kinds of shapes can be seen in it?

19.   If a solid melts at a low temperature, it is more likely to be
      (a)   composed of covalently bonded molecules than of ions
      (b)   an ionic bonded substance than a metal
      (c)   a mixture than a pure substance
      (d)   a good conductor of electricity than a poor conductor

20.   A live electron charge cloud
      (a)   repels all other charge clouds, dead or alive

(b)   repels some other charge clouds
(c)   repels no other charge clouds
(d)   repels live clouds
(e)   repels dead clouds

21.   Which of the following properties will be useful in determining the bond type of a substance?
    (a)   melting point
    (b)   electrical conductivity
    (c)   polarity

22.   The Rutherford experiment was the crucial test for
    (a)   the fact that gold can be made in very thin sheets
    (b)   the validity of x-ray diffraction
    (c)   the conservation of charge
    (d)   *Answer*   None

23.   Charging bodies by rubbing involves
    (a)   the conservation of charge
    (b)   the conservation of mechanical energy (i.e., large scale kinetic and potential energy)
    (c)   a change in potential energy
    (d)   none of the above

24.   As you know, a battery can produce an electric current in a circuit. The production of the current involves a chemical process inside the battery. Which of the following questions would be appropriate questions to ask if you wanted to learn more about the *chemical process* involved?
    (a)   Is the temperature significant?
    (b)   Does it matter, with respect to the chemical process, what the battery terminals are connected to?
    (c)   Is energy involved?
    (d)   Does water enter the chemical process?
    (e)   Is the presence of air (oxygen) necessary?
    (f)   Is the size of the battery significant?

25.   Some of the characteristics of all crystals are
    (a)   regularity
    (b)   cleavage
    (c)   solubility in water
    (d)   solidity
    (e)   nonconductivity

26.   Which of the following phenomena give us information about the regularity of arrangement of the constituents of crystals?
    (a)   cleavage
    (b)   electrical conductivity
    (c)   x-ray diffraction
    (d)   sharp melting point
    (e)   solubility

27.   The chlorine atom may be represented by $\cdot \ddot{\underset{..}{Cl}} :$

    Any other atom or atoms that can be represented by an identical electron-dot arrangement has or have atomic numbers of
    (a)   5
    (b)   7
    (c)   9

(d)   11
(e)   13

28. Two of the following refer to the same chemical process. Which two?
  (a)   electron transfer
  (b)   ionization potential
  (c)   polar bonds
  (d)   oxidation-reduction

29. Electrolysis of ionic solutions is always related to
  (a)   chemical combination
  (b)   chemical replacement
  (c)   oxidation-reduction

30. The process of ionization is always accompanied by
  (a)   an energy transfer
  (b)   a charge transfer
  (c)   the emission of light
  (d)   electrolysis

31. The process of electrolysis is always accompanied by
  (a)   an energy transfer
  (b)   charge transfer
  (c)   the emission of light
  (d)   evolution of gas

32. Entropy is a measure of
  (a)   the total energy of a system
  (b)   how fast a chemical reaction occurs
  (c)   how difficult it is to distinguish one particle from another
  (d)   the energy distribution within a system

33. You have a sample of an unknown substance which you know is soluble in water. Which of the following experiments will be useful if you want to discover whether the bonds in the substance are ionic or covalent?
  (a)   an analysis of its spectrum in a flame
  (b)   a conductivity experiment
  (c)   crystallization by evaporation of the water
  (d)   placing a stream of it in an electric field

APPENDIX III

FILM EVALUATION

The number and types of films to be used in the teaching of PSNS must be left to the individual instructor. It is hoped that this list and evaluation will help the teacher to make a choice.

Both the longer 16-mm films and the so-called single-concept 8-mm loops have been reviewed and evaluated. Because these two types of films serve different purposes, they are grouped separately.

Many excellent films exist and new ones are rapidly being produced. Since it is a fair generalization that the newer a film the better it is likely to be, a teacher really interested in using films ought to keep abreast of these by getting on mailing lists of distributors and ordering for preview new films that might serve his purpose.

The selection criteria for the films listed were: Can this film fill a gap in the teaching of PSNS as outlined in the text by an imaginative presentation of experiments or models that would be impractical for the average PSNS teacher to carry out because of a lack of time, funds, or inclination? Can the film, by its very nature and because of its appeal to students, possibly do a superior job of presenting, or reinforcing material that is relevant to a real understanding of the subject matter?

Because PSNS has, in many instances, its own way of presenting materials, most films do not fit in entirely with either subject material or philosophy of presentation. In many cases the instructor has the option of turning off the sound and providing his own commentary.

For detailed comments on the various uses of films in class, the Commission on College Physics publication, **Production and Use of Single Concept Films in Physics Teaching,** is a useful guide. In many cases it has been found worthwhile to set aside time outside the regularly scheduled classes for film showings on an optional basis. Many of the suggested 16-mm films are 30 minutes or longer and, while very useful, the instructor may not have the time available in class. It is recommended that for optional showings the first few films be particularly good and possibly compulsory. Usually, an unmotivated student has to be convinced that it is worth his time to view films.

Films were selected from a wide group of sources. In many cases a film was produced for an entirely different audience. In some of the cases, especially where the audience was a grade lower than college, it would be a good idea to start the film after appropriate comments are made about the level of the film.

In general, if a film is lively, up to date, and visually good (fulfilling requirements that it be non-authoritarian and good science), then it is useful. If it is dull and tedious, then its use is not recommended, even if the material is relevant and the presentation accurate.

Only films actually reviewed are included in the lists. There are other films for which a review copy could not be obtained or which are not easily available; these are not listed.

Detailed descriptions of reviewed films are not given in most cases. A recommended film should be previewed by the teacher, if possible, before showing. Because the length of delivery time of film suppliers varies, an instructor interested in ordering films should do so as early as possible.

The following publications include valuable information about the use of films in the teaching of physics and chemistry as well as extensive lists of available films:

Ealing Cartridged Film-loops, 1968 Science Catalog for College and Universities, Ealing Film-Loops, 2225 Massachusetts Avenue, Cambridge, Mass. 02140.

"Films (16 mm) for Students of Physics," Robert L. Weber, *Am.J.Phys.* **36**, 302-326 (1968).

Films as a Lecture Aid, Alfred Leitner, Physics Demonstration Experiments, Chapter 21, Ronald Press, New York (1968).

"Physics Films," Robert L. Weber, *Physics Teacher,* 6, 224-257 (1968).

Production and Use of Single-Concept Films in Physics Teaching, Commission on College Physics, University of Maryland, 4321 Hartwick Road, College Park, Maryland 20740.

Resource Letter B S P F - 1. "A Bibliography of Selected Physics Films," William R. Riley, *Am. J. Phys.* 36, 475-489 (1968).

Short Films for Physics Teaching, Commission on College Physics, University of Maryland, 4321 Hartwick Road, College Park, Maryland 20740.

Source Directory of Educational Single-Concept Films Available in Magi-Cartridges, Technicolor Corporation, Commercial and Educational Division, Box 517, Costa Mesa, California 92627 (25 cents).

Teacher-produced Instructional Films in Chemistry (8 mm and super 8), R. O'Connor and W. Slabaugh, Advisory Council on College Chemistry, Department of Chemistry, Stanford University, Stanford, California 94305.

Films can be obtained directly from the distributor, or they may be obtained from one of the university film libraries. Below is a list of some of these audio-visual libraries that have sizable film collections available for rental. Many libraries issue catalogues:

Audio-Visual Center
Arizona State University
Tempe, Arizona 85281

Film Library Supervisor
Extension Division
University of California, Berkeley
Berkeley, California 94720

Audio-Visual Center
University of Connecticut
Storrs, Connecticut 06268

Audio-Visual Center
Florida State University
Tallahassee, Florida 32306

Georgia Center For Continuing Education
University of Georgia
Athens, Georgia 30601

Audio-Visual Aids Service
Southern Illinois University
Carbondale, Illinois 62903

Visual Aids Service
University of Illinois
Champaign, Illinois 61820

Audio-Visual Center
Indiana University
Bloomington, Indiana 47401

Audio-Visual Center
Purdue University
Lafayette, Indiana 47907

Bureau of Audio-Visual Instruction
Extension Division
State University of Iowa
Iowa City, Iowa 52240

Bureau of Visual Instruction
University Extension
University of Kansas
Lawrence, Kansas 66045

Abraham Krasker Memorial Film Library
Boston University
School of Education
765 Commonwealth Avenue
Boston, Massachusetts 02215

Audio-Visual Education Center
The University of Michigan
Ann Arbor, Michigan 48104

Audio-Visual Center
Michigan State University
East Lansing, Michigan 48823

Audio-Visual Extension Service
University of Minnesota
2037 University Avenue, S.E.
Minneapolis, Minnesota 55414

Audio-Visual Center
University of New Hampshire
Durham, New Hampshire 03824

Audio-Visual Education
State Department of Education
Trenton, New Jersey

New York University Film Library
Washington Square
New York, New York 10033

Educational Film Library
Syracuse University
Collendale Campus
Building D-7
Syracuse, New York 13210

Bureau of Audio-Visual Education
University of North Carolina
Chapel Hill, North Carolina 27514

Audio-Visual Services
Division of Continuing Education
Coliseum 131
Corvallis, Oregon 97330

Audio-Visual Aids Library
The Pennsylvania State University
University Park, Pennsylvania 16802

School of General Studies
Audio-Visual Aids Bureau
University of South Carolina
Columbia, South Carolina 29208

Visual Instruction Bureau
University of Texas
Austin, Texas 78712

Audio-Visual Center
Brigham Young University
Provo, Utah 84601

Audio-Visual Services
University of Washington
Seattle, Washington 98105

Bureau of Visual Instruction
University of Wisconsin
1312 West John Street
Madison, Wisconsin 53706

For each film listed the following information is given:

1. PSNS film code number

2. *Film Title*

3. Series — PSSC: Physical Science Study Committee, produced by Educational Development Center and distributed by Modern Learning Aids (*MLA*).

    Chem Study: Chem Study Chemistry Films distributed by Modern Learning Aids (*MLA*).

    YCF: Yale University Chemistry Films, produced by the Sterling Chemistry Laboratory and distributed by Association Films Inc. (*AFI*).

    ETS: Horizons of Science Film Series, produced and distributed by the Educational Testing Service (*ETS*).

    Ripple Tank Series: Ripple Tank Wave Phenomena Series; five films produced by Educational Development Center, narrated by James Strickland and distributed by Universal Education and Visual Aids (*UEVA*).

4. B-W (black and white) or color

5. Running time, in minutes

6. Silent if not a sound film. All 16-mm films have sound unless noted. All 8-mm loops are silent unless noted.

7. Author of film, if known, and his affiliation; or producer.

8. *Distributor abbreviation* (such as *MLA*). See list of distributors at the end of this appendix. In general films should be ordered from the distributor and not the producer.

9.   Comments on the film and its usefulness in PSNS.

10.   PSNS chapter number.

11.   PSNS evaluation according to the following ratings:

A*   Highly recommended for showing, fits in with subject matter, and an excellent film visually and pedagogically

A   Recommended for showing; a good film that fits in with subject matter

A'   Recommended for showing; a good film on supplementary subject matter

B   An acceptable film, fits in with subject matter

B'   An acceptable film on supplementary subject matter

C   Not recommended for PSNS; the film may still be good for other purposes

16-mm FILM LIST

1.   *Action and Reaction,* color, 15 min, *FA.* Visually and pedagogically beautiful with special techniques that make visible the presence of macroscopic forces inside solid objects. Chapter 8, A*.

2.   *The Balance and its Use,* color, 20 min, United Kingdom Atomic Energy Authority, *GATE.* Historical development from 6000 years ago to the present. A careful discussion of design but too much detail for PSNS at the end on the use of the modern chemical balance. Chapter 2, B'.

3.   *Behavior of Gases* (PSSC), B-W, 15 min, L. Grodzins, M.I.T., *MLA.* Brownian motion of smoke particles and mechanical analogue for molecular motion. Chapters 7 and 10, B.

4.   *Boiling From a Liquid-Liquid Interface,* B-W, 7 min, silent, United States Atomic Energy Commission, Argonne National Laboratories, *AFI.* Water boiling from a liquid mercury surface, then n-hexane from the same surface. A fine illustration for students that the closer you look at "simple" things the more you see. Chapters 1, 10, and 16, A'.

5.   *Bragg Reflection* (Ripple Tank Series) B-W, 10 min, EDC, *MLA* and *UEVA.* The reflection of waves scattered from a two-dimensional lattice is studied. The narrative is very technical for PSNS students. Chapters 5 and 15, C.

6.   *Bubble Model of a Metal Structure,* Sir Lawrence Bragg, The Royal Institution. This film in its entirety is not useful for PSNS. Two 8-mm film loops are based on this film, one of which is of interest to us. See film loop number 3 on page 316.

7.   *Catalysis* (Chem Study), color, 17 min, R. Powell, Berkeley, *MLA.* Demonstrates and interprets three simple catalyzed reactions. Animation shows what takes place on the molecular level in a catalyzed reaction. Potential energy curves show the relationship between uncatalyzed and catalyzed reactions, a concept important to PSNS. Chapter 15, A.

8.   *Chemical Bonding* (Chem Study), color, 16 min, G.C. Pimentel, Berkeley, *MLA.* Explains chemical bonding in terms of the electric interactions that cause the bonding in the hydrogen molecule. Through animation, the quantum mechanical view of electron distribution is portrayed. Chapter 16, B.

9.   *Color Television,* color, 20 min, *FACSEA.* Technical in spots but may be useful. Uses many ideas developed in PSNS: color, filters, electrons, waves. Chapters 3 and 4, B'.

10.   *Combustion,* color, 8 min, Sutherland Educational Films, *FA.* Candle, phosphorus, charcoal, kerosene, and gasoline are pictured. It is recommended that this film be used without sound. Chapters 7 and 16, B.

16-mm FILM EVALUATION SUMMARY

Chapter	A*	A	A'	B	B'	C
1	79	22, 74	4, 70			
2	30	52, 76	31		2, 40, 42, 72	47, 49, 50, 54
3			17, 20, 73	64	9, 48	58
4	80		34, 68		9	
5		13, 16				5
6			46			
7	56	22, 52	53, 65	3, 10		
8	1, 30			32, 33		
9				51		
10	56	27, 38, 57	4, 23	3		
11			24, 25, 77	11, 21, 61	55	
12					29	
13	12, 59, 69		26, 43, 60, 66	19, 44, 67		
14		14	53		18	36
15		7, 16, 71	15, 46, 62	35		5, 83
16			4, 62, 65 82	8, 10		
17		22, 63, 74, 75	53, 78	28		
18	81		23			
Acids and Bases	45		39			
Magnetism				41		
Astronomy		37				

11. *Coulomb's Law* (PSSC), B-W, 30 min, Eric Rogers, Princeton, *MLA*. Summary of electrostatics with helpful presentation of the inverse square law. Discussion of charge distribution inside a charged hollow sphere is too long for PSNS purposes. Chapter 11, B.

12. *Crookes Tube* (YCF), color, 8 min, silent, A. Patterson, *AFI*. Crookes tube demonstration with all the standard variations beautifully, carefully, and colorfully done. Chapter 13, A*.

13. *Crystals* (PSSC), B-W or color, 25 min, Alan Holden, Bell Telephone Laboratories, *MLA*. Demonstrates the nature of crystals and how they are formed. Shows actual crystal growth under a microscope. Formation of grain boundaries is also illustrated. Chapter 5, A.

14. *Crystals and Their Structures* (Chem Study), B-W, 22 min, J.A. Campbell, Harvey Mudd College, *MLA*. Starts by looking at NaC1 crystals and cleaving, shows attempts to cleave glass and gives a simple model of a glass. The film includes good ripple tank pictures. An x-ray beam is aimed at a model and its structure is predicted from the diffraction pattern produced. This film ties much of course material together. Chapter 14, A.

15. *Crystals, an Introduction*, color, 25 min, Elizabeth Wood, Bell Telephone Laboratories, *BELL*. The orderly arrangement of atoms in crystals is described, It clearly relates symmetries of the unit cell to the physical properties of the crystal. Some parts of this film are beyond the scope of the PSNS course. Chapter 15, A'.

16. *Crystal Structure*, color, 12 min, H. Powell, Oxford University, *ICI*. Shows the growing of various crystals. The film includes electron photomicrographs of tobacco mosaic crystal, the cleaving of calcite, and good ripple tank pictures of interference. An optical diffractometer, and an x-ray goniometer are illustrated, including excellent photographs of x-ray diffraction patterns. This film fills a real gap in the PSNS presentation. Chapters 5 and 15, A.

17. *Color Quality of Light in Photography*, color, 9 min, *THORNE*. Pictures the relationship between color and temperature, as well as the use of filters. Chapter 3, A'.

18. *Definite and Multiple Proportions* (PSSC), B-W, 30 min, *MLA*. A demonstration of what made Dalton believe that matter is composed of atoms. While technically good, the film is not appropriate in its presentation of the material for PSNS. It does document, however, many experiments very valuable in our discussions. The film could be used in parts and modified by the teacher to fit our purposes; it could then be used successfully. Chapter 14, B'.

19. *Discharge Through Gases*, B-W, 11 min, Educational Foundation for Visual Aids, England, *MGHT*. Shows the pressure in a discharge tube being progressively reduced. The film seems too technical and pedantic for PSNS but has a good model for the description of what is happening in this PSNS demonstration. Chapter 13, B.

20. *Doppler Effect and Shock Waves* (Ripple Tank Series), B-W, 8 min, *UEVA*. A good introduction to waves, very good to stimulate interest in wave phenomena. While Mach number and shock waves, mentioned in the film, are not a part of the PSNS course, the student is very likely to have heard of these concepts. Chapter 3, A'.

21. *Electrostatics,* B-W, 11 min, *EBF*. Useful recapitulation after finishing PSNS electrostatic experiment though the discussion is not in the PSNS style. Chapter 11, B.

22. *Elements, Compounds, and Mixtures* (PSSC), color, 33 min, *MLA*. We recommend showing this film several times during the course. Discussions and demonstrations of the difference between elements, compounds, and mixtures. Includes time lapse photography of putting things together and taking them apart by chemical methods with identification of components by means of the physical properties such as melting point, boiling point, solubility, color, etc. Chapters 1, 7, and 17, A.

23. *Exploring the Edge of Space* (ETS), color, 19 min, *ETS*. Use of polyethylene plastic film in giant balloons to make measurements in the upper atmosphere at 100,000 ft. Could be used as an interest stimulator for the effect of air temperature and pressure on the polyethelene balloons. The interdependence of scientific disciplines is shown. Chapters 10 and 18, A'.

24. *Forces* (PSSC), B-W, 23 min, Jerrold Zacharias, M.I.T., *MLA*. For discussion see next film.

25. *Forces* (taken from above film), B-W, 8 min, *EDC*. The excerpt presents the Cavendish experiment in qualitative fashion, and in an engagingly informal style. The torsion pendulum is made of plastic tape and two bottles of water, while the large masses are cardboard cartons filled with sand. The scene which follows the experiment is especially valuable. The Cavendish balance had been enclosed in an electrostatic shield made of copper screens. When this shield is removed, and a rubber rod (rubbed with fur) is brought near, the much greater strength of electrical relative to gravitational forces is dramatically demonstrated. The complete film surveys electric, magnetic, gravitational, and nuclear forces in an equally informal set of experiments and discussions. Some of these parallel our Experiments 11-1 to 11-3. Chapter 11, A'.

26. *Frank-Hertz Experiment* (PSSC), B-W, 30 min, Byron Youtz, Reed College, *MLA*. Several extraneous calculations and discussions but some valuable and well-done demonstrations, including a model for the mercury atom using dry ice pucks and a ping pong ball. A mechanism for energy transfer is discussed. The epilogue by James Frank does not seem particularly interesting and may be omitted. Chapter 13, A'.

27. *Gas Pressure and Molecular Collisions* (Chem Study), color, 21 min, J.A. Campbell, Harvey Mudd College, *MLA*. The film explores the relationship between gaseous pressure and molecular collisions. Pressure is measured as a function of temperature by a method similar to the one used in PSNS. Mechanical models illustrate experimental observations. The model illustrating the relative escape velocities of gases with different molecular weight at the same temperature is valuable to our students. The film is highly recommended although occasionally it gets too wordy and there are too many calculations. Chapter 10, A.

28. *Gases and How They Combine* (Chem Study), color, 22 min, George C. Pimentel, Berkeley, *MLA*. The film includes useful material on the growth of the particle model to explain the behavior of gases. The grouping of gases according to their solubilities is shown and various tests to distinguish gases, both qualitatively and quantitatively, are discussed. In the beginning of the film, viewers are told what an exciting part of science this topic really is; the approach used here does not seem appropriate for our students. It is hoped that our students will discover this themselves; if not, they will not believe it when told. Chapter 16, B.

29. *Genesis of the Transistor,* color, 15 min, *BELL*. Good demonstrations of the effect of heating on conductors, semiconductors, and nonconductors. Unfortunately, some good material is marred by poor music, over dramatization, and commercials for the Bell Telephone System. The film is available free of charge which might be a compensation for this. There often arise questions about transistors and this film may help to answer some of these if time is available. Chapter 12, B'.

30. *Gravity, Weight, and Weightlessness,* color, 11 min, C. York, U.C.L.A., *FA*. Beautifully explores the relationship between gravity and weight. This film fills a great gap in the perception and understanding of weight and weightlessness. Chapters 2 and 8, A*.

31. *Heat and Cold – Very High Temperature,* color, 20 min, *CENCO.* Excellent color photography. The film includes discussions of optical pyrometers, fusion, and plasma, and the fourth state of matter. Useful in discussion of temperature measurement. Chapter 2, A$'$.

32. *Inertia* (PSSC), B-W, 26 min, E.M. Purcell, Harvard, *MLA.* See next film.

33. *Inertial Mass* (PSSC), B-W, 19 min, E.M. Purcell, Harvard, *MLA.* The film *Inertial Mass* is a continuation of the film *Inertia.* Among the topics covered in this sequence are: effects of forces applied to frictionless puck; relation between acceleration and applied force when mass is constant; dynamical behavior of different objects under the influence of a constant force. Inertial and gravitational masses are compared. Chapter 8, B.

34. *Interference and Diffraction* (Ripple Tank Series), B-W, 19 min, James Strickland, ESI, *UEVA.* Two-source interference patterns reveal effects of varying wavelength, separation of sources, and phase. Diffraction is presented as a form of interference. Useful supplement to PSNS materials. Chapter 4, A$'$.

35. *Introduction to Reaction Kinetics* (Chem Study), color, 13 min, *MLA.* All animation. Recommended to be shown without sound track which does not fit in with PSNS course presentation. Good pictures of models of potential energy barriers and clouds. Chapter 15, B.

36. *Ionization Energy* (Chem Study), color, 22 min, *MLA.* The film presents two methods of measuring ionization energy: photoionization, and electron bombardment. Animation shows what occurs on the atomic level during the ionization process. The film seems too technical and not on a PSNS level. Chapter 14, C.

37. *Jupiter, Saturn, Mars in Motion,* color, 8 min, silent, *EBF.* Excellent time-lapse photographs taken through the 60-inch Mt. Wilson telescope. Supplementary Chapter on Astronomy, A.

38. *Kinetic-Molecular Theory,* color, 15 min, *MGHT.* Excellent Brownian motion footage of smoke particles. Includes cloud formation upon combination of NH_4OH and $HC1$ and a mechanical model for the bromine diffusion experiment. Chapter 10, A.

39. *Let Us Teach Guessing,* color, 61 min, A Demonstration with George Polya, *MLA.* Professor Polya lectures to his undergraduate college class in a style that is precisely hoped for in PSNS. His students deduce for themselves a theorem in solid geometry. "If a problem is too hard, try an easier one," which is what we are constantly trying to do. This film would be helpful to show students who are confused and unhappy with this open-ended style. Discussing this technique might make them a little more relaxed with the course. This is an award winning film produced by the American Mathematical Association. Any time after Chapter 1, A$'$.

40. *Long Time Intervals* (PSSC), B-W, 25 min, *MLA.* Discusses the significance of long time intervals and demonstrates how radioactivity in rocks can be used to measure the earth's age. The section on radioactive dating is too long and detailed for PSNS but of possible interest to some students. Chapter 2, B$'$.

41. *Magnetism and Electricity,* color or B-W, 17 min, Science Education Dept., Teachers College, Columbia University, *MGHT.* Of possible interest for elementary education majors. Supplementary Chapter on Magnetism, B.

42. *Man is the Measure,* color, 23 min, *FORD.* Interesting, artistic, good photography, many excellent models and things to "put on the shelf." Some advertising but film is free. Chapter 2, B$'$.

43. *The Mass of Atoms* (in 2 parts), B-W, each about 47 min, R. Hertz and C. Brewer, Monsanto Research Corp., *UEVA.* An experiment is performed in which the masses of helium and polonium

atoms are determined. The discussion is inte.esting but very detailed and sometimes complicated. It might be useful for students who are sufficiently interested. For a detailed review see *Am. J. Phys.* 36, 772 (1968). Chapter 13, A'.

44. *Mass of the Electron* (PSSC), B-W, 18 min; Eric Rogers, Princeton, *MLA*. Electron motion in a cathode-ray tube encircled by a current carrying wire leads to the determination of the mass of the electron. The calculations are brought out step by step, probably too detailed for PSNS. The visual part of the film is not particularly interesting for our students. Chapter 13, B.

45. *The Mathematician and the River* (ETS), color, 19 min, *ETS*. A fine film convincingly illustrating the use and meaning of mathematical models in understanding the physical universe. Flood control on the Mississippi River is used as an example. Any place where models are discussed, A*.

46. *Matter Waves* (PSSC), B-W, 28 min, Alan Holden and Lester Germer, Bell Telephone Laboratories, *MLA*. Demonstration of the wave behavior of electrons and of an optical analogue. X-ray and electron diffraction are discussed as well as the wave behavior of other particles. Chapters 6 and 15, A'.

47. *Measurement* (PSSC), B-W, 21 min, William Siebert, M.I.T., *MLA*. The measurement of the speed of a rifle bullet is used to emphasize that the accuracy of a physical measurement depends on many factors. This film is specifically keyed to the beginning of the PSSC course. Chapter 2, C.

48. *Measurement of the Speed of Light,* B-W, 8 min, A.A.P.T. College Physics Series, *MGHT*. Methods of Fizeau, Foucault, and Michelson for the measurement of the speed of light are included. Well illustrated. Chapter 3, B'.

49. *Measuring Large Distances* (PSSC), B-W, 29 min, Fletcher Watson, Harvard, *MLA*. Earth, moon and star models are used to illustrate celestial distance-measuring techniques involving triangulation, stellar parallax and brightness of stars. Chapter 2, C.

50. *Measuring Short Distances* (PSSC), B-W, 20 min, Dorothy Montgomery, Hollins College, *MLA*. Moves from the centimeter scale to microscopic dimensions and atomic dimensions revealed by the field emission microscope. Chapter 2, C.

51. *Mechanical Energy and Thermal Energy* (PSSC), B-W, 22 min, Jerrold Zacharias, M.I.T., *MLA*. With models this film demonstrates the transfer of the kinetic energy of bulk motion to the energy of random molecular motion. Models used are very good. The film includes the PSNS pressure-temperature experiment. Chapter 9, B.

52. *Melting Points* (Relation to Periodic Table) (YCF), color, 3 min, *AFI*. Excellent demonstration of the determination of the melting point of chlorine and bromine. This is of particular interest because the PSNS student may doubt that matter he knows as a gas is ever a liquid or a solid. The film includes an excellent picture of a three-dimensional bar graph. Chapters 2 and 7, A.

53. *Metals and Nonmetals* (YCF), color, 9 min, *AFI*. Compares physical properties of metals and nonmetals such as malleability, conductivity, thermal conductivity, and acid and base properties. The periodic table is used to organize the information. Chapters 7, 14, and 17, A'.

54. *The Metric System,* color or B-W, 13 min, *MGHT*. High school level. Chapter 2, C.

55. *Millikans Oil Drop Experiment* (YCF), B-W, 6 min, silent, *AFI*. Shows experiment to determine the charge on the electron. Includes formulas for an analysis of the data. Chapter 11, B'.

56. *Molecular Motion* (Chem Study), color, 13 min, J. Arthur Campbell, Harvey Mudd College, *MLA*. Excellent demonstrations; $KMnO_4$ in water; bromine diffusion. Many properties of matter lead to the idea of molecular motion. Translational, rotational, and vibrational motions are discussed. The film includes animation and dynamic models. Chapters 7 and 10, A*.

57. *The Molecular Theory of Matter,* color or B-W, 11 min, *EBF.* Includes demonstration of the bromine diffusion experiment, as well as Brownian motion and crystals growing from melt. Chapter 10, A.

58. *The Nature of Color,* color, 11 min, Ira Freeman, Rutgers, *CORF.* Color presented as a property of light. Selective absorbtion and reflection are discussed. Additive primaries, complementaries and subtractive mixtures are demonstrated. Chapter 3, C.

59. *A New Reality,* color, 51 min, International Council for Educational Films, *IFB.* Follows the development of the structure of the atom with particular emphasis on the contributions of the Danish physicist, Niels Bohr. The film includes: patterns in a piece of wood; salt crystals growing; different orders of magnification up to the electron microscope which can see "molecules piled up like oranges in a shop window"; cloud chamber photographs; incredibly good, long segment of an atomic model in a series of semianimated sections. Electric discharge glow and spectra are beautifully demonstrated. Discussion of: causality, particles, wave diffraction pattern; models of atoms in which the electron is represented as a particle or a wave; the growth of natural science. Complementarity is discussed clearly and significantly with extensions to philosophic and human implications. Produced at the Niels Bohr Institute, Copenhagen by Laterna Films, Copenhagen. Chapter 13, A*.

60. *On the Stability of Matter* (Part 1 of the series "The Fabric of the Atom: An Introduction to Quantum Mechanics" by Philip Morrison, M.I.T.), B-W, 30 min, BBC-TV, *ROBECK.* Discussion of the identity and stability of atoms and the resolution of problems by quantum mechanics. Of interest to better students after a discussion of atomic models. Chapter 13, A′.

61. *Patterns of Scientific Investigation* (YCF), color, 22 min, *AFI.* Harold G. Cassidy illustrates each step in a typical pattern for scientific work. The film consists of lecture demonstrations in static electricity. Chapter 11, B.

62. *Physics and Chemistry of Water,* color, 21 min, *FA.* Visually beautiful; excellent time lapse photography of ice formation. Chapters 15 and 16, A′.

63. *Physical Chemistry of Polymers,* color, 22 min, *BELL.* Excellent models, both moving and static. Interesting segment on cotton in which the polar bonds are so strong, that it doesn't melt, it decomposes. Chapter 17, A.

64. *Progressive Waves: Transverse and Longitudinal* (AAPT series), B-W, 9 min, *MGHT.* Animated presentation of one-dimensional sinusoidal transverse and longitudinal waves. Contains extraneous material, but includes many good models. Chapter 3, B.

65. *Properties of Mixtures and Compounds* (YCF), color, 4 min, *AFI.* Mixing and combining sulfur and iron. Chapters 7 and 16, A′.

66. *Positron-Electron Annihilation,* B-W, 28 min, Stephen Berko, Brandeis, *UEVA.* If the question of anti-matter and mass-energy conversion is raised, this film could be used to answer interested students. Chapter 13, A′.

67. *Random Events* (PSSC), B-W, 31 min, Hume and Ivey, Toronto, *MLA.* Shows how the overall effect of a very large number of random (unpredictable) events can be predictable. The film includes the model for the conduction of electricity in metals used in PSNS and discusses the decay of polonium. It seems long and repetitious, but could be useful if shown in segments. Chapter 13, B.

68. *Reflection and Refraction* (Ripple Tank Series), B-W, 17 min, James Strickland, EDC, *UEVA.* Circular and straight pulses are reflected from various shaped barriers; refraction, focusing and total internal reflection are demonstrated. Chapter 4, A′.

69. *Rutherford Atom,* B-W, 40 min, Robert Hulsizer, M.I.T., *MLA.* Excellent reinforcement of PSNS development of atom models using alpha particles scattered by gold foil. Unusually good model of gold foil atom. All kinds of scattering demonstrations. This film easily makes the transition for our students from the marble scattering experiment to conclusions about some atomic models. There will be a significant number of students that will really want to know all of this and it would be unfortunate to let them down. Chapter 13, A*.

70. *Scientific Method in Action,* color, 19 min, Winnetka and Glencoe, Illinois School Boards, *IFB.* Demonstrates that pure reasoning of Aristotle is insufficient — one must experiment. Film uses examples from physics, biology, and even a pitcher learning to throw a baseball. Chapter 1, A'.

71. *Shapes and Polarities of Molecules* (Chem Study), color, 18 min, David Dows, University of Southern California, *MLA.* Fits in very well after the PSNS experiment on the electrical attraction of water and CCl_4. Good emphasis on molecular models. Chapter 15, A.

72. *Short Time Intervals* (PSSC), B-W, 21 min, Campbell Searle, M.I.T., *MLA.* Studies in great detail how one would go about measuring the time of an average lightning flash. The film is overly long but may be useful if enough interest is shown in just how such short times can be measured. Chapter 2, B'.

73. *Similarities in Wave Behavior,* B-W, 26 min, J. N. Shive, Bell Telephone Laboratory, *BELL.* Uses Shive-Bell wave demonstrator which is a wave machine similar to that used on the Gateway 8-mm film loops on wave behavior. Emphasis on similar behavior of waves in acoustical, electrical, mechanical, and optical systems. "Nature really is consistent." Useful after the PSNS spring experiment. Good for students interested in more details. Chapter 3, A'.

74. *Solution, Evaporation, and Crystallization* (YCF), color, 3 min, silent, *AFI.* Sulfur powder is dissolved in carbon disulfide, then allowed to evaporate in a hood. Stop-motion and close-up photography are used to observe the formation of crystals. Excellent eye opener and follow up to PSNS sulfur experiment, especially if it does not "work." Chapters 1 and 17, A.

75. *Sulfur, Its Physical States and Properties* (YCF), color, 9 min, *AFI.* Shows that the physical transformations of sulfur are functions of both temperature and time. Changes are explained in molecular terms by animated sequences. Chapter 17, A.

76. *Time and Clocks* (PSSC), B-W, 28 min, John King, M.I.T., *MLA.* Good PSNS-type approach including slow motion of milk droplets and fast motion of rose opening. The film discusses standards as well as Galileo and pendulums. High-speed photography is used to slow down a flying bird, a tennis ball hitting a racket, and a bursting balloon. Chapter 2, A.

77. *Universal Gravitation* (PSSC), B-W, 31 min, Hume and Ivey, Toronto, *MLA.* The law of gravity on planet X is described. Long segments of calculations could be excluded but are valuable to clarify the inverse square law. Film includes interesting, computer-generated, satellite orbits. Chapter 11, A'.

78. *Vibration of Molecules* (Chem Study), color, 12 min, Linus Pauling and Richard Badger, *MLA.* All animations. Excellent models; energy levels; strength of chemical bonds related. Chapter 17, A'.

79. *Visual Perception* ETS, color, 20 min, Hadley Kantrell, Perception Demonstration Center, Princeton University, *ETS.* Pictures the way the eye and mind combine to create awareness. The question is asked, "How closely does objective reality correspond to what we see?" The film demonstrates that perceptions of motion, due entirely to the assumptions within the observer, may prove satisfactory to a student and that only by making mistakes can one learn. It ends by pointing out that scientific research is based on observation and unless we are aware of our assumptions, we may miss clues leading to new discoveries. Chapter 1, A*.

80. *Wave Motion,* B-W, 7 min, *GATE.* Excellent Schlieren photographic technique of ripple tank interference pattern of two sources. Excerpts of these are available on 8-mm loops (Loops 11, 12, 14, 17, 40). Chapter 4, A*.

81. *The Worlds of Dr. Vishniac* (ETS), color, 20 min, *ETS.* What it means to be a scientist. This particular well-known microbiologist functions completely in his apartment in Manhattan with occasional excursions into Central Park. Although the subject matter is not the study of solids, as we approach it, this film may actually convince our students that, as Dr. Vishniac says, "it is so important to be interested, to look around ... the world will be bigger ... the world around us." The microphotography (cinemicroscopy) is extraordinary. Chapter 18, A*.

82. *Xenon Tetrafluoride,* color, 6 min, Argonne National Laboratories, *CALVIN.* Demonstrates combination of xenon and another element. Shows the formation of xenon tetrafluoride crystals. "Opened up a new area for the study of chemical bonding." Chapter 16, A'.

83. *X-Ray Crystallography,* B-W, 21 min, Educational Foundation for Visual Aids, London, England, *MGHT.* Illustrates the production of x rays; discusses x-ray diffraction. Shows many models and Laue patterns but of no particular interest to PSNS. Chapter 15, C.

8-mm FILM LOOP LIST

The production of single-concept film loops is in its infancy. There are several serious problems with the mass production of these loops and with the durability both of the loops and their packaging. This could be corrected in the near future because of the rapidly growing interest in their production and use. Similar problems exist with the projectors, which were developed as a clever gadget for home movie showing. There are many places where short loops will be most helpful, mainly in the area of picturing demonstrations that are too impractical to perform for the average teacher of PSNS. Many of the existing loops, however, have been produced for special purposes that do not necessarily add to the presentation of the PSNS course.

The next few years should see a great improvement in equipment and packaging; in the interim there are several loops that do fit in; some rather well. These are listed in the same format as the 16-mm films above in this appendix, except that for most loops the catalog number is given following the distributor.

None of the following loops has sound; they are generally available in 8-mm or Super 8. In the near future, however, the regular 8-mm format may be dropped by the distributors.

1. *Barrier Penetration,* B-W, 2 min, E.S.I., *EFL 80-2355.* Ripple tank phenomena. Chapter 4, A.

2. *Bragg Reflection of Waves,* B-W, 4 min, *EFL 80-2363.* Bragg reflection is demonstrated in a ripple rank using a two-dimensional array of pegs. A needed supplement to PSNS ripple tank demonstrations. Chapter 6, A*.

3. *Bubble Model of a Crystal Structure and Boundaries,* B-W, 2 min, Sir L. Bragg, The Royal Institution, *EFL 84-0116.* Bubble rafts are used to simulate a two-dimensional crystal structure. Chapter 5, B.

4. *Bunsen Burner,* color, 4 min, R.M. Whitney, Roxbury Latin School, *EFL 84-0025.* Although alcohol burners are used for PSNS, many schools may have bunsen burners and some PSNS experiments call for these. This is an extremely useful and well-produced loop describing the assembly, adjustment, and operation of a Bunsen burner. Any Chapter, A*.

5. *Changes on Mixing,* color, 4 min, *UNESCO.* Four different, visually striking changes occur. A good use of this medium. Chapters 1 and 16, A.

8-mm FILM LOOP EVALUATION SUMMARY

Chapter	A*	A	A′	B	B′	C
1	20	5	52			
2	29, 30, 31					33
3		6, 40, 55, 59, 60, 63, 64	19, 27, 51, 58			
4	13	1, 6, 11, 14, 16, 35, 36, 40, 41, 55, 60	39, 51	15, 57	12, 17	
5				3		
6	2					
7	20		54			
8	26, 61, 62		8, 32, 56			10, 42, 43
9			53	7		22
10	25, 50	18, 49	8, 9, 23, 24, 28			
11		34, 37	44	21		38
12						
13						
14						
15	20					
16		5	23			
17	45, 46, 47, 48					
18						
Acids and Bases	4					

6. *Circular Wave Reflection from Various Barriers,* B-W, 3½ min, E.S.I., *EFL 80-2322.* Ripple tank phenomena, Chapters 3 and 4, A.

7. *Conservation of Energy,* color, 4 min, J.L. Stull, Alfred University, *EFL 80-2769.* Examples of transforming potential to kinetic energy on a linear air track. Mostly useful. Chapter 9, B.

8. *Conservation of Momentum-Elastic Collisions,* color, 4 min, J.L. Stull, Alfred University, *EFL 80-2777.* Compares elastic and inelastic collisions. Several examples of elastic collisions are introduced as problems. Chapters 8 and 10, A′.

9. *Conservation of Momentum-Inelastic Collisions,* color, 4 min, J.L. Stull, Alfred University, *EFL 80-2751.* Includes a series of quantitative demonstrations. Visually appealing although rather slow in drawing interest at beginning. Chapter 10, A′.

10. *Constant Velocity and Uniform Acceleration,* color, 4 min, J.L. Stull, Alfred University, *EFL 80-2728.* Photocells are used for measurements of the passage of gliders along a linear air track. Does not seem appropriate for PSNS. Chapter 8, C.

11. *Diffraction at an Aperture,* B-W, 1 min, *GATE.* Excerpt from 16-mm film number 80. Demonstrates the optical effect caused by a light shining through a vertical slit, opened at various widths. Then waves in a ripple tank are shown as they encounter a fixed narrow aperture, two apertures side by side, a wider aperture, a very wide aperture, and a varying aperture. This helps to make the transition for students from two-source interference to two-aperture interference. Chapter 4, A.

12. *Diffraction at an Aperture-Variable,* B-W, 1 min, *GATE.* Excerpt from 16-mm film number 80. Waves in a ripple tank are passed through an aperture of constant width. λ is doubled and then tripled. Chapter 4, B′.

13. *Diffraction – Double Slit,* color, 4 min, F. Miller, Ohio State University, *EFL 80-2074.* Excellent diffraction patterns produced by varying the slit width and the wavelength. Chapter 4, A*.

14. *Diffraction at a Narrow Obstacle,* B-W, 1 min, *GATE.* Excerpt from 16-mm film number 80. A vertical pin lit by a narrow vertical source is moved into view, and the diffraction is observed. Then parallel waves are interrupted by a straight obstacle placed at the center of a ripple tank. Diffraction occurs around each side of the obstacle and the resulting interference fringes behind the obstacle and on either side are seen. Chapter 4, A.

15. *Diffraction and Scattering of Waves Around Obstacles,* B-W, 3 min, E.S.I., *EFL 80-2447.* Ripple tank pictures of the diffraction patterns due to obstacles. Chapter 4, B.

16. *Diffraction – Single Slit,* color, 3 min, F. Miller, Ohio State University, *EFL 80-2066.* Good after our experiment as reinforcement and for post-laboratory discussion. Chapter 4, A.

17. *Diffraction at a Straight Edge,* B-W, 1 min, *GATE.* Excerpt from 16-mm film number 80. First a vertical straight edge is illuminated by light from a narrow vertical source. Then a single barrier is moved sideways into the path of waves traveling across a ripple tank and the diffraction pattern is observed. Chapter 4, B′.

18. *Diffusion,* color, 3 min, H.A. Daw, New Mexico State University, *EFL 80-2959.* Visually stimulating. A gas model consisting of different colored pucks on an air table is used. Chapter 10, A.

19. *Doppler Effect,* B-W, 3½ min, E.S.I., *EFL 80-2363.* Ripple tank phenomena. Chapter 3, A′.

20. *Drops and Splashes,* color, 4 min, G. Grey, Newton Schools, *EFL 80-0076.* An extremely beautiful loop, using some of the latest high-speed photographic techniques by H. Edgerton and T. Uyemura of M.I.T. A great question stimulator. Chapters 1, 7, 15, A*.

21. *Electrostatic Induction,* color, 4 min, A. E. Walters, Rutgers, *EFL 80-2835.* May be useful after PSNS experiments have been performed. Chapter 11, B.

22. *Energy and the Pendulum,* color, 2 min, Eothen Films, *FA P/M/1.* All this loop does is to tell you that $\frac{1}{2}mv^2 = mgh$. A transparency could take its place. Chapter 9, C.

23. *Energy Transformations I,* color, 3 min, *UNESCO.* The idea that energy derived from a chemical reaction may appear as thermal energy and as work is presented, using a zinc-silver nitrate solution system. Chapters 10 and 16, A′.

24. *Equipartition of Energy,* color, 3 min, H.A. Daw, New Mexico State University, *EFL 80-2934.* Heavier blue pucks moving slower than lighter yellow ones on a two-dimensional air table. Chapter 10, A'.

25. *Finding Absolute Zero,* color, 4 min, *EFL 80-3395.* Uses PSNS-type pressure-temperature apparatus; this loop is a very valuable supplement for laboratories not equipped to reduce temperatures below $0°C$. Chapter 10, A*.

26. *Force, Mass, and Acceleration,* color, 4 min, Eothen Films, *FA P/M/5.* Parallels PSNS experiment on force and motion. Chapter 8, A*.

27. *Formation of Shock Waves,* B-W, 3½ min, E.S.I., *EFL 80-2389.* An excellent eye-opener for introducing waves. Chapter 3, A'.

28. *Gravitational Distribution,* color, 4 min, H.A. Daw, New Mexico State University, *EFL 80-2942.* Too technical for PSNS although partially useful because a good two-dimensional gas model on an air table is used to explain the variation in density of the atmosphere. Includes good model of boiling and settling of heavier particles. Chapter 10, A'.

29. *Handling Solids and Liquids,* color, 4 min, R.M. Whitney, Roxbury Latin School, *EFL 84-0017.* The film presents both correct and incorrect techniques for handling chemicals. Includes many useful laboratory techniques. Chapter 2, A*.

30. *Heating Liquids,* color, 3 min, R.M. Whitney, Roxbury Latin School, *EFL 84-0041.* The film demonstrates four techniques utilized in the heating of liquids. Includes valuable laboratory techniques. Chapter 2, A*.

31. *Heating Solids,* color, 4 min, R.M. Whitney, Roxbury Latin School, *EFL 84-0033.* The film presents four different techniques associated with heating solids and emphasizes the selection of appropriate apparatus for the temperatures to be encountered. Includes useful laboratory techniques for PSNS students. Chapter 2, A*.

32. *How an Air Track Works,* color, 4½ min, J.L. Stull, Alfred University, *EFL 80-2801.* Useful to illustrate to students another way to simulate frictionless motion. A visually interesting loop. Chapter 8, A'.

33. *Identifying Solids by Density,* color, 4 min, D. Herbert and M.H. Shamos, *EFL 80-3262.* Uses displacement (Archimedes principle) not discussed in PSNS; while visually pretty, the loop has too many ideas compressed into the four minutes. Chapter 2, C.

34. *Insulators and Conductors,* color, 3 min, A.E. Walters, Rutgers; *EFL 80-2827.* Useful after PSNS experiments have been performed, or in case the electrostatic experiment does not work properly. Chapter 11, A.

35. *Interference,* B-W, 2 min, *GATE.* Good model for reinforcement and cancellation of waves; needed by many students. Chapter 4, A.

36. *Interference of Waves,* B-W, 4 min, E.S.I., *EFL 80-2405.* Two-source interference patterns in a ripple tank. Still pictures taken from the apparatus used are included in the PSNS text. Chapter 4, A.

37. *Introduction to Electrostatics,* color, 4 min, A.E. Walters, Rutgers, *EFL 80-2819.* Useful after PSNS experiments have been performed. Uses the same graphite coated styrofoam ball and other materials as PSNS. Chapter 11, A.

38. *Measurement of "G" – The Cavendish Experiment,* color, 4 min, F. Miller, Ohio State, *EFL 80-2124.* A good film including time-lapse photography, but too detailed a measurement on the torsion pendulum for PSNS. Chapter 11, C.

39. *Microwaves,* B-W, 5 min, *GATE.* The wavelength of 3-cm microwaves is measured by interference. Excellent supplement. Chapter 4, A′.

40. *Movement of Two Sources,* B-W, 1 min, *GATE.* Excerpt from 16-mm film number 80. Uses the Schlieren technique to demonstrate interference patterns with one and both sources moving. Chapters 3 and 4, A.

41. *Multiple-Slit Diffraction,* B-W, 3 min, E.S.I., *EFL 80-2439.* Ripple-tank interference patterns due to 2, 3, 4, and 8 slits. Chapter 4, A.

42. *Newton's First and Second Laws,* color, 4 min, J.L. Stull, Alfred University, *EFL 80-2736.* Using a linear air track, the motion of various gliders is studied. The loop seems too detailed for PSNS and somewhat confusing. Chapter 8, C.

43. *Newton's Third Law,* color, 3 min, J.L. Stull, Alfred University, *EFL 80-2744.* Two gliders are used on a linear air track for various experiments. The calculations seem too involved for PSNS. Chapter 8, C.

44. *Paramagnetism of Liquid Oxygen,* color, 3 min, F. Miller, Ohio State, *EFL 80-2041.* The topic is not included in PSNS, but this loop could be used in a discussion of different kinds of forces as an interest stimulator, or in connection with the optional package on magnetism. Chapter 11 or supplementary chapter on Magnetism, A′.

45. *Polymer Science I, II, III, IV,* color, 4 min each, *ACCC.* These four loops are a good supplement to
46. the section on polymers. The first one is especially useful and contains excellent models to account
47. for the melting points, elasticity, and ductility of polymers. Number II contains models of cross-
48. linking, cross branching, copolymers, random copolymers, etc. The third loop contains models of the glassy state, rubbery state, crystallization by chain folding, crystal melting by unfolding, use of crossed-polaroid filters to observe breakdown, glass-transition temperature, viscous flow, chain translation, and disentanglement. Number IV contains step polymerization models, chain polymerization, decomposition, elasticity, thermal effects, and bulk polymerization. Chapter 17, A*.

49. *Properties of Gases,* color, 3½ min, H.A. Daw, New Mexico State University, *EFL 80-2967.* Pucks on an air table are used to demonstrate pressure and force as well as isothermal and adiabatic compression and expansion of gases. Chapter 10, A.

50. *Random Walk and Brownian Motion,* color, 4 min, H.A. Daw, New Mexico State University, *EFL 80-2926.* Uses pucks on an air table for molecular motion models and ends with a picture of Brownian motion of smoke particles. Chapter 10, A*.

51. *Reflection of Waves from Concave Barriers,* B-W, 3½ min, EDC, *EFL 80-2330.* Ripple tank phenomena. Chapters 3 and 4, A′.

52. *Rotating Reference Frames,* color, 4 min, H.F. Meiners, Rensselaer Polytechnic Institute, *EFL 80-3015.* Uses a can of spray paint on a moving cart to produce patterns on a rotating disc. Illustrates that things look different from different viewpoints. Chapter 1, A′.

53. *Sand Pendulum 5 – Pouring Sand into Soda Straws,* color, 4 min, E.S.I., *EFL 80-0888.* Useful after the pendulum experiment to demonstrate another method of determining the pendulum velocity. Chapter 9, A′.

54. *Solid Solutions,* color, 4 min, *UNESCO.* Shows the manufacture of bronze in Thailand. Interesting, both for unusual method of demonstrating importance of knowledge of melting points, and for attempt to present material in fashion relevant to it. Chapter 7, A′.

55. *Straight Wave Reflection from Straight Barriers,* B-W, 3½ min, EDC, *EFL 80-2314.* Ripple tank phenomena. Chapters 3 and 4, A.

56. *Stroboscopic Photography,* B-W, 4 min, *GATE.* A camera and an electronic flasher are used to photograph a tennis service. From the photograph the speed of the ball as it leaves the racket can be calculated. A useful supplement illustrating velocity measurements. Chapter 8, A'.

57. *Superposition of Pulses,* B-W, 3 min, E.S.I., *EFL 80-2397.* Ripple tank pictures of the patterns due to single and multiple pulses. Chapter 4, B.

58. *Temperature Waves,* color, 3½ min, F. Miller, Ohio State, *EFL 80-2165.* May raise good questions such as "What is a wave?" Why doesn't everything have wave behavior? Chapter 3, A'.

59. *Transverse Waves,* B-W, 5 min, *GATE.* Uses lines of dynamics carts, similar to PSNS carts, linked by coiled springs for wave model. Chapter 3, A.

60. *Two Sources in Phase,* B-W, 1 min, *GATE.* Excerpt from 16-mm film number 80. Uses the Schlieren technique in a ripple tank to demonstrate steady interference pattern of waves from two sources. Chapters 3 and 4, A.

61. *Uniform Acceleration,* color, 4 min, Eothen Films, *FA P/M/3.* Fits in perfectly after PSNS experiment; almost essential as a supplement to our post-laboratory discussion. Produces same graph as PSNS experiment. Chapter 8, A*.

62. *Uniform Linear Velocity,* color, 2 min, Eothen Films, *FA P/M/3.* Clearly demonstrates uniform linear velocity and inertia. Chapter 8, A*.

63. *A Wave Equation,* B-W, 4 min, *GATE.* Animation compares two imaginary waves on the wave machine traveling side by side. The relationship between speed, wavelength, and frequency is shown. Chapter 3, A.

64. *A Wave Machine,* B-W, 5 min, *GATE.* Similar to two-dimensional Shive-Bell Wave Machine. An excellent supplement to class demonstrations. Chapter 3, A.

ABBREVIATIONS USED FOR FILM DISTRIBUTORS

ACCC	Advisory Council on College Chemistry, 701 Welch Road, Palo Alto, California 94304.
AFI	Association Films, Inc. Executive Office: 600 Madison Avenue, New York, N.Y. 10022. Library: 600 Grand Ave., Ridgefield, New Jersey 07657.
BELL	Bell Telephone Company. Apply for films at your local telephone business office.
CALVIN	Calvin Productions, 1105 Truman Road, Kansas City, Missouri 64106.
CENCO	EDUCATIONAL Films, 1800 Foster Ave., Chicago Illinois 60640.
CON	Contemporary Films Inc., 267 West 25 Street, New York, N.Y. 10001.
CORF	Coronet Instructional Films, Coronet Building, 65 East South Water Street, Chicago, Illinois 60601.
EBF	Encyclopedia Brittanica Films, Inc., 4424 Oakton Ave., Skokie, Illinois 60076.
EDC	Education Development Center, Inc. (formerly Educational Services, Inc.), 39 Chapel Street, Newton, Mass. 02160.
EFL	Ealing Film-Loops, 2225 Massachusetts Ave., Cambridge, Mass. 02140.

ESI	See EDC.
ETS	Educational Testing Service, 20 Nassau Street, Princeton, New Jersey 08540.
FA	Film Associates, 11559 Santa Monica Blvd., Los Angeles, California 90025.
FACSEA	French American Cultural Services and Educational Aid, 972 Fifth Ave., New York, N.Y. 10021.
FORD	Ford Motor Co. Film Library, The American Road, Dearborn, Michigan 48121.
GATE	Gateway Educational Films Ltd., 470 Green Lanes, London N13, England.
ICF	Communication Films, International Communications Foundation, 870 Monterey Pass Road, Monterey Park, California 91754.
ICI	Imperial Chemical Industries, Ltd., London, S.W. 1, England. Film Library: 444 Madison Ave., New York, N.Y. 10022.
IFB	International Film Bureau, Inc., 332 South Michigan Ave., Chicago, Illinois 60604.
MGHT	McGraw-Hill Book Co., Text Film Division, 330 West 42nd Street, New York, N.Y. 10036.
MLA	Modern Learning Aids, 1212 Avenue of the Americas, New York, N.Y. 10036. Offices or libraries also in Atlanta, Boston, Buffalo, Cedar Rapids, Chicago, Cincinnati, Cleveland, Dallas, Denver, Detroit, Honolulu, Kansas City (Mo.), Los Angeles, Milwaukee, Minneapolis, Omaha, Philadelphia, San Francisco, St. Louis, Summit (N.J.), Toronto, Washington (D.C.).
MSC	Macalaster Scientific Corporation, 60 Arsenal Street, Watertown, Massachusetts 02172
NBS	National Bureau of Standards, Office of Technical Information and Publications, Washington, D.C. 20234.
PURDUE	Purdue University, Audio-Visual Center, Lafayette, Indiana 47907.
ROBECK	Peter M. Robeck Company, 230 Park Ave., New York, N.Y. 10017.
TFI	Tribune Films Inc., 141 East 44 Street, New York, N.Y.
THORNE	Thorne Films, Inc., 1229 University Ave., Boulder, Colorado 80302.
UEVA	Universal Education and Visual Aids (formerly United World Film, Inc.), 221 Park Avenue South, New York, N.Y. 10003.
UNESCO	United Nations Educational, Scientific and Cultural Organization; Pilot Project for Chemistry Teaching in Asia. P.O. Box 1425, Bangkok, Thailand.

APPENDIX IV

REFERENCE LIST

Andrews, D. H., and R. J. Kokes
Fundamental Chemistry, Second Edition
John Wiley and Sons, New York, 1965

Baez, A. V.
The New College Physics
W. H. Freeman and Co., San Francisco, 1967

Campbell, J. A.
Why Do Chemical Reactions Occur?
Prentice-Hall, Englewood Cliffs, N. J., 1965

CBA Chemical Bond Approach Project
Chemical Systems
Webster Division, McGraw Hill Book Company, St. Louis, 1964

Chem Study
Chemistry, an Experimental Science
W. H. Freeman and Co., San Francisco, 1963

Christiansen, G. S., and P. H. Garrett
Structure and Change
W. H. Freeman and Co., San Francisco, 1960

Feynman, R. P., R. B. Leighton, and M. Sands
The Feynman Lectures on Physics, Volume 1
Addison-Wesley Publishing Co., Reading, Mass., 1963

Greenstone, A. W., F. X. Sutman, and L. G. Hollingsworth
Concepts in Chemistry
Harcourt, Brace and World, Inc., New York, 1960

Holden, A. and P. Singer
Crystals and Crystal Growing
Anchor Books, Garden City, New York, 1960

Lehrman, R. L., and C. Swartz
Foundations of Physics
Holt, Rinehart and Winston, New York, 1965

Mason, S. F.
Main Currents of Scientific Thought
H. Schuman, New York, 1953

PSSC — Physical Science Study Committee
College Physics
Raytheon Education Co., 1968
Note: This reference is to the *college* edition, *not* to the high school edition.

Resnick, R., and D. Halliday
Physics, Part I and Part II
John Wiley and Sons, New York, 1966

Shamos, M. H., Editor
Great Experiments in Physics
Holt-Dryden Books; Holt, Rinehart and Winston, New York, 1959

Sienko, M. J., and R. A. Plane
Chemistry: Principles and Properties
McGraw-Hill Book Co., New York, 1966

Stevenson, R., and R. B. Moore
Theory of Physics
W. B. Saunders Co., Philadelphia, 1967

Toulmin, S. E,, and J. Goodfield
The Architecture of Matter
Harper and Row, New York, 1963

Wood, E. A.
Crystals and Light
D. Van Nostrand Co., Princeton, New Jersey, 1964